Saves Union

Slaves to Fashion

Poverty and Abuse in the New Sweatshops

Robert J. S. Ross

The University of Michigan Press
Ann Arbor

331.25
Ros

"/05

A CIP catalog record for this book is available from the British Library.

Library of Congress Cataloging-in-Publication Data

Ross, Robert J. S., 1943–
    Slaves to fashion : poverty and abuse in the new sweatshops /
Robert J. S. Ross.
        p.   cm.
    Includes bibliographical references and index.
    ISBN 0-472-10941-3 (cloth : alk. paper) — ISBN 0-472-03022-1
(cloth : alk. paper)
    1. Sweatshops. 2. Clothing workers. 3. Clothing trade—Corrupt
practices. I. Title.   4 Labor Laws
HD2337.R67   2004
331.25—dc22   2004004960

Grateful acknowledgment is made to the following publisher for
permission to reprint previously published material: HarperCollins
Publishers Inc. for "Shirt," from *The Want Bone* by Robert Pinsky
(New York: HarperCollins Publishers, 1991). Copyright © 1991 by
Robert Pinsky. Reprinted by permission of HarperCollins
Publishers, Inc.

Shirt

by Robert Pinsky

The back, the yoke, the yardage. Lapped seams,
The nearly invisible stitches along the collar
Turned in a sweatshop by Koreans or Malaysians

Gossiping over tea and noodles on their break
Or talking money or politics while one fitted
This armpiece with its overseam to the band

Of cuff I button at my wrist. The presser, the cutter,
The wringer, the mangle. The needle, the union,
The treadle, the bobbin. The code. The infamous blaze

At the Triangle Factory in nineteen-eleven.
One hundred and forty-six died in the flames
On the ninth floor, no hydrants, no fire escapes—

The witness in a building across the street
Who watched how a young man helped a girl to step
Up to the windowsill, then held her out

Away from the masonry wall and let her drop.
And then another. As if he were helping them up
To enter a streetcar, and not eternity.

A third before he dropped her put her arms
Around his neck and kissed him. Then he held
Her into space, and dropped her. Almost at once

He stepped up to the sill himself, his jacket flared
And fluttered up from his shirt as he came down,
Air filling up the legs of his gray trousers—

Like Hart Crane's Bedlamite, "shrill shirt ballooning."
Wonderful how the pattern matches perfectly
Across the placket and over the twin bar-tacked

Corners of both pockets, like a strict rhyme
Or a major chord. Prints, plaids, checks,
Houndstooth, Tattersall, Madras. The clan tartans

Invented by mill-owners inspired by the hoax of Ossian,
To control their savage Scottish workers, tamed
By a fabricated heraldry: MacGregor,

Bailey, MacMartin. The kilt, devised for workers
to wear among the dusty clattering looms.
Weavers, carders, spinners. The loader,

The docker, the navvy. The planter, the picker, the sorter
Sweating at her machine in a litter of cotton
As slaves in calico headrags sweated in fields:

George Herbert, your descendant is a Black
Lady in South Carolina, her name is Irma
And she inspected my shirt. Its color and fit

And feel and its clean smell have satisfied
both her and me. We have culled its cost and quality
Down to the buttons of simulated bone,

The buttonholes, the sizing, the facing, the characters
Printed in black on neckband and tail. The shape,
The label, the labor, the color, the shade. The shirt.

Contents

Contents

Acknowledgments

This project began during one sabbatical leave and was substantially finished during another. Clark University granted the sabbatical, and a Clark faculty development grant helped me comb the files at the Cornell University School of Industrial and Labor Relations library. I am grateful, but in truth the work was accomplished despite the duties I have gladly shouldered at Clark University.

The librarians are another matter. Mary Hartman, Ed McDermott, and Irene Walch of the Robert Goddard Library responded to every inquiry and tracked down each article or book—and did it with humor. Professors are often well served by librarians but have rare occasions to say so. This is mine. The small-town librarians in Southborough, Massachusetts, also have big hearts: to Judy Williams, Peggy Tuttle, Clare Curran-Ball, and Heidi Lindsey—hats off!

When I chose it during my first sabbatical, the topic of garment industry labor abuse arose from a series of speaking and conference engagements. This topic was the one that united heart and intellect. The heart part was an act of filial loyalty: my father, Irving Barrett, was a garment cutter, a member of Local 10 of the International Ladies Garment Workers Union, and his father had been an early organizer of the union. After my father's death, my father-in-law, Ben Levenson, became a kind, wise, and loving father figure. It is to these two men who volunteered their care for me that I dedicate this book.

Numerous colleagues and informants ease the way of works like this. Those who I leave out will, I hope, forgive the protracted nature of the project. Prof. Altagracia Ortiz led me to her work and that of other Puerto Rican colleagues to help me in my first try at understanding the Puerto Rican role in New York's garment industry. Ellen McCormack, an undergraduate student at Clark and now a faculty member at Wellesley College, collaborated with me, as did Ellen Rosen, on our first sweatshop paper in 1995. Rich Appelbaum and Chris Chase-Dunn have given me opportunities to set my thoughts out in talks and on paper, as have Jim Russell, Richard Peet, Jerry Lembcke, Gary Gereffi, Arno Tausch, and Gernot Kohler.

Apo Leong of the Asia Monitor Resource Center facilitated a trip to Beijing that induced an important writing project that my new collaborator, Anita Chan, and I have accomplished. I am indebted to them both. The Ford Foundation paid for a trip that made all that possible. Monina Wong of the Hong Kong Christian Industrial Commission showed me the scene in Shenzhen and Guangdong.

Edna Bonacich showed grace under pressure when, as she generously showed me around the Los Angeles garment district, she coolly talked down an overheated street person. She and Rich Appelbaum wrote a great book on Los Angeles's garment industry that inspired me to labor on. Jeff Hermanson entertained my questions from the Workers Justice Center in New York and by e-mail from his AFL-CIO office in Mexico City. Ginny Coughlin of UNITE kindly answered questions and paid for lunch. Carl Proper opened his files and lent me his desk at ILGWU headquarters. Ann Hoffman of UNITE's Washington office was interesting on and off the record. Jerry Fishbein, then of UNITE, showed me my first sweatshop—its picture is in this book—and Alan Howard was helpful and encouraging.

One Monday afternoon in July 2000 Charlie Kernaghan called me and barked, "Bob, I want you come to Managua with me . . . on Wednesday." I took a leap of faith, paid for the ticket, and haven't regretted it for a moment. Barbara Briggs, Kernaghan's associate at the National Labor

Acknowledgments

Committee, was willing coolly to inform me of the politics of things I did not understand. She is one of this world's unheralded but true heroes.

Herb Spivack gave me insight to U.S. brand names' relations with their Chinese contractor counterparts: and he gets to fly first class.

The Executive Committee of the Greek Federation of Textile Workers answered my questions for an hour, and I learned three different parties' views of the idea of a social clause. Rick Van den Braber taught me about the Clean Clothes Campaign in Amsterdam—among the many charms of that city. Peter Liebhold of the Smithsonian was an attentive listener and a good teacher and had great files. Nancy Green told me where to go in Paris garment districts and where to have a really nice meal I could afford. Her book was a source of vital information. The staff of the Kheel Center for Labor-Management Documentation and Archives at Cornell University helped me find transcripts of Frances Perkins's talks to her students; Hope Nisely helped me locate photographs. Numerous people at the Department of Labor's Office of Public Affairs and Wage and Hour Division office facilitated my research.

Summer interns of the International Studies Stream at Clark University, Kendra Fehrer, Johann Walczak, and Adam Tomczik produced meticulously documented drafts of the Kukdong and BJ&B cases.

Peter Dreier commented on the first draft manuscript in exquisite and sometimes painful detail. I took almost all of his advice.

When one labors in obscurity, the helping hand of people who publicize one's work is welcome and often decisive. Clark's former director of communications, Kate Chesley, liked the idea of sweatshop research and publicized my first few papers. Tim Boulay, associate director for media relations, did likewise. The upshot was that Ellen McCarthy, an editor at the University of Michigan Press, took notice and approached me about writing this book. I appreciate all of this attention and initiative. Ellen stayed with me through many delays as civic responsibilities and faculty leadership competed for my time.

Marion Levenson Ross continued to respond to drafts and ideas long after the novelty wore off: when I count blessings she is the first. Rachel I. Ross brings the right books to my attention and a host of other good things. Gabriel M. B. Ross has a mission to have me read things of higher quality than I might otherwise devolve toward, and he expects me to run with him in each of his many cities. All of this is too much goodness to have been earned.

As I close this work, we come to the second year after the premature death of John O'Connor, organizer, environmentalist, former student, and philanthropist. Before it became a major public issue, John and his wife, Carolyn Mugar, understood the importance of the work I had begun on sweatshops in the apparel industry, and they helped me to get the research done. John was so happy about the work: he would playfully punch me on the arm and say, "Hey, we figured that one out, didn't we?" as news of the movement spread. Carolyn has my undying gratitude, and John's memory lives brightly in my heart.

It is well known that titles are more than titles. As the introduction to this book suggests, I lived with the title *Hearts Starve* for many years. Ellen McCarthy gently dissented, and Marion Ross did so more clearly. I thank them. When shove came to push I polled the troops and lost the vote. Then I picked up a voice mail message while white-water rafting in West Virginia: "Bob," said Suzanne Gordon, "Steve [Early] and I have been talking, and the title is *Slaves to Fashion*." She was right, and she wins my gratitude for caring and also a copy of the book.

There is a long line of women toilers behind this book. My father's mother, Molly, was the last sewing machine operator in our family; my mother, Marsha, taught small children how to read in school and taught her own children to stand up for themselves; her mother, Irene, took her own name, worked her whole life, and had a terrific sense of humor. My sister, Linda, has prevailed and has also brought me a lot of fun software. It is probable that somewhere in every family of American Jews there is someone whose life was touched by the rag trade. The era of sweatshops and immigration at the turn of the twentieth century is part of the lore of many other immigrant groups as well. It is a sadness that new groups of immigrant women—fighting for their families and struggling in their new lives—face conditions that have advanced so little since those days. They are our metaphorical grandparents, these strong women, and they deserve a whole world more than they get.

Introduction

Sweatshops Are
Where Hearts Starve

it is the afternoon of Passover in 1998. Our home is busy with preparations as the feast that celebrates the liberation of Hebrew slaves is nearing readiness. Our guests have not yet arrived, and I am listening to a tape that I plan to play as people arrive. It is a recording of Judy Collins singing a poem—written in 1911 to celebrate women workers on strike—"Bread and Roses." I want to play this song for our guests because for me it knits the pieces together—the ancient festival of liberation; my father's work as a cutter in the garment industry and his mother's and father's work there too; and my work and mission since 1995 on the new sweatshops in the apparel industry.

Dressed and ready, the festive table set, the house warm and aromatic with traditional foods, I find myself focused on the tape player, playing the song over and over again, trying to memorize it. But why am I doing that, now of all times? I can't sing and won't venture to try for our friends and relatives. Over and again the tape plays, and my lips move with the words as Judy Collins's brilliant soprano brims my eyes. And then a phrase leaps at, springs at, dives at, tears at, attacks, and enters my soul.

> Our lives shall not be sweated from birth until life closes;
> *Hearts starve* as well as bodies; give us bread but give us roses!

Slaves to Fashion

Hearts starve. You arrive at work in a cramped and mean little shop at seven in the morning. The boss has told you not to punch in until eight. He or his wife screams at you all day—"Hurry up, you idiot!" "Can't you sew a straight line?" "You're as clumsy as a dog." At five he punches out your time card, but you work until six or even later past evening and into night. Paid by the piece you have been a bit slower today, bothered by a puncture from a needle last week. If the multiplication was done you did not make the $5.15 an hour that is the legal minimum wage—though the official records will show you did because two of your hours are not recorded. The work is boring, repetitive, extremely uncomfortable, but it requires absolute attention. Should your thoughts stray for but a moment, should you wonder how your boy is doing in the first grade or if you might get nice weather to take a walk on Sunday, you will get injured. A robot may bring a stiff fender to a hard chassis, but as yet only a human hand can guide two limp pieces of fabric to be machine-sewn together in an arc or a tight corner.

Hearts Starve. When things are busy you will do this six days a week. You might work later than six o'clock in the evening. Then you might consider yourself lucky. Overtime is an opportunity to get another few dollars. You need them all. Rent takes most of what you get.

Hearts Starve. You have to use the toilet, but the washroom makes you nauseous and you are scared of the dark corridor and of catching some disease. The bathroom is filthy. The boss screams if you take enough time to try to clean it yourself.

Hearts Starve. There is a course for finishing high school at night in the neighborhood, but you never know when the overtime will come. You can't plan. If you say no to overtime you'll get fired. Will it always be like this? Can you ever breathe free?

Throughout the developed world, in Europe and North America, closets of clothing are stuffed with the changing demands of fashion. We slaves to fashion rarely wear out clothes in the physical sense: instead, we grow tired of them. The next new thing adorns our bodies in each season. Thousands of commercial messages remind us in each season that we are perceived as we dress. How devastating it is to be told one is dressed "so eighties." As we are slaves to fashion as consumers so too are the producers. The flood of clothing demanded by consumerist culture is not necessarily paid for with a flood of new purchasing power: clothing costs less as a portion of family budgets now than it did a generation ago. In New York and Bangladesh, in Los Angeles and Managua, hearts starve for the finer things in life as we slaves to fashion reap the product of those enslaved to fashion.

In January 1912 textile workers in Lawrence, Massachusetts, struck against a cut in their pay. The mill owners had lowered their pay in response to a Massachusetts law that reduced the workweek from fifty-six to fifty-four hours.

The workers were mainly immigrants, the largest number Italian. They were considered unskilled. The craft-oriented labor movement of the time thought these workers, many of them women, could not be organized. But the radical Industrial Workers of the World—the Wobblies of fame and song—were successful in organizing the women across ethnic and linguistic lines. A hard strike ensued, immortalized in a stirring, evocative painting by the artist Ralph Fasanella.[1]

The women took the lead in the strike. They were set upon with violence. They had to send their children away to protect them—and by doing so they won sympathetic hearts to their cause as photographs of the children stepping down from trains, gazing out at strange cities, were carried in the newspapers of the day.[2] The workers suffered betrayal, and attempts were made to frame them through outrageous schemes. Their Italian leaders were charged with the murder of Alice LoPezzo when police killed her. They maintained their unity and their dignity and finally in March 1912 won their demands.

The Lawrence strike began less than two years after the end of the "Uprising of the Twenty Thousand" shirtwaist makers in New York. The uprising was the largest ever industrial action by women at that point, and the Lawrence strike continued the story—immigrant women fighting for their rights. Even today, in New York's labor lore, the 1910 "Great Revolt" of sixty thousand largely male cloakmakers is a story somehow subordinated to that of the women.

As Abraham Lincoln put it, "The mystic chords of memory" call forth "the better angels of our nature."[3] We seem to need the story of those women to tell us something or perhaps instruct us about ourselves. And so, for many years now, we have come to believe that during one of their marches the Lawrence textile workers carried a sign that, by this *act* of constructively remembering, has become the special emblem of women workers and of all who strive for dignity in their labor. Many speakers and writers have passed on the cultural memory that a Lawrence sign read, *"We want bread and roses too."* Such a sentiment reminds us that those poor immigrant laborers—in Lawrence or in New York or in Los Angeles this morning as you glance at this page—were not just victims, not merely recipients of the good conscience of their allies, not merely reflexes of a market demand for clothing and fashion. They were fully human, with fully noble hopes and dreams even in their miserable stinking shops at six o'clock in the morning on cold days. The enslaved yearn for the finer and better things of life.

Memory has joined the Lawrence strikers to James Oppenheim's poem "Bread and Roses." Yet there is no evidence that the sign "We want bread and roses too" was ever carried by a Lawrence striker. Most recently Jim Zwick discovered Oppenheim's poem was written and published *before* the Lawwrence strike (in December, 1911), and he thinks the origin is in a Chicago garment strike in 1909–10 (Zwick 2004).[4]

The oppressed and exploited have always wanted not just tomorrow's bread but Sunday's roses too. The big struggles of working people involve "the individual awakening of 'illiterates' and 'scum' to an original, personal conception of society and the realization of the dignity and the rights of their part in it."[5] When Rose Schneiderman, a garment worker unionist and suffrage campaigner, the great orator after the Triangle fire of 1911, gave a series of 1912 lectures on behalf of voting rights for women, she used the slogan to emphasize the need for working-class women to have a voice in public life (Harney 1999).

The International Ladies Garment Workers Union (ILGWU, or ILG) sponsored a Broadway musical, *Pajama Game* (beginning in 1954), which addressed the question of the meaning of small advances from a worker's point of view. "Seven and a Half Cents" is a song about an hourly raise. Trivial, perhaps. But as the song says, "Give it to me every hour of every day. . . . Soon I'll be livin' like a king." Well, if not a king or queen, then, anyhow, as Woody Guthrie said about Pete Seeger's vision for America, "All union, all free, all singing."[6]

Hearts Starve. Around the world sewing-machine operators toil day after day. In China's privately owned export factories they may work twenty-seven of thirty days, eleven hours a day. Economists and journalists from the West seem to be impressed that the apparel toilers of the developing countries are better off than indentured prostitutes or their sisters who remain on farms without electricity. They are not better off for long.

After ten years or perhaps a bit more, they return to the villages. They leave behind a mountain of jeans, a skyscraper of blouses, icebergs of fleece, and *Titanic*-sized piles of silk ties. An Everest of dress shirts anchors continents of sneakers. Then they are gone. There are hardly any forty-year-olds in China's export factories or in the export processing zones of the developing world. Spent and discarded, the women move on.

Hearts Starve. As I end my writing of this work of fealty to family and tradition, the U.S. Census is releasing the new figures for immigration in the decade from 1990 to 2000. It is as we knew. This has been the greatest era of immigration in our history. Just as the wave of immigrants at the turn of the twentieth century first brought the ready-to-wear clothing business to our shores, the Russian Jews and the Italians, the sewing-machine operators and the cutters, so now Hispanic and Asian migrants populate the shops and factories of the rag trade. It has ever been the merciless devourer of immigrants. It takes whole lives but doesn't say thanks. Those Jewish and Catholic and Orthodox immigrants from Southern and Eastern Europe were different from the Protestant and Western Europeans who preceded them. And now still darker hued people come to make our dresses and slacks, and they are also different from the Europeans who preceded them. But not so different.

Hearts Starve. They come to earn a decent life. To avoid a bomb or a bullet late at night. To make a safe place for their children and, if they are very lucky, to have a moment or two to rest in the sun. They are just like us. They are our grandparents and parents and great-grandparents. We owe them what we owe them.

This book has a lot of numbers in it. But it has only one vision. Behind

Slaves to Fashion

every chart or table and fact and policy is a woman or a man at a sewing machine and a cutting table. Whose hearts starve.

As we go marching, marching in the beauty of the day,
A million darkened kitchens, a thousand mill lofts gray,
Are touched with all the radiance that a sudden sun discloses,
For the people hear us singing: "Bread and roses! Bread and roses!"

As we go marching, marching, we battle too for men,
For they are women's children, and we mother them again.
Our lives shall not be sweated from birth until life closes;
Hearts starve as well as bodies; give us bread but give us roses!
—James Oppenheim, 1911

Part 1 The Fall and Rise of Sweatshops
in the United States

1 What Is a Sweatshop?

Images in the Wrong Place

A young girl looks into the camera, her dark eyes wide, her posture a bit uncertain, her hands holding the pieces of clothing she is about to push toward a sewing machine needle. She is Latina, her hair dark, her features vaguely Indian. Cara Metz's photo of an underage girl in a Brooklyn sweatshop is a haunting image of the new sweatshops in North America (Metz 2001). This girl's gaze, without a friendly smile for the camera but with her body awkwardly posed for its sake, speaks to us, as if from the beginning of the century. From that time, we vaguely recall Jacob Riis's *How the Other Half Lives* (1890). The women in their dark, small Lower East Side room of New York's Manhattan are "Sewing and Starving in an Elizabeth Street Attic," as depicted in one of Riis's photographs.

There is something wrong in this juxtaposition. Sweatshops are the past, or they are elsewhere: they are not *us,* not now. In the United States, as in Europe and Asia, most audiences assume that an address about the contemporary sweatshop problem will be about some place other than the United States. Sometime in 1890 or 1911 in the United States, perhaps, yes, in Jacob Riis's time, but not now. Extreme labor abuse must be in Central America, perhaps, or China. My neighbors in a quiet village at the very edge of metropolitan eastern Massachusetts, many employed in

An underage worker in New York's Manhattan garment district, 1991. Courtesy of Cara Metz, for UNITE.

computer-related businesses, are at first surprised when they learn that a "sweatshop book" is going to start with conditions in the United States. Their confusion is understandable. The United States is a rich nation, perhaps the most affluent in the world. We are not supposed to have sweatshops, places of work so bad that they remind us of the bad old days that we were supposed to have left behind. *We* have improved so much.

Understanding our society as a place where the bad old days of labor exploitation and injustice are over sustains our positive sense of our march through history. It also allows those of us who are employed and adequately fed to feel proud of our own accomplishments. The poor, many think, have only themselves and their self-inflicted joblessness to blame (Wilson 1996, 159–64). Yet, a combination of political, economic, and social trends has come together to recreate working conditions that are nearly as bad as those of the early twentieth century. Sweatshops are back, and they are right here.

Many people will object that to be exploited in the United States may still leave a worker better off than he or she might be elsewhere. Comparative and competitive suffering, what one writer termed "the oppression sweepstakes"(Leo 1995), is not a pretty game, nor fruitful, nor honorable. Does a person deemed poor in America eat better than a person starving in the Horn of Africa? (Yes, but his or her diet and life circumstance will lead to premature death, more frequent chronic illness, and more serious acute episodes of illness [See Daniels, Kennedy, and Kawachi 2000; FRAC 2001].) Does a child born in one of the poorest communities in New York have a better chance of survival than the average child in El Salvador? (Perhaps not; see Ross and Trachte [1990], who found that 1980 infant mortality rates in the poor sections of New York were comparable to third world rates of death of those below one year of age.) Do American sewing machine operators in New York or Los Angeles have more electronic *things*, or *stuff*, and live in better housing than the shanty dwellers of Nicaragua or the factory dorm residents in China? Yes, most probably, but they may also be further from the average living circumstance of people in their society. Poor people in the United States, including the working poor, may be more deprived relative to the standards of decency that we have set ourselves than workers elsewhere in relation to their own societies. As many have noted, in addition, the United States has more inequality and deeper poverty than the other rich nations (see, e.g., Smeeding and Rainwater 2001).

This chapter will discuss the meaning of the term *sweatshop*, paying close attention to the United States and its history, and it will put the term in a global context as well. My goal is to give this highly charged word an objective meaning, one that goes beyond expressing disapproval or standing as a colorful metaphor for "lousy work." The larger context is the apparel industry worldwide. The "rag trade" merits this attention for historical, cultural, and economic reasons. Historically and culturally, English language speakers have associated the term *sweatshop* with clothing manufacture from the time the phrase was widely understood and almost from the beginning of the ready-to-wear clothing industry.

In North America garment making is closely associated with the idea of the sweatshop—in part, as we shall see in the next chapter, because of the particular history of triumphs and tragedies in New York, the world's largest media market for most of the last century. In economic terms the apparel industry is among the world's largest manufacturing industries and is among those very few industries where extreme exploitation of vulnerable labor is central to the labor process and to the chain of profit making.

There are other industries in which the extremes of exploitation approach those of the rag trade. In the United States some segments of the restaurant industry, as frequently as the apparel industry, meet the (U.S.-based) formal criteria of "multiple labor law violator" (U.S. GAO 1989). Restaurants, however, do not make products that enter into world trade: by definition, they are not part of the problem of global labor standards, a central concern of this book. The human and labor rights violations of agribusiness and its use of migrant labor are somewhat notorious but also outside the scope of this work. Nonetheless, in common with labor abuse in the apparel industry, labor law reform and labor standards enforcement would be important steps to improve conditions in these industries. But that gets ahead of the story; for now we leave aside in this book the restaurant and agricultural industries.

Footwear production in the developing world has been the focus of much antisweatshop agitation and concern—especially in regard to Nike, whose contractors often engage in exploitative labor practices (Connor 2001, 2002). In many countries data from footwear production are combined with textile and apparel data. Therefore, information about this industry is sprinkled throughout this book. When data do distinguish footwear from apparel workers, however, it usually shows an advantage to footwear workers. The reasons are easy to understand. Footwear products are, on the whole, more expensive and are made with more machinery; they are more "capital intensive." There are hardly any stages of footwear production that can be regularly done by workers at home. So the factory workers hardly ever compete with unregulated (and more frequently exploited) homeworkers.

Another industry that has been the focus of charges of labor abuse is the toy industry, especially in China, where up to 70 percent of the world's toys are made (Bezlova 2002; Hong Kong Christian Industrial Committee 2003). As is true in the apparel industry, toy making suffers from the relative weakness of contractors who make toys for name brands and the additional weakness of the workers, who are often inexperienced. Outside of China, toy industry workers in factories may compete with homeworkers, especially for the assembly of plastic parts. Much of the global situation of toy workers is therefore similar to apparel workers, and so are the forces that impoverish them. Yet there are very few workers in the U.S. toy industry (fewer than twenty-five thousand by the end of 2002), and the logic of our inquiry is to explain how an industry and its workers are enmeshed in global capitalism. In the interest of clarity and relevance, therefore, the focus of this work is on the apparel industry. Not only does this make our story compact, but it focuses attention on the industry most likely, of all the world's globalized export industries, to systematically incorporate sweatshop labor in its products.

Eleven million people worldwide made clothes in 1998; when combined with textile and footwear workers, the total was over 29 million workers worldwide (29,387,000; see ILO 2000, 14–22).

The Sweated Trades

Understanding what a sweatshop is requires a brief look at history and the evolution of the language used to describe industrial conditions.

Sweatshop: A First Definition

The idea of the sweated trades reached its modern form in the mid-nineteenth century in Britain (MacLean 1903). By the late Victorian period there had been repeated investigations of them, and a general—somewhat impressionistic—definition emerged. In the first instance, those who were "sweated" were the workers, the direct producers, while those who extracted their labor were the "sweaters," the employers or direct purchasers of their work. Charles Booth found in the sweated trades the common threads of "overcrowding, irregular hours, low pay; periods of terrible strain, overtaxing the powers and exhausting the vital forces" (Booth 1902, cited in Bythell 1978, 11). The quasi-official definition came from an otherwise unsuccessful House of Lords inquiry. Sweating was no particular method of remuneration, no particular form of industrial organization, but certain conditions of employment, viz., *unusually low rates of wages, excessive hours of labour, and unsanitary workplaces.* (emphasis mine; cited in MacLean 1903, 290; see also Bythell 1978, 232)

The conditions of the sweated trades were (and are), in Britain and America, particularly associated with a certain industrial organization. The sweated trades were those branches of industry characterized by middleman contractors standing between the direct producers and the commercial customers who bought the product, coordinated the various vendor contractors, and then sold the commodity to the public. Then, as now, the commercial buyer, usually the larger, more powerful partner in the chain of commodity production, managed to evade legal and public accountability for the conditions of the laborers by insisting that these were the responsibility of the middleman contractor.

The contractor function may itself be subdivided among subcontractors—for example, when a shop contracts to sew already cut clothing, the owner may subcontract any part of the sewing to another shop or some part of the process, such as embroidery, if it is required, or button sewing. Again, the "sweater" in the term *sweatshop* was not necessarily she who sweats but rather he who makes others sweat.[1] In Britain, before the explosive growth of the ready-to-wear clothing industry at the end of the nineteenth century, the sweated trades might have connoted furniture making, shoe and boot making, spinning and weaving, and other trades. Bythell (1978) adds nail and chain making to this list. These were the trades in which workers toiled at home at the behest of contractors, who commissioned and then collected the "outwork" and delivered it to jobbers. Then, as now, the labor-intensive sweated trades were typically paid a "piece rate"—for each unit of work they performed rather than by the hour. In the apparel industry the piece rate may be so many cents per collar sewn to the yoke of a shirt or per sleeves sewn to a body. The homeworkers, who were always paid a piece rate, were so dispersed as to make it impossible to regulate wages and conditions even if the political will to do so had been present.

Industrial homeworkers, or "outworkers," were understood to be an alternative—a less costly one—to factory labor. MacLean (1903, 290) traces the usage to "the troublous times" in England in 1847–48, "when the working people were in the direst straits and commenced taking work home for a mere pittance rather than sit quietly waiting starvation." Her language is instructive in the context of today's discussion of the labor conditions in developing nations. MacLean refers to a choice workers in sweatshops make—and those who give "two cheers" for today's sweat-shops often emphasize the idea of choice (Kristof and WuDunn 2000). MacLean states it clearly: the choice to work for a pittance is an alternative to "sit . . . waiting starvation" (290). When the alternative is starvation, the decision to work under abusive conditions is closer to coercion than choice—though it may be rational to choose life over starvation.

The workers drawn to the growing ready-to-wear clothing industry from 1870 to 1900 were similar and similarly driven in Britain and America—indeed, the similarities are very close, down to the ethnicities of the workers, and one history could be another. In both places, Jews fleeing the pogroms of Eastern Europe concentrated in poor neighborhoods and disproportionately in the burgeoning ready-to-wear clothing industry. In both London and New York immigrant Jews were both workers and bosses. Most decisively, in both cities in the rapidly expanding apparel business, especially in its largest and most volatile branch, fashion-sensitive women's outerwear production was the site of the contractor sweating system (Garnett 1988).[2]

The earliest markets for ready-to-wear clothing in the United States were those in which the consumer had no woman who could sew his clothes—slaves and sailors. The decisive factor in the creation of a mass market for ready-to-wear clothing, however, was relative population growth in cities—urbanization. Urbanization involved the transformation of the nation from one characterized by rural households that made their own clothes to urban and rural households that bought ready-made clothes.

The concentration of wageworkers in physically compact urban areas created the possibility of a market for ready-to-wear clothes. The technology of cutting and sewing then made the exploitation of this market profitable and efficient. In the 1860s women's cloaks began to be made in long production runs. In the 1880s suits were added, and then in the 1890s dresses and "waists" began to be made. At the end of the Civil War, there were, according to Best (1919, 777), about six thousand wage earners in women's clothing production; by 1919 there were about two hundred thousand. New York City was the titan of the industry, with over 70 percent of its value produced there and over 50 percent of its labor force working there.

Although simplified histories of the process of industrialization often contrast domestic handwork with factory manufacture, the sweating system and outwork grew along with the ready-to-wear industry (Bythell 1978; Schmiechen 1984). Schmiechen estimated the number of clothing outworkers in London in 1901 at 125,000–90,000 (1984, 283). The new technology of clothing production—band-saw cutting (1860) and the Singer sewing machine (1851)—allowed unskilled workers to increase their productivity and to work at home. This "decentralized mode of production," Schmiechen notes,

> was a distinct financial advantage to the employer because it made up for the lack of capital and space and allowed the employer to expand production without expanding facilities. (1984, 283)

The use of the term *sweatshop* and the associated *sweated trades* came to be highly associated with the system in which a manufacturer used an agent to assign or otherwise distribute work to workers laboring in their homes, producing relatively low-value goods and paying at a piece rate. The sweatshop itself was, at the turn of the century, the sweater's own home, where he might assemble workers to do work for which he had contracted to a manufacturer. So Jacob Riis's early pictures of "sweaters" were of multiple adults, including men, working in domestic rooms, but not necessarily members of the same family.[3] Later, the word *sweatshop* migrated to crowded and dangerous—and low-paying—workshops.

The link between sweated working conditions and outwork, outsourcing, or homework consists of a number of independently operating factors. In the first instance the homeworker is isolated and usually desperate for work. MacLean wrote in 1903 (about the 1840s) that workers took such jobs "for a pittance" because they were in danger of starvation. Spurred by the whip of penury, workers with few choices will take unfair conditions

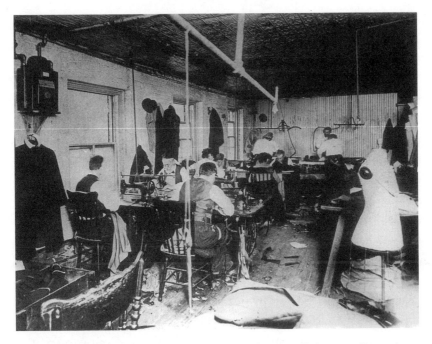

Early twentieth-century sewing shop: gas lighting and foot-treadle sewing machines. Note both men and women sewing machine operators. Courtesy of Kheel Center for Labor-Management Documentation and Archives, Cornell University.

of work to survive. Thus, the homeworker is subject to (as is the factory wage worker who earns but a pittance) a strategic game in which he or she has few choices but the employer has many.

For immigrants who move to big cities in the garment-making centers of the world, there may be major barriers to their participation in regular jobs. These barriers to participation in the mainstream economy may include language difficulties and lack of knowledge of local legal rights. In some cultures, patriarchal norms restrict where married women, or young women still in their father's homes, may work. These restrictions may include working outside of family enterprises or among those of different ethnic backgrounds. Around the world immigrants are often of uncertain legal status, what we now call in the United States "undocumented," and are thus reluctant to take formal jobs and timid when they do. For all of these reasons homework may appeal, but the workers' bargaining power is low.

In addition, homework disperses and divides workers, making it likely that they will compete with one another for the work rather than cooperate to increase rates of pay (Schmiechen 1984). Finally, because of the physical dispersion of homeworkers it is difficult, if not impossible, to enforce the legal minimum standards for their work. This creates another dimension to competition among workers. Because homework labor standards are apt to be low, industries with large amounts of homework are apt to suffer a drag on labor standards and rates of pay. The homeworkers drag down the factory workers. Indeed, when minimum compensation laws were passed in Britain, at least two economic historians claim that manufacturers, attempting to evade them, moved work from factories to home laborers (Bythell 1978; Schmiechen 1984).

If the sweated trades were centered in the nineteenth and early twentieth centuries on industries with large numbers of outworkers, that relationship, nevertheless, was the essence of the matter and not, as the House of Lords Select Committee on the Sweated Trades pointed out, a matter of definition. Over time, the defining core of the idea of a sweatshop became centered on conditions of work rather than on location of workplace or organization. By the early twentieth century, in New York the idea of the sweatshop no longer automatically referred to a tiny hovel in which outworkers sweated for a petty contractor. Rather, the term was now broadly applied to any factory workplace, as the *Encyclopedia Britannica* (2001) puts it in its modern definition, "in which workers are employed for long hours at low wages and under unhealthy or oppressive conditions."

By 1909, when shirtwaist makers went out on strike to improve their conditions (see the next chapter), a few large "inside" manufacturers—like Leisorson's and the Triangle Shirtwaist Factory—about whose terrible fire we will learn in the next chapter—had very large factories. Tens of thousands of other sewing machine operators were employed in small contractor shops. Still further down the food chain were subcontractors who gave work out to the homeworkers. Packed into small apartments, whole families bent over their work all day every day, paid by the piece, paying for their own heat and light as best they could and for their own sewing machines as well. The pathetic wage slaves Jacob Riis pictured in *How the Other Half Lives* (1890) were really "Sewing and Starving in an Elizabeth Street Attic" and "Trousers for 7 Cents" were but a pittance.

Then, as now, the pyramid of the apparel industry rested on a broad base of direct producers: sewing machine operators made up over half of the workers in the industry. In the Triangle Shirtwaist Factory, there were about five hundred employees on that fateful Saturday of March 25, 1911, and over 240 sewing machines on the main sewing floor. The cutters, pressers, trimmers, cleaners, and transporters of all kinds filled the production worker complement. Above the workers in the pyramid of power were contractors, their most frequent employers. The contractors employed them to sew clothing at the order of those called "jobbers" in New York for most of the twentieth century. Nowadays, confusingly, the term used for the entity that designs and causes garments to be assembled under its name is *manufacturer*.

In 1901 the labor economist John R. Commons described the garment contractors this way:

> the contractor or sweater now in the business in American cities is peculiarly . . . an organizer and employer of immigrants. The man best fitted to be a contractor is the man who is well acquainted with his neighbors, who is able to speak the language of several classes of immigrants, who can easily persuade his neighbors or their wives and children to work for him, and in this way can obtain the cheapest help. (quoted in Howard 1997, 152)

What Is a Sweatshop? Meaning and Metaphor

New York state license superintendent Daniel O'Leary in 1900 expressed his horror at "Workers toiling in dark, humid stuffy basements on Division Street, children of eight years, and women, many of them far from well, sweating their lives away in these hellholes" (quoted in Howard 1997, 152). The Frenchman Emile Levasseur similarly depicted the bottom of the "sweating system" in New York at the turn of the century:

[I]n dilapidated-looking buildings; the wooden steps shook, narrow and nause-ating toilets were in the stairway, medium-sized rooms where some twenty workers worked like demons, cutting, placing buttons, ironing, each according to his specialty. . . . [T]he spectacle of such feverish activity, of all those hands following the movement of the machines made me think of one of the circles of hell in Dante. (quoted in N. Green 1997, 137)

These two quotes illustrate some of the main themes by which the world of reform, of "enlightened" opinion, came to characterize and understand for itself the meaning of the term *sweatshop*. The economic dimensions of the meaning of *sweatshop* are measurable. According to some standard—a minimum wage law or the cost of a standard market basket of necessities—pay may be judged to be low, hours may be long, overtime pay may be (illegally) withheld, or benefits like holidays or health insurance may be deficient or absent. Common understanding goes further, as these quotes suggest, for they imply a workplace that is physically unhealthy or dangerous. Yet, all these definitions or observa-tions include the idea of "oppressiveness," and this, while it has physical meanings, is also cultural, psychological, and emotional. For example, a dirty, unswept floor, while it may be nasty or dangerous, may finally be tolerable.

Overflowing toilets, or insufficient numbers of them, enter a different realm of oppressiveness. Indeed, in almost all accounts of sweatshop con-ditions, especially those given by women workers, bathroom conditions and the regulation of bathroom visits—usually by men—figure vividly in workers' heartfelt complaints. Abusive language and even hitting—an emotional as well as physically cruel environment—also strip dignity from workers as they are used as punishments to drive production. The theme of grievance about toilet facilities is a striking continuity in the complaints of women workers throughout the twentieth century. A woman who worked in Manhattan's garment district described her fac-tory in a 1998 testimony:

When it's busy, we work up to sixty to sixty-three hours. The conditions in the factory are not very good. There's no air circulation. The bathrooms are outside on our floor. In the factory where I work almost everyone is from Ecuador. Those people work hard. And since they are very far from their land, they come and are afraid of losing their jobs, so they enslave themselves. Almost no one goes to the bathroom, they feel embarrassed. The bathroom is outside. They have to leave the factory, go to the hallway. It's a bit dangerous because anyone can enter the bathrooms. (Meza 1997, 5)

Union staffer Jo-Ann Mort interviewed a worker named Aracely, who works in Los Angeles's garment district, now a larger apparel-producing region than New York and described recently as the sweatshop capital of the United States. She is a presser who works twelve hours a day, seven days a week. She has untreated burns on her hands and complains that the bathroom is wretched. "You want to get out of there as quickly as possible" (Mort 1997, 193). Mort also interviewed Leticia, a sewer in Los Angeles. Leticia described a shop she visited where the workers had a union contract:

> "[It] is like a dream shop. Even the bathrooms are so beautiful you could eat there." By contrast, where she works, "We don't even have toilet paper, you have to bring it from home."
> "There is no space to walk in the shop. Everything is on top of you. When it rains, you have to cover yourself because the roof has a lot of holes. Rats come out. But the pressure is the worst. They won't even let you go to the bathroom— 'I need this work and I need it now' they say." (Mort 1997, 196)

This dimension of abuse—oppressiveness as emotional degradation, including rigorous regulation of toilet access and miserable sanitary conditions—is related to the extraction of profit from the workers, who are kept strictly at their jobs and are driven to produce more (a form of "speed up"). This is simply and obviously a *quantitative* aspect of exploitation: less time in bathroom breaks, more production; less desirable facilities, less use of them, more time sewing. Let us call this the "economistic" explanation of this abuse. The alternative explanation includes the economistic one but goes further, adding as motivating cause the *qualitative* dimension of the relation between employer and worker— that of control.

Successful employers are able to hire workers at a wage and set them to work at machines where the total cost of these is less than the revenue earned from selling the good or service that the wage earners produce. The contractor prices the piece rate he pays the workers after he has taken the contract for a certain amount per thousand dozen. More work, more

Old office building in the Los Angeles downtown, near fashion wholesale centers. Photographer: Robert J. S. Ross.

profit. Undergirding the contractor's ability to keep the pace up, to keep the "girls" and "boys" at their tasks, to accept the piece rate and thus the intensity of their work and the total wage possible to them, underneath the *leverage* the employer has, is—of course, once we examine it—not *free choice* but the constrained choice really available. Sweatshop workers are not free to be CEOs for Disney or high school art teachers or translators at the United Nations (UN). To keep his workers at their stations the sweat-shop operator must maintain his laborers as people—as women, as "girls"—who will return the next day. In turn, they must be people whose understanding of their choices is so limited that the boss's offer of employment remains acceptable the next day. A woman whose sense of herself is as a weak, vulnerable, constrained, abused, defenseless person is more apt to come back to X's Sewing Shop, even after being told she is a child for needing to pee.

The object of such humiliation is, however, not merely one individual worker but rather all of her co-workers, actual and potential. The objects of the humiliation are those groups of workers that a given type of

What Is a Sweatshop?

Adapted office space creates awkward workshops. Here is the locked back door in the office building—the only exit except for the entrance through the reception office. Photographer: Robert J. S. Ross.

employer, just like the cowboy at the roundup, is cutting out for his industrial niche's brand.

In social science terms, the hypothesis is that the regulation of bathroom behavior, the use of foul and demeaning language, even the neglect of bathroom facilities all dehumanize and intimidate workers, especially women, and keep them feeling weak and thus without recourse. Control and degradation of the woman worker's body are part of a regime of . . . control. To have control over a person is to exert power. Here is how a famous French philosopher put it, denying that the nineteenth and twentieth centuries were notable for their control over people's ideas:

In fact nothing is more material, physical, corporal than the exercise of power. What mode of investment of the body is necessary and adequate for the functioning of a capitalist society like ours? From the eighteenth to the early twentieth century I think it was believed that the investment of the body by power had to be heavy, ponderous, meticulous and constant. Hence the formidable disciplinary regimes in the schools, hospitals, barracks, factories, cities, lodgings, families. (Foucault 1980 [1975])

The strategic game of profit is a power game: those who have it take it.

The use of the term *sweatshop* historically is tied, then, to material deprivation and extreme exploitation and to abusive relations and degrading conditions on the job. In its extreme, sweatshops summon up our deep historical fears of fire and death and, more, our consciousness of ourselves, here in the United States and perhaps more broadly the West, as people in a civilization that no longer uses people up or degrades fellow humans in such systematic ways. *Sweatshop* means fear and hope.

Sweatshop: The Metaphor

It is no wonder then that the word *sweatshop* is as nimble, supple, and dynamic as our languages generally are. Words serve us, not we them. Metaphors mobilize emotion and connect by connotation the new with the familiar. When we say a dancer, gymnast, or baseball outfielder is as graceful as a gazelle, we concisely evoke in our listener an image of long-legged stride, great leaps, and a lean fluidity of line. When someone tells us she works in a sweatshop, she tells about a job where normal expectations of economic, environmental, and humanly dignified treatment have been radically disappointed. Implied too is a kind of fear—of unsanitary taint or of fire and even death. Rich with historical meaning the usage also implies that something barbaric and old has been summoned up from extinction, the progress of the century for ordinary folk turned back, the beast arisen that won't stay killed. If there is fear in workers' use of the word, there is also hope. By making the term *sweatshop* relative to our current expectations and by using it to evoke feelings about older "badder" days, modern language and we humans who use and make it suggest to our listeners and to ourselves that these are things that can or should be overcome. The statement "That place is a sweatshop!" implies that the workplace is damnably archaic. In modern Greek usage *tsekouzisma,* "to squeeze the juices out," communicates the brutality of what has come to be seen as an older transcended moment in capitalist development.

In the course of mid-century American (and, more broadly, Western) capitalist development, therefore, the word broadened. Now the word *sweatshop,* as Nancy Green points out, has become a metaphor for bad conditions and pay that is below standard (N. Green 1997, 160). An example of this expansive metaphorical use of *sweatshop* is an article in the *New York Times* on July 10, 1998, by Steven Greenhouse, who reported on a long simmering labor dispute in a New Orleans shipyard. Pay ranged there from eight dollars to over thirteen dollars per hour—hardly illegal. But the shipyard had a bad safety record. And the pay was about two dollars per hour less than a comparable yard in Mississippi. In addition, the compensation at this company included benefits that were meager by industry standards. " 'It's a sweatshop, with such low wages,' said Mike Boudreaux, a mechanic" (Greenhouse 1998).

Mike Boudreaux is undoubtedly correct that his shipyard is a lousy employer. Yet, by the criteria of the antisweatshop campaigners, eight dollars per hour in 1998 may have been a living wage in New Orleans. It would have provided, for example, income above the poverty line for a family of three, using national and official guidelines.[4] Boudreaux's place is lousy, but it is different from—better than—conditions in the U.S. apparel industry ninety years ago or, in many cases, now.

Going beyond Metaphor

From a research point of view and perhaps from a law enforcement perspective, neither of which is ethically complete, the metaphoric usage "sweatshop as lousy job" is problematic. One may agree with Boudreaux that his employer misuses him. There is, however, no objective criterion to show that, just because one person considers a job lousy, it is compellingly barbaric, exploitative, or abusive. More importantly, as *sweatshop* becomes more metaphoric and poetic, the usage invites a subjective relativism: one woman's sweatshop is another person's hard job is another one's job. At the end, a mere matter of opinion is at issue.

Among the important questions social research can answer about a matter that seems troubling or unjust is this: How big a problem is it? While one outrage is a misery, it is hard to mobilize change in the law and in the practice of a nation of a quarter of a billion souls on behalf of one or a dozen or even a few hundred unjustly abused workers. An objective definition of a problem allows an answer to the question: How prevalent are sweatshop conditions in the United States? How big is the problem? If the problem is big, the nation may be moved.[5]

Sweatshop: The Definition

Insofar as conditions in the American apparel industry are concerned, this research adopts a restrictive but objective definition of a sweatshop: *"a business that regularly violates both wage or child labor and safety or health laws"* (U.S. GAO 1988). The definition depends on the Fair Labor Standards Act (FLSA), which establishes a minimum wage and requires premium pay for hours over forty in one week. In addition, the FLSA prohibits child labor and industrial homework in large branches of apparel making. Violations of state and federal workplace safety laws—for example, the regulations enforced by the Occupational Safety and Health Administration (OSHA)—are also part of the definition. The Wage and Hour Division (WHD) of the U.S. Department of Labor (DOL) is responsible for enforcing the FLSA. Local authorities, for example, fire departments, are also responsible for enforcing some safety laws. The U.S. DOL and the apparel workers' union—Union of Needletrades Industrial and Textile Employees (UNITE)—often summarize the definition of a sweatshop as "multiple labor law violator" or "chronic labor law violator." By emphasizing persistent violations the definition includes nontrivial behavior and excludes occasional lapses.

A clear logic led the General Accounting Office (GAO) of the U.S. Congress to invent this definition. As early as 1979 the first reports of the "new sweatshops" were in the New York press. For example, *New York* magazine published an investigative piece by Rinker Buck (1979). In 1988 Congressman (now Senator) Charles Schumer (D-NY) asked the GAO—an agency of Congress that investigates executive branch spending and program performance on behalf of the Congress and at the behest of its members—to look into the sweatshop problem around the country. The GAO report to Congressman Schumer was entitled "Sweatshops in the U.S.: Opinions on Their Extent and Possible Enforcement Options" (1988). As is customary when congresspersons request reports from them, the GAO opens with a letter of transmittal. Here is the key excerpt from that letter:

> Because sweatshops are not defined in federal statute or regulation, we developed a definition in cooperation with your office. We defined a sweatshop as a business that regularly violates both wage or child labor and safety or health laws. As synonyms we used the terms "chronic labor law violator" and "multiple labor law violator." (U.S. GAO 1988, 1)

This definition has the same virtue for researchers as it has for the GAO: one can objectively define a law violator and thus count (or estimate) the number of violators. It is much harder to study the prevalence of a condition if each of its defining characteristics is subjective and totally contextual. The term *sweatshop* is a vivid metaphor for a lousy job: the challenge for research is to turn metaphor into something measurable.

There is a cost to the clarity thus gained. Even if an employer does pay the minimum wage and does pay overtime premiums for longer hours, the ordinary moral sensibility of our culture might still judge the wage too low. For example, the minimum wage will not lift a family of three out of poverty. By moving the word *sweatshop* from the realm of metaphor and subjective moralism to that of a legalistic test, the GAO's definition leaves many low-paying jobs with lousy conditions unsullied by the label *sweatshop*. Principally for this reason many people disagree with the GAO's definition (Rothstein 1996b; N. Green 1997; Waldinger and Lapp 1993; A. Ross 1997, 296).

The most common criticism of the legalistic definition is that, on the one hand, it is arbitrary and, on the other, it confers moral dignity to bad pay. Besides the fact that the GAO's definition is most useful for research purposes, there is, however, another defense for it. The framework of social protections embodied in labor and public health law defines what Marx would have called the "historical" or "social" element that is part of the determination of the value of labor power (Marx 1998). By reserving the term *sweatshop* for those workplaces that do not meet even the low standards of public law, the definition denotes "super exploitation," that is, something even more extreme than low pay.

In practice, shops in the apparel industry that violate the wage or over-time laws almost always violate both of these, which are known collectively as the "monetary provisions" of the FLSA. An even higher proportion violates OSHA safety regulations. Thus, in the ordinary discourse of enforcement—for example, when the U.S. DOL released quarterly enforcement reports as part of its "No Sweat" program in the 1990s—chronic and nontrivial minimum wage violations are taken as *indicators* of sweatshop conditions.

Sweatshops in the U.S. Apparel Industry: How Many?

Clarifying the definition of sweatshops in terms of U.S. law is important because at least one other approach came up with very different results. In an important article, Waldinger and Lapp (1993) used an indirect and indeed ingenious method to claim that there was little sweatshop labor in the New York region's apparel industry. A discussion of their method and findings illustrates the ambiguity of the idea of "informal economy" and the dangers inherent in its literal use.

Waldinger and Lapp argue that the consensus-estimating technique that suggested as many as fifty thousand sweatshop workers in New York in the 1980s was based on erroneous guesses. They point out that in the decade of the 1980s a series of scholars (including myself) generated estimates by citing each other's guesses. The authors proceed to examine whether indirect measures of sweatshops indicate a marked increase in "covert" workers. The authors' definition of a sweatshop is one that is "covert" or in the "informal sector."

They argue that a marked decrease in manufacturing wages as a proportion of value-added[6] in manufacturing would indicate an increase in covert production workers. The proportion of production workers to all workers should also decrease if a substantial fraction of production workers are working "off the books"—paid in cash by contractors. They demonstrate that wages as a proportion of value-added declined by about 10 percent in the 1970s and 1980s in the nation as well as in New York and California. This decline indicates productivity gains but no differences between the nation as a whole and the areas likely to have been impacted by sweatshops. Furthermore, they find no reduction in the number of production workers as a proportion of all workers in the garment industry. They conclude that there is a low-wage immigrant garment industry but that estimates of large increases in covert sweatshop employment are overstated.

While there is reason for skepticism about estimates based on anecdote and even on informed opinion, there are severe methodological problems with Waldinger and Lapp's approach. The most important problem is embedded in their definition of shops that are "off the books" and thus in the informal sector. The "informal sector" refers to economic activity that is not officially recorded or registered and so remains untaxed. In developing countries, examples would be homeworkers and street vendors. In developed countries, it would include off-the-books activity. Many illegal enterprises would therefore be included in the informal sector, such as prostitution or illegal drug sales, but it would also include activity that intends to evade some laws in otherwise legal activity. Waldinger and Lapp assume that the bulk of sweatshop workers will not show up as workers in tax or other official payrolls. Yet, investigators from the WHD of the U.S. DOL and from the New York Labor Department often find that shops that are multiple labor or health and safety law violators do show up in official records.

Evidence that the majority of sweatshops may be visible to some official records appears in the GAO study of tax compliance of sweatshops in New York and California (U.S. GAO 1994a)—published after Waldinger and Lapp's 1993 article. In that study, composed of the violators *known* to the Departments of Labor of the two states, the GAO found that in New York City fifteen out of twenty-one sweatshops filed state taxes at least once between 1990 and 1994; in California thirty-eight out of forty-four had done so. Of the ninety-four places in the two states (which included restaurants), only eight had not filed unemployment payroll taxes.[7]

The idea of an informal economy does not require total invisibility. In apparel shops, for example, workers are often asked to start work before they punch in on the legally required time clock. Castells and Portes note "the systematic linkage between formal and informal sectors, *following the requirements of profitability*" (1989, 12, emphasis added). The informal sector, they say, "is unregulated by the institutions of society in a legal and social environment in which similar activities are regulated." Indeed, as we see in the apparel industry, the subcontracting system allows for an elaborate and complex texture in which the formal and informal, the recorded and unrecorded, are woven among closely related though fictively distinct entities. As between manufacturers and contractors, some contractor practices are closely inspected—quality control—while others "escape" the notice of the commissioning principal; and the contractors and their subcontractors record some activities that are legal, while other activities that may be illicit are "cash only."[8]

This last practice is especially significant for Waldinger and Lapp's method because it subverts the statistical underpinning of their conclusion. Indeed, their conclusion results, in large part, from their definition of sweatshops as referring only to firms that are totally covert. They write, "While Chinatown's garment contractors may include many firms that cheat on hours and wage laws . . . they are clearly not underground" (15). Violations among New York's Chinatown contractors are difficult to find. Yet Zhou (1992) surveyed over four hundred Chinatown women workers and found that their average wage was below the legal minimum.

When the U.S. DOL constructed a baseline survey in New York, it found that, in a sample of firms, 90 percent of New York City's Chinatown shops were labor law violators (U.S. DOL 1997). Yet, according to Waldinger and Lapp, these are not sweatshops because they are not "underground."

Waldinger and Lapp used a highly advanced statistical technique and found no evidence for a completely off-the-books apparel sector.[9] Instead of concluding that there is no significant sweatshop sector in the apparel industry, they should have found that the concept of the informal sector is relative, not absolute.

What Is a Sweatshop?

The New Sweatshops: Prevalence

The evidence of sweatshop prevalence consists of reports from state and federal Departments of Labor and GAO surveys that, unlike Waldinger and Lapp, examine compliance with the FLSA and OSHA regulations.

Los Angeles and Southern California, 1994–2000

Four times in the 1990s the U.S. DOL, the California state labor commissioner's office, and Cal/OSHA cooperated in surveys of garment contractors in southern California and in particular in the Los Angeles region. The California Division of Labor Standards Enforcement (DLSE) initiated a Targeted Industries Partnership Program (TIPP) in 1992, and these surveys have been a cooperative program of TIPP (California State DLSE 1996). In 1994 and 1996 the firms surveyed were randomly selected from California Employment Development Department records of firms in Standard Industrial Classification (SIC) 2300 (apparel manufacturing).[10] Since the first survey (1994) showed that 80 percent of the firms were in the five-county area of the Los Angeles Basin, the 1996 survey focused on this region. The data were then reanalyzed to make comparisons between them. In 1994, 78 percent of the firms had either minimum wage or overtime violations of the law—that is, "monetary provisions." Ninety-eight percent had some kind of violation, most frequently record keeping. The average number of violations (out of ten categories) was 4.5.[11] By 1996, 61 percent of the seventy-six firms studied had monetary violations (the reduction was not statistically significant at the 90 percent confidence level, according to the DLSE). In 1996 almost three-quarters of the firms (72 percent) had serious OSHA violations, 43 percent had minimum wage liabilities, and 55 percent had overtime liabilities. The average back pay owed due to minimum wage violations in 1996 was $1,592 for each worker; the average back pay owed for overtime violations was $1,643. At minimum wage ($4.75 in 1996) the most a fully employed worker would receive for standard workweeks would have been $9,500. The back pay due was almost 17 percent of base pay; the overtime pay due was just over 17 percent. If a worker were subject to both violations, she would have been short 34 percent of potential base pay. None of these numbers is trivial for the working poor, although they were lower than the numbers for 1994 (U.S. DOL 1996).

A voluntary program of compliance monitoring, in which the manufacturers—that is, jobbers who hire contractors—undertake to monitor the labor law compliance of their agents, has been the primary enforcement innovation of the DOL. Compliance monitoring does, according to these surveys, reduce violations noticeably. The percentage of firms with wage liabilities was significantly less for monitored firms (48 percent) than for those not monitored (78 percent). A little less than half of the firms (48 percent) were monitored.[12]

In 1998 the DOL found compliance rates in Los Angeles had not appreciably increased (U.S. DOL 1998). In August 2000 the DOL and the cooperating California agencies released the results of their latest study to date: only one-third of garment contractors complied with labor law and only 37 percent of a random sample of previously cited violators complied with the law (U.S. DOL 2000).

In summary, considerably over one-half of the random samples of firms engaged in apparel manufacturing in southern California had multiple labor law, in particular monetary and environmental law, violations in the mid-1990s. Estimates of the number of apparel workers in the region run between 120,000 and 150,000. These data justify an estimate that 70,000 to 90,000 workers labor in sweatshop conditions in southern California.

San Francisco, 1995–97

In the smaller labor market of the San Francisco Bay Area, in surveys whose details have not been released, the U.S. DOL found FLSA (wages and hours) violations at lower levels—43 percent in 1995 and only 21 percent in 1997 (Fraser 1998). No improvement had been made in that small labor market (ten thousand workers) by 1999: 74 percent of "Bay Area garment businesses comply with the minimum wage, overtime pay and other requirements of the Fair Labor Standards Act, not a significant change from a similar 1997 survey, and up . . . from 57 percent in 1995" (U.S. DOL 1999).

What Is a Sweatshop?

New York, 1997, 1999

A U.S. DOL 1997 survey of New York City garment shops included ninety-four firms. According to the DOL, the study was intended, as was the 1994 Los Angeles one, to create a baseline for future findings.

> The New York City survey consisted of a random sample of the latest available information regarding known garment contractors in all five boroughs. Among other purposes, this and other investigation-based surveys help establish a statistically valid baseline of compliance in order to track industry compliance over the long term. (U.S. DOL 1997)

In this study the DOL found that 63 percent of the firms violated the minimum wage and overtime provisions of the FLSA and that 70 percent violated the record-keeping requirements of the law. In Chinatown, 90 percent of the firms violated the monetary provisions of the law. In 1997 there were somewhat over seventy-five thousand garment workers in the New York area. A sweatshop population estimate based on the gross number of employees would range from 63 percent down to 40 percent: between forty-seven thousand and thirty-three thousand workers (without taking into account invisible home sewing machine operators). The same method produces a range of forty-eight thousand to seventy-six thousand sweatshop workers based on New York's 1983 employment base. This is close to the fifty thousand worker estimate (Ross and Trachte 1983) that Waldinger and Lapp (1993) criticized so harshly.[13]

Throughout the period under discussion (1970s–90s) employment in the apparel industry declined drastically, and that is particularly so in New York City. Apparel employment in New York City declined from 340,000 in 1950 to 140,000 in 1980 to 59,000 in 2000 to 40,000 in 2002 (Ross and Trachte 1983; Bureau of Labor Statistics 2004b). The fifty thousand sweatshop worker estimate of the early 1980s was probably low.[14]

In 1999 contractor violations of the FLSA in New York continued at an unchanged rate (U.S. DOL 1999). In 2001, according to the Bush administration's DOL, now backing off from the more aggressive stance of the Clinton administration, the rate of New York violator contractors had fallen to 48 percent (U.S. DOL 2002).

Underestimation? Estimation!

While Waldinger and Lapp (1993) exaggerated the invisibility of the sweatshop sector of apparel manufacturing, the U.S. DOL and California DLSE data almost certainly underestimate the size of the sector. The official agencies base their violation data exclusively on firms that, as mentioned previously, have *some* legal visibility to authorities. Contractors who are totally cash based, with no legal existence, will not appear in their data; more importantly, the labor force toiling for contractors who illegally give workers bundles to sew at home are largely obscured from these data. Large segments of the Dallas and Miami (U.S. GAO 1994b) garment industry employment may be invisible to official records, as may be segments of New York's Chinatown and Mexican workers in Los Angeles.

In the two leading production centers of the industry, Los Angeles and New York, more than 60 percent of contractor shops in the visible industry provided sweatshop conditions through the year 2000.[15] In the year 2000 there were just under 760,000 recorded apparel workers in the United States (Bureau of Labor Statistics 2001a), including workers both in the apparel manufacturing industry and those in the smaller knitted mill products industry (see appendix 1). This number included over 287,000 sewing machine operators and another 148,000 jobs in categories likely to take place in contractor shops, such as dry cleaners. There are, then, about 435,000 recorded workers in apparel jobs vulnerable to sweatshop conditions. In addition, it is likely that another 20 percent of the sewing machine operators are homeworkers or unrecorded.

Informants and industry experts believe that the sweatshop violation rates are lower in the modern factories outside the fashion production centers, such as those in the mid-south. The overall violation estimate for workers in vulnerable occupations is, therefore, held at 50 percent (rather than at the 60 percent rate used in earlier work). For knitted wear, except for sewing machine operators, the estimate is lower, 20 percent, based on the lower probability of contractor shops being employed in this whole industry fragment.

What Is a Sweatshop?

Adding 50 percent of the recorded base in apparel, 20 percent of those outside of sewing machine operators in knitted wear, and all of the unrecorded sewing machine operators produces an estimate of about 265,000 workers laboring in sweatshop conditions in the United States in 2000. Strikingly, employment declined in the central apparel production part of the industry (the given estimate includes a small portion of knitted products) by over 100,000 workers between 1998 and 2000 (Bureau of Labor Statistics 2001a). The number of sweatshop workers may, therefore, have declined.

This procedure was a detailed replication of 1998 work that produced an estimate of 400,000 sweatshop workers. The difference is that the current estimate uses somewhat more cautious estimators for sweatshop prevalence for the year 2000 and takes into account the reduction in employment base of 165,000 workers in the apparel industry and knitted wear industry in three years. This resulted in the estimated number of sweatshop workers in the United States in the year 2000 of 265,000. The method is explained in detail in appendix 1.

For the year 2000 this "occupational" method of estimation was supplemented with an "establishment" method. This method approximates the number of workplaces that fit the definition of a sweatshop and then the number of workers involved in them. The establishment method, also outlined in appendix 1, produced a low-range estimate of 229,000 workers and a high-range estimate of 256,000 workers. This is encouraging: if two rather different techniques produce very similar results, one feels more confident in one's estimate. The midpoint of the establishment-based estimates is 243,000; the midpoint between this and the occupational estimate (264,000) is about 254,000. *There are, therefore, approximately 255,000 sweatshop workers in the United States.*

The global context here is relevant. If we go back to 1998 employment levels, using the 1998 American sweatshop estimate, the United States was the second largest employer of clothing workers in the world (after China). Its 400,000 sweatshop workers, if they were in a separate national economy, would be the world's fourth largest mass of clothing workers. Alternatively, ignoring employment level changes elsewhere around the world, the estimate of 255,000 sweatshop workers for the year 2000 would place the United States' victims of labor abuse as the eighth largest mass of clothing workers in the world (see table 3).

Sweatshops Abroad: The Global Context

There are no universally accepted, objective, measurable criteria for defining a workplace as a sweatshop around the world. There is a wealth of information that allows us to make cautious judgments, however, and an emerging international consensus about what constitutes labor abuse. Many countries have national minimum wage and maximum hours laws—and they are violated often, as are ours. In addition, minimum wage provisions of the law in many national jurisdictions are even more inadequate than our own. Starting with the problem of our own minimum wage law as the definition of decency reveals the American problem and the global one.

This book uses a legalistic definition for U.S. sweatshops—the core of the definition is violations of the FLSA as an operational measurement of the broader ideas of low pay and long hours. In addition, our discussion acknowledges, though it did not attempt to directly measure, the idea of unhealthy or unsafe conditions and oppressive violations of human dignity. If one took this approach to a world scale, it would first encounter an inherent difficulty: is any given nation's minimum wage law a good indicator of low wages?

To work with this idea fairly the first matter is the adequacy of the U.S. minimum wage. Table 4 shows the value of the U.S. federal minimum wage in relation to the official poverty level for different sized families and households, all corrected for the year 2000. For example, a mother supporting one child employed full-time, year round, would earn $10,712, about 11 percent ($1,100) below the poverty level. The minimum wage produces income that is $3,100, or just under 30 percent, short of official poverty for a family of three.

Analysts of living costs and American popular opinion think decency requires much more than the official poverty level. In one study, a sample of Americans told interviewers how much they thought the minimum a family of four needed to get by: this was 24 percent above the official poverty level. Strikingly, this coincides with at least one school of thought as to how to revise the official poverty line (Wilson 1996, 254–56).

If the poverty line for the United States was expanded by 25 percent, the average wages of all legal apparel workers in the country in 2000 ($22,000) would fall below the revised poverty level for a family of four ($22,200) and would be barely above that required for a three-person family ($20,500). This average includes the managers, designers, and other higher waged persons in the industry. So we must drill more deeply into the material and take this a bit further.

There were over 300,000 visible sewing machine operators in the United States in 1999. Official statistics necessarily overstate their average wages because the official documents show them earning an average hourly wage of $7.74 and a median wage of $7.25. Since, as estimated earlier, as many as half of them or more earn less than the minimum wage, it is likely that the DOL's survey method includes data that are falsified by employers. Even setting aside this matter, if one employs the expanded definition of poverty, *legal* sewing machine operators, working above the *legal* minimum wage, earned an average of $16,090 in 1999. This was over $650 short of the 1999 expanded poverty definition for a family of three and 15 percent above that standard for a family of two (see table 5 for the calculations and references).

It is clear that any fair-minded international comparison of apparel industry labor conditions and labor rights positions will find the United States wanting in law and law enforcement along with many other countries. Nevertheless, as grinding and as unfair as U.S. apparel industry conditions may be, the world at large, with the apparent exception of Western Europe, is no better and often worse. These conditions are highly related: around the world there is extreme competitive pressure to find ever cheaper pools of labor to serve the apparel export markets.

In the face of competitive pressure, there is, as the critics of global capitalism call it, a "race to the bottom" (of labor standards). In response to this there is mounting social movement pressure in North America and Europe forcing an emerging consensus that defines the outer limits of decency in apparel industry conditions. The substance of this broad consensus does not define adequacy. In a fashion similar to the flawed American minimum wage law, the emerging international consensus defines the boundary of civilized economic behavior. One can discern the consensus by examining the various codes of conduct that industry and advocacy groups have proposed. The corporations themselves have directly influenced some of them, and these codes are now the subject of fierce controversies. The controversies mainly concern the monitoring of standards, transparency (meaning how much information the public will get), and enforcement or sanctions. What is interesting is the degree of content overlap among them. The provisions of these codes and references to the Web sites where they may be directly accessed are found in table 6.

Among the four most prominent code-making groups is the Clean Clothes Campaign (CCC), based in Amsterdam and at the center of a broad European network of consumer groups committed to improving the lives of garment workers worldwide. The CCC "model code of conduct" was put forward for adoption by individual firms in 1998; in 2000 the CCC embarked on a pilot project to test its implementation with European retailers and manufacturers. They have not yet reported how many or which firms have adopted it. The CCC model code incorporates by explicit reference the idea of core labor rights put forth by the UN-affiliated International Labor Organization (ILO). The Fair Labor Association (FLA) is an American industry nongovernmental organization (NGO) project originally initiated by Secretary of Labor Robert Reich under President Clinton. In an unanticipated turn of events (see chapter 7) the FLA was, at first, the affiliation of choice for universities trying to placate antisweatshop student campaigners. As of the summer of 2003, 178 universities that license or sell apparel with their imprinted logos have joined the FLA, along with twelve large clothing and footwear firms and a number of NGOs. The FLA became embroiled in a major controversy when the American garment workers union, UNITE, refused to sign its final report and walked out. A student-initiated competitor was developed, with UNITE's blessing, the Workers Rights Consortium (WRC), that put forward a similar code of conduct with a very different monitoring approach. A business standards group, Social Accountability International (SAI), has promulgated a code—called SA8000—that is notable for being based on ILO conventions on labor rights. Finally, the Ethical Trading Initiative (ETI) is a British organization "of companies, non-governmental organisations (NGOs), and trade union organisations committed to working together to identify and promote good practice in the implementation of codes of labour practice" (ETI 2003). Twenty-four large retailers and manufacturers with significant British operations, including Marks and Spencer and Levi Strauss, and over a dozen major NGOs, including Oxfam, are signatories to the ETI. In addition, the British Trades Union Conference and the international apparel worker confederation based in Brussels—the International Textile, Garment, and Leather Workers' Federation (ITGLWF)—have adopted the base code of the ETI. Notably, the International Confederation of Free Trades Unions (ICFTU) and International Union of Food, Agriculture, Hotel, Restaurant, Catering, Tobacco and Allied Workers' Associations (IUF) have also endorsed this initiative.

Each of the organizations and codes regards compensation at least as high as the national legal minimum wage as a requirement of good behavior. This seems obvious—but in many countries' export sectors, enforcement of local legal minimum standards is weak or nonexistent.

In addition, as is also the case in the United States, the minimum wage is often inadequate to support a family and sometimes inadequate to support an individual worker. This is true in Mexico (U.S. Department of State 2001), for example, which is tied with China as the biggest exporter to the United States and is one of the top ten clothing exporters in the world. Lack of enforcement is a frequent complaint of workers rights watchdogs about mainland China, the world's largest exporter of clothing, where the laws are good but enforcement scarce.

Acknowledging the frequent inadequacy of national legal minimum wage legislation, the CCC, the WRC, the ETI, and SA8000 all call for a wage standard that meets the workers' basic needs and some discretionary income available for saving. Only the WRC code adds language recognizing that average family size in different countries should be taken into account. The more industry-oriented FLA code of conduct softly "recognize(s) that wages are essential to meeting employees' basic needs" (FLA 2003b).

Each of the codes puts forth a standard workweek of forty-eight hours (except where national legislation is lower), and all but the WRC notes that up to twelve more hours may be requested by the employer. The WRC makes no mention of the number of overtime hours it considers legitimate, but, along with all but the FLA, the WRC states that overtime should be voluntary and paid at a premium (for example, 1.5 times the regular pay). The FLA does not require that overtime be voluntary but merely says it should be paid at least regular rates. Strikingly, this language is necessary in the garment industry because almost everywhere workers are paid by the piece; if they fail to meet a quota for the day to make their minimum wage, they may be (legally or illegally) required by their employers to work extra time without additional pay.

All of the codes include language prohibiting discrimination on a variety of ascribed characteristics—such as race, nationality, religion, and gender. All reject "harsh punishment" or harassment (sexual included) and/or corporal punishment, and all state that forced, bonded, or indentured labor should be rejected.

Each code adopts similar language restricting child labor. Children under the age of fifteen should not be employed in factories, unless national law allows this, in which case, for developing countries, the ILO exception is recognized. Where the compulsory school-leaving age is higher, firms should use that standard in a given country.

Each code includes a positive obligation to provide a safe and healthy work environment. All but the FLA include language indicating that this should be according to current knowledge; in addition, SA8000 and the ETI make explicit mention of clean and healthy dormitories where they are provided and, notably, bathrooms and toilets as well. The WRC code makes particular mention of women's reproductive health protection.

In addition, each code makes mention of a right of association and collective bargaining. But they do so differently. The FLA does not mention ILO conventions on the right to form and join a union or protection against discrimination as a member or official of a union. Nor does the

What Is a Sweatshop?

FLA put a positive obligation on its signatories to facilitate representative institutions for workers in countries where trade unions are not legal or are otherwise repressed. The codes of the WRC, SA8000, CCC, and ETI each provide language about these matters.

Among these codes there is no consensus about the need for reporting violations or about the identification of subcontractors in a public fashion. These are major issues among American activists, and only the American student-labor organization, the WRC, requires such transparency in its model code.

There is, then, a bare-bones consensus definition of a standard; falling below it will make a place of work a sweatshop.

On a world scale, in regard to pay, a sweatshop is a place where workers are paid below the local minimum wage or where, at that wage, they are unable to meet their basic needs. Left without broad agreement is the size of family for which the wage should provide. In regard to hours of work, forty-eight hours seems to be the developing country standard, with a near consensus that overtime hours, as many as twelve additional, should garner premium pay. The codes all acknowledge discrimination and personal abuse as oppressive conditions, and they universally affirm, albeit with degrees of clarity, a right to association. They all call for healthy and safe work conditions, and two mention toilets and dorms as part of these concerns.

These standards would allow a researcher, in principle, to report, as I have done in this chapter for the United States, the number of sweatshop workers in the world. But the task is too big. Later chapters, however, will show why sweatshops are so prevalent in the United States—and the most important single reason is because they are so prevalent in the world. This definition of the line between merely poorly paid work and a sweatshop is capable of objective measurement—it allows us to go beyond metaphor and subjective disapproval. But it is not exorbitant.

Imagine a fifteen-year-old girl working sixty hours a week at a minimum wage that might be just enough to feed herself and pay for fuel to cook the food. Charles Kernaghan, one of the great American campaigners on this issue, paraphrases a Salvadoran worker in his speeches when he says: "they want to rise from misery to poverty."

Appendix 1. Estimating the Number of Sweatshop Workers in the United States in 2000

Method 1: Occupational Estimation

Table 1 gives the detailed numbers for the steps described in the following estimation. See chapter 1 references for the origin of violation rates.

1. Begin with a survey regularly published by the U.S. Bureau of Labor Statistics: the Occupational Employment Survey, last done in 1999 and available on-line at <http://stats.bls.gov/oes/1999/oesi2_23.htm>. This source also gives median and mean hourly wages and annual earnings for each occupation. From that list of hundreds of detailed occupations in apparel manufacture (SIC 23), the estimate took production occupations that were apt to be located in contractor shops. The violation rate of the FLSA that the DOL had found in major garment-making centers was known; in addition, the estimate added those other low-income occupations (below nine dollars an hour) that were likely to be associated with these operations. I performed the same operation for SIC 225—knitted mill products.

2. Sum the percentage of total industry employment of occupations vulnerable to sweatshops for SIC 23. These are occupations apt to be in contractor shops.

3. Since the survey was for 1999, the percentage of vulnerable workers was applied to the total employment of the industry for the year 2000. This, of course, reduced the estimate of potential sweatshop workers because the industry is shrinking.

4. The number of vulnerable workers established by this number was multiplied by an estimated 50 percent violation rate.

TABLE 1. Estimating the Number of Sweatshop Workers in the United States in the Year 2000: Occupation Method

A. Standard Industrial Code (SIC) 23

Vulnerable Occupation	% of Total Industry Employment
Janitors and cleaners, except maids and housekeeping cleaners	0.0067
Maids and housekeeping cleaners	0.0002
Laundry and dry-cleaning workers	0.0044
Pressers, textile, garment, and related materials	0.0175
Sewing machine operators	0.4226
Shoe and leather workers and repairers	0.0028
Sewers, hand	0.0145
Tailors, dressmakers, and custom sewers	0.0049
Textile bleaching and dyeing machine operators and tenders	0.0025
Textile cutting machine setters, operators, and tenders	0.0236
Cutters and trimmers, hand	0.0032
Cutting and slicing machine setters, operators, and tenders	0.0042
Inspectors, testers, sorters, samplers, and weighers	0.0313
Packaging and filling machine operators and tenders	0.0022
Cementing and gluing machine operators and tenders	0.0011
Helpers—production workers	0.0143
Laborers and freight, stock, and material movers, hand	0.0225
Machine feeders and offbearers	0.0044
Packers and packagers, hand	0.0366
Total % vulnerable occupations in SIC 23, 1999	61.95

Calculation of SIC 23 Estimated Number of Sweatshop Workers

Year 2000 SIC 23 annual employment	633,200
Vulnerable visible workers (633,200 × 61.95%)	392,267
Visible sweatshop workers (392,267 × 50%)	196,134
Invisible sewing machine operators (633,200 × 42.26 × 20%)	53,518
Total estimated SIC 23 sweatshop workers (196,134 + 53,158)	249,652

B. Standard Industrial Code (SIC) 225

Vulnerable Occupation	% of Total Industry Employment
Pressers, textile, garment, and related materials (3)	0.0225
Sewing machine operators	0.1594
Sewers, hand	0.0137
Textile bleaching and dyeing machine operators and tenders	0.0547
Cutters and trimmers, hand	0.0004
Helpers—production workers	0.0236

(continued)

TABLE 1. *Continued*

Laborers and freight, stock, and material movers, hand	0.0210
Machine feeders and offbearers (3)	0.00049
Packers and packagers, hand (3)	.0453
Total % vulnerable operations in SIC 225, 1999	34.55

Calculation of SIC 225 Estimated Number of Sweatshop Workers

Year 2000 SIC 225 annual employment	125,600
Vulnerable visible workers	
(125,600 × 34.55%)	43,395
Vulnerable visible workers minus sewing machine operators	
(43,395 – 20021)	23,374
Estimated nonsewer sweatshop workers	
(23,374 × 20%)	4,675
Estimated sewing machine operations when violation rate is applied	
(20,021 × 50%)	10,010
Total estimated SIC 225 sweatshop workers	
(4,675 + 10,010)	14,685

Grand total estimate of number of U.S. sweatshop workers in year 2000

Total estimated SIC 23 sweatshop workers	
plus total estimated SIC 225 sweatshop workers	
(249,652 + 14,685)	264,337

    a.   This is based on the 61+ percent violation rates in New York and Los Angeles and estimates equally high in, for example, El Paso, Miami, and Dallas (see chapter 1). The lowered overall rate corrects for the fact that contractor shops are smaller than other shops. A 50 percent rate was used to estimate the numbers of vulnerable workers actually in sweatshops.

  5. To this number was added an estimate of the invisible home sewing machine operators, taken to be an additional 20 percent of the total number of visible sewing machine operators.

  6. The same operation was performed to establish vulnerable occupations for SIC 225 (knitting mills) as a percentage of total industry employment, available on-line at <http://stats.bls.gov/oes/1999/oesi3_225.htm>. Once again I multiplied the percentage of total industry employment in vulnerable occupations in 1999 by the total industry employment in 2000 to get the vulnerable worker base number.

    a.   For this industry group I then removed the sewing machine operators and took an estimated 20 percent of remaining vulnerable occupations as sweatshop workers.

    b.   For sewing machine operators, I estimated a 50 percent violation rate and added this number back.

  7. I added the SIC 23 and 225 figures for the total estimate: 264,337 ≈ 264,000.

44

Method 2: Establishment Estimation

Table 2 summarizes this procedure.

TABLE 2. Estimating the Number of Sweatshop Workers in the United States in the Year 2000: Establishment Method

	Number of Establishments	Industry Average Establishment Size
SIC 23 data		
(633,200 workers)	22,947	27.6
Contractor shops per SIC 23	16,603	
data (202,393 workers)	(22,947 × 70%)	21.0
Contractor shops per NAICS 315 data		
(175,545 workers)	13,768	25.5

Calculation of Estimated Numbers of Sweatshop Workers Using SIC 23 and NAICS 315 Data

(a) Before inclusion of estimated number of invisible sewing machine operators

	Number of Sweatshops	Number of Workers
SIC 23 data, applying violation rate		
(16,063 × 60%)	9,638	202,393 (at 21 workers per establishment)
NAICS 315 data, applying violation rate		
(13,768 × 50%)	6,884	175,545 (at 25.5 workers per establishment)

(b) Adding estimated number of invisible sewing machine operators

Estimated number of invisible sewing machine operators	53,500
Low estimate of total number of sweatshop workers (175,545 + 53,500)	229,045
High estimate of total number of sweatshop workers (202,393 + 53,500)	255,893

Note: Discrepancies in total numbers of workers are due to rounding.

Note: 71% of women's outerwear establishments are contractors, and their average size is 21 employees; 59% of total cut and sew apparel manufacturing, as measured by the newer (NAICS) classifications, which count fewer establishments and workers in the industry, are contractors. These include 199,807 workers at an average establishment size of 25.5. See U.S. Census Bureau 1998.

1. Estimate the number of contractor shops in the industry. There are different databases with somewhat different total numbers of establishments. The older SIC 23, apparel manufacturing, had 22,947 establishments in the year 2000. This older system does not clearly separate contractor shops from other establishments. The newer North American Industry Classification System (NAICS) substantially revises the SIC system. For 1997, for example, the year of the last published Economic Census, there were 25,068 SIC 23 establishments and 17,065 NAICS 315 establishments. The NAICS system, however, identified contractors versus manufacturers in some of the major divisions of the industry; and it included large elements of the older SIC 225—knitting mill products.

The U.S. Census Bureau publishes a "Bridge" document that helps show the relation of the old to the new system. This was used to establish alternate estimates of the number of shops in the apparel industry that were contractors and to whom known violation rates could be applied.

2. Seventy percent of the older women's outerwear division establishments were contractors; 59 percent of the entire new NAICS 315 are contractors. I took these as the parameters of the high and low estimates. To the high estimate I used a 60 percent violation rate—that found by the DOL in the large garment centers. To the lower estimate I applied a 50 percent violation rate, correcting for potential regional variation.
3. These procedures produced a range of 175,545 to 202,393 workers. To this number I added the same number of invisible home sewing machine operators as I had to the first method. The result is a range of 229,045 to 255,893, whose midpoint is 242,469 (243,000).

TABLE 3. Comparison of Number of U.S. Clothing Sweatshop Workers (1998 and 2000) with World Levels of Employment in Clothing Manufacturing in 1998

Rank	Country	Clothing Employment (in hundred thousands)
1	China[a]	3,677.8
2	United States	793.0
3	Mexico	567.7
4a	U.S. Sweatshop Workers (1998 estimate)[b]	400
4	Russian Federation	392.8
5	Japan	319.0
6	Bangladesh	316.5
7	Indonesia	289.3
8a	U.S. Sweatshop Workers (2000 estimate)[b]	255
8	Poland	250.0
9	Italy	213.5
10	United Kingdom	201.0
11	Brazil	185.9
12	Romania	180.0
13	Philippines	178.1
14	Korea, Republic of	177.6
15	Turkey	166.1
16	Thailand	160.0
17	South Africa	145.8
18	Portugal	136.7
19	India	133.2
20	Tunisia	125.4

Source: Data from ILO 2000, 19.

[a]Data for China include clothing and footwear.

[b]See tables 1 and 2 and discussion in this chapter for derivation of estimated numbers of U.S. sweatshop workers.

TABLE 4. Annual Income from Minimum Wage and Poverty Levels in 2000

	Two Adults, under 65 Years Old	One Adult, One Child	Two Adults, One Child	One Adult, Two Children	Averages for Family of Four
Poverty level income ($)	11,531	11,869	13,861	13,874	17,761
Poverty gap ($)[a]	−819	−1,157	−3,149	−3,162	−7,049
Poverty gap (%)[b]	7.65	10.80	29.40	29.52	65.80
Hourly wage required to reach poverty level income ($)	5.54	5.71	6.66	6.67	8.54
Hourly wage required to reach 125% of poverty level income ($)	6.93	7.13	8.33	8.34	10.67

Source: Author's calculations from official poverty thresholds: http://www.census.gov/hhes/poverty/threshld/thresh00.html; accessed 4/28/01.

[a]Poverty gap ($) is calculated by comparing gross annual income at minimum wage (40 hours per week × 52 weeks × $5.15 = $10,712) with poverty level income.

[b]Poverty gap (%) is calculated by determining the raise (%) required to bring a family up to poverty level income.

TABLE 5.   Comparison of Annual Income from Minimum Wage and Sewing Wages with Poverty Levels in 1999

	Two Adults, under 65 Years Old	One Adult, One Child	Two Adults, One Child	One Adult, Two Children	Averages for Family of Four
Poverty level income ($)	11,214	11,483	13,410	13,423	17,029
Poverty gap at minimum wage (%)[a]	4.69	7.20	25.19	25.31	58.97
Hourly wage required to reach poverty level income ($)	5.39	5.52	6.45	6.45	8.19
Hourly wage required to reach 125% of poverty level ($)	6.93	7.13	8.33	8.34	10.67
Poverty gap ($) for sewing machine operator ($)	+4,885	+4,616	+2,689	+2,676	−929.80
Poverty gap for sewing machine operator at 125% of poverty level (%)	+2,082	+2,745	−6,630	−680	−5,187

Source: Author's calculations from official poverty thresholds for 1999 (U.S. Census Bureau 2001c).

Note: Gross annual income at minimum wage is $10,712 (40 hours per week × 52 weeks × $5.15). Gross annual income for sewing machine operator is $16,099 (40 hours per week × 52 weeks × $7.74).

[a]Poverty gap (%) is calculated by determining the raise (%) required to bring a family up to poverty level income.

TABLE 6. Comparison of International Codes of Conduct for Manufacturing

(a) Wages and Hours

	Minimum Wage/Compensation	Overtime	Hours/Day Off
Fair Labor Association	minimum legal or prevailing wage: "Employers recognize that wages are essential to meeting employees' basic needs. Employers shall pay employees, as a floor, at least the minimum wage required by local law or the prevailing industry wage."	paid; premium if law requires	48 hour week plus 12 hours overtime; 1 day in 7 off
Clean Clothes Campaign (CCC)	legal or industry minimum and basic needs: Wages should meet "at least legal or industry minimum standards and always be sufficient to meet basic needs of workers and their families and to provide some discretionary income."	voluntary; always premium	48 hour week plus 12 hours overtime; 1 day in 7 off
Social Accountability International code (SA8000)	legal minimum and basic needs: "wages paid for a standard working week shall . . . always be sufficient to meet basic needs of personnel and to provide some discretionary income."	voluntary; always premium	48 hour week plus 12 hours overtime; 1 day in 7 off
Workers Rights Consortium	legal minimum, dignified living wage, and needs: "provide for essential needs and establish a dignified living wage for workers and their families."[a]	voluntary; premium	48 hour week plus 12 hours overtime; 1 day in 7 off
Ethical Trading Initiative	legal minimum plus needs: "Wages and benefits paid for a standard working week meet, at a minimum, national legal standards or industry benchmark standards, whichever is higher. In any event wages should always be enough to meet basic needs and to provide some discretionary income."	voluntary; premium	48 hour week plus 12 hours overtime; 1 day in 7 off

(continued)

TABLE 6. *Continued*

(b) Restrictions on Certain Types of Labor

	Child Labor	Forced Labor
FLA	at least age 15 (14 in developing countries) or school leaving age if higher	no prison, indenture, bonded labor
CCC	at least age 15 or school leaving age	forced labor not allowed; ILO standards 29, 105
SA8000	at least age 15 (14 in developing countries) or school leaving age if higher	forced labor not allowed; no worker deposits of money or identity papers
Workers Rights Consortium	at least age 15 (14 in developing countries) or school leaving age if higher	forced labor not allowed
Ethical Trading Initiative	15 (14 in developing countries) or school leaving age if higher	forced labor not allowed

(c) Other Provisions for Worker Protection

	Safety/Health	Discrimination	Harassment/Abuse	Right of Association	Public Disclosure of Violations
FLA	safe and healthy working environment	discrimination by race, nationality, ethnicity, disability, gender, age, political opinion, etc., prohibited	prohibited	right to association and collective bargaining	no
CCC	safe and hygienic working environment according to prevailing knowledge	similar to FLA standard: ILO 100, 111	prohibited	right of association and collective bargaining; ILO 87, 98	for monitoring purposes

SA8000	safe and healthy working environment according to prevailing knowledge; same for dormitories; clean bathrooms	similar to FLA	prohibited	right to join a union and bargain; alternatives to be facilitated where unions and collective bargaining are illegal	yes if establishment successfully achieves certification; no if establishment fails certification
Workers Rights Consortium	safe and healthy working environment; protection for women's reproductive health	similar to FLA	prohibited	right to association and to join a union; not facilitate state action against unions where unions are not legal	yes
Ethical Trading Initiative	safe and healthy working environment according to prevailing knowledge; same for dormitories; clean bathrooms required	similar to FLA	no harsh punishment or intimidation allowed	if right to freedom of association and collective bargaining restricted under laws, employer should facilitate, and not hinder, development of parallel means for independent and free association and bargaining	no

Source: Data from Fair Labor Association: http://www.fairlabor.org/all/code/index.html; Clean Clothes Campaign: http://www.cleanclothes.org/codes/cccode.htm; SA 8000: http://www.cepaa.org/SA8000/SA8000.htm; Workers Rights Consortium: http://www.workersrights.org/coc.asp; and Ethical Trading Initiative: http://www.eti.org.uk/pub/home /welcome/main/index.shtml. Accessed January 21, 2004.

[a]"A living wage is a 'take home' or 'net' wage earned during a country's legal maximum work week, but not more than 48 hours. A living wage provides for the basic needs (housing, energy, nutrition, clothing, health care, education, potable water, childcare, transportation and savings) of an average family unit of employees in the garment manufacturing employment sector of the country divided by the average number of adult wage earners in the family unit of employees in the garment manufacturing employment sector of the country" (Workers Rights Consortium 2002).

2 Memory of Strike and Fire

1909: Clara Lemlich

In the fall of 1909 young women sewing machine operators—"girls" they
were called, and many were but fourteen or fifteen—began a strike against
two New York City garment firms. The Triangle Shirtwaist Company and
Leisorson's were two among the very large "inside" or factory-based manufacturers. Almost two years later a fire at the Triangle Factory would sear
American memory, forever joining the word *sweatshop* to the image of
women and children trying to escape fire by jumping to their deaths. It
was, however, the heroism of the girls of 1909 that drew such sympathetic
attention to the victims of 1911 (McClymer 1998).

The operators wanted their desperately low wages raised; they wanted
recognition of their union, the embryonic ILGWU; and they wanted
health and sanitary provisions, such as clean restrooms and fire sprinklers.
Soon word of the strike spread throughout the garment shops of New
York, concentrated in Lower Manhattan, and the small group of activists
who led the tiny Local 25 determined that to spread the movement beyond
their initial group they needed a general strike, which in turn required a
community meeting. The small ILGWU was barely prepared to help its

even smaller Local 25—the women shirtwaist makers. Some thought the men were insensitive to the needs of the women workers.

With the strike growing and more of the women in the small contractor sewing shops leaving their shops, the men of the ILGWU and the leadership of Local 25 were at a crossroad. They called for a meeting at the Cooper Union Hall in Lower Manhattan, the site of many prominent civic events, not the least of which was Abraham Lincoln's 1860 address "Right Makes Might," which cemented his campaign support in New York.

The big meeting at Cooper Union was held on November 22, 1909. Over two thousand sewers—operators—crowded the hall. Speeches were translated among English, Italian, and Yiddish. Samuel Gompers, the American Federation of Labor (AFL) president, whom historians consider notable for both his eloquence and his moderate views (Buhle 1999; Greene 1998), was a major speaker. Gompers expressed his ambivalence about strikes in general but urged the workers to be determined if they did go on strike. According to the *New York Call,* reporting the day after the meeting, Gompers said: "I have never declared a strike in all my life. . . . but there comes a time when not to strike is but to rivet the chains of slavery upon our wrists."

> "Yes, Mr. Shirtwaist Manufacturer," Gompers went on, "it may be inconvenient for you if your boys and girls go out on strike, but there are things of more importance than your convenience and your profit. There are the lives of the boys and girls working in your business."
> Gompers appealed to the crowd to stand together.
> "If you had an organization before this, it would have stood there as a challenge to the employers who sought to impose such conditions as you bear. This is the time and the opportunity, and I doubt if you let it pass whether it can be created again in five or ten years or a generation. I say, friends, do not enter too hastily but when you can't get the manufacturers to give you what you want, then strike. And when you strike, let the manufacturers know you are on strike!"
> "I ask you to stand together," said Gompers in conclusion, "to have faith in yourselves, to be true to your comrades. If you strike, be cool, calm, collected and determined. Let your watchword be: Union and progress, and until then no surrender!" (Stein 1977)

As the debate wore on, a "girl" who called out from the back interrupted a speaker: "I want to say a few words." That the girl was a young woman and that her placement at the back of the hall bore no relation to her importance is part of the fabric from which selective memory weaves legend.

Clara Lemlich was twenty-three years old in 1909 (Orleck 1997). She had come from Russia six years earlier. Her father was learned, a rabbi, and she had received a high school education. Clara was, therefore, more educated than the vast majority of her fellow immigrant workers. Fiery and altruistic, Lemlich had already been on strike at Leisorson's dress-making company and was on the executive board of Local 25. Short and described as frail, contemporary accounts say the crowd lifted Lemlich over their heads and then onto the stage. Lemlich spoke to the point in Yiddish and with the militancy that history records as characteristic: "I have listened to all the speakers and I have no patience for talk. I am one who feels and suffers for the things pictured. I move that we go on a general strike." (Call 1909 as cited in Stein 1977, 70).

The shirtwaist makers were, as the social movements scholars might say, prepared to be mobilized (see McAdam 1982, 20–58, esp. 48–51). The *New York Call* melodramatically recorded the moment:

> As the tremulous voice of the girl died away, the audience rose en masse and cheered her to the echo. A grim sea of faces, with high purpose and resolve, they shouted and cheered the declaration of war for living conditions hoarsely. (Stein 1977, 70)

That Clara Lemlich, whose married name was to become Shavelson, is often reported to have been a "girl" and that her intervention came from the "back" of the hall mixes the stereotyped language of the day and industry with a tendency to hallow big moments in working-class history by making leaders seem naive or spontaneous. Women workers in those days did tend to withdraw from the workplace upon marriage; and they were young. Hence the usage of "girl" as in "factory girls." The expectation that factory girls were young, in addition to Clara's short stature, explains perhaps why she was often and plausibly reported to be a sixteen-year-old, "a wisp of a girl." And in each rendition of the story, no doubt accurately but hardly ever analyzed, we hear Clara's voice from the back of the hall.

A jaded culture yearns for the unpracticed voice of the spontaneously

The heroine of 1910: Clara Lemlich, later Shavelson (center), and comrades of the Local 25 of the ILGWU. Courtesy of Kheel Center for Labor-Management Documentation and Archives, Cornell University.

aggrieved. We associate the qualities of authenticity with amateurs, not professional organizers or functionaries; with youth (or old age); and with regular members rather than with those in leadership roles in organizations.

The girl from the back of the hall was a young woman of more than ordinary education among her peers and was also one of the organizers of the strike and the meeting. She was a member of the executive board of Local 25, which had called the meeting. Staying in the background, as Clara did at the back of the hall, until a meeting has raised many issues and the time is ripe for intervention—this is part of the lore of organizers of mass organizations everywhere in the world. Clara Lemlich Shavelson was to become a lifelong working-class organizer, joining the revolutionary parties of her era and then, even in her retirement home in the 1980s, assisting the nurse's aides to form a union (Orleck 1997). So our young tribune was authentic, all right, and also strategic. As the story develops, she and her comrades also understood the culture of their fellow workers.

Then came a legendary moment in labor history, American Jewish history, and industrial history: the chairman of the meeting, Benjamin Feigenbaum, led the assembly in an oath to stay true to the strike: "If I turn traitor to the cause I now pledge, may this hand wither from the arm I now raise" (Stein 1977, 71). Described as an "old Jewish oath," the wording no doubt resonates in Jewish history from the Babylonian exile and from Psalm 137:5: "If I forget you, O Jerusalem, let my right hand whither!"[1] "Here," writes McClymer (1998, 31), "was the stuff of romance: Veteran labor leaders waffle over the crucial question of the general strike until a 'girl' galvanizes the meeting with her impromptu eloquence and her fellow workers rise as one. . . . [A]n inspiring story. . . . Her speech, the vote, and the taking of the oath were almost certainly all planned carefully in advanced by the committee."

And so the factory girls went out on strike. The few hundred from Leisorson's and the Triangle Factory were joined by more than twenty thousand others. Their endurance carried them through thirteen weeks of fall and winter and early spring. The young women were remarkable to a world in which massive industrial employment of women was not new but union and class-based political organization of women was. The workers, Lemlich not least, were articulate about their grievances. Here is young Clara, now a figure of curiosity to the newspapers, in the *New York World* in the first week of the strike:

> There are two kinds of work—regular, that is salary work, and piecework. The regular work pays about $6 a week and the girls have to be at their machines at 7 o'clock in the morning and they stay at them until 8 o'clock at night, with just one-half hour for lunch in that time. . . . there is just one row of machines that the daylight ever gets to—that is the front row, nearest the window. The girls at all the other rows of machines back in the shops have to work by gaslight, by day as well as by night. Oh, yes, the shops keep the work going at night, too. . . . The shops are unsanitary—that's the word that is generally used, but there ought to be a worse one used. (Stein 1977, 12–13)

Theirs was the largest industrial strike by women known to their times. Although the *New York Times* tended to report industrial issues from a perspective sympathetic to employers (McClymer 1998), the strikers obtained support from influential middle-class and upper-class women organized under the rubric of the Women's Trade Union League (WTUL), and this was to prove crucial.

The New York police brutally harassed, jailed, and beat the strikers. The network of establishment forces—Tammany Hall politicians, the criminal fringe they protected and upon whom they fed, the commercial leadership of the city, all the forces that depended on a quiescent mass of workers—set upon them. For the young women the taunts and jeers of prostitutes and street ruffians were particularly trying.

The fines and bail payments were out of reach for the working girls, so the union raised money to pay their fines—but with difficulty. The arrests arose out of picketing activity. Picketing occurred when sign-carrying workers attempted to dissuade—or even block—strike breakers from entering their shops. It was also used as a demonstrative form of public education. Under a variety of pretexts police harassed the picketers. This harassment eventually became a weakness for the forces arrayed against the workers.

A critical moment came when the affluent women of the WTUL chose to join the picketers. In a story line now familiar, the police hit and jailed the more privileged women, and media coverage changed. With the jailing of middle-class supporters, such as WTUL member Mary Dreier, public opinion began to turn toward the strikers.

Union activists regularly met with sympathetic women of the city's wealthy families. The support of "liberal reformers" was in 1910, as it was to be in the New Deal period, part of the formula for workers' advances. In this instance a sympathetic sisterhood was extremely useful to the strikers—for example, in raising bail money for those detained. The WTUL was composed of middle-class women and some very affluent ones as well. It supported the union organization of women and was particularly sympathetic to immigrants and the industries that exploited them. It was part of the middle-class reform culture of the period, one that, for example, supported things like Florence Kelly's National Consumer League, which campaigned against sweatshops. The WTUL employed staff members who then helped organize unions. For example, Rose Schneiderman, who was to earn fame for her oration after the Triangle Factory fire and was later a prominent spokeswoman for women's right to vote, was an early organizer of the ILGWU and was then employed by the WTUL.

Eventually smaller contractors signed agreements with the union, though at that point the larger ones, including, tragically, the Triangle Shirtwaist firm, did not. The contracts included provisions for better pay, limits on hours, and prohibition of homework. Over three hundred contracts with small firms provided for union shops (that is, the hiring of union members). All of the provisions of the settlement proved hard to enforce, however. Yet two immediate results were more powerful than the gains made in the contracts. The union's membership greatly grew, and the action of the women emboldened the men in the industry. The strike became known as the "Uprising of the Twenty Thousand." It was the making of the ILGWU.

The "Great Revolt" of sixty thousand cloakmakers, primarily men, followed the "Uprising of the Twenty Thousand" only months later in 1910. More planned and prepared, the cloakmakers strike ended with the signing of the Protocols of Peace. Drafted by mediator (and future Supreme Court justice) Louis Brandeis, the Protocols became a blueprint for bringing "stability" out of the "chaos" of an industry notorious for its volatility, cutthroat competition, and ferocious exploitation (see N. Green 1997, 54–56). The Protocols called for a fifty-hour week, the abolition of homework, minimum-wage scales, and union preference hiring. It also created a Joint Board of Sanitary Control and a Board of Arbitration for settling major disputes.

The defenders of the ILG and those who lionize its history take the Protocols as both a key step and a model for defending workers in a highly competitive and usually small-scale industry. There were and are critics. The Protocols were a long step toward institutionalizing collective bargaining and moving away from strikes as the key means of working-class self-defense. The evolving structure of industrial relations in the women's apparel business, with New York at its center, would pit the union and its larger manufacturer base against the small shop contractors who subverted labor standards.

The larger manufacturers were the more powerful enterprises in the various links in the chain of production. They sent work to smaller shops for various tasks—sewing or cutting, for example. They forced the smaller shops to compete with one another for lower piece rates. The union could get the manufacturers to agree to use union contractors—but it could not force the manufacturers to share profits with them.

Soon the Protocols produced a thicket of procedures by which disputes were settled and relations between various parts of the industry were governed. This turn to formal procedures and the union's focus on gaining contracts at the top of the power pyramid tended to draw the young ILG toward a more bureaucratic style, and its officers became more distant from its base of working-class activists.

The Protocols caused a lively debate within the union itself. Its early organizers were socialists and radicals of a variety of descriptions. They envisioned a new order for workers. Their dilemma to this day is still with working-class activists and trade unions: if revolution is not imminent, if workers require defense inside capitalist society, then a structure that defends them in an industry notable for volatility and dispersion will necessarily place a premium on stability and central leverage. This the new union did.

The Union

The "Uprising of the Twenty Thousand" marked the beginning of twenty years of seesaw growth for the ILGWU and later for the organized men's clothing industry—the Amalgamated Clothing Workers of America (ACWA). Formed in 1900 as part of the AFL, the ILGWU focused on women's clothing production—slightly more than half of all clothing employment and production. Its immediate and historically largest base was New York City—where about one-half of all garment production took place (N. Green 1997, 46–55). By 1908 the ILG had but 7,800 members though the industry employed about 100,000 workers in New York alone.[2] The strikes of 1910 brought ILG membership from 58,000 in 1909 to 84,600 in 1912. Nancy Green reports that in 1911 an immigration commission claimed that 36 percent of clothing workers and 80 percent of the cutters were organized—rates much higher than today (N. Green 1997, 53). By early 1912, Green reports (55), the union claimed that it had contracts with 1,796 out of 1,829 shops—an industry 98 percent organized. The demand for ready-made clothing during World War I and the union's relative success in organizing boosted membership still further: by 1917 there were 128,000 ILGWU members. In nine years, through two major strikes and a world war, the membership had grown more than sixteen times as large as it had been before the shirtwaist makers' strike.

There would be many defeats before the industry was finally tamed; industrial conditions and internal fights brought membership down to 30,000 by 1931. Before these see-saws of fortune, back in 1911 in the midst of growth came the defining iconic moment in the century-long fight against sweatshops: the Triangle Factory fire.

The Fire

The fire at the Triangle Shirtwaist Factory, located in the Asch building on Washington Place and Greene Street in New York's Greenwich Village, broke out on Saturday, March 25, 1911, just after 4:40 P.M. (the first alarm was turned in at a box at 4:45 P.M.). The first of the five hundred men, women, girls, and boys employed at the factory were leaving on this Saturday workday at that time (Stein 2001 [1962], 14).[3] Some of the women were in the dressing room, tidying up before they went down to the street. Perhaps a cigarette ignited the cloth scrap (remnants) heaped under the eighth floor cutting tables arrayed along the Greene Street side of the building (34). The fire began there below the ninth floor main sewing room.

The Triangle firm occupied the three top floors of a then modern industrial building—steel and brick and fireproof. When the fire broke out on the eighth floor, it filled the workroom with smoke. The fire soon blocked the staircase on Greene Street—the freight staircase where a guard checked the purses of the women as they left. The canvas fire hoses, grabbed from the wall, had no water pressure. The door to the second stairway—sometimes referred to as the rear stairs—on Washington Place initially was locked on the eighth floor, but the key was left in it, and one of the male supervisors finally opened it with much difficulty. Despite the building code, it opened inward, not outward, and the press of bodies prevented him from getting to it. Many of the eighth floor workers eventually escaped down the Washington Place stairs; others were cut off from it and were burned while others were forced out the windows to die of the fall. The workers on the ninth floor, where there were 240 sewing machines and 260 workers, had the least notice.

The management group on the floor above them, the tenth floor, had been warned by phone; but the next call to the ninth did not go through. The elevators went first to the tenth floor, and many got down through the courageous work of two elevator operators. Others from the tenth floor went to the roof and jumped onto other buildings. New York University law students, attending a lecture in the adjacent building, saw the flames and organized a ladder rescue to get fire victims from the roof of the Asch building to their own building thirteen feet higher. One hundred and fifty workers were thus rescued.

The women on the ninth floor had the least warning and the fewest exits. The phone call had not come to warn them, and the gradual realization of fire that had alerted those on the eighth floor was not their lot. Suddenly everything was black and hot and burning. Those near the Greene Street side used that exit, but the flames from the eighth floor had lapped into that side of the ninth floor through the windows. Quickly the staircase on the Greene Street side became inaccessible. The girls ran to the elevator, but after they had completed a few trips, the elevators could no longer function. Women were found crushed and burned by the elevator door; others were found in the shaft, having fallen to their deaths; a few survived that fall.

On the ninth floor the Washington Place door was locked. Piled against it were later found many bodies. The owners of the Triangle Shirtwaist Company, Max Blanck and Isaac Harris, were eventually charged with homicide. Their defense—famous among lawyers of the day—claimed that the door was not locked and, if it was, they had not locked it and, if they had locked it, the death of the individual in whose name the case was brought, Margaret Schwartz, could not be shown to have been caused by the locked door. Finally, they claimed, even if Schwartz had died because the door was locked, they had had good reason to lock the door to protect their property (Stein 2001 [1962], 177–203).

The fire department arrived quickly, but its ladders did not reach as high as the eighth floor. Trapped by flames forcing them to the windows, the women, girls, and some boys were seen by observers to look back and then, resolving themselves, to step out into the air against the hope that the flimsy firemen's nets would save them. The nets did not. They fell to the sidewalk, those who did not suffocate or burn. Reporters wrote that the bodies lay in heaps.

Journalist William Shepherd described "a love affair in the midst of all the horror." A young man out on the ledge of the ninth floor helped first one girl, then another, then a third girl out onto the ledge as the flames licked at their clothing and heat forced them away from the window. Each jumped to her death. Then a fourth girl came to the window. "I saw her," dictated Shepherd to the *New York World*, "put her arms around him and kiss him. Then he held her into space—and dropped her." The young man then jumped himself: "Together they went into eternity" (Stein 2001 [1962], 19, 20). One hundred and forty-six people died as a result of the fire on March 25, 1911.

The fireproof building survives to this day, two plaques reminding the casual wanderer and the history seeker alike that this really is the place, surrounded by New York University's Washington Square campus and occupied by the Chemistry Department.

The Triangle Fire. It seems self-defining now: a firm of callous owners who had neglected fire equipment, who murderously allowed the back door to be locked, who employed children and worked their people seventy or eighty hours a week. The fire is a metaphor for the bad old days of sweatshops, a day we were to have overcome, a past whose horror only illumines the civilized nature of contemporary life.

Even the locked back door is the subject of layers of social meaning. Most accounts (e.g., McClymer 1998; N. Green 1997; Stein 1977) take for granted that the vital second exit was locked because the owners feared the girls would steal shirtwaists, would walk out with them—so poor, their employers knew them to be, that the girls would risk job and freedom to heist a little dress out the back door. At their trial in their defense, Blanck and Harris's brilliant lawyer, Max Steuer, demonstrated that the large pocketbooks carried by the women could hold as many as four shirt-waists. Yet in garment workers' families, across the generations, no such demeaning account is given. Families such as my own knew that the back door was locked so that union organizers—known as "delegates" in those days—couldn't sneak up the back way to chat up the operators and keep the union alive in this nonunion factory. For our family, which included two generations of cutters and sewing machine operators, the memory that the Triangle shirtwaist makers' strike had happened just a year before the fire made this version more concrete.

It bears some thinking: How did the fire at the Triangle Shirtwaist Factory come to be *the Triangle*—the self-defining icon of the bad old sweatshop days? John McClymer points out that only a month before the fire, a terrible disaster in Pennsylvania, a mine fire, killed more people, but we know about it now only because John's grandfather was in it (McClymer 1998, vii). Those miners speak to us from their graves only through McClymer family memory—not through the public consciousness. By contrast, the Triangle Fire has been the subject of countless stories, films, and, for example, an evocative poem by the poet laureate Robert Pinsky (1996, 84). In his poem "The Shirt" Pinsky writes:

> Of cuff and button at my wrist. The presser, the cutter,
> The wringer, the mangle. The needle, the union,
> The Treadle, the bobbin. The code. The infamous blaze.

That women and child workers were victims brings special sympathy to an industrial or any other accident—such is the bent of our culture. That New York has long been a very loud amplifier in the recording of our nation's social history and in the production of mass culture also contributes to the Triangle's stature.

McClymer has yet another answer to his own question. The dead of the Triangle burn in our memory because they were familiar to the people of their city. They had so recently been the leaders of the heroic strike. These were not unknown miners in a firm no one knew about. The Triangle dead worked at the place where the factory girls had first ventured forth on their own. They had persevered on picket lines through the New York winter, maintained their dignity through attempts at humiliation, been jailed and seen again and again on the city's front page. The public grieved them because in some collective sense the public knew them.[4] As he watched the girls drop from the windows to their deaths, journalist William Shepherd dictated his story over the phone from a nearby shop.

> I remembered these girls were the shirtwaist makers. I remembered their great strike of last year in which these same girls had demanded more sanitary conditions and more safety precautions in the shops. These dead bodies were the answer. (Stein 2001, 20)

The dead of the Triangle suffered the irony that, while the strike succeeded in launching the ILGWU, the strikers failed to reform the practices at the firm that employed their strike's leaders. Rosy Safran told the *Independent* on April 20, 1911:

> I was in the great shirtwaist strike. . . . Our bosses won and we went back to the Triangle Waist Company as an open shop. . . . If the union had had its way we would have been safe in spite of the fire, for two of the union's demands were adequate fire escapes on factory buildings and open doors giving free access from factories to the street. The bosses defeated us and we didn't get the open doors or the large fire escapes and so our friends are dead and relatives are tearing their hair. (quoted in McClymer 1998, 90)

Chaos and Order

After the "Uprising of the Twenty Thousand," which established the union with 312 shops under contract, the cloakmakers, mostly men, struck in 1910—the "Great Revolt"—formally mandating a schedule of wages and hours and principles of health and safety. The apparel industry, the "rag trade" in bittersweet familiarity, is structurally at once most modern and archaic. In this, its protean shape, lies coiled the possibility of sweating a new generation of workers even as the old has freed itself.

The Protocols of Peace under the "Great Revolt" created a track along which the union would run, attempting to regulate the chaotic structure of the contractor-subcontractor market of the garment business. Collective bargaining replaced—gradually—strike action, to the distress of the more militant socialists among the garment workers. The bargaining itself helped to reduce some of the cutthroat elements of the industry because the union forced the employers to unite for industrywide or branchwide negotiations. In addition, the union over the long generation to follow would try to control conditions at the shop level by forcing the manufacturers to take responsibility for labor conditions in the contractor shops—"joint liability." This was the workers' part of the sweatshop solution—union action, collective bargaining, joint governance of the industry. The strikes of 1909–10 launched the unions on their modern trajectory. Eventually they (that is, the separate unions in the men's clothing industry and the women's clothing industry) became the rocks upon which industrial progress was founded. They were not alone.

The fire of 1911 stirred the conscience of the city of New York and the state. The middle- and upper-class reformers who were thus inspired learned, in the next generation, to work with politicians based in immigrant working-class communities. The result, eventually, was the public policy half of the solution. Both parts—the workers' own unions and the political reforms—are central to the story of the ascent to decency for garment workers.

This story is important, for the sweatshop phenomenon in the American apparel industry is not, as Jesus said of the poor, a condition "always ye have with you" (John 12:8). In the present moment, this is doubly important: the story of the American garment workers, their progress, and their losses has critical lessons for the now global industry.

After the Fire

In the aftermath of the fire, marches, demonstrations, and spontaneous outrage were plentiful. A public funeral on April 5 drew 400,000 marchers in a steady downpour. Earlier, at a protest meeting called by the Shirtwaist Local 25—the local of the strike of 1909 led by Triangle shirtwaist workers— fifty women fainted, gripped by grief and outrage and by socialist oratory.

Eight days after the fire, on April 2, 1911, the WTUL held what appears to be the memorial meeting that had the most long-run influence. Called by the WTUL, it was therefore sponsored not by the immigrant working-class movement but by their more affluent allies. Held at the Metropolitan Opera House, which had been rented by a WTUL member, this memorial meeting was an interfaith ceremony featuring impassioned speeches by the Roman Catholic Diocese of Brooklyn's Director of Charities, Msgr. White, by Bishop David Greer, and by Rabbi Stephen Wise. The most famous of the addresses, though, came from another short immigrant sewing machine operator, the red-haired Rose Schneiderman. Described by the *New York Times* as "a slip of girl," she had been an organizer for the ILGWU and was on the WTUL staff. However slight, she too had been among the organizers of the Triangle workers' strike. She would soon become a tremendously effective orator on behalf of women's suffrage.

Schneiderman's speech at the Opera House memorial meeting was a classic. Short and powerful, it started with these memorable lines:

> I would be a traitor to these poor burned bodies if I came here to talk good fellowship. *We have tried you good people of the public and we have found you wanting.*

Schneiderman ended her statement not merely with an appeal to bourgeois conscience but with a demand that her audience respect the labor movement:

> Too much blood has been spilled. I know from experience it is up to the working people to save themselves. And the only way is through a strong working-class movement." (Stein 2001 [1962], 144; emphasis added; also available at <http://www.ilr.cornell.edu/trianglefire/texts/stein_ootss/ootss_rs.html>; see also McClymer 1998, 99–102)

The Opera House meeting pledged to enact and enforce fire safety laws. It symbolized both an awakened conscience among those outside the ambit of working-class politics and unions and their alliance with unionists and reformers.

Factory Investigating Commission

The fire was a scandal; it was a media event and a humiliation to those responsible for the public's safety. Frances Perkins, then a social reformer and activist, put it this way:

> This made a terrible impression on the people of the State of New York. I can't begin to tell you how disturbed the people were everywhere. It was as though we had all done something wrong. It shouldn't have been. We were sorry. Mea culpa! Mea culpa! We didn't want it that way. We hadn't intended to have 147 [sic] girls and boys killed in a factory. It was a terrible thing for the people of the City of New York and the State of New York to face. (Perkins 1964)

The reformers—Progressive era political and social policy advocates—leaped to the occasion. They caused the legislative leaders in Albany, the capital of New York, to form the Factory Investigating Commission. New York assemblyman Al Smith, until the fire a very ordinary "machine" politician, was majority leader of the assembly. Described by Robert Caro as the best bill drafter ever, Smith had a congeniality that was exceeded only by his attention to details (Caro 1974). He appointed himself to the commission as he became aware of the fact that the dead of the fire were disproportionately immigrants from the districts he represented. Smith came under the influence of reformers, including Frances Perkins, who was chief investigator for the commission and later became a counselor to Smith. Smith, elected governor of New York in 1918 (and reelected four times), would come to embody the modern, liberal face of the Democratic Party. Politicians based in immigrant neighborhoods, unions, and social reformers all in coalition—this was the Al Smith formula, even before Franklin Roosevelt's New Deal coalition two decades later. Smith shepherded, as speaker of the New York Assembly and then as governor, the most progressive social legislation of the time. He was the first Catholic nominated for president, in 1928.

The Factory Investigating Commission revealed the extent of the extreme abuse of workers—especially women workers—in the service and manufacturing sector of the New York economy and proposed aggressive safety and wage regulations. It even proposed a minimum wage—a legislative achievement Perkins was to cherish only later, as Roosevelt's secretary of labor.

World War I brought full employment and rising wages to New York's garment workers, as it did throughout the nation. At the end of the war union membership peaked at 129,000 (N. Green 1997, 56). In the postwar 1920s, union membership declined. This was a result of the manufacturers' responses to union strength and to a period of "civil war" among factions of the ILGWU. The manufacturers moved away from the union areas, resisted signing contracts, and evaded the agreements they had made.

In the meantime, within the union, factional disputes reached critical levels. After the Russian Revolution many American Socialists were drawn to the Communist banner; the vision of a world remade by working-class revolutionaries inspired groups of trade unionists and many within the New York labor movement. The ILGWU was a notable center of Communist strength. Other figures within the union, though, remained oriented to a more gradualist and pragmatic view of the union's role in society and in the industry. The combination of manufacturer evasion and internal fighting drastically weakened the union. By 1927 ILGWU membership was only one-fifth of its 1918 strength (28,000) (N. Green 1997, 56). After another increase, union membership declined to 24,000 under the early impact of the Depression in 1931.

The men's and women's unions were able, after the strikes before World War I and under the full employment conditions of the war, to both increase membership and bring some degree of control over their respective industries. The ways structural change affected worker organizing in that period facilitated union advance. From the 1890s on there had been a gradual growth in larger factories, and the balance of work between homeworkers and factory workers shifted toward the factory. By 1913 over half of all dress and shirtwaist workers toiled in factories with over seventy-five workers; 27 percent worked in factories with one hundred to two hundred employees. This concentration (as compared to the early period of the ready-to-wear industry) made the dynamics of working-class self-defense similar to other industries. Sociologists from Karl Marx on have noted that large workplaces (and enterprises) have tended to produce more class consciousness and unionization. The classical explanation for this is at least twofold.

Larger workplaces make objectively clear to workers that their fates are determined in common. In a small office or business, one may believe that one's own effort, or one's relation to the boss, or the fate of the enterprise will determine one's material fate and the possibility for fair treatment on the job. In a factory of hundreds, a worker realizes that—on average—the amount of money, autonomy, or justice that one receives is going to be shared by those hundreds. Thus, cooperation with one's fellow workers is among the very logical possibilities for improvement.

Marx and subsequent observers of working-class self-defense have also thought that larger workplaces facilitate communication between workers. Research has shown that this proposition, while relatively true, also has high variability. For example, John Cumbler (1979) showed that, under conditions where noise and intensity of the pace of production prevented workday conversation, worker organization was slower and less successful than under the obverse conditions.[5] Still, the tendency for workshops and enterprises to grow larger favored union organization. By drawing work away from homeworkers and into factories, the evolving industrial structure of garment production also cut down on the invidious effects of exploited homeworkers competing with factory-based sewing machine operators for the same work.

As the 1920s progressed, however, manufacturers reevaluated the advantages of centralized production and control. They began to prefer the jobber-contractor-subcontractor system. The jobber might have the cutting and sewing done in a submanufacturer shop or the sewing done by a contractor. In every case, though, the workshop was smaller and the legal subcontracting relationship allowed the manufacturer (now a jobber) to evade the conditions of the union contract. The decentralization of the industry also allowed some shops to migrate out of the garment district and out of Manhattan—and thus away from the venerable concentrations of experienced (and union-friendly) workers.

The increasing fashion consciousness of mass-market clothes in the 1920s also favored the decentralization of the industry. Mass media advertising was on its way to creating the "consumer culture" that matured later in the twentieth century. Status attached to the purchase of certain objects—conspicuous consumption—was not new (see Veblen 1902), but appealing to wider and larger parts of the population including middle-income workers was.

Fashion in a mass market and with mass communications means change; change requires flexibility. Successful flexibility from the perspective of an enterprise means shifting risk to other links in the production chain, or commodity chain, of the industry. Rather than tie themselves to big inventory or large fixed capital, manufacturers contracted out for production, shifting contracts as need demanded.[6]

As garment firms responded to union threats and fashion trends, the women's industry of the 1920s also experienced a period of intense political infighting between Socialists and Communists. This eventually contributed to the crash of union membership. In New York, as around the world, the Russian Revolution sparked sympathetic interest among Socialist-minded workers. Jewish workers in New York's garment districts were among the clusters of American workers who responded to the revolutionary fervor of the early Bolsheviks. As early as 1917 some members of the old Local 25, which had led the "Uprising of the Twenty Thousand," formed a study committee on the Russian events. When the Communist Parties were formed, Jewish garment workers along with other clusters—for example, Finnish workers in the iron country of the Upper Great Lakes—were early adherents. In the 1920s, the Communists embarked first on a strategy of militancy within the old unions. A number of New York locals of the ILGWU elected executive boards dominated by Communist supporters.[7] They were opposed quite ruthlessly by Socialist loyalists who were reformers but not as radical as the Communists. A 1926 cloakmaker's strike, largely thought to be unsuccessful (N. Green 1997, 60; but see Nadel 1985), was followed by the expulsion of three locals in which the Communists had a majority. Thereafter Communist strategy changed—from "boring from within" the old unions to "dual unionism," that is, the creation of militant alternatives to the Socialist and other unions. As many as twenty-five thousand garment workers followed their lead—and left the ILGWU in control of the more reformist-minded Socialists led by David Dubinsky.

At the brink of the Great Depression, then, the condition of garment workers (in New York) presented a small paradox. Their union was significantly weaker than it had been ten years earlier at the end of World War I. On the other hand, through prior strikes and existing contracts, conditions (at least in the organized shops) had improved. The workweek had declined from between fifty-six and sixty hours at the turn of the century to fifty hours under the Protocols of Peace and nominally to forty hours in 1928 (N. Green 1997, 62).

The strikes of the prewar period, the fire, and the subsequent reforms of the Progressive era had had a larger impact on factory safety. Sprinklers were now mandatory in factories, standards for exits had improved, and inspections were more serious and professional.

Many of these gains were to be extinguished by the Depression, but the Progressive era formula—unionization, progressive middle-class alliance, and proworker public policy—would combine after 1938 to change the face of the industry.

3 The Decline of Sweatshops in the United States

> The red silk bargain dress in the shop window is a danger signal. It is a warning of the return of the sweatshop, a challenge to us all to reinforce the gains we have made in our long and difficult progress toward a civilized industrial order.
>
> Secretary of Labor Frances Perkins, 1933

As Franklin Roosevelt was inaugurated in 1933, the working class of the United States was becoming poorer and more desperate. The cowboy humorist Will Rogers, whistling in the dark, said, "America is the first country to drive to the poor house." In cities, where workers certainly did not have cars, the apparel unions in particular lost the strength they had gained earlier, but new militancy was brewing.

Unemployment had soared to over 33 percent nationally; in New York 38 percent of the working population could not find jobs (Committee on Economic Security 1935, table 6). Prices dropped about 25 percent from 1929 to 1933. One could buy with seventy-six cents in 1933 what had cost one dollar in 1929.[1] If a worker still had a job, he or she desperately needed to hold onto it. If one did not have a job, as Annie MacLean (1903) noted about the century before, a worker would work for a pittance rather than starve quietly. Of course, some of those who worked and others who faced starvation acted in a decidedly unquiet manner and fueled the marches and protests and the socialist and communist responses to the collapse of the economy. This working-class movement was the basis for the political and organizational gains that were to remake conditions of work for the apparel industry and for the country (Goldfield 1989).

The pressure on the labor-intensive garment industry was a disaster. Manufacturers evaded the old union contracts by giving work to contractor shops, and the old-style competition among contractors drove standards through the floor. The loss of market for new clothes was compounded in New York City by the contractors' setting up outside the city, migrating to New Jersey and to Pennsylvania.

Campaigning amid and against these conditions, Franklin Roosevelt brought to Washington a pragmatic outlook and a raft of idealistic reformers. Among the reformers were veterans of his own New York State administration. He asked Frances Perkins, his New York industrial commissioner, to be Secretary of Labor. Perkins became the first female cabinet member, and to this day her years of service, over twelve as Secretary of Labor, are unequaled. Perkins had been closely involved with the New York State Factory Investigating Commission, formed after the Triangle Fire. This led directly to Perkins's becoming part of what really was the direct grandparent of the vaunted Roosevelt New Deal—the Al Smith administration of New York State. The story of the policies of the New Deal, and the long struggles against labor abuse, is a story of the people who made those policies and who engaged in those struggles. From the perspective of the apparel industry, it is a narrative with surprising continuities—surprising anyhow to those accustomed to thinking of the New Deal as a sharp break with the past.

Alfred Emanuel Smith had been a straight-ahead Tammany Hall Democratic machine politician before 1911; one group of reformers named him the worst legislator in Albany. He came from Lower Manhattan, famously working as a dockhand unloading ships at the Fulton fish market. Smith worked his way up the political machine ladder the old-fashioned way, doing menial errands for politicians, being silently loyal, and waiting his turn. He eventually gained, as Robert Caro (1974) notes, a tremendous command of the mechanics of legislation and the terrific geniality that made him the Happy Warrior.[2]

The Triangle Fire had struck a powerful chord in Smith, when he discovered that so many of his constituents were among the dead. He had by then a somewhat unusual profile—well liked, he was known to be a knowledgeable legislative authority on the state constitution and the New York City charter, and he championed some changes the reformers liked—self-rule for New York, for example. With the Triangle Fire and its aftermath, though, Smith turned a corner.

Smith was, at the time of the fire, Chair of the New York Assembly's Committee on Ways and Means and Majority Leader as well. He arranged to be made vice-chair of the Factory Investigating Commission, with state senator Robert Wagner as chair, which was set up to investigate industrial conditions. In the next year, he became speaker of the assembly. On the commission and in the assembly he worked closely with Frances Perkins.

Frances Perkins was born in Boston and raised in the industrial town of Worcester, Massachusetts. After graduating from Mt. Holyoke College, she returned to Worcester, volunteering for work with "factory girls." She soon went to the Chicago area and became interested in social work after exposure to, among other experiences, Jane Addams's Hull House. She left Chicago to study economics and sociology at the Wharton School in Philadelphia. From there she went to New York City and earned a social work degree from Columbia University in 1910. Shortly after graduation, Perkins went to work as Executive Secretary for the National Consumer's League (NCL) in New York. The antisweatshop campaigner Florence Kelly, an early influence on Perkins's focus on labor and factory issues, had founded the NCL.

For Frances Perkins, too, the Triangle Fire marked an emotional reference point in her life. She had "watched the factory girls leaping to their deaths from the flaming building," and she formed and led, among the reform and social work agencies of the city, a Committee on Factory Safety. As such, she was a key support person for the Factory Investigating Commission (Brody 1981).

The Factory Investigating Commission undertook an intensive and extensive examination of industrial conditions. It proposed changes in the state industrial code, including many safety measures such as mandatory sprinklers for factories, as well as minimum wages. Smith and Perkins developed a partnership: he taught her about the practicalities of politics and legislation. She took Smith and the other commissioners in hand and by the hand and taught them, through field trips and research, the realities of labor abuse in their times. At Smith's funeral in 1944, the Social Security Administration official history reports,

> [T]wo of his former Tammany Hall political cronies were overheard to speculate on why Smith had become a social crusader. One of them summed the matter up this way: "I'll tell you. Al Smith read a book. That book was a person, and her name was Frances Perkins. She told him all these things and he believed her." (Social Security Administration n.d.)

Smith was elected governor in 1918, and he asked Perkins to serve on his Industrial Commission, which governed the New York Labor Department. Elected again in 1922 Smith made Perkins a member and then chair of the reorganized Industrial Board, again facing opposition from business interests.

From the vantage point of over eighty years later, it is either very easy or very hard to see the changes marked by the Smith administration in New York State. It is hard to see the changes because of the ways historians have lionized the national administration of Smith's successor, Franklin D. Roosevelt. Everything positive that the government did before 1932 was, in popular imagery, the work of Theodore Roosevelt or Abraham Lincoln. Franklin D. Roosevelt stands over his era as a titan, dwarfing those who came immediately before him and casting a shadow over those who succeeded him. It was Al Smith, however, who cast the die of alliance among reformers, immigrants, and labor that was to be the hallmark of the grandly understood New Deal coalition. After the Factory Investigating Commission, New York State—under Smith's governorship, Perkins's tutelage, and the urging of what may have been the most mature of the nation's regional labor movements—took the lead in proposing hours limitations and attempting to legislate minimum wages.

As an activist and an official, Perkins had become acquainted with state senator Franklin Roosevelt by the time she first came to the Smith administration. After Roosevelt was elected governor in 1928 (while Smith was running unsuccessfully for president), he made Perkins the industrial commissioner to head the New York Labor Department. Then, when he was elected president in 1932, Roosevelt asked Perkins to become his Secretary of Labor. In her person, Perkins bridged the Smith-Roosevelt transition. More to the point, so did the New York labor movement and the immigrant labor it represented. Basing their gubernatorial careers on the reformers and their discourse, on labor, and on immigrants, however different the Irish pol and the Dutch aristocrat were, Smith and Roosevelt shared a path to the future. Perkins was the Girl Guide[3] down that path.

Perkins's appointment was that of the first woman in the cabinet and of the first nonunion member to be Labor Secretary. When Franklin Roosevelt asked her to serve, Perkins said she would serve on condition that she would get the opportunity to work for minimum wages, hours limitations, prohibition of abusive child labor, unemployment insurance, and social security. Roosevelt agreed (Berg 1989).

The National Recovery Administration

Among the earliest pieces of legislation passed in the famous First Hundred Days of the New Deal was the National Industrial Recovery Act (1933), which created the National Recovery Administration (NRA). Controversial throughout its short life, the NRA was an American experiment, albeit without much forethought, in corporatism—the variant of capitalism that seeks to regulate the political economy through the mutual decision making of business, labor, and government.[4]

What the European Social Democrats and moderate or "social" Christian Democrats now call the "social partners"—business and labor, usually facilitated by government—were invited to sit together and compose industrial codes for each industry. These codes regulated hours, minimum wages, and other aspects of the competitive arena in each industry. Among the agendas built into the legislation was the legitimation of unions as part of the American landscape—embodied in Section 7(a)—a process begun by federal policy here but bitterly fought out in industry in the next ten years.

The NRA codes commonly created agreements for forty-hour workweeks. The eight-hour day had been part of the labor movement's core aspirations since the middle of the nineteenth century. Many occupations had attained it by the 1930s—for example, federal government workers and certain skilled trades with high bargaining power. For the women and men of the sweated trades, the forty-hour week, forty-cents-an-hour wage was an important guarantee and prop.

The fundamental insight of the industrial policymakers who cobbled the National Industrial Recovery Act (NIRA) together was not altogether different from that which animates labor and social policy critics of today's global capitalism. Under conditions of cutthroat competition, with a vast reservoir of unemployed workers, a race to the bottom was driving wages and standards downward. If a level playing field of agreed standards could be enforced, not only would employers be more restrained but workers' purchasing power would be an engine of economic recovery.

The conditions of deflation and unemployment had indeed created a race to the bottom. Though many parts of the labor movement viewed the new law with suspicion or hostility, it was useful to garment workers. Cloakmakers gained control of subcontracting (though dress makers did not); the regulations brought homeworkers back to shops in menswear (Greene 1997, 63).

Even as the NRA generated codes and regulations that improved conditions in the garment industry—and elsewhere—its corporatist structure ran afoul of the U.S. Supreme Court. The law had passed early in the new Roosevelt administration—during the famous First Hundred Days—on June 16, 1933. In accordance with the law, on April 13, 1934, the president signed an executive order establishing, among other things, health and inspection standards for the live poultry industry. The Live Poultry Code provided for a forty-hour workweek and fifty cents an hour minimum wage.

A New York City poultry wholesaler, the A.L.A. Schechter Poultry Company, was subsequently indicted for violating the code, for selling uninspected chickens, for failing to keep required records, for failing to pay the minimum wage, and for selling an "unfit" chicken to a retailer. The case thus earned the nickname the "sick chicken" case. After conviction on most but not all of the original charges, Schechter appealed, and the Supreme Court agreed to hear the case in April 1935. The Court rendered its decision on May 27, 1935. The Court set aside the NIRA on the grounds that it granted an unconstitutional delegation of congressional authority to the president. The sick chicken case thus killed one of the mainstays of the early New Deal (*A.L.A. Schechter Poultry Corp. v. United States*, 295 U.S. 495 [1935]).

Not everywhere was the NRA as effective in protecting workers' rights as it was in the apparel industry. The enforcement of the industry codes had been cumbersome, and Section 7(a), using language that "guaranteed" a right to organize, had not been universally effective. A wave of strikes as early as August 1933 caused the president to ask his fellow New Yorker, now a U.S. senator, Robert Wagner to head a commission looking into labor law revisions.

Neither the administration nor the labor movement was thus surprised or particularly unprepared when the Supreme Court set aside the NIRA. By the end of the year the Wagner Act—the National Labor Relations Act (NLRA)—established the right to join a union and created the beginning of the modern industrial relations framework. The same language was used in Section 7 of the new law as had been in Section 7(a) of the old one. Simon Rifkind had drafted the original language while he worked for Senator Wagner; Leon Keysersling, later chairman of the Council of Economic Advisers under President Harry Truman, told an interviewer that the NLRA was written in Wagner's office and implied that he had inserted Rifkind's language into the new bill (St. Antoine 1998).

It stated once again in Section 7:

> Employees shall have the right to self-organization, to form, join, or assist labor organizations, to bargain collectively through representatives of their own choosing, and to engage in other concerted activities for the purpose of collective bargaining or other mutual aid or protection. (See NLRB 2001.)

Arguably the most important piece of legislation for the next generation, the Wagner Act, by facilitating the organization of workers, allowed American workers to develop the strategic capability through the use of which they would then obtain public policies that defended and furthered their security and decency. Amendments and hostile courts, Congresses, and administrations have long since eroded that accomplishment, but in its time the Wagner Act was a great leap forward for American workers. Its passage did not, however, solve the problem of the race to the bottom in the apparel industry.

Ms. Perkins's Thrift Shop

By 1936 conditions in the needle trades were again terrible. Contractor shops were proliferating, moving away from the geographic centers of union strength, and the union was not successful in ensuring that manufacturers held contractors and subcontractors to union standards (N. Green 1997). Roosevelt and the Democratic platform in the presidential election year called for minimum wage and hours legislation (Douglas and Hackman 1938, 492). In his second inaugural speech, on January 20, 1937, Roosevelt claimed that "I see one-third of a nation ill-housed, ill-clad, ill-nourished" (Roosevelt 1937). Repeating that phrase in a message to Congress on May 24, 1937, Roosevelt called for the passage of a bill his administration, some labor leaders, and congressional leaders had introduced (Douglas and Hackman 1938, 493).

As early as 1935, during the procession of the Schechter case through the federal courts, Secretary of Labor Perkins had begun to prepare for the nullification of the NIRA. Never persuaded, as she later put it, of the virtue of the "informal cooperation between industries and the President and labor to achieve by agreement and not by law some better pattern of hours and wages," Secretary Perkins also knew that the Schechter case threatened even the advances that had been made by the NRA (Perkins 1965, 4). She told a seminar at Cornell in 1965 a version of the drafting of the FLSA:

> Therefore . . . I had caused to be written, and had written a large part of it myself, a kind of a . . . bill, which, although far too elaborate[5] . . . attempted to cover every objection that the courts had raised to this sort of legislation earlier. . . . [T]his bill . . . had been introduced into Congress and was sitting there comfortably before a committee, but it was in Congress already. This was a bill which one of the counselors said *was just . . . my thriftshop, I put it there just in case we should need it at some time or other.* . . . I was very glad I had done so when this Schechter decision came down. (Perkins 1965, 3–4; emphasis added)

The fight for what became known as the FLSA was long and ferocious and involved deep compromises. Even the "natural" constituency of the bill, the labor movement, was divided. Understanding this division requires a brief excursion into the structure of the labor movement then and now.

The Structure of the American Labor Movement:
A Conceptual Excursion

Until the very historical moment we are now discussing, the mid-thirties, the numerically dominant mode of labor union structure in the United States was what analysts call "craft unions." Workers had built their associations around distinctive occupations: cigar makers, bricklayers, printers, ladies' dressmakers, men's suit makers, and so on. The more skilled workers tended to have the most bargaining power, and they tended to have organized their unions earlier than had less skilled workers. Out of the complex historical forces of the fifty years from 1880 to 1930, filled with exceptions and colorful moments, the dominant tendency among organized labor in the United States was an apolitical "business unionism." Rather than fostering worker militancy or a broader vision of a just society, this form of trade union consciousness and practice stolidly worked to advance wages and working conditions. Business unionism was not as politically activist as its competitors, nor was it highly oriented to building a community-based workers' movement. Despite his moments of rhetorical flourish, the famous Samuel Gompers embodied this approach during the years in which he led the AFL.[6]

By the mid-thirties, and with the suffering those years of the Depression had brought, working-class radicals, militants, and intellectuals had long nurtured a different vision of how to organize unions. This concept—industrial unionism—called for organizing all the workers of a given employer and industry into "One Big Union."[7] The relatively more skilled and the relatively less skilled, united, in this view, would be more effective, would embody the larger egalitarian goals of labor as a social movement, and would overcome the divisions of race and ethnicity that so divided American workers. In addition, the industrial union strategy tended to be adopted by those of leftist political views and thus usually implied a more politicized vision of how labor unions would behave in the larger body politic. The Depression united three trends that brought industrial unionism to timely emergence: mass production, immigrant integration, and the sudden, massive reversal of progress in working conditions accompanied by mass suffering.

The middle third of the twentieth century was a period in which mass production manufacturing became the dominant center of the economy and of wealth making in capitalist countries, including the United States. There the great corporations came to dominate the landscape and to employ by hundreds of thousands the men and women working at assembly lines making millions of uniform commodities.[8] The majority of such workers were semiskilled and unskilled in that their employers accomplished job-specific training in short periods. From the employers' point of view the workers were like the commodities they produced: indistinguishable and replaceable. It was in the mass production industries, therefore, that workers most clearly perceived that their earnest efforts and their skills or experience would not guarantee them consideration from the employer. Their ability to advance their interests lay in their ability to unite and to compel employers to deal with them as collective equals.

Modern American social science, supported culturally by the mass media apparatus, has enjoyed "proving" Karl Marx wrong because the working class of the capitalist countries did not make a revolution. Error, just as virtue, in the social sciences is relative and probabilistic. The rise of industrial unions, their relatively higher level of politicization, and the relatively higher level of class awareness of the workers in them were all developments that Marx's sociology would have explicitly predicted.[9]

Other factors were also part of the sociology that made the time ripe for industrial unionism—factors similar to those that elected Roosevelt in 1932. From 1880 to World War I, and ending formally in 1924, the United States received what was, until the turn of the twentieth century, the largest immigration wave in its history. The immigrants of that period came from Southern and Eastern Europe and were in their majority Catholic, Orthodox, and Jewish—they were not the Protestants of Northern and Western Europe who had founded the nation. In 1900–1910, the last uninterrupted decade of this epochal movement of peoples, 8.8 million people immigrated to the United States.[10] The great flow of European migration to American cities was interrupted by the submarine warfare of World War I and then was formally ended by the Immigration Quota Act of 1924. This act severely restricted immigration numerically and, inspired by racist hostility toward Eastern and Southern European non-Protestants, divided the new, small quota of those who could enter the country by their proportion of the population in 1890 (and subsequently 1920)—that is, it strongly favored natives of Northern and Western Europe.

By 1928 many of the immigrant workers who had, in the words of the labor anthem, "dug the mines and built the railroads" (Chapin 1915), assembled the cars and sewed the dresses, of America had obtained citizenship. When Governor Al Smith ran for president as a Democrat, presumably many Catholic immigrants and their children voted for the first time—the electorate grew by 8 percent over 1924. Then, with the coming of the Great Depression, these new voters, combined with converted Republicans, elected Roosevelt (Brown 1988). With the landslide of 1936, having proved himself a president who would help workers, Roosevelt encouraged a whole new cohort of new voters. In addition, in the workplaces of America in the previous fifty years, outlines had been sketched of accommodation and unity regarding ethnic difference—religious, linguistic, cultural. The Congress of Industrial Organizations (CIO) was the expression, then, of immigrants who had worked out their relations with each other and of the sons and daughters of immigrants who had taken fully to thinking of themselves as American.

Finally, for most American workers, while unions were weak in the 1920s employment was high and productivity gains were under way. State legislation and federal inroads had limited the workday for many subgroups of workers—such as federal employees, women, and children. Average working hours were going down. But the brutality of the Depression reversed the relative improvements workers had experienced. Losing something you once had may be more infuriating than not having what you want. This was one of the classic theories of revolution, now somewhat discredited, but it still makes sense in understanding the upsurge of class militancy in the 1930s (Davies 1962).

Based at first in the United Mine Workers (UMW) union, the movement for industrial unionism had another strong base in the men's clothing union, the ACWA, led during the 1930s by Sidney Hillman. The ILGWU was also a multicraft union, and its leader, David Dubinsky, also supported, at first, the fledgling CIO.

Hillman was an experienced political operative who had known Roosevelt from the time he was governor. Given his industry's low wage and exploitable profile, Hillman was a long-term supporter of minimum wage legislation. But ominously, as late as 1936, when Roosevelt saw to it that a wages and hours plank had been put in the Democratic party platform, the AFL sent communications to both political conventions calling for "minimum wage legislation for women and children but not for men" (Samuel 2000).

By 1937 the AFL position was softening; a large division within it called for a minimum wage (Samuel 2000). Nevertheless, as Frances Perkins later wrote,

> many AFL officials privately expressed the traditional Gompers doctrine against minimum wages, repeating the old adage that "the minimum tends to become the maximum." (quoted in Samuel 2000)

When the FLSA came before the Congress in 1937 and 1938, the AFL and the CIO still had different positions on how to accomplish the minimum wage concept, and this allowed the congressional conservatives to delay, obstruct, and then extract concessions in the final product. The main arena was the House of Representatives: the Senate passed a bill in 1937, but the House did not. The AFL opposed the administration's and the CIO versions, which contributed to the bill's defeat twice. Finally, in 1938 a bill was passed with both Democratic and Republican support. Among the concessions were exemptions for agricultural workers and intrastate retail workers.

It is inconceivable that Washington—where the AFL, the New Deal reformers, the Southern Democrats, and the Republicans faced each other in the arena—would have passed both the Wagner Act and the FLSA. The critical margin was the threatening context of the sit-down strikes of the mid-thirties and the radical influence in the CIO that had led those strikes. Hillman, the political point man for the CIO, had unique access to Roosevelt's inner circle—for example, to Secretary Perkins; but behind Hillman were the sit-down strikes, and behind them were the revolutionaries Washington so wanted to deflect.[11]

By the glorious alchemy in which a victory has a thousand fathers, the AFL by 1939 was saying the bill should not be changed and by 1944 was vowing to defeat attempts to undermine it. By 1946 the AFL had campaigned to raise the minimum—which had begun at twenty-five cents and had risen to forty cents an hour—to one dollar an hour. By 1955, on the eve of their eventual merger, the AFL and the CIO had formed a coalition to raise the minimum wage. Even the meager twenty-five-cent minimum immediately raised the wages of 300,000 workers in 1938 (Berg 1989, 31).

Ms. Perkins's thrift shop had become an American institution.

Homework and Child Labor

Section 8 of the FLSA gave the secretary of labor

> the authority to make such regulations and orders regulating, restricting, or prohibiting industrial homework as are necessary or appropriate to prevent the circumvention or evasion of and to safeguard the minimum wage rate prescribed in this Act, and all existing regulations or orders of the Administrator relating to industrial homework are hereby continued in full force and effect. (29 U.S.C. 201, et seq.)

After the law was passed, Secretary Perkins and her aides experimented with industrial homeworkers by tracking their hours in log books. However, in hearings held in the early 1940s DOL spokespersons claimed that they could not account for the hours of homeworkers and thus could not enforce a minimum wage (Boris 1985, 1994). In 1942, Perkins banned industrial homework in women's apparel and related branches of the industry.

It is easier to enforce the laws that few want to break than to do otherwise. World War II created both an economic and a regulatory environment favorable to labor. Full employment, especially the employment of women, drained the reservoir of labor that abusive employers had usually relied on to subvert labor standards in the apparel industry. When Rosie the Riveter went to work, so too did Sadie the Sewing Machine Operator.

In addition, wartime production focused on military uniforms, not fashion goods. These were, inherently, factory-based production items. Furthermore, war production contracts favored unionized contractors. The FLSA's ban of child labor, outside of agriculture, was not a contentious matter during the war years.

By the end of World War II, sweatshop abuse in the apparel industry was becoming a memory of the past. Workers may not have been treated justly or allotted their fair share of the nation's bounty, but, nevertheless, apparel workers looked forward to a new life of relative decency as the "Greatest Generation" headed home from war.

4 The Era of Decency and the Return of the Sweatshop

with World War II came full employment. The apparel industry turned decisively toward factory employment as uniforms made up a larger fraction of its production and women's styles were simplified and limited by wartime restrictions on fabric use. Both of these factors would have reduced sweatshop conditions, but in addition there were now the homework bans, the restrictions on child labor, and the wages and hours standards of the FLSA. On top of all these propitious conditions was the growing power of the garment unions within their industries. The War Production Board also helped: defense contracts were given to union plants (see N. Green 1997, 65–67).

The Era of Decency: 1940s–1970s

With the FLSA as a floor and with a large fraction of the industry unionized, the union contracts in both men's and women's clothing pioneered benefits in prepaid health insurance and retirement pensions. The full employment during the war period and then the expansion in consumer demand after it afforded apparel workers unprecedented opportunity for income and leisure. Already in 1938 *Life* magazine had jumped the historical gun and prematurely announced, following a fetching front cover picture of "Garment Workers at Play": "Thirty years ago the industry stank of the sweatshop and the cruelest kind of exploitation. . . . Still numerous in 1933, the sweatshop is virtually gone today" (*Life*, August 1, 1938 as cited in Smithsonian Institution 1998).

By the end of World War II, even union leaders and commentators began to refer to sweatshops in the past tense.

The Union Perspective

Publications from and statements by the ILGWU support the view that sweatshops declined for roughly a thirty-year period. As early as 1944, a historian closely associated with the apparel unions wrote in the past tense: "In the old sweatshop days the garment worker lived in an environment, industrial and social, which was a major outrage to every rule of public health" (Stolberg 1944, 299). Stolberg, it is interesting to note here, is associating the term *sweatshop* with the tenement apartment workshop rather than the later association with abusive labor conditions in any given setting. Even in that case, though, Stolberg's perception is a kind of evidence: homework was shrinking.

In a report prepared for the ILGWU somewhat later, in 1951, Emil Schlesinger[1] also spoke of the sweatshop and sweatshop-related conditions in the past tense. His emphasis is mostly on the union's success at countering the effects of the "outside system of production," that is, the nonunion subcontracting firms that once were the sweatshops of the apparel industry. Schlesinger remarks on how "in the past" an employer would pay his overhead expenses and then, "with what little there was left, he would pay his workers. If nothing was left, his workers were not paid" (Schlesinger 1951, 6). More clearly, Schlesinger states, "The sweatshops have been wiped out; the days of their existence are among the most shameful pages of recorded history" (90).

Schlesinger's proposition is significant because he attributes the end of abusive conditions to the union's control over the subcontracting system.

LIFE

GARMENT WORKERS AT PLAY

AUGUST 1, 1938 **10** CENTS

Life celebrates—a little early—the end of sweatshops.

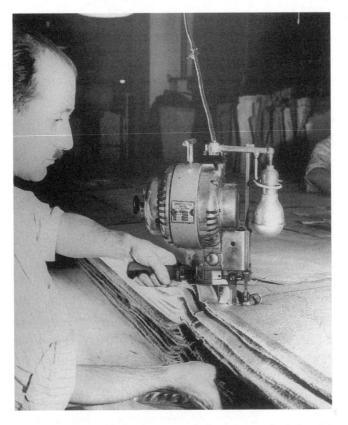

A cutter works with his blade. Courtesy of Kheel Center for Labor-Management Documentation and Archives, Cornell University.

For Schlesinger, the lawyer son of an early ILGWU president, it was not the FLSA, not the expanding consumer economy, but instead control over cutthroat competition that reformed the industry. The mechanism of this control was the joint liability contract and the union's ability to force jobbers to give work only to union contractors and thus to force contractors to allow their workers to join the union. The former protected wage levels and benefits by making the jobber responsible for them even if the contractor couldn't make the payments; the latter led to top-down organizing.

Controversial among critics of the ILGWU, top-down organizing occurred when the union extracted from the jobber an agreement to give work, for example, sewing already cut garments, only to union contractors. "Once the union organized the big manufacturer or jobber, all the workers in the contracting shops working for that company became union members—sometimes overnight" (Tyler 1995, 263). The strength of this strategy was its ability to overcome the evasion inherent in the labyrinth of contract and subcontracting relations in this amoeboid industry of shape changers. The weakness of this way of building a union was that the new workers who thus became members may have had little commitment to the union or knowledge of it and were not likely to become part of a democratic internal life. When large numbers of members are in this situation, sloth and corruption are constant temptations. Those were to occur later.

In the 1940s and early 1950s, in addition to these chroniclers close to the union, union officials also considered the sweatshop problem behind them. Speaking at the groundbreaking ceremony for a union-sponsored housing project, ILGWU president David Dubinsky said, as reported in the union's newspaper, "Now 50 years later, the garment workers return to their place of origin. We have wiped out the sweatshop. Now we return to wipe out the slum" (Dubinsky 1977 [1953], 268).

When Dubinsky referred to this ceremony again in 1955 he wrote of its Lower East Side site: "only a few of the old structures remain standing on this site. When their walls come tumbling down the last sign of the slum and the sweatshop will disappear for ever from this corner of Manhattan" (Dubinsky 1977 [1955], 267). Dubinsky described these sweatshops of the past:

> There were rooms in these houses where the sun never shone. There were rooms in these houses in which children slaved over bundles of garment work, breathing in the foul air that made them tubercular before they were grown up. There were rooms in these houses in which, in a not too distant past, men and women worked to the point where they dropped. (267)

In conclusion, David Dubinsky stated, "We cannot forget the poverty, the sickness, the homework shops, the child laborers of their neighborhood" (268). These statements suggest that, in the eyes of the union leadership of the 1950s, sweatshop conditions, as early as the 1940s and certainly by the early 1950s, had been but were no longer characteristic of the apparel workers' conditions in New York's industry.

Such claims might be viewed skeptically by those knowledgeable about union politics. Dubinsky had risen to political dominance in his union through a bitter struggle with Communist rivals who had a political following among Jewish garment workers in particular. They had been militant in the 1920s and bitterly critical of him in the 1930s. With Dubinsky ascendant while the Red Scare harassed his erstwhile enemies, some might claim that he was merely self-congratulatory.[2]

Other Views

Certainly Herbert Hill, labor secretary of the National Association for the Advancement of Colored People (NAACP), thought Dubinsky and his union were puffed up and evasive, for he accused them of tolerating and even endorsing sweatshops for Black and Puerto Rican workers (Hill 1974). In testimony before Congress (U.S. Congress 1963), Hill railed against the political exclusion of Puerto Ricans and Blacks from the leadership of the ILGWU. He discussed the "callousness" with which union leaders tolerated very low (but, according to my calculation, lawful) wages in those branches of the industry in which minority people were concentrated. At one point in his testimony Hill refers to the ILGWU acceding to another union's sweetheart contract with a "sweatshop"[3] employer.

Hill's main purpose in his testimony to Congress and in his provocatively entitled article "Guardians of the Sweatshops: The Trade Unions, Racism, and the Garment Industry" (1974) is to condemn the ILGWU for discrimination and political exclusion of Puerto Ricans and Blacks—a matter I am not disputing. In his article, Hill cites low wages in those branches of the New York garment industry where production workers were predominantly Puerto Rican or Black. He also cites a case history of the ILGWU in the late 1950s *opposing* a New York City minimum wage law that was higher than the federal minimum. Yet Hill never indicates that the examples of low wages he offers were illegal. Indeed, by using the term *sweatshop* in quotation marks, Hill indicates he is employing the term as a metaphor for low wages and lousy conditions.

Nevertheless, at least some feminist historians in this branch of scholarship appear to have concluded that sweatshop conditions were indeed prevalent in New York's garment industry in the 1950s in shops where Puerto Rican women worked. One of these researchers, Altagracia Ortiz (1990, 1996), has studied the history of Puerto Rican women in the New York apparel industry and in the ILGWU. While her main concern is the creation of a historical and political narrative of Puerto Rican women, rather than analytical theory building in political economy, Ortiz's conclusions pose a challenge to our contention.

There are two separate bases for Ortiz's claim that Puerto Rican women encountered sweatshop conditions in the 1950s. First, there are oral history interviews of a half dozen women performed by Ortiz and others.[4] In these interviews workers told of hard work for little pay. Yet her report does not allow us to judge whether these women were paid below the minimum wage of that era; were denied overtime payment; were subject to extensive health or safety hazards; or were employed at a place with child labor infractions. That is, the interview material as cited in the published work is too imprecise to allow a positive judgment about the existence of sweatshops *as we have defined them.*

The other source of Ortiz's claim is the journalist Dan Wakefield's 1959 book on New York City's Puerto Ricans—*Island in the City.* Wakefield's fifth chapter is provocatively entitled "Sweat without Profit." The chapter tells of the new garment contractors in Spanish Harlem employing Puerto Rican women at low wages. This chapter also questions the motivation of the ILGWU in addressing these problems.

Wakefield does not provide much information about wages actually earned by the women sewing operators. One example he gives is that of a woman who was told she would earn forty-two dollars a week (the minimum union scale—slightly higher than the U.S. minimum wage of a dollar an hour at the time). Her weekly take-home pay was only twenty-nine dollars. Wakefield quotes the woman's employer as making a vague reference to taxes, suggesting that he was keeping the money that legally should have been set aside for taxes. Yet the narrative does not demonstrate that he was paying subminimum wages.

Wakefield's chapter does offer some quantitative insights into this issue. An interview with a business agent of the ILGWU in East Harlem reveals the assumption that a union shop is ipso facto not a sweatshop. The union agent says there are thirty-five steadily operating shops in East Harlem (where the Puerto Rican population was then concentrated). Yet only a total of twenty-five shops were organized (Wakefield 1959, 201). Wakefield also notes that there were unknown others—too marginal to keep track of or to organize. Despite the tenuousness of these facts we can nevertheless produce some estimates of sweatshop prevalence in 1950s New York City.

If six of the ten unorganized shops were substandard, then there were six sweatshops.[5] If, in Spanish Harlem of the late 1950s, there were about six *known* sweatshops, let us further estimate that another four were undetected, for a total of ten.[6] There are about seventeen employees per contractor shop. Since this number is larger than the anecdotal reports of ten or a dozen workers, we err only in overestimation. This calculation would yield 170 sweatshop workers in Manhattan according to our definition.[7] If we assume equal numbers in the Bronx, Brooklyn, and Manhattan, the total number of workers in apparel sweatshops in New York City in the mid-1950s would then be 510.

The estimated number of sweatshop employees in the 1980s in New York City was about fifty thousand (U.S. GAO 1989); the estimated number in the mid-1950s would be under 1.5 percent of that estimate. Even if we double the 1950s estimate to one thousand sweatshop workers and use the low end of the current sweatshop workforce estimate as the denominator (100/33,000), the result is 3.3 percent of today's number. If this estimate is anywhere near correct, the problem was *not* quantitatively significant. We can therefore conclude that sweatshops were not a major social problem in the New York City apparel industry in the 1950s despite the employment of large numbers of poor women who had recently emigrated from Puerto Rico.

In summary, despite Herbert Hill's claims and despite associated uses of the term *sweatshop* made by a historian of Puerto Rican people in New

York and by the journalist Wakefield, by the strict definition of *sweatshop* we are using here, the problem of extremely abusive conditions was relatively minor. There is evidence that the ILGWU was less aggressive in its collective bargaining on behalf of local unions with concentrated minority populations than it was for its traditional base of Jewish and Italian workers. But the wages and conditions of Puerto Rican and African-American sewers, about which Hill and Ortiz complain, do not fall below legal minima and do not meet an objective definition of *sweatshop*. Thus, while there may have been strategic and moral error by the union, the migrants to the industry of the 1950s were not subject to conditions as bad as those earlier in the century or, more ominously, later.

Academic Observations of the 1950s

However skeptical we might be about Dubinsky's political motives, others more removed from the ambit of his political career have come to similar conclusions about sweatshop decline.

Documentary and Economic Evidence

In her extensive research on apparel workers in Paris and New York, the historian Nancy Green surveyed union records exhaustively. Her conclusion was that "the labor history of the industry as constructed through union records contrasts the sweatshops of the 1900s to the subsequent amelioration of conditions, thanks to union efforts and especially the legendary 1909–1910 strikes" (N. Green 1997, 158).

Green found corroborative evidence for the union's view. Among this evidence is the decline of homework. The worst abuses of physical environment and low pay occurred in the crowded tenements of the immigrant neighborhoods like the Lower East Side of New York in the first years of the twentieth century.

While New York State, in the years directly after the Triangle fire of 1911, attempted to regulate and partially abolish homework, these laws

94

were ineffective in eliminating substandard conditions (N. Green 1997). As we have seen, under the authority of the FLSA, in 1942 Secretary of Labor Frances Perkins prohibited industrial homework from most branches of the apparel industry, except under permits, and these only under such special circumstances as that of a handicapped worker (Boris 1994). Green reports that "it was estimated between 1935 and 1955 the number of homeworkers in New York State had dropped from 500,000 (in all fields) to less than 5,000" (N. Green 1997, 64). Furthermore, "in 1962, the New York State Department of Labor abolished its special homework unit due to 'apparent success' in policing homework and enforcing sanctions" (152, citing New York State Department of Labor 1982). With unregulated homeworkers disappearing as a low wage alternative to workshop labor, it is fair to infer that conditions in the New York apparel industry had improved by the 1950s.

There is statistical evidence that supports this conclusion even as it documents later decline. As of 1947 garment workers' average hourly wages were 95 percent of manufacturing workers' hourly wages—and despite declines these wages would not go below 60 percent of manufacturing wages for twenty-five years (see fig. 1). In the post–World War II era, garment workers participated in the fabled "American Dream."

Along with other unions the apparel unions had adapted to World War II wage policies by bargaining for a large raft of new benefits. While the socialist leadership of the apparel unions had always been highly oriented to their members' outside-of-work lives with educational programs, summer camps, and benefits, the wage and price controls of the early 1940s pushed collective bargaining toward benefits. The ILGWU secured an early form of the HMO for its members, retirement plan contributions were locked into jobber/manufacturer contracts, and union pension funds were invested in such ambitious projects as affordable housing. Employment in the garment industry was mainstream. While a single operator wage package would not put a family in the middle class, two such earners would constitute middle income by the standards of the day. Ten years after *Life* magazine declared their victory, apparel workers were poised to enjoy the fruits of American life.

Slaves to Fashion

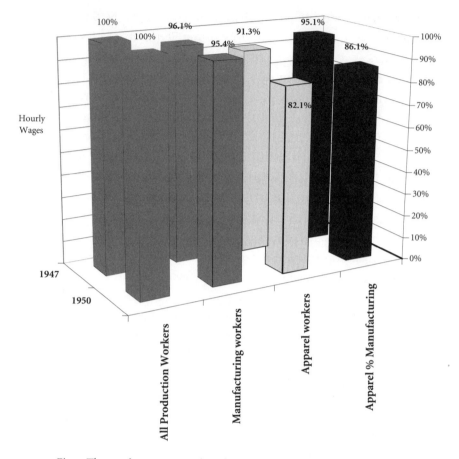

Fig. 1. The good years: Apparel workers' wages in context, 1947 and 1950.
Source: Bureau of Labor Statistics 2001a.

The Rise of the New Sweatshops

Early in the 1970s Jacob Petofsky of the ACWU warned at an AFL-CIO conference that imports from countries paying nine cents an hour would bring back sweatshop conditions to the United States (*New York Times,* July 14, 1971). Even earlier, while the total value of imports was still low, certain lines of production were highly impacted by imports. In a pattern that was repeated many times, American policymakers—and union officials—traded domestic jobs for Cold War politics.

Gus Tyler, the ILGWU's resident historian, in-house intellectual, and assistant to President Dubinsky, tells the story in vivid fashion. Tyler begins his discussion by noting that "outside production," meaning contractor shops, had always been the structural feature of the industry that eroded labor conditions. By 1966, he goes on to say, "outside" became "outside of the United States" (Tyler 1995, 265). Earlier, the first local of the ILGWU to experience the onslaught to come was the neckwear local. Its manager proposed a convention resolution to stop or restrain imports of silk scarves from Japan, imports that were "choking his members to death." Tyler articulated to him the union's traditional position in favor of free trade and working-class solidarity—but with a social democratic Cold War twist. Tyler "explained to [the union official] the war had badly damaged the Japanese economy, that such economic distress would breed communism, that [the union official's] protectionism would put him, an old Socialist, on the side of the American capitalists and the Japanese Communists" (266).

The Cold War rationale for fostering labor-intensive apparel and textile employment was to be repeated in successive waves: after Japan came Korea and Taiwan, then Hong Kong and Singapore, then Central America (Rosen 2002). It is a bit odd to read the statements of apparel industry union officials a generation after their predictions turned out to be true and then to hear them excoriated as mindless protectionists. What they really were were willing victims of the Cold War.

Apparel workers' wages, buoyed by wartime conditions and government policies that supported unionization, began a long slide toward inferiority. In 1947 (as far back as this government time-series goes) apparel workers, as we saw earlier, earned 95 percent of manufacturing workers' hourly wage and 85 percent of their average weekly earnings; by 1950 they had slipped to 86 percent of their hourly wage and 77 percent of weekly earnings. By 2000 apparel workers averaged only 63 percent of the hourly manufacturing wage and only a bit more than half (57 percent) of the average weekly earnings in manufacturing. Figure 2 shows the decline of apparel workers' wages relative to fellow workers in the manufacturing sector.

The story of apparel workers is part of the larger story of the growth of inequality in the last generation. If we compare the wages of the men

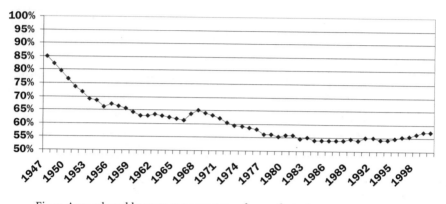

Fig. 2. Apparel weekly wage as percentage of manufacturing wage, 1947–2000

and women who make our clothes with the median in the family income distribution, we see a sharper relative decline. In 1947 apparel workers' average weekly wage multiplied out (optimistically) to about 72 percent of the American family median wage. By 1977 it had fallen to 42 percent. By 2000 the average apparel worker, working full-time, earned but 36 percent of the median family income. Figure 3 depicts this decline graphically. The international standard for comparing poverty rates regards households with 50 percent of a nation's median income as poor. My calculations do not correct for family size or for the number of workers, but they indicate that the average garment worker is among the working poor.[8]

By 1979 reports of sweatshop conditions in New York's still nationally dominant garment industry had begun to accumulate. Official, not union, sources estimated the number of sweatshops—paying below the minimum wage—at five hundred factories (Stetson 1979). Unannounced, a joint task force of state and federal officials was formed in February of that year to investigate and crack down on massive labor law violations in the flourishing Chinatown sewing industry. The task force found that 35 percent of the five hundred small shops in Chinatown had violations of the FLSA. Almost twenty years later, joint task force to the contrary notwithstanding, a DOL survey (U.S. DOL 1997b) found a 90 percent violation rate in Lower Manhattan's Chinatown.

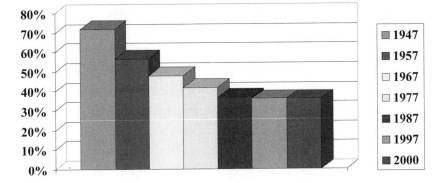

Fig. 3. Losing ground: Apparel as percentage of family median income. Source: Calculated from U.S. Census Bureau 2002a and Bureau of Labor Statistics 2001a.

In that same year, 1979, a long feature on sweatshop conditions appeared in New York City's glossy magazine *New York* (Buck 1979). By 1980 liberal Democratic assemblyman Frank Barbaro proposed legislative action against homework and sweatshop conditions in the New York State legislature, but it was defeated by a coalition of conservative Republicans and Latino Democrats, each defending (illegal) homeworkers (Meislin 1980).

In 1959 an average apparel worker's weekly earnings—which few garnered for a full fifty-two weeks each year—would have produced an annual income about 27 percent above the poverty line for a family of three. This was not much, especially since the official poverty line was so low. By 2000 such a worker's earnings would have put her 33 percent above this nominal poverty line. The difference between the eras is not the 6 percent improvement. Rather, the difference lies in the very high probability that the earlier era data were more or less accurate, while the latter period is almost certainly an inaccurate result of falsely high reporting of payments by businesses. Since very substantial fractions of the employers of apparel workers fail to pay the minimum wage (see chapter 1) and even larger numbers fail to keep proper records of their payments to workers, there is good reason to believe that formally employed apparel workers actually endure worse pay situations than the official data report.

It was, then, during the 1970s and 1980s that multiple factors converged to reproduce sweatshops in the apparel industry. Imports were not the only force that eroded the garment workers' American moment. The next few chapters in part II will analyze these forces in detail. In addition to the primary force—the globalization of production and free trade without labor standards—the decline of U.S. apparel workers' economic position was influenced by the decline of the apparel unions' power in the industry; by de facto deregulation of labor standards and privatization of law enforcement; by massive structural change in the industry causing concentrated power in an industry previously dispersed and competitive; and, finally, by a new workforce of undocumented, and therefore disempowered, immigrants exploited by unscrupulous and desperate entrepreneurs.

Part 2 Explaining the Rise of the New Sweatshops

when Clara Lemlich and her sisters struck in 1909, the brutal conditions they faced were a result of competition only barely restrained by law. The miserable conditions in the apparel industry were probably worse than average for American or, for that matter, London and Parisian workers, but they were produced as well by a general weakness on the part of workers. The legal framework of the day did not support workers' rights of association—trade union rights. Few communities of workers had managed to obtain collective bargaining contracts, and most found the courts and the law hostile to their interests. The idea of a social safety net had only begun to be articulated in Europe, where the labor movement was stronger and workers somewhat more unified. At the end of the nineteenth and the beginning of the twentieth centuries, migrants—most of whom were rural to urban migrants and many of whom crossed frontiers to become immigrants—were a vulnerable category of workers wherever they found themselves and their employers found them.

The sweatshops of the early twentieth century in the United States, therefore, were the product of cutthroat competition and a lack of social regulation of working conditions, including health, safety, wages, and hours. Also facilitating those extremes of exploitation was the large pool of labor available to employers—what Marx called the "reserve army of the unemployed." In addition, political leaders could ignore the needs of working people with relative impunity: workers' interests were not well represented by political parties, and a relatively small proportion of immigrants voted.

Some of these conditions are the same and some are different as we examine the turn of the twentieth century into the twenty-first. In the United States and in most countries, including developing nations, the laws are better than they were a century ago. They appear to protect workers from overly long hours and provide for legally mandated minimum wages, and they usually include health and safety standards. The problem now is law enforcement—or its absence. In the United States there is the superficial appearance in law that union rights—labor rights—are protected. That these nominal legal protections are flimsy is among the reasons why conditions in the industry have become so bad. Part 2 will include an analysis of one aspect of law enforcement—de facto deregulation.

In both periods, a pool of immigrant labor is available to unscrupulous employers. In the current period, however, many of the toilers in garment shops are not legal immigrants—making them doubly vulnerable on the labor market.

The chapters in part 2 will explore these matters. The analysis begins with the most massive differences between the contexts of exploitation then and now. The central concept uniting the most important causes of the rise of the new sweatshops is the shift in power and the potential resources for power brought about by the connected processes of globalization, particularly dramatic in the apparel trade, and concentration in the retail sector. Together these trends create the terrible competition that erodes labor standards in some places and retards progress in others. Part 2 begins with an analysis of how unrestrained global capitalism drives a ferocious race to the bottom in labor standards among the world's apparel producers. Then it turns to the strategic and accountable actors in this system of production—the concentrated retail chains and a handful of manufacturers that dominate the rag trade.

5 Global Capitalism and the Race to the Bottom in the Production of Our Clothes

early in the era of global capitalism Raymond Vernon (1979) used the term *global scanning* to convey the process by which the large multinational corporations systematically searched the globe for the most propitious sites on which to place their production facilities and to target their sales efforts. Ross and Trachte adopted this concept when they wrote in 1990:

> The global firm . . . is a design for survival under competitive conditions of the new era. Its ability to "scan" the globe for investment possibilities makes possible a rational assignment of resources and a ruthless pursuit of the exact combination of local policies, labor conditions, transport considerations, and so forth for any commodity or part. (66)

Unions and labor-rights activists have long argued that investors and corporations seek out the places where unions are weakest, labor protections are least enforced, workers are most repressed, and, consequently, labor is cheapest. While scholars would want to hedge and qualify the extent to which this proposition is true, political leaders around the world try to hold down what they antiseptically call "local costs of production" in an attempt to attract the proverbial golden goose of capital investment. In much of Europe, this may take the form of cutting back on employers' payroll taxes or severance costs (Hooper and Connolly 2001). In Burma

(Myanmar), it takes the form of forced labor under a brutally repressive military dictatorship (Commission of Inquiry 1998). Labor activists have called this process the "race to the bottom." More formally, the race to the bottom implies a process of competition between jurisdictions sparked by investors, the object of which is to hold down or reduce such costs of production as labor costs and social protections. The European usage concerning social policies is vivid: there analysts refer to "social dumping" as the process by which employers move plants or contracts to jurisdictions with less social insurance, fewer pensions, fewer health costs, and so forth. The general proposition is that, as investors favor locations that are cheaper or that afford workers fewer rights, the more well-paid and protected workers tend to lose those advantages. The process produces a decline in labor standards understood qualitatively and/or quantitatively.

How can we tell if the race to the bottom is really taking place? One way is to look at the average wage in industries that export goods to the United States. If there really were such a "race," we would expect export production to shift from higher-wage countries to lower-wage countries. Many countries import clothing to the United States. Italy, where apparel workers earned an average of $12.55 per hour in total compensation (wages and benefits) in 1998, accounts for about 2.5 percent of imported clothes (Office and Textiles and Apparel [OTEXA] 2001a). Meanwhile, garment workers in Burma—which accounted for 0.75 percent of U.S. clothing imports in mid-2001, its share tripling since 1998—earned about $.04 per hour in 1998 (OTEXA 2001a; NLC 1998). If we weight the wages in Italy, Burma, and all the other countries that send clothing to the United States according to the percentage of U.S. imports coming from each country, we can then estimate the average hourly wage for imported garments in general. By comparing the results over a period of years we should be able to get an idea of the general trend.[1]

Despite certain limits (see chapter 12), using this method for the thirty-four suppliers that cover about 94 percent of American imports, the average wage for U.S. apparel imports appears to have declined by about 6 percent from 1998 to 2001. The method used is based not on changes in the wages in a given country but on changes in the mix of countries contributing to the U.S. import stream. That is, the race to the bottom involves investors deserting countries as lower-waged ones become available as export platforms. Since 1998 the mix of imported clothing to the United States has changed. Indonesia, Bangladesh, Guatemala, Nicaragua, Peru, and Burma—all low-wage countries—have increased their shares. Meanwhile, Canada, Italy, the United Kingdom, and Israel have declined. As we shall see in the next chapter, this cheapening of imported clothing is the result of a rational process largely controlled by a handful of firms. The final result, however, is deterioration of the working conditions of apparel workers.

As discussed in chapter 4, we have witnessed the decline in American apparel workers' relative economic position in comparison to other American workers as well as the reappearance of sweatshop abuse in the North American apparel industry. While there are many contributing factors to this decline of labor standards, none is larger than the globalization of the apparel industry under conditions of a race to the bottom. Figures 4, 5, and 6 show the rise of imports to the United States and the decline of apparel workers' jobs and wages.

The story these figures tell is a capsule of the way globalization affects workers in much of the world. As apparel imports grew through the 1950s and 1960s they were as yet not large enough to compromise employment levels of the whole industry—though assuredly certain specialties were affected (as attested to by the leader of the neckwear local of the ILGWU; see chap. 4). By the late 1970s, as imports steeply sloped upward, employment in the apparel industry began a precipitous drop and so did real (inflation-adjusted) hourly wages. It is not accidental that the earliest accounts of the new sweatshops stem from this period.

The Price of Clothes

Supporters of the current form of globalization often defend the "neoliberal" trade regime as one that favors consumers by keeping prices low. The availability of goods from low-wage countries has certainly kept

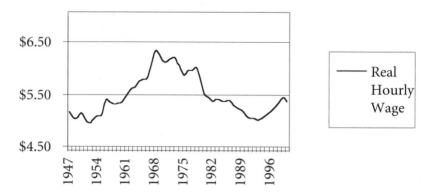

Fig. 4. Real value of officially recorded hourly apparel wage (1982–84 dollars), 1947–2000. Sources: Calculated from Bureau of Labor Statistics 2001a, 2001e.

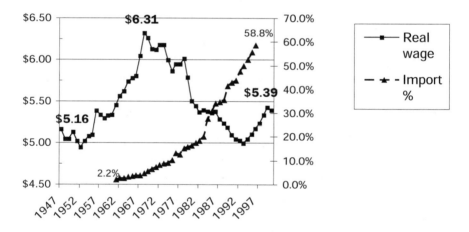

Fig. 5. Real hourly apparel wages (1982–84 dollars) and import percentage, U.S. production, 1947–2000. Sources: Bureau of Labor Statistics 2001a, 2001e.

clothing prices down—and apparel wages as well. Imagine a shirt bought for $10 in 1970. By 2000 that $10 shirt would have cost about $21.90—an increase of 219 percent. But the general cost of living went up about twice as much during that same period—440 percent.

So clothing increased in cost only about half as much as the average cost of living. This accounts in part for the fact that the legally recorded

Global Capitalism and the Race to the Bottom

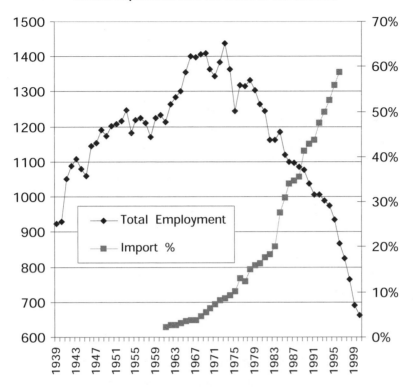

Fig. 6. Apparel employment (in thousands) and import penetration (in percentage). Source: Calculated from Bureau of Labor Statistics 2001a.

average apparel wage increased less than the cost of living: for every $10 an apparel worker earned in 1970, the official—that is, the overstated—weekly earnings indicate she would have earned $40.20 in 2000; yet it would have required $44.40—10 percent more—just to have remained with the same purchasing power. While the official weekly earnings of apparel workers were falling behind the cost of living during this period, they were falling further behind the median family income in the United States. Apparel workers lost 10 percent of their purchasing power throughout those decades; the median family gained about 14 percent in purchasing power. Figure 7 depicts these changes.

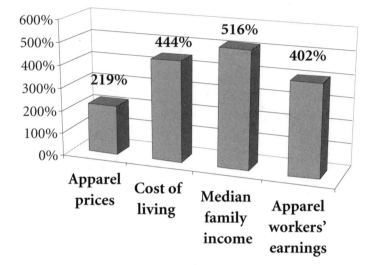

Slaves to Fashion

Fig. 7. Apparel costs in context, 1970–2000. Sources: Bureau of Labor Statistics 2001a, 2001e; U.S. Census Bureau 2002b.

The Way the Race to the Bottom Works:
China versus Mexico

Worldwide, apparel production has been shifting dramatically to low-wage countries. Much of this shift has been to China, and most of that to the less regulated "special economic zones" (ILO 2000). Figure 8 shows hourly wages (including all benefits) around the world as of circa 1998. It shows China, Indonesia, and Vietnam near or at the bottom of the list. By the mid-1990s China held about one-quarter of the world export market in clothing and footwear combined (ILO 2000).

In the meantime, beginning in the 1970s and dramatically accelerating after the passage of the North American Free Trade Agreement (NAFTA) in 1993, Mexico vigorously has joined the competition for the clothing markets of the rich countries. Mexico, as of 2000, produced a little below 15 percent of all clothing imported to the United States; China was the origin of a bit over 15 percent. Figure 9 shows the data on Mexico and China apparel imports combined for the U.S. and European Union (EU) markets (other data on this relationship is illustrated in chapter 13).

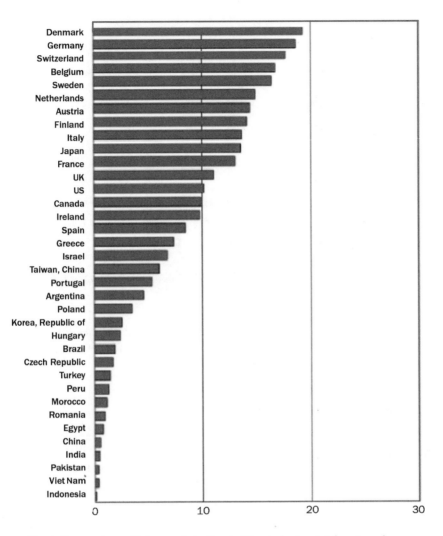

Fig. 8. Comparison of labor costs in the clothing industry, total cost per hour (U.S.$) in 1988. Source: ILO 2000.

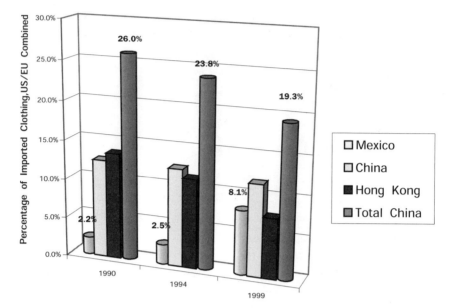

Fig. 9. China and Mexico in U.S./EU apparel imports. Source: Office of Textiles and Apparel (OTEXA) 2002 and International Textile and Clothing Bureau 2001.

A ferocious competition is now under way for the American and European market.

In China's export factories, the hours are long, workers toil in grim compounds, and union rights are nonexistent. Guangdong Province, bordering Hong Kong, is notorious for high accident rates and a bleak landscape of foreign-owned factories and dormitories.

During a field visit in January 2001, the absence of a normal community life for the workers was striking. With long workweeks and few days off, the workers had little leisure time, even if there were facilities for gathering or informal recreation. Separated from the outside world by walls with guards at the gates, the workers could leave when they were off from work, but within quite long distances of these compounds there was literally nothing but more factories. An example of the atmosphere of surveillance to which these workers are subject occurred as our research group and a guide from a Hong Kong NGO stopped to talk to two women outside their factory.

Global Capitalism and the Race to the Bottom

The women wore uniforms with the logo of the factory at which they worked—as is typical in these factories. We asked why they were out in the street in the middle of the afternoon, and they told us they were on short time since the factory had fewer orders from the United States that month. We discovered that they were, as were the vast majority of the workers in the export factories of Guangdong, migrants from a small village. Atypically, one of the workers was married, and she was looking forward to seeing her husband on her annual New Year's journey home. The second woman, who was younger, was not married and did not think she'd be able to meet anyone as long as she worked in the factory. They declined to have their pictures taken, and we shortly thereafter said goodbye. As we walked away down the barren industrial street, bereft of people, stores, or facilities, we glanced back and noticed that the uniformed (and armed) guard from the factory gatehouse had walked out into the street and was talking to the women, even as he turned toward us, indicating our retreating forms. We imagined he was asking the women who we were and what we wanted.

Systematic data are hard to retrieve for China, but the overall picture is one of workers without rights enduring extremely harsh conditions, even while economic growth creates a new, affluent middle class. Many sources report workweeks of over eighty hours (Chan 2000, 2001; NLC 2000). Wages seem to be in the neighborhood of twenty-five cents per hour, but living costs require as much as eighty-seven cents per hour (NLC 2000). While local newspapers publicize stories of worker abuse (Chan 2001) and the official union sometimes does act for workers, independent worker organization is not allowed (NLC 2000).

China and its special administrative region, Hong Kong, have been major sourcing areas for U.S. apparel firms for quite a while. However, among the more dramatic increases in the origin of exports to the United States are those from Mexico. NAFTA really has worked—for U.S. retailers and importers. Close enough to the major markets of the United States so that clothing can be trucked to warehouses in one or two days from completion, Mexico's *maquiladora* factories rapidly accelerated their imports to the United States after 1993, rising from 4 percent of the U.S. import flow in 1994 to 15 percent in 2000 (calculated from OTEXA 2001b).

Mexican factory owners in the apparel export sector are well aware of the global competition for the U.S. and EU markets. While Mexico has an advantage of fast turnaround time due to market proximity and increasing technical sophistication in filling North American orders, the vastly lower Chinese wages loom as a threat to Mexico's newly won market share. Consequently, factory owners in Mexico, and throughout the Western Hemisphere, are notorious for their hostility to unions and for the lack of enforcement of Mexico's quite good labor law. In fact, the official data on Mexico's wages may be as undependable as are those for the United States: they overstate wages because employers falsely report paying the minimum wage when they do not. Despite this official overstatement, Mexican apparel wages earnings did increase about 217 percent from 1994 to 1999 (ILO 2001). However, Mexican prices increased almost 300 percent during the period 1995–99 (U.S. Census Bureau 2001d, 834). In 1993 Mexico's officially reported apparel wages were 17 percent of U.S. wages. By 1998 that number had fallen to 10 percent—even while U.S. apparel workers were falling behind their local cost of living (U.S. DOL 2001).

William Greider put the matter of the China-Mexico confrontation in the context of the larger race to the bottom:

> [T]he downdraft on wages and competing economies induced by China's ascendancy may produce a terrible reckoning. For many poor nations that thought they had gained a foothold on the ladder, the reversal will be quite ugly.
>
> This is the "treadmill" that ensnares developing countries—writ large. If they attempt to boost wages or allow workers to organize unions or begin to deal with social concerns like health or the environment, the system punishes them. The factories move to some other country where those costs of production do not exist. (Greider 2001)

The competition between Mexico and China and, by implication, among all the poor countries striving to fill orders from rich country buyers threatens the small signs of progress that their workers may have made. Examples, small and fragile, from Mexico and China illustrate this problem. The Chinese use little child labor in the export factories because the vast pool of underemployed rural dwellers offers ample labor supply. The rural to urban migrants live in single-sex dormitories with mostly single women; family-oriented communities do not surround the export factories.

In the meantime, Mexico's tentative steps toward political and civil reform are symbolized ambiguously by the election to the presidency of Vicente Fox, who, however conservative, was free of the corrupt practices of the Institutional Revolutionary Party (PRI). During 2001 a symbolic victory of an independent union making college sweatshirts, aided by solidarity from North American activists, suggested that the further development of an autonomous labor movement might be imminent (Vickery 2001; McCall 2001).

Imagine now the cutthroat competition in which ferocious resistance counters each advance by Mexican workers as factory owners and managers look, as it were, to the cost of labor to their east and worry over each penny. At the same time, squeezing each penny out of the cost of a pair of jeans, Chinese managers in Guangdong Province worry over the cost of freight to America and the time it takes to get denim products across the sea. Might not some managers look aside as an obviously underage girl appears, in all her willing docility, to take a job sewing or trimming? In both countries, neither with very good records for workers' rights or standards of living for workers in the export sector, there is something to lose from a race to the bottom.

The Race at the Bottom: The Chentex Factory in Nicaragua

In May 2000, the U.S. Congress enacted an extension of NAFTA benefits to Caribbean nations. Similar apparel and textile product access to U.S. markets, earlier obtained by Mexico under the NAFTA treaty, was granted to the Caribbean countries. Before that time, Reagan administration policy embodied in the Caribbean Basin Initiative (CBI) had implanted what scholar Ellen Rosen calls a "planned sweatshop" economy in Central America (Rosen 2002). With few exceptions (e.g., Costa Rica and Jamaica), the CBI countries were low wage and agrarian. The Reagan administration of the 1980s used trade concessions to anchor to U.S. interests the Central American bourgeoisie; and they did it by creating an apparel export sector. The cold war was hot in Central America, and it inspired U.S. decision makers to sacrifice American Latino garment jobholders to the interests of U.S. retailers and their Central American suppliers (who were frequently Korean and Taiwanese investors).

When the United States, through its sponsored terrorists ("contras"), forced the insurgent Nicaraguan Sandinista government to hold elections in 1990, the result was a succession of conservative governments closely tied to the United States and, interestingly, to the government of Taiwan. Among the initiatives of the new, neoliberal regime was the creation of free trade zones that would participate in the U.S. market access of the CBI.

Nicaragua is one of the poorest countries of the Western Hemisphere. Per capita income is about $470 annually; most economically active workers do not hold regular wage jobs but work in the informal economy. So the paychecks of the free trade zones factories, now received by about thirty-five thousand workers, are highly valued—even when they are earned under sweatshop conditions.

In July 2000 a delegation of labor union leaders, NGO representatives, and a member of the U.S. Congress visited the Las Mercedes free trade zone. It was among the numerous delegations that the National Labor Committee (NLC) organized in the summer and fall of 2000. What follows is adapted from notes and from an article published shortly after the visit (Ross and Kernaghan 2000).

6 A.M., July 13, 2000: Las Mercedes free trade zone, Managua

A river of people, nineteen thousand workers, packed ten or twelve across, pours slowly through a bazaar of hawkers toward the gates of Las Mercedes free trade zone located about two kilometers from Managua's airport.

Headed for twenty-three factories that open at 7 a.m., the workers will stay until at least 5:15 p.m.; many will be forced to work until 7 p.m., and others until 9 p.m. The hawkers sell them fried bread, fruit, meat sandwiches, caffeine, and vitamin B pills. The workers suck neon-colored sweet drinks from sandwich bags as they flow to the gates.

I traveled to the Zona Franca with a delegation of unionists and student activists at the request of the Managua union confederation (CST-JBE). They asked us to investigate their charges of violations of internationally recognized labor rights and Nicaraguan labor law, especially at the Chentex factory, the last of two Las Mercedes factories with functioning unions. In all of Central

Global Capitalism and the Race to the Bottom

America there were then no other unions functioning in free trade zones. Between the fall of 1999 and the spring of 2000 a multiemployer offensive in the zone had eliminated two other unions.

Nien Hsing, the Taiwanese company that owns the Chentex plant, as well as two others in the zone and three in Mexico, launched in the fall of 1999 a brutal offensive to crush the union in its Chentex plant. The Chentex management fired workers who were members of the union and even those seen as friendly to it. They charged union leaders with serious criminal offenses carrying potential seven-year sentences. In response, the union reached out to allies in North America, including the NLC, the AFL-CIO, the United Steelworkers, UNITE, Witness for Peace, and the Campaign for Labor Rights.

On the first morning our delegation visits the zone, the Chentex workers tell us of behavior that is evidence that "the Chinese," as they refer to the management, act with lawless impunity. Amid the dust and rotten fruit of the bazaar's trash, a knot of activists pass out leaflets. People gather, drawn by their leaders and eddying around us.

A slim young man reading from some notes on an envelope introduces a woman who says her supervisor at Chentex hit her. She tells of complaining to the Ministry of Labor after she was verbally abused and then hit and says that she was fired when she made the complaint. The young man, the financial secretary of the Chentex workers union, introduces us to Jessica, a fired union activist who was hit by the same man in 1997.

The workers are mostly young women, and single mothers are numerous, although an experienced observer notes that it seems as if the number of men has increased among the mass trudging toward the gates. Elsewhere—in the United States, too, as Bonacich and Appelbaum (2000) report about the Los Angeles apparel industry—the proportion of men in this basically female industry rises when work becomes more scarce.

Out of the crowd now comes a young man, muscular, in a red football jersey, his black hair shining in the morning sun. He is among an estimated three hundred workers fired at Chentex.[2] One afternoon his supervisor handed him a photocopied note written by hand. There was a blank space for his name. Addressed to the director of human resources, the letter stated that the young man was writing to resign from the Chentex union and asked the firm to stop deducting union dues. He refused to sign, as many others did, and was fired on the spot.

Nicaraguan labor law nominally protects workers like this young man as well as the women who were hit. But, in addition to being bureaucratically slow, the Ministry of Labor processes complaints as directed by the government (at that time President Aleman), openly siding with the employer. Time, in Managua as in New York, is the great ally of the employer in industrial disputes. The Las Mercedes and Chentex workers have no savings. So, fired unjustly, they have few resources that might support a patient wait for the legal procedures. Into this desperate gap between resources and justice the employer sometimes offers a Faustian deal: they will release them and give them the legally entitled severance pay (accrued at one month per year of service) if they withdraw their complaint of unfair practices. Thus, impunity is purchased.

Slaves to Fashion

Now one of the activists brings to us another woman, a pretty but sad-looking girl. "I lost my baby because Los Chinos abused me," she says. She is finishing the night shift. They are, these days, working 7 p.m. to 7 a.m., with a break at midnight. They work six days each week. This girl was pregnant in the spring, and her supervisor yelled at her when she lagged, calling her names like "dog face," saying she was dumb as a horse. She says, "I lost my baby in May. Because they harassed me so much."

Yet another woman comes forward. She works in the embroidery area. They have been on twelve-hour shifts for weeks, including many Sundays. She was told not to join the union or she would be fired. Now even more girls come up. They are not on the night shift; they were sent back from the gate because they were late. We ask if they could get in trouble for talking to us. "Claro"—of course—they could be fired for talking to union people.

The Nicaraguan apparel industry has grown rapidly in just a few years—from $73 million in 1995 to $375 million in 2001—and the vast majority of its production is bound for U.S. markets (OTEXA 2001a). The factories in Las Mercedes are contractors who work for name brands and retail stores.

Global contract production is a cutthroat business. About 30 percent of the apparel sold in the big stores is store-brand merchandise, where the chain acts as the initiator of the production process—"the manufacturer." The actual production enterprises such as the Nien Hsing Company—however tyrannical they are to their workers—dwell in the middle of a steep pyramid of power rising above them. At Chentex, as of the summer of 2000, they made store-brand jeans for Kohl's retail stores (Sonoma), J.C. Penney (Arizona), Kmart (Route 66), and Wal-Mart (Faded Glory), as well as the brand-name jeans Gloria Vanderbilt, Bugle Boy, and Cherokee. Though the smallest of the four retail chains with major orders at Chentex, Kohl's had a 1999 revenue stream of $4.6 billion ($6.1 billion in 2000)—more than double Nicaragua's 1999 and 2000 GDP. Kohl's profits of $258 million ($372 million in 2000) were more than double Nien Hsing's 1998 sales of $127 million. Nien Hsing's growth to $245 million in sales in 1999–2000 still made it considerably smaller than Kohl's (Kohl's Department Stores 2000; World Bank 2001a; Nien Hsing 2001).

Chentex workers earn less than 1 percent of the retail price of the jeans they stitch—between thirty and forty cents an hour. This compares to the 10 percent typical of the global north and the 5 percent ratio in U.S. sweatshops.

When we visit the workers' homes we can see the result. Tipitapa is a sprawling town twenty minutes from the free zone. There we meet a woman, Cristina, who was fired from Chentex, unjustly she thinks, for low production. Her sister, who lives across town, was fired for being a union member. Cristina's home is a wooden frame, ten-feet square, hung with plastic sheeting for two of the walls and with cardboard boxes that once held shirts shipped from the free zone in Panama for the rest. Her shack has a dirt floor and holds one large bed and (barely) two chairs for herself, her husband, and their baby. Her toilet is a hole in the ground surrounded by a shower curtain hung from a rack. We are shocked to learn that her husband works seven

Cristina in her one-room, one-light-bulb home, Tipitapa, Managua region, 2001, interviewed by Alan Howard of UNITE. Photographer: Robert J. S. Ross.

Rear view of shack with plastic basin and shower curtain around privy to left, Tipitapa, Managua region, 2001. Photographer: Robert J. S. Ross.

days a week at another of the free zone plants, but even with his overtime pay they can only afford this bare shelter.

Important increases in workers' pay would have small impact on the final retail price. The Chentex workers earned but twenty cents for a pair of jeans selling for between twenty-one and thirty-four dollars.

In 1998–99 workers at Chentex succeeded in obtaining legal status for their union and in negotiations won relief from forced overtime. They began a discussion of wages in 2000 by proposing a base pay increase of 40 percent, but management would not negotiate. On April 27, 2000, the union called a one-hour stoppage to emphasize their seriousness. Then the employer embarked upon a serious campaign to rid itself of the union. Nien Hsing filed criminal charges against the Chentex union officers and systematically began to fire union activists and intimidate union supporters.

As the workers reached out to contact their international allies Nien Hsing unsheathed its longest sword. They told the Nicaraguan government that if the Ministry of Labor forced them to drop the criminal charges against the union leaders they would drop their plans to build a new $100 million free trade zone (industrial park) in the city of Leon and would pull their three factories out of the country (Ruiz 2000; Nicaragua Network 2000). The union leadership, while combative even in the face of this threat, was nevertheless mindful of the problem created by threats of a capital strike. When we discussed pressure from the United States they were wary of being politically vulnerable to the charge of jeopardizing "thirty thousand jobs" (Ruiz 2000; Barbosa 2000).

The union attempted to preserve its base of supporters among the workers still inside the plant by giving members license to sign the letters renouncing the union. But the firings continued. The enthusiastic spirit of the workers was impressive. I imagine it was a residue of the movement that brought the Sandinistas to power in 1979 but also a result of that period in Nicaraguan history. Yet these reserves were not bottomless.

The union's legal status was jeopardized because the employer used the renunciations as evidence of its minority status, and the Ministry of Labor gave copies to the U.S. Embassy to claim its innocence (Ruiz 2000).

The NLC continued to organize delegations to Nicaragua throughout the summer and fall of 2000, including a group of prominent religious leaders. Each of these garnered local and some national media exposure. After the July 2000 visit, Congressman Sherrod Brown organized a letter signed by over sixty congresspersons asking President Clinton to look into labor standards violations in Nicaragua. President Clinton's trade representative, Charlene Barshefsky, wrote to the Nicaraguan government, threatening that trade access to the U.S. market

> may be in jeopardy in light of the government's failure to protect the labor rights of the Chentex employees as required by the CBTPA [Caribbean Basin Trade

Partnership Act] as well as the Conventions of the International Labor Organization. (quoted in NLC 2000)

Still, Nien Hsing, the largest original equipment manufacturer (OEM) of jeanswear in the world, selling to firms even larger than itself, continued to block settlements that its local manager proposed after negotiations with the union and with other government and commercial interests (e.g., the administrative head of the free trade zone). Finally, a Nicaraguan court ordered the firm to reinstate the union leaders, and they eventually agreed to rehire four out of nine fired leaders and seventeen fired workers (out of hundreds). Upon rehiring the leaders in May 2001, the Chentex plant management then embarked upon a campaign of isolation, intimidation, and harassment. They fired any workers who spoke to the former union leaders inside the factory; they surrounded the four leaders with hostile people, for example, officials of the "company union." They denied the four activists access to overtime. They repeatedly interviewed them and asked when they would quit.

Finally, on June 13, 2001, after a yearlong struggle that included extensive international support and also a victory, albeit a deeply compromised victory, the union leaders were forced to resign. They explained that their presence was a threat to any worker in the plant who befriended them (Parsons and St. Louis 2001).

The international solidarity movement had adopted the Chentex struggle, and the NLC was able to reach out to contacts in Hong Kong and from there to Taiwan to develop support for the Chentex workers in Taipei, even in the Taiwanese legislature. For a time it seemed a textbook lesson in the how and why of international solidarity. Despite this formidable campaign, by midyear of 2001, a small victory had been vitiated.

Arrayed against the Chentex workers was the highly related web of a world structure, a regional market, and domestic demography and politics. In the world structure, ferocious competition for the rich countries' markets gives even relatively large multinational operators like Nien Hsing little leeway. Should their plants falter in timeliness or cost, J.C. Penney, Kohl's, or Wal-Mart has a world of poor countries in which they can make their jeans. Some of these choices are regional. Though

Nicaraguan workers are paid much less than Mexicans, Mexican plants are more efficient and closer to U.S. markets. They are real competitors with the *Nica* workers. For every proud and righteous union supporter in the Managua region, too, there are legions of even poorer urban and rural workers who, in order to have a regular paycheck, will accept conditions that more experienced workers fight against. Two-thirds of economically active *Nicas* were in the informal economy in 2000—street vendors, for example. When the Chentex management threatened some of the union supporters, trying to get them to renounce the union, they would say, one woman told me, "The union is dead. If you don't renounce it you will be selling tomatoes on the street corner tomorrow."

The race for the rich country markets is on, with China and Mexico vying for supremacy in the U.S. market and with labor standards of all put at risk. These two countries are going head-to-head for the U.S. market—and are neck-and-neck in the race to the bottom.

Imports and Investors

One measure of low-wage competition is the level of import penetration. Table 7 reports the increase in clothing imports to the United States. Apparel imports, largely from low-wage producers, went from 2 percent of apparent consumption in 1961 to over 52 percent in 1999. These are very conservative estimates. The analysis does not correct, for example, for reimportation of material cut and then exported to be sewn and reimported ("9802" items). In addition, the data in table 7 are by value of shipments, not numbers of items. When the U.S. Census analyzes particular clothing lines, rather than the whole industry with all of the data aggregated, major product lines show much higher levels of import penetration. For example, 87 percent of men's sweaters (82 percent by dollar value) were imported in 1999, as were 66 percent of suits and 75 percent of sport coats. Ninety-two percent of women's suits, 69 percent of skirts, and 59 percent of women's dresses were imported in 1999 (U.S. Census Bureau 2000). As many have argued (Ross and Trachte 1990; R. Ross 1997a; Bonacich and Appelbaum 2000), the availability of a global pool of cheap

TABLE 7. Import Penetration in U.S. Apparel Market in 1961–99 (in $ millions)

	Domestic Production ($)	Imports ($)	Exports ($)	Import Penetration[a] (%)	Import/ Domestic Production (%)
1961	13,088	283	159	2.1	2.2
1962	13,948	374	152	2.6	2.7
1963	14,818	400	158	2.7	2.7
1964	15,514	481	196	3.0	3.1
1965	16,426	568	177	3.4	3.5
1966	17,308	637	188	3.6	3.7
1967	18,483	692	207	3.6	3.7
1968	19,628	900	220	4.4	4.6
1969	21,045	1,149	242	5.2	5.5
1970	20,394	1,286	250	6.0	6.3
1971	21,687	·1,574	258	6.8	7.3
1972	23,914	1,967	300	7.7	8.2
1973	25,970	2,261	381	8.1	8.7
1974	26,855	2,465	593	8.6	9.2
1975	27,098	2,775	602	9.5	10.2
1976	30,019	3,912	740	11.8	13.0
1977	35,323	4,393	859	11.3	12.4
1978	37,845	5,722	1,035	13.5	15.1
1979	37,350	5,902	1,387	14.1	15.8
1980	40,293	6,543	1,604	14.5	16.2
1981	44,074	7,752	1,628	15.4	17.6
1982	46,681	8,516	1,236	15.8	18.2
1983	49,423	9,976	1,049	17.1	20.2
1984	50,672	14,002	1,026	22.0	27.6
1985	50,784	15,711	991	24.0	30.9
1986	53,323	18,171	1,178	25.8	34.1
1987	62,119	21,503	1,490	26.2	34.6
1988	62,750	22,363	1,988	26.9	35.6
1989	61,447	25,372	2,362	30.0	41.3
1990	61,962	26,602	2,864	31.0	42.9
1991	62,649	27,377	3,746	31.7	43.7
1992	68,844	32,644	4,659	33.7	47.4
1993	70,986	35,475	5,433	35.1	50.0
1994	73,258	38,561	6,009	36.4	52.6
1995	73,780	41,208	6,979	38.2	55.9
1996	73,319	43,075	7,836	39.7	58.8
1997	68,018	50,191	9,279	46.1	73.8
1998	64,932	55,838	9,474	50.2	86.0
1999	62,798	59,156	8,541	52.2	94.2

Source: U.S. Industrial Outlook, various years. 1991–99: *U.S. Statistical Abstract,* 1998, 2000. Production, 1997–99: U.S. Census Bureau 2001a.

[a]Import penetration = imports/([domestic production + imports] – exports).

labor has had a powerful effect by weakening workers' bargaining power everywhere and by subverting the higher standards of compensation and benefits in the older industrial regions. This has had an even more powerful effect in labor-intensive industries like apparel.

In 1990 Ross and Trachte wrote one of the earliest books on global capitalism. There they argued that a search for cheaper labor was a basic dynamic of the internationalization of manufacturing and thus of globalization itself. The argument was mildly criticized as too one-sided. Of course, there are political constraints apart from economic ones, and there are infrastructural requirements for successful exporting—ports, telecommunications, and so forth. Further research has allowed the deepening of the analysis of the noneconomic dimensions of foreign investment in developing countries. It reinforces the original argument.

While the effects of multinational corporations on developing nations is the subject of a vast literature, London and Ross (1995) analyzed the reverse: the determinants of foreign investment in developing countries. They found that foreign corporations were more likely to invest in countries that had fewer protests and strikes; that had less democracy; and, within limits, had more repression. In addition, nations with relatively "inexpensive" urban labor forces (and, perhaps, high levels of class exploitation) attracted more investment than did nations with high rural-urban productivity disparities (and low levels of exploitation). All of these findings were independent of the consistently positive (and expected) effect of the level of technological development and/or market size.

Global capitalism (as a new moment in the history of capitalism) began in a transition period that is being accomplished through new kinds of competition on a world scale. The internationalization of capital and the creation of global chains of manufacturing production bring new areas of the globe into the industrial system. By the 1970s, the worldwide pool of industrial labor expanded beyond the boundaries of those states with an enfranchised working class and high levels of reproduction—that is, standards of living. Employers seeking to reduce their direct employment costs and their indirect political burdens sought out communities of workers who were politically less potent than those in the older industrial states and whose costs of reproduction were lower.

Global Capitalism and the Race to the Bottom

The London and Ross study (1995) tested one dimension of a theory of global capitalism: its political sociology. They found consistent support for that part of the theory that emphasizes the *control* of labor. This finding, using a quantitative cross-national method, confirmed the many interpretive case studies that portrayed the era of transition from monopoly to global capitalism—the 1970s to roughly 2000—as one in which authoritarian states with subordinated working classes were attractive to investors seeking relief from the political and economic environments of social democratic and Keynesian liberal core states. In the context of global capitalism as it emerged in the 1970s, civil and political rights and vigorous expressions of dissent were not virtues in the eyes of investors.

The central finding about the control of labor and its positive attraction for capital puts some other work in a more global context. For example, O'Donnell (1973) argued that the bureaucratic-authoritarian model of the deepening of development in South America required political exclusion of the "popular" sector to give foreign capital confidence. O'Donnell's model of the requisites for industrialization included, then, both Foreign Direct Investment (FDI) and the political repression implied by our findings. Writing during the period of transition to global capitalism O'Donnell proposed for South America the generic form of the relation of labor control and FDI suggested by our findings (London and Ross 1995).

It is interesting that this quantitative study of where investors choose to put their export platforms should be so close to the impressionistic reportage of the current moment: China, Indonesia, and Vietnam and, before them, South Korea (under the colonels) and Taiwan (under the Kuomintang). Of course, in the last decade or more the form of foreign investment has changed almost as drastically as its geography. Nowadays, big rich country global firms do not necessarily own contractor factories—in apparel, footwear, electronics, and many other commodities. The corporations that own the actual production facilities are often large and multinational, but they may be headquartered in Asian countries, as are the Korean, Taiwanese, and Hong Kong apparel firms, and they are usually smaller than their clients. To study the equivalents of investment for the more recent period, one would have to develop measures consistent with the contract economy.

As the river of goods flows to the rich country markets, it scours its own channel. In part, the globalization of the rag trade erodes standards in older industrial countries, creating sweatshops in New York and Los Angeles and weighing down the hope of advance in Nicaragua and Mexico. In the long run this tide may create even more lasting and positive social effects. The tide of imports that eroded the American garment workers' hard-fought gains is a signal of the creation of a truly worldwide pool of industrial labor. The realization that the condition of advance for each is advance for all is a dawning—if not fully lit—realization of today's labor movement (see Ross 1995a, 1995b).

In the meantime, apparel workers around the world are part of an industry whose power structure is heavily influenced by the fact that the major retailers are also major importers. Among the top one hundred importers of apparel, retail chains controlled 48 percent of imports as of, roughly, 1995 (Jones 1995).

The power of retailers and the market share of imports from countries where workers' material levels of living are considerably poorer than working-class standards in the older industrial nations compose the most important strategic *differences* between the new sweatshops of the late twentieth century and the old ones of its early years. Among the *similarities* of these two eras is that in each case the most exploited workers have been immigrants. Popular and journalistic accounts of contemporary sweatshops are well aware of, if not obsessed by, this parallel.[3] To acknowledge the contribution of a reserve of labor to worker vulnerability is not, however, to accede to the proposition's primacy. The immigration issue is addressed directly and separately. In the meantime, the basic dynamic behind the rise of sweatshops in the United States—and the dispersal of the apparel industry to places where workers are treated poorly—is the overall structure of global capitalism and the specifically neoliberal trade regime it has fostered. At the top of that system in the apparel industry are the eight-hundred-pound gorillas of the rag trade—the retail chains.

6 Retail Chains

The Eight-Hundred-Pound Gorillas of the World Trade in Clothing

Where the Power Is: Brand Names and Retailers

The global commodity chain of the apparel industry consists of fiber production, textile manufacture, design, cutting, sewing, marketing, and retail (see, e.g., Gereffi 1994; Appelbaum and Gereffi 1994). These stages in the production process may be, and in apparel typically are, disaggregated over space (Ross and Trachte 1990). The most powerful actors in the global commodity chain of the apparel industry—the retailers—have used their strategic power to capture the largest share of profits (Gereffi 1994; Appelbaum and Gereffi 1994). By sourcing clothing in very low-wage areas of the global economy, the name brand manufacturers and the big private label retailers are able to appropriate the lion's share of the markups; the direct producers, including their direct supervisors—the contractors—obtain but small shares of the consumer's dollar.

Let us propose a simple proposition about power in a global commodity chain: wherever there is relative concentration there is relative power. In automobile production, there are very few major producers, relatively many dealerships, and potentially many parts manufacturers. The automakers are powerful relative to these other partners.[1] In the apparel business, among the great changes in the last thirty years has been the rise of concentration in the retail apparel sector. If we can imagine a conceptual (if fictitious) vice president for clothing manufacturing and sourcing for each retail chain, then ten individuals control almost three-quarters of the U.S. clothing supply. The dollar amount is staggering: $130 billion.

The complex global contracting system produces grimly humorous oddities: In 1998 a pair of Britannia relaxed fit boys' jeans—selling for $17.99 at Kmart and "produced," that is, contracted for, by the giant Vanity Fair (VF) Corporation—may have been made in Nicaragua or in the United States. In the United States the NLC estimated the (U.S. industry standard) labor cost as $2.08; in Nicaragua $0.14. The NLC purchased these garments, made in different places, selling for the same price, at the same store. Levi Strauss & Co., which sold the Britannia brand to the VF Corporation, closed eight U.S. plants and three in Europe, laying off seventy-three hundred U.S. workers and seventeen hundred French and Belgium workers in 1998 (Tomkins and Buckley 1998).

The terms used to describe links in the clothing commodity chain may be confusing. In the contemporary apparel industry, the largest group of workers, approximately 343,000 in the United States and tens of millions around the world, are sewing machine operators.[2] In the typical contractor shop, there are also cutters (though cutting may be done separately), pressers, and trimmers.[3]

Just above these direct producers on the pyramid are their fictively direct employers, the contractors. Contractors directly assemble clothes. In the United States, there are about twenty-three thousand production sites for clothing, most of them small contractor shops with seventeen or twenty workers.

The structure is often different in the developing nations. There, for example, in China or Central America, large factories and foreign capital stand in contrast to the small shops and immigrant bosses of the U.S. industry. Some of the Asian corporations that contract clothing manufacturing are very large indeed. Nien Hsing, the Taiwan-based corporation that makes denim and jeans in Nicaragua, Mexico, and Lesotho, claims to be the largest maker of jeans in the world. Among the customers of their

Nicaraguan plants in 2000 were Kohl's, J.C. Penney, Wal-Mart, Target, and Gloria Vanderbilt (Ross and Kernaghan 2000). On their Web site Nien Hsing says they also have "close" relations with Levi Strauss & Co., Lee, and Edwin (a Japanese-based international seller of high-end jeans).

Standing above the contractors in power, and much fewer in numbers, are what are now called manufacturers, what Emile Schlesinger and the New York regional usage called jobbers. In the rag trade manufacturers make designs, marketing plans, and profits: contractors make clothes. While there are thousands of clothing manufacturers, only a handful of them make the brand name clothing that is recognizable. The brand name Fruit of the Loom, for example,

> has an estimated 45% domestic mass market share in men's and boys' under-wear and an estimated 13% domestic mass market share in women's and girls' underwear. [They report that their nearest competitor had only 6 percent of the women's and girls' market.] In 2000, Fruit of the Loom's domestic activewear market share was approximately 28% for T-shirts sold through wholesalers and 20% for fleecewear. (Fruit of the Loom 2000)

Ninety-nine percent of Fruit of the Loom production was in Mexico, Central America, or the Caribbean Basin (Fruit of the Loom 2000).

To take another example, consider the largest apparel company in the world, the VF Corporation. VF had revenues of $5.7 billion in the fiscal year 2000. These revenues included the sales from Lee, Wrangler, Rider, Rustler, Chic, Gitano, and Britannia jeans, among others. VF brands held 27.5 percent of the U.S. jeanswear market. Over two-thirds of VF's U.S. sales were derived from apparel made abroad, in both their own and in contractor factories (VF Corporation 2001, 2, 17).

Given its sheer size, any one of VF's orders might utilize a given factory's annual output. One might imagine that VF agents in the free trade zone in Managua, Nicaragua, or in Mexico's maquiladora sector would have a certain leverage in their discussions when they bargain for a price per thousand dozen of a given garment. In 2001 VF ranked 309th in the Fortune 500 listings and second (to Nike) in revenues among the top ten apparel/footwear firms (*Fortune* 2001).

VF analyzed its costs in its 2001 annual report in terms of the location of its own plants and its contract operations—noting that it was moving operations to lower cost locations, for example, out of Europe. Even so, management of VF discussed its sales in terms of the fate and fortune of the department stores to which it sold. For example, VF discussed its different brands of jeans in terms of the mid-tier versus the mass merchandise stores to which they sell Lee and Wrangler, respectively. Management attributed 1999 declines in Lee brand jeans sales to "overall softness in retail sales in mid-tier department stores in the U.S." (VF Corporation 2001, 18).

So, as powerful as the big manufacturers are in terms of the contractors below them, looming above even the great manufacturers are the great merchant empires of the retail chains: Wal-Mart, Sears, Kmart, Target, and J.C. Penney. The top ten apparel manufacturers in the U.S. had $34.1 billion in sales for the fiscal year 2000. The biggest retailer, Wal-Mart, alone had sales of $193.2 billion—more than 5.5 times as much. Wal-Mart sold, according to *Fortune* (2001), $33 billion in clothing in 2000. That is at the retail level; assuming their wholesale cost of clothing was about $17 billion, Wal-Mart alone made outlays for clothing as large as half the entire output of the top ten manufacturers.

The second largest retail chain, Sears, had gross sales of $40.9 billion. Passing down past Kmart and then Target, one reaches the fifth largest retail chain, J.C. Penney, before approaching the same order of magnitude of total sales as the total of the top ten brand name manufacturers ($32.9 billion). Together, the great retail chains dominate the entire retail business, with the top group controlling most clothing sales (see table 10).

Beyond the sheer magnitude of their orders from a given manufacturer, however, the retailers attempt to capture more of the markup by directly commissioning the production of store brand, or private label, clothing. These brands account for as much as 30 percent of their clothing sales, and they give them additional leverage in their relations with manufacturers. The manufacturers, in turn, open up their own branded outlets in their attempt to keep as much of the markup as possible.

Returning to the contractors, most of these businesses—in the domestic U.S. market—are small. Many are owned and operated by recent immigrants attempting to become capitalists. The apparel business at the production base of the pyramid has very low barriers to entry. A few hundred square feet and a few sewing machines, and you're in business. In this U.S. context, the cost of textiles is not part of the contractor's burden because the so-called manufacturer delivers sometimes cut goods, sometimes fabric, but never loses legal title to the parts or the finished product. In the current sweating system of North America, the contractor is the fictional employer, not the manufacturer or jobber. In California, the standard form of agreement between manufacturer and contractor is called the Adams contract, and it reads, in part, like this:

> >5. Contractor acknowledges that it is an independent contractor and not an employee of MANUFACTURER, and that it is contractor's sole responsibility to comply with all City, County, State and Federal laws applicable to employers. Contractor expressly represents that all persons who perform work for the contractor under this agreement are solely employees of the contractor and not employees of the MANUFACTURER. . . .
> >9. In the event that contractor is found to be in violation of any City, County, State or Federal law, contractor agrees to indemnify, hold harmless and defend MANUFACTURER from any liability that may be imposed on MANUFAC-TURER as a result of such violation. . . .
> >14. Contractor agrees to indemnify, hold harmless and defend MANUFAC-TURER from any liability that may be imposed on MANUFACTURER arising out of any claim made by an employee of contractor against the MANUFAC-TURER. (cited in Bonacich and Appelbaum 2000)

The Adams contract preserves the legal fiction that the contractor, as the direct employer, is responsible for the conditions of employment of the workers. The pyramid of power puts the giant retail chains, which are significant manufacturers themselves, in the most concentrated position. They are the price makers, not the price takers.

Sammy Lee, a retail executive, described the system in an interview conducted by Bonacich and Appelbaum (2000) for their book on the apparel industry in Los Angeles. When interviewed in 1993, Lee was vice president of Contempo Casuals, a subsidiary of the Nieman Marcus Group, which had a large private label program. Lee told the authors that retailers

> can calculate how many minutes it takes to sew a particular garment and, based on the minimum wage, can figure out how much they need to pay per garment in order to cover it. However, for large orders, the retailer can simply cut back the price he is willing to pay, forcing the contractor to pay less than the legal

minimum. . . . The pressure goes right down the line. Pricing starts from the retailer and moves down. It doesn't start from the bottom, from the real costs of making the garment. The retailer can always go down the street and find someone who can make it for less. The manufacturers and contractors are stuck. Everyone down the line is squeezed. (Bonacich and Appelbaum 2000, 90)

Some trend data on retailing will show how power has steadily accumulated at the top of the pyramid. *Census of Retail Trade,* published every five years by the U.S. Census Bureau, allows an estimate of the apparel market share of the top stores in each category using the publicly available U.S. Census data. The concentration ratio that results is *much lower* than those obtained from proprietary sources based on direct surveys of chains. Nevertheless, the data permit over-time trend comparison.

For the top twenty department store chains (including discounters) and the top twenty apparel chains, their market share of apparel was assumed to be the same as their market share of all sales in the retail category. This is not necessarily accurate for department stores or discount chains. Their share of clothing sales may be (and apparently is) larger than their share of total retail sales. The resulting estimate is that about 57 percent of apparel sales were sold by the top forty chains in 1992 and in 1997. This is, as we shall see, a gross underestimate. What is certainly a reflection of reality, whatever the precise level, is the *growth* in concentration of about 1 percent each year from 1972 to 1992.

By 1993, using proprietary data from the Kurt Salomon market research firm, Jones reported that the top five retail organizations held 48 percent of the apparel market, or $168 billion in sales (Jones 1995). Using another private firm's estimate of total apparel sales, and yet another source of

TABLE 8.   Apparel Sales in Top 20 Specialty Apparel Chains plus Top 20 Retail Department Stores, 1972–97[a]

	1972	1977	1982	1987	1992	1997
Retail value ($ billions)	15.5	25.1	41.6	66.9	92.3	106.6
% of gross apparel sales	37.9	42.4	47.8	52.6	56.9	56.9

Source: Author's calculations from U.S. Census Bureau, *Economic Census,* "Retail Trade," "Merchandise Line Sales," and "Establishment and Firm Size," various years.
[a]Includes discount chains.

store-by-store sales, results in an estimate that the top ten chains sold 72 percent of American clothing in 2000 and that the top five controlled 49 percent of the market (Welling 2000). The top five clothing retailers in order are Wal-Mart, J.C. Penney, Federated Department Stores, Gap, and Target. (Table 9 gives the affiliated stores of each chain.) Together they sold $90 billion of clothing in 2000. At wholesale, that is more than the entire output of the top ten U.S. manufacturers.

In 2000 Wal-Mart alone sold about eighteen of every one hundred dollars of clothing sales. Second only to Exxon in gross revenues, at $193.3 billion, Wal-Mart employs 1.2 million people worldwide, significantly more than its nearest U.S. rival, General Motors (which employs a mere 386,000). Wal-Mart is the largest retailer in the United States, Canada, and Mexico. It confidently predicted it would be the second largest in the United Kingdom when fiscal year 2001 results were tabulated.

TABLE 9.   Affiliated Stores of the Top Five Sellers of Apparel[a]

Wal-Mart (apparel sales: $33,002.5)	Wal-Mart stores Supercenters (include groceries) Neighborhood Market Sam's Club Wal-Mart International (Operating in Argentina, Brazil, Canada, China, Germany, Korea, Mexico, Puerto Rico and the United Kingdom)
J.C. Penney (apparel sales: $22,757)	J.C. Penney stores and catalogue Renner stores Brazil) Eckerd Drugstores
Federated Department Stores (apparel sales: $12,401)	Bloomingdale's The Bon Marché Burdines Goldsmith's Lazarus Macy's (East and West), incorporating Jordan's Rich's Fingerhut catalogue and e-commerce
The Gap (apparel sales: $11,635)	Gap Banana Republic Old Navy
Target (apparel sales: $10,110.6)	Target, Super-Target Mervyn's Marshall Fields, incorporating Dayton's and Hudson's

Source: Apparel Industry, August 2000, and company Web sites
[a]Apparel sales in $ millions.

Threatened by discounters like Wal-Mart and Target, clothing retailers mimic their pricing and procurement strategies. With an era of aggressive pricing has come an aggressive search for sources of supply that are ever cheaper than the sources of one's competitor in any given category. Two strategies have resulted, usually in combination: private label production and a restless search for less costly contractors.

At J.C. Penney, for example, and only there, one may buy Arizona-brand jeans. Arizona jeans will sell at a lower price than Wrangler jeans or Levi's. J.C. Penney commissions the production of Arizona jeans from contractors around the world. Another example is Sears, where one can buy a variety of goods in the Kenmore brand, usually variants of name brand goods, made to slightly less costly specifications. These two approaches embody the two distinct ways in which store brands, or private labels, are produced.

In one mode of store brand procurement and production, the large retailer does a deal with a name brand manufacturer, who then produces an item similar to the branded one, with perhaps some slightly less expensive features. Many of the big brand clothing manufacturers do private

TABLE 10.   Market Share of U.S. Apparel Sales, 2000, Top Ten Retailers

	Apparel Sales ($)[a]	Cumulative Sales/Share ($)[a]	Market Share (%)	Cumulative Share (%)
Wal-Mart	33,002.50	33,002.50	18.1	18.1
J.C. Penney	22,757.00	55,759.50	12.5	30.6
Federated Department Stores	12,401.20	68,160.70	6.8	37.4
The Gap	11,635.00	79,795.70	6.4	43.8
Target	10,110.60	89,906.30	5.5	49.3
The Limited	9,723.00	99,629.30	5.3	54.6
May	9,706.20	109,335.50	5.3	60.0
Sears	8,214.20	117,549.70	4.5	64.5
Kmart	7,185.00	124,734.70	3.9	68.4
TJX	6,156.50	130,891.20	3.4	71.8
Top Ten Total	130,891.20			71.8
Total U.S. Sales	182,306.00			100.0

Source: Apparel sales and cumulative sales/share from *Apparel Industry*, August 2000. Total U.S. sales from NPD Group 2001.

[a]In $ millions.

label production for the big chains. This requires that they sell the garment at a wholesale price less than their own comparable branded items. Apart from the price competition between national brands, the price pressure from the chain store buyers is fierce. Here is the way it seemed in the summer of 2001 to a VF executive, as told by Scardino (2001):

> While private-label jeans performance has retailers pleased—including Wal-Mart with Faded Glory and Kmart with Route 66—suppliers are getting squeezed.
> "There's definitely margin pressure," says LaGrega [president of the VF mass market jeanswear division]. Yet vendors are stepping up to the challenge. "We're continuing to produce much better products, values and quality at the same prices as last year."

Private label clothing is produced in another way, one that puts even more price pressure on the industry. A retail chain may generate a design for a garment or for a family of fashion garments. These designs may be created by either in-house or consultant designers. With designs in hand, the firm or its agents will then search for contractors (factories) and subcontractors that can produce the garment. The result is a commodity from which the retailer can capture even more of the value—eliminating more middleman steps between itself and consumers' purchasing price. Private label production allows the retailer to retain more of the final value of the product.

The power structure of the industry is heavily influenced by the fact that the major retailers are also major importers. As noted in chapter 5, by the mid-1990s among the top one hundred importers of apparel, retail chains controlled 48 percent of imports (Jones 1995). This is a river of clothing from contractors located throughout the world ferociously competing with one another to serve the North American and EU markets. Pressure from the top is relayed down the pyramid of clothing to the direct producers, the majority of whom are women sewing machine operators in poor countries.

In the early 1990s, 25 percent of women's apparel sales were private labels (Palpacuer 1997, citing Kurt Salomon Associates 1992). By the mid-1990s private labels accounted for 25–36 percent of a selected list of

apparel items (*Apparel Industry* 1996, 54). In 2001 the private label proportion of Sears's $8.2 billion in apparel sales was about 50 percent—$4.1
billion! As early as the mid-1990s the very upscale Barney's of New York
and Henri Bendel reported private label sales of 16–50 percent (Nicholson
1997). In 1998 the May department store chain (including Filene's, Lord
and Taylor, Robinson-May, and others) reported that 17 percent of its
clothing sales were in private labels. In its annual report for 2000, May
reported:

> We have undertaken three strategic initiatives to better position May for this
> decade. First, in merchandising, we are conceptualizing and implementing
> stronger, exclusive proprietary brands, segmented by age and lifestyle. We will
> build our private label capabilities. (May Department Stores Company 2001)

With $9.7 billion in apparel sales in 2000 and assuming that the 17 percent
of 1998 is now around 20 percent, May's worldwide purchasing for its own
brands would now be about $1.94 billion.

Scanning the Globe for Sources of Cheap Clothing

At their corporate headquarters, we can imagine the retail grandees
squeezing the numbers. Where is the next 1 percent of margin? Over the
last generation, this decision has been accomplished with dreary similarity: we can get the savings by procuring the goods in an ever cheaper location. As early as 1979, Rinker Buck first exposed the dynamics and the
structure of the new sweatshops in New York. This is the way the system
looked at street level to a contractor:

> A manufacturer will tell me he has 2,000 twelve-piece blouses he needs sewn. I
> tell him I need at least $10 per blouse to do a decent job on a garment that com-
> plicated. So then he tells me to get lost—he offers me $2. If I don't take that, he
> tells me he can have it sent to Taiwan or South America somewhere, and have it
> done for 50 cents. So we haggle—sometimes I might bring him up to $4 per
> blouse.
>   Now you tell me, how can I pay someone "union scale" [$3.80 in 1979] or
> even the minimum wage [$2.90 as compared to $5.15 in 2003], when I'm only
> getting $4 per blouse? With overhead and everything else, I may be able to pay
> the ladies $1.20 per blouse, but that's tops. There's nothing on paper. I get it in
> cash. (Buck 1979, 46)[4]

Proximity, Time, Quality, and Efficiency

As the big firms make sourcing decisions, a number of factors, in complex interaction, may influence their choice of producer locations. These considerations include proximity, time, and quality—as well as labor cost. New information technologies have revolutionized many practices in the relationship between retailer and manufacturers. Some have even thought they would save the American apparel industry.

A manufacturer or chain may value proximity to a contractor shop or factory if a style is new, the work is elaborate, or rapid changes are in process. In those cases, quality control personnel and/or designers will want to check the work early and often. The proximity consideration is separable from a straight timeliness or speed consideration. It concerns the convenience of executives and the closeness of control. If there is instability in a style—innovations are being made rapidly, for example—or if the very newness of a style means that sewing machine operators and cutters will take some time to learn it properly, then repeated visits to the place of production may be desirable. There is a difference between going across town in Manhattan or downtown in Los Angeles and taking a twelve- or sixteen-hour journey to southern China. Proximity of buyers to manufacturers to contractors in New York and Los Angeles is literally by taxi.

Similar considerations surround speed of delivery. If a contractor can promise delivery of an order in ten days as opposed to two months, that is an advantage in the technological environment of contemporary retailing. The willingness of contractor shops to work all hours and to accept madly tight deadlines, based on the willing work of eager immigrants, bodes well for the speed of delivery.

Finally, independent of speed and convenience, manufacturers want contractors to be able to deliver goods with a minimum of defects. While quality design features may be greater or lesser for different garments—for example, single- or double-needle stitching or more or less elaborate tucks or pleats—for any given simple or complex garment, the contractor nevertheless must produce it correctly. Returns hurt stores and reputations of the brands. For these reasons many analysts, optimists and pessimists, labor, and management have guessed or hoped that there was some minimum level of American production (and employment) below which the industry would not sink.

On top of everything else, the culture of the American garment centers is resourceful and teachable: American shops are significantly more productive, measured by time per garment, than their low-wage competitors. Productivity increases in the apparel industry consistently outdistanced the U.S. economy as a whole in the 1990s, and unit costs fell. Unit labor costs in women's outerwear[5] were 13 percent lower in 1999 than they were in 1992; output per hour was 49 percent higher. This compares to a 5.2 percent increase in unit labor costs in nondurable manufacturing in this period and a 17.8 percent increase in output per hour.[6]

The new information technology of the retail-manufacturing relationship, according to one influential and massively funded study of the U.S. apparel-textile-retail complex, has offered an opportunity for American manufacturers to reap "new competitive advantages" (Abernathy et al. 1999, 1). The authors of *A Stitch in Time,* who include John Dunlop, former secretary of labor, garnered attention and awards for their optimistic analysis of the apparel-textile-retail complex. This conclusion about new information technology is based on technological relationships that begin with the real-time information about the status of inventory that managers obtain from bar code scanners at checkout counters. The scanner reports the specifics (color, size, and so forth) of garments sold in the last day, week, month, season, or year. A manager can thus discern the level of inventory on hand in stores and warehouses and know to a day or so when to reorder and which styles and variants are succeeding. The impact of this information retrieval is very large.

The seasonality of the apparel business has ever been the curse of the garment worker, and the uncertainty of the business has been the worry of the manufacturer. These concerns have changed in the new regime of inventory control ("lean retailing") but not always as the players would have imagined. In the old days, firms made samples and buyers made orders many months in advance. Large orders would cause employers to drive the workers into overtime as they worked to complete orders by shipping dates. As the goods went out the door, the manufacturer would often have nothing else or little else for the workers to do. Thus commenced the prosaic slack or slow season—or in French, the more vivid *la morte-saison,* even shortened to *la morte*—"the death"—in the *Sentier* garment district in Paris (N. Green 1997, 140). Then while the workers went on short time or layoff, worrying about their rent, their bosses worried about returns: if the stores did not sell the goods, they could return them.

It is no wonder that garment firms went in and out of business and that both workers and their bosses had a certain cultural veneer of toughness: it was not an easy business.[7] The four seasons included a cycle of reorders (when things were going well), and long-term employees learned to ride the storm while their employers learned to value their skills. The new technology has created the possibility to change this pace—but not with nearly so much change as Abernathy and his colleagues thought it would.

Retailers, with much more information than ever before, have used the new technology in two distinct ways. First, they keep much less inventory: a request for the salesperson to look in the back room for a specific size is an archaic memory. In the discount stores at the mall, what you see is what is there. This "lean retailing" conserves retailer capital and reduces risk. As stocks run low, the firm requests reorders. In the most efficient case, where business partners have built up trust and dependability, there may be an automatic reorder process by which retailers give suppliers access to their computer data and networks.

For the manufacturer and even the contractor, there are at least two sides to the lean retail coin. The technology makes possible a more even annual flow of work. Three-week cycles of reorder are smoother than four seasons. On the other hand, on-time delivery is now critical: if a manufacturer fails to put goods in the warehouse by a certain date, the cupboard will be bare at the mall. At the bottom of the pyramid, where computerized access to the big chain inventory is but a newspaper story, orders come down the line: we'll take five thousand dozen if you do it in a week or ten days. What looked to Abernathy's Harvard Business School research team as the creation of a more orderly industry becomes, at the bottom of the food chain, even more time pressure.

Second, the *Stitch in Time* researchers point out that the new technologies have also spurred and supported another feature of the retail revolution. There is a stunning multiplication of styles, colors, and sheer numbers of items. The number of separate bar codes in a store may be in the tens of thousands. Kmart (now in bankruptcy protection) has seventy thousand items in each store. Keeping just the right level of inventory requires the ability swiftly to change a product mix. Wal-Mart, the earliest of the general merchandisers to adopt bar code technology, turns its inventory over 7.29 times each year; the failing Kmart does it 4.39 times a year. In mid-2000, as a new team of executives began to try to rescue Kmart, they discovered fifteen thousand truckloads of unsold merchandise outside of Kmart stores waiting for backroom space (Gallagher 2002).

Given the advantages of proximity, time, quality, and a decade-long record of improved productivity, "the story of how information technology enabled the American garment industry to triumph over low-cost competition overseas," according to *New York Times* reviewer Fred Andrews (1999), should have been written on the logbook of the U.S. apparel industry. But it was not. In the three brief years between the time Abernathy and his colleagues mailed in their manuscript (1998) and 2002, the American apparel industry lost another 281,000 jobs (from 639,000 to 358,000) (extracted from Bureau of Labor Statistics 2004).

What went wrong with the calculations of Abernathy and his colleagues? First, they failed to separate those fashion items that were either (a) design stable, (b) time insensitive, or (c) so inexpensively designed that both quality and time could be sacrificed. In today's world of jeans, informal casual wear, and growing inequality (where the working classes are forced to shop "down," e.g., at Wal-Mart), Chinese or Nicaraguan suppliers at twenty-five cents an hour are "competitive" sources. The second failure of the *Stitch in Time* authors was their miscalculation, in their optimism, of the meaning of *proximity*. More rapidly changing fashions, if they are not made to rigorous or complicated standards, may be made in the Western Hemisphere; but *proximity* may not mean "internal to the continental United States." Mexico, the Dominican Republic, or the Caribbean, in general, are much closer to the United States than are China or Asia and serviceably close to the fashion centers of the East and West

Coasts. So, what remains for U.S. production? Technically demanding innovative styles and ordinary work that competes in price with the Western Hemisphere—at sweatshop wages and conditions.

In chapter 5, we saw how some big chains—J.C. Penney, Wal-Mart, Kohl's, and Kmart—used a repressive Nicaraguan factory to make jeans for the American market. Consider now how the Gap, the fourth largest seller of clothing in the United States with $11 billion in 2000 sales and $13 billion in 2001, uses the complexity of the legal and contracting system to procure cheap goods for sale.

The Gap in Saipan

In 1999 a group of labor rights organizations—including the apparel workers' union UNITE and the West Coast advocacy group Global Exchange—sued eighteen apparel retailers and manufacturers for gross labor and human rights violations.[8] The legal action included two federal lawsuits and one California suit. In summary, the accused included six of the top eight apparel retailers (Gap, Dayton-Hudson [soon to be Target], J.C. Penney, Sears, May, and Limited). Five of the top ten manufacturers (Jones Apparel Group, Liz Claiborne, Phillips Van Heusen, Polo Ralph Lauren, and Warnaco) were also among the firms accused of racketeering, wholesale violations of the FLSA, and violations of the Anti-Peonage Act of 1992, causing the use of indentured or bonded labor.

These offenses were committed inside the jurisdiction of the laws of the United States—in the Commonwealth of the Northern Mariana Islands (CNMI), the island of Saipan principally. The public faced once more the implication of forced labor in the United States, evoking for many the images of the dreaded El Monte slave labor case.

Saipan is one of the fourteen Northern Mariana Islands located in the northern Pacific Ocean, west of the Hawaiian Islands, about three-quarters of the distance between Hawaii and the Philippines. After World War II, the Northern Mariana Islands became part of a United Nations Trust Territory of the Pacific Islands. In 1975 the citizens of the Northern Mariana Islands voted in a plebiscite to be joined to the United States as a commonwealth, under the sovereignty of the United States, as the CNMI. Congress granted the CNMI local control over immigration and, in order to spur economic development, control over the local minimum wage. Citizens of the CNMI are, as are citizens of the Commonwealth of Puerto Rico, U.S. citizens. The laws of the United States, including labor laws, otherwise rule the CNMI. Therefore, clothing made in Saipan is "Made in the USA."

In the 1980s Korean and Chinese contractor corporations and U.S. brand name producers discovered that goods made in the Marianas enjoyed duty- and quota-free access to the U.S. market. This offered relief to firms that were already filling quotas in, for example, China, Hong Kong, and the Philippines. The CNMI also has a lower legal minimum wage than the United States (presently $3.05). With control over its own immigration, the CNMI places few restrictions on the number of temporary (guest) workers, thus enabling vigorous recruitment of contract workers from China. Saipan became an export platform for "Made in the USA" goods to be sent to the United States.

By the late 1990s, Saipan and the CNMI had turned themselves into a giant dormitory compound for temporary, low-wage garment workers. More specifically, the CNMI had become a factory dormitory for young Chinese women, duplicating the industrial practices of the Chinese special economic zones: a place where young Chinese women sell their labor cheaply, desperately seeking financial help for their poor peasant families.

With a total employment of almost 47,000 workers in 1999, over 35,000 (76 percent) CNMI employees were non-U.S. citizens.[9] In 1980 there was no garment sector—total manufacturing employment was 110 persons. As of 1999 there were 14,708 manufacturing workers, and almost all of these were in nondurable manufacturing (Central Statistics Division 2001, 50, 51), and almost all of these were in the garment sector.[10] From 78 garment workers in 1980, garment employment grew to 7,700 garment workers in 1995 and then exploded to over 14,000 in the next four years. The majority of these workers are noncitizen, temporary Chinese women workers: over 11,000 workers in the apparel sector are from China; over 9,000 of these are women (Central Statistics Division 2000, 58). These few workers move a lot of goods: $1 billion in 1999 (Burger and Comer 2000, 5).

Taken from their homes in China to restricted dormitory compounds on a small island in the middle of the Pacific, the young women brought to make clothing in Saipan are only a shadow removed from indentured servants. Although the Saipan minimum wage is lower than that of the mainland United States, the workers say that contractor factories often fail to pay it.[11]

The contractor factories in Saipan accomplish evasion of minimum wage and overtime pay provisions of the FLSA in much the same way as sweatshop operators in the smaller mainland American factories do it. Workers are required to work "off the clock" if they have not met the (unrealistic) quota for the day or if repairs are required. The employer calls these hours "voluntary."

Working conditions include

> lack of safety equipment on sewing machines, fire exits that are either blocked or chained shut, extreme heat with poor ventilation, hazardous fire conditions, and air choked with dust, synthetic and cotton fibers from cutting machines. Dust masks frequently are not supplied except immediately prior to pre-announced OSHA inspections—when health and safety conditions are temporarily improved, although they return to their previously unlawful state when the inspectors leave. (*Doe I et al. vs. The Gap et al.* 2001)

The workers pay for the right to come to Saipan. Their dormitories are in compounds, sometimes locked down in curfews. They eat at company refectories (for which they are charged $100 per month). Some of the dorms, for which the workers are charged another $100 per month,

> are overcrowded, vermin- and insect-infested employer-owned barracks. At night, many workers are either not allowed to leave the barracks or must return by a specific curfew or suffer disciplinary action. Workers are also required to pay up to an additional $100 each month for food, but often go hungry or are fed insufficient quantities of poor quality, poorly prepared, unhygienic food. Several incidents of mass poisoning have occurred at the Contractors' factories. (*Doe I et al. vs. The Gap et al.* 2001)

For these and other recruitment fees, the Saipan workers' first-year debt is estimated by a human rights group at $3,604, but others suggest the range is $2,000–$7,000 (Witness 2001; Global Exchange 2004). First-year wages, not counting overtime or taxes but deducting room and board, for a minimum wage worker being paid for fifty weeks at forty hours per week would be about $3,700 ($6,100 - $2,400). It is no wonder that the workers seem to accept workweeks of seventy and eighty hours: an immense amount of overtime work is the only way they can escape from crushing debt. This debt composes the heart of the slavelike conditions the workers face. According to the U.S. DOL:

> Alien workers in the CNMI, who usually must pay substantial fees to middlemen to secure a job in the CNMI, are indentured because they are in the territory solely by virtue of their employment contract with a specific employer who is in control of the duration of the stay of the alien worker. Generally when an alien worker's contract is terminated, the employee must leave the CNMI. Local employers are forbidden by CNMI law from paying alien workers more than that stipulated in their original contract, which is usually, or very close to, the CNMI minimum wage. (Schoepfle 2000, 249)

According to the workers' attorneys, the threat of deportation and the consequent failure to pay the debt of their recruitment jeopardizes the workers' freedom and further threatens the workers' relatives, who, having guaranteed their debt, may be imprisoned. This claim is made more plausible by the fact that the recruitment companies that supply workers to the Saipan contractors are co-owned by the Chinese government (*Doe I et al. vs. The Gap et al.* 2001).

Early reports by Congressman George Miller (D-CA) and his staff found massive labor law violations and terrible conditions in the Saipan garment industry (see, e.g., Democratic Staff 1997). In January 1999, on behalf of a class of these workers, federal and California suits were brought against the contractor factories and the retailers for whom they worked, including Gap. The plaintiffs charged that they were victims of indentured or bonded labor, of obstructions of their right to association under the Wagner Act, and of violations of minimum wage and overtime provisions of the FLSA.

Among the precedent-making aspects of the lawsuit was the naming of the retailers as responsible for the labor conditions of the contractors they had engaged to make their branded clothing. Nineteen of the retailers settled with the plaintiffs, agreeing to $8.75 million in damages. Refraining from the settlement, however, were Gap, Levi Strauss & Co., Limited, Lane Bryant, Abercrombie & Fitch, Target, J.C. Penney, May, Talbots, and more than a dozen Saipan factory owners (Global Exchange 2002b; Strasburg 2002).

Gap drew the most attention in the Saipan matter for two reasons: it was the most adamant in blocking the settlement reached by the other nineteen retailers and manufacturers, and it was the defendant with the most at stake.

Gap has the largest volume of production in Saipan—$200 million (Global Exchange 2002b)—about one-fifth of the total CNMI garment export. Though Nike has become the "bad boy" of the footwear industry—largely because of its size, not because its practices are more terrible than the others—Gap appears to be a special case of abusive practice and arrogance combined. Not only is Gap among the largest retailers and the largest customer in this abusive environment, it is also in perennial difficulty in other locations around the world. The human rights group Global Exchange claims news of Gap abuses in Russia, Macao, Honduras, Hong Kong, and Indonesia.

> In Russia we were notified that Gap pays factory workers just 11 cents/hour and keeps them in slave-like conditions. Workers from Macao contacted the Asia Monitor Resource Center in Hong Kong complaining of abusive treatment by factory managers, who forced them to work excessive overtime and cheated them out of their pay. A delegation from the National Labor Committee in June 1999 reported that Honduran Gap factory workers are subjected to forced pregnancy tests, forced overtime, exceedingly high production goals, locked bathrooms, and wages of $4/day, which only meet 1/3 of their basic needs. The workers said that if they tried to organize a union or even become more informed of their rights, they would be fired. They had never heard of Gap's code of conduct. In Indonesia, 700 workers went on strike in July, 1997 protesting miserable wages and the factory management's refusal to recognize their independent union. (Global Exchange 2002b)

Gap was first involved in a public imbroglio about the sweatshop issue when revelations about its contractor, the Mandarin factory in El Salvador, led the NLC to lead a campaign against the firm in 1995. Gap agreed to a first ever experiment in independent monitoring of factory conditions (Krupat 1997). Since that time Gap has been very sensitive to charges that it is implicated in abusive labor practices. This sensitivity has not led to as much change in sourcing as it has in public relations.

Gap had $13 billion in retail sales in 2000, making it the 147th largest corporation on the Fortune 500 list. It is the 4th largest apparel retailer in the United States, and the 31st in number of employees. Gap is the 384th largest corporation in the world (ranked by revenue) (*Fortune* 2001). Despite—or perhaps because of—its size, Gap took the lead in resisting the settlement in the Saipan case. The plaintiffs' lead lawyer, Michael Rubin, wondered: We're alleging an overarching conspiracy, a scheme. . . . I don't mind Gap fighting this case and taking it to trial . . . [but] what I don't understand is: Why is Gap blocking these other companies from settling? (Strasburg 2002).

On September 26, 2002, Gap joined other holdouts, including local Saipan contractors, in a settlement of the class actions suits against them. Only Levi Strauss & Co. still held out. The thirty thousand past and present workers would have access to $6.4 million in back wages; three thousand dollars would be available to current workers for repatriation; and a monitoring system would enforce an agreed conduct code in the Marianas. Altogether it was a $20 million settlement (Collier and Strasburg 2002). As this book was going to print the suit was withdrawn, and the settlement was final.

Power and Accountability

Among the themes of the new antisweatshop movement at the turn of the twentieth century has been one that is shared with conservatives: accountability. The retailer and brand name manufacturers contend that they are not the employers of the workers in New York, Los Angeles, Saipan, or Guangdong Province. Retail executive Sammy Lee, quoted earlier, rejoins: the retail buyer sets the price. The retailers are responsible for the parameters in which the contractors are forced to work (Bonacich and Appelbaum 2000).

The ability of the big chains to dictate terms—prices—reflects a new distribution of power—the last generation's *redistribution* of power—in the textile-apparel-retail complex. This joins unregulated globalization as a cause of sweatshop labor. Lee testifies to the power and to the pressure emanating from the chains to reduce the labor cost in garments. Industry and management consultants Deloitte and Touche make a similar point somewhat more broadly:

> To reduce costs, many companies are being forced to relocate or outsource pieces of their supply chain. One big reason: In a world where mega-retailers like Wal-Mart and Carrefour have amassed enormous buying power, cost pressures for manufacturers in most industries are immense. (Deloitte Touche Tohmatsu 2003, 4)

The proposition made at the opening of this chapter was that where there is concentration in a supply (commodity) chain there will be a node of power. Power in a commodity chain, Lee and the consultants tell us, is price-dictating ability. In this era, concentrated price-making ability by the chains has forced manufacturers into a global search to cheapen labor and to collaborate with sweatshops in America. Consider, by contrast, the period 1940–70. In that period the concentrated links in the commodity chain were the unions; manufacturers and retailers were relatively dispersed. For most of that era American apparel workers enjoyed wages much closer to the manufacturing norm than they do today.

In other industries with concentrated producers, for example, automobiles, a unified union has been able to maintain a semblance of economic decency for its workers—though not without relative losses (see Ross and Trachte 1990).

Responsibility and Accountability

"Responsibility walks hand in hand with capacity and power." Josiah Gilbert Holland (n.d.) thus succinctly summarized the relation between resources and morality. Almost every idea of moral behavior has this interesting empirical connection: we are morally accountable for that which we are empirically responsible. We are not held to account for the weather, but we are accountable for that part of our behavior about which we may reasonably presume to have some discretion. We are not morally accountable for the fact of having to breathe. We are accountable for putting things in the air that other people must breathe.

It was their insight into the relation between capacity to act and accountability that led the tycoons of a hundred years ago to worry in public about their obligations or to preach to others in self-contradiction. Even as his agents shot and killed miners in Ludlow, Colorado, John D. Rockefeller, Jr., felt obliged to declare, "I believe that every right implies a responsibility; every opportunity, an obligation; every possession, a duty" (Rockefeller 1941; Daugherty 2000).

It is against the standard of responsibility and accountability that Big Retail fails. The big chains have the power to extract concessionary prices from their suppliers. As they do so, they are driving forces in the race to the bottom—for workers in New York, in Saipan, and around the world. The alternative is not to appeal for more "soulful" executives; one doubts that classes in ethics in business schools will redress these abuses. The real alternative is new (i.e., old) sources of countervailing power and laws that protect them and restrain the abuses.

7 Firing Guard Dogs and Hiring Foxes

Introduction: Cutting the Federal Budget and "the Dead Hand of Regulation"

Among the thousands of small contractor shops where workers sew clothing—in New York, Los Angeles, New Jersey, and around the United States—six out of every ten persistently break the labor laws by failing to pay minimum wages or overtime.[1] Over the last three decades, though, the government has gradually undertaken unilateral disarmament in the fight against labor lawbreakers. Understanding how and why this has happened is part of the solution to the puzzle of the rise of the new sweatshops. The story is part of a larger one: a shrinking federal government, deregulation, and privatization.

When Ronald Reagan campaigned for the presidency in 1980 he did so against a swollen federal bureaucracy, and in the midst of the inflation of the late 1970s he specifically targeted the favorite bogeyman of the American conservative movement of his era: the federal deficit. In his first State of the Union Address, on February 18, 1981, President Reagan grieved, "Can we who man the ship of state deny it is somewhat out of control? Our national debt is approaching $1 trillion. A few weeks ago I called such a figure—a trillion dollars—incomprehensible." In this speech he unveiled his "plan . . . aimed at reducing the growth in Government spending and taxing, reforming and eliminating regulations which are unnecessary and unproductive, or counterproductive." Five years later in his 1986 State of the Union Address, he looked back on "Government growing beyond our consent [that] had become a lumbering giant, slamming shut the gates of opportunity, threatening to crush the very roots of our freedom."

Ronald Reagan also orchestrated the most vigorous expansion in the U.S. military budget since World War II. The defense budget increase from Reagan's inauguration to its apogee in 1989 was $146 billion (from $157.5 billion to $303.6 billion). This compares to the Vietnam War increase from $50 billion in 1961 to $83 billion in 1969 (Council of Economic Advisers 2002, 415).[2]

In the eight years of Ronald Reagan's and then the four years of George H. W. Bush's presidencies, the nation witnessed a moderately successful Democratic Party defense of some social spending, wildly effective Republican tax cutting, and a more than doubling of military spending. The result was a tripling of the federal budget deficit in six years (1981–86)—from $79 billion to $221 billion (Council of Economic Advisers 2002, 413, 415). The national debt soared from the $1 trillion ($994 billion) that so grieved Ronald Reagan to a tripled $2.9 trillion. The national debt as a fraction of the GDP zoomed from 33 percent to 54 percent (Council of Economic Advisers 1997, B-76).

Reagan, as the slayer of the national debt, was a failure. Yet, in that failure his two terms created the crucible of twenty years of worried budget cutting. Every federal budget for the next twenty years had then to cope with the Reagan legacy. As Ronald Brownstein (1998, 30) noted in a *U.S. News and World Report* column, there had been a "two-decade-long period in which the deficit has largely defined the competition between the two parties. For years, conservatives have used public support for a balanced budget as a vise to squeeze government spending." Throughout the Reagan, George H. W. Bush, and Clinton administrations, cutting discretionary (mainly domestic) spending to bring the deficit under control became one of the centerpieces of presidential performance. In this regard, Reagan's obvious failure at budget balancing led to long-term success in his role as the dragon slayer of big government.

Firing Guard Dogs and Hiring Foxes

In the wake of Reagan's political success, Presidents Bush and Clinton (mainly Clinton) set about cutting the budget—and the number of federal employees. The federal government cut 359,000 jobs between 1989 and 1999.[3] In 1981 the 2.9 million federal civilian employees were 2.9 percent of U.S. employees; by 2000 federal employees were 2.1 percent of the employed (calculated from Council of Economic Advisers 2002, 375–76).

The conservative movement's campaign against "the size of government" and "the dead hand of bureaucracy" was not as popular as its mobilization of resentment against idleness. Playing upon the stereotype of welfare recipients as "welfare queens"—portrayed as Black, fraudulent, and exploitative of the good intentions of the public—the conservative movement managed to mobilize a mass voter base on behalf of cuts in social spending, in taxes, and in the budget in general (Edsall and Edsall 1992). These aided the broad objectives that the conservative movement's business class sponsors deeply cherished. Those objectives included deregulation and its twin, the privatization of government functions. The welfare issue cloaks these politics: the old Aid to Families with Dependent Children (AFDC) was a tiny fraction of the discretionary domestic budget.[4]

Each year presidential budgets and Republican congressional leadership called for "trimming" excess spending and excess personnel from the federal government. By 1990 a *New York Times* reporter noted, "Over the last decade, the discretionary programs, accounting for roughly 17 percent of Federal spending, have borne the brunt of budget-cutting" (Rasky 1990). By the mid-1990s Clinton had made the issue his own, and many Democrats followed his lead. Vice President Al Gore attempted to claim he was a master budget and cost cutter (Getter 1999, A6).

When the Congress and a president announce they have agreed on a package of budget cuts and tax changes to reduce the deficit, we (the broad public) rarely hear about, inquire into, or comprehend the details of hundreds of people and functions that are to be excised from the government. Retiring or resigning staff members are not replaced. Vacant positions are left unfilled. Workloads of individuals increase. Growth in a bureau's responsibility in a given region, say, the garment industry in Los Angeles, is not paralleled by growth in the personnel responsible for enforcing the FLSA. Over time, a policy of budget cuts may amount to a de facto policy of deregulation.

Deregulation may be an explicit and conscious policy to leave more of the behavior of an industry to market forces. This has been the famous case in the airline industry, for example, and more recently in telecommunications. An associated policy—privatization—allows private industry to offer for profit goods or services that only the government has previously offered.[5] An example of this would be turning over the cleaning of government office buildings to private cleaning firms rather than hiring janitors and cleaners as public employees. Another example would be President George H. W. Bush's intention to provide more housing for military families through private construction and by provision of vouchers for use on the private market (Bush 2001, 39).

Deregulation policies can be accomplished without being announced—and arguably without their administrators envisioning the long-term results of their actions. From the time of the Eisenhower administration to the present, the federal government has, without announcing a policy of deregulation, allowed the number of investigators in the WHD of the DOL to fall in relation to employment growth and, in fact, to fall in absolute numbers. If the number of "cops" on the fair labor enforcement beat had kept up to the standards of the 1950s, there would be almost two thousand more investigators than there are now.

When Dwight Eisenhower was president of the United States in 1957, the WHD of the DOL had one investigator for every forty-six thousand employees in the economy; by 1972, after a brief deterioration, the level was similar. This level of enforcement was apparently adequate, and it was among the contributions that led, in the long generation from 1938 (when the FLSA was passed) to the late 1970s, to the defeat of the worst and widespread cases of the sweatshop problem in manufacturing industries, such as garment making.

After the mid-1970s, successive federal budgets chipped away at this level of law enforcement. As table 11 shows, during the presidency of Ronald Reagan, the ratio of WHD investigators to employees rose past 1:97,000–110,000. When President George H. W. Bush left office, the ratio was 1:130,000. Still, the combination of budget cutting and antigovernment rhetoric continued; by 1996 the ratio of enforcers to workers was at its high of over 1:150,000. If the number of investigators had kept pace with the growth of employment, there would have been over 2,500 officials whose job it was to stop sweatshop abuses and other violations of the labor laws. Instead, table 11 indicates that by 1996 there were only 781 investigators (Eisenhower had over 1,100).[6] This is like firing two out of every three cops and then wondering why there are more traffic accidents and robberies. These data are portrayed graphically in figure 10.

Of course, actual investigators visit establishments, firms, or branches of firms, and only then do they examine records of individual workers. Therefore, the workload of investigators is really defined by the number of establishments—business locations—subject to the FLSA. In 1974 the U.S. Census Bureau changed the definition of *establishment,* which resulted in a marked increase.[7] However, it is possible to construct a time-series with a consistent definition for many of the years since 1983. The story is the same, but it allows imagery that is more precise.

Each Wage and Hour investigator had nominal responsibility for an average of over fifty-seven hundred locations by 1983. This was high enough that law breaking had become noticeable—it was well into the era of the new sweatshops in the apparel industry, and violations in the restaurant business were also becoming well known (U.S. GAO 1988). By 1996, however, the ratio had soared to about eighty-seven hundred. If an investigator can visit and thoroughly analyze three to five establishments a week (not likely since they visit in teams) and worked forty-eight weeks per year (with two to three weeks of vacation plus time off for national holidays), it would have taken that worker fifty-eight years to visit his or her caseload. Therefore, discovery was not much of a threat to the over twenty-three thousand small contractor shops in the apparel industry.

Reversing the Tide? From Deregulation to Privatization

In the summer of 1996 Congresswoman Nydia M. Velazquez (D-NY) successfully proposed a $5 million increase in appropriations "to the Wage and Hour Division, to specifically fight sweatshop violations in the gar-

TABLE 11. Wages and Hours Investigators and Employed Population: Selected Years 1957–96

	Investigators (I)	Establishments[a] (Es) (in hundred thousands)	Ratio: Es/I	Employment (Em) (in hundred thousands)	Ratio: Em/I
1957	1,146	3,219	2,730	52,855	46,121
1964	954	3,458	3,625	58,283	61,093
1965	969	3,522	3,635	60,763	62,707
1966	969	3,542	3,655	63,901	65,945
1967	969	3,511	3,623	65,803	67,908
1971	1,572	3,511	2,233	71,211	45,300
1972	1,594	3,541	2,221	73,675	46,220
1983	928	5,307	5,719	90,152	97,147
1984	916	5,518	6,024	94,408	103,066
1985	960	5,701	5,939	97,387	101,445
1986	908	5,807	6,395	99,344	109,410
1987	951	5,937	6,243	101,958	107,211
1988	952	6,019	6,322	105,209	110,514
1989	970	6,107	6,296	107,884	111,221
1990	938	6,176	6,584	109,403	116,634
1991	865	6,201	7,169	108,249	125,143
1992	835	6,318	7,566	108,601	130,061
1993	804	6,403	7,964	110,713	137,703
1994	800	6,509	8,136	114,163	142,704
1995	809	6,613	8,174	117,191	144,859
1996	781	6,739	8,629	119,608	153,147
1997	942	6,895	7,320	122,690	130,244
1998	942	6,942	7,369	125,865	133,615
1999	937	7,008	7,479	128,916	137,584
2000	942			131,759	139,872
2001	940			132,213	140,652

Source: Statistical Abstract of the United States (various years); Department of Labor budget documents and interviews.

[a]Prior to 1974, figures are based on reporting units. For all but manufacturing industries a reporting unit counted an establishment as one no matter how many different locations it may have had within a county. The number of establishments counts each location with a single owner within a county as one establishment. In all years separate manufacturing locations in a county are counted as establishments. Thus, the number of reporting units prior to 1974 is a smaller universe than the number of establishments after and is not strictly comparable.

ment industry" (Velazquez 1996, H7234). This is a story of mass media, congressional gumption, and presidential politics. It is also a story of a road not taken and the sorry consequence of indiscriminate budget cutting. The number of investigators went from 781 to its current 940 because in that particular summer media attention and presidential and congressional politics came together; they froze at that level (940) for all of those reasons too.

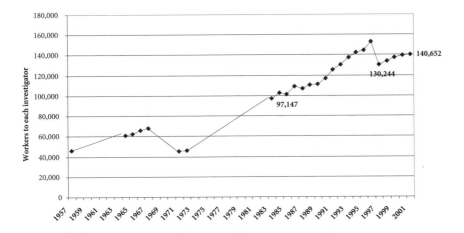

Fig. 10. Wage and hour investigators in the United States, 1957–2001, selected years

The way the scene was set in a manner that allowed Congresswoman Velazquez to prevail is an interesting tale. It is equally important to understand how advances are made as well as how labor abuse spreads. Figure 10 shows a small recovery in FLSA enforcement efforts in the late 1990s. This is the story of how it happened—and how it stopped happening.

During the spring of 1996 a celebrity scandal developed as television and newspaper stories focused on Kathie Lee Gifford, the popular cohost of a television chat show. Gifford, a former model, endorses a line of "Kathie Lee" clothes, and Wal-Mart had, at that time, an exclusive contract to manufacture and sell them. On April 29, the NLC revealed that child labor was used in the Kathie Lee clothing production lines in a contractor factory in Honduras; then weeks later, UNITE discovered that workers for another Kathie Lee clothing sub-subcontractor, in Manhattan, had been jilted out of their pay.

Chapter 10 tells this story in greater detail, along with a detailed analysis of the media coverage of the sweatshop issue, but briefly the Gifford affair more than doubled and in some cases tripled media coverage of the sweatshop issue. By July 1996, Congresswoman Velazquez could address a visible issue without fear of being obscure. DOL and Capitol Hill informants confirmed in 1997 interviews the importance of the Gifford matter in putting the sweatshop issue on the map (Hoffman 1997; Seiden 1997; Gohl 1997; S. Green 1997).

Another support for congressional action was the context of the presidential campaign and of Senator Edward Kennedy's fight to increase the minimum wage. Even with a Republican majority in the House, the looming election campaign found Republicans leery of being seen as miserly or mean-spirited.[8] Kennedy's staff also thought the minimum wage struggle was aided by the publicity given to the sweatshop issue by the Gifford affair.

Finally, there is Congresswoman Velazquez. Elected in 1992, Velazquez was the first Puerto Rican woman in the U.S. Congress. Her district, including parts of Brooklyn and Manhattan, may be second only to the Los Angeles fashion district for having the most sweatshops in the United States. Known in the 1980s as a "fiery orator" (Newfield 2002), Congresswoman Velazquez told her colleagues on July 10, 1996:

> Sweatshops have spread like wildfire, Congress has turned a blind eye and ignored this problem. This has caused millions of workers and American businesses to suffer. . . . fly-by-night kingpins open sweatshops for just a few months and then close without warning. They collect money from manufacturers and pay workers a pittance—if anything at all. . . . They operate a classic shell game, with women, immigrants and children as their pawns. These crooks must be stopped and we must begin by adopting this amendment. (Velazquez 1996, H7235)

Velazquez was born in Puerto Rico, where her father was a sugar cane worker. She was educated there and in New York City, where she earned a M.A. degree in political science at Hunter College of the City University of New York. She paid her dues as a member of the city council of New York and earlier as a representative of the Puerto Rican government in New York. As a result of her initiative the number of investigators was increased, and the ratio of workers to investigators dropped for the first time in decades. It did not continue to improve, however, and the political and policy strategy the Clinton administration chose embodied a different path.

Firing Guard Dogs and Hiring Foxes

The Privatization of Labor Standards Enforcement

Upon his inauguration in 1993, President Bill Clinton appointed a law school friend, the prominent liberal intellectual Robert Reich, as secretary of labor. Responding to advisers, including Maria Echaveste, the appointee who headed the WHD, Reich and the WHD began a new wave of aggressive—and publicity-conscious—enforcement on the sweatshop issue before it became a big media issue.

The "discovery" of the new sweatshops had begun, as noted earlier, in the late 1970s and early 1980s. The GAO published a major report on the issue in 1988. Already under the Bush administration, some rethinking of enforcement strategy was under way. Beginning in 1991, 157 manufacturers in southern California were told "to stop doing business with contractors violating labor laws" (Silverstein 1993, D1; Sward 1993, A1). It was Reich, however, who cared to make a public issue of labor abuse in the apparel industry.

As early as 1994, for example, the DOL used, and threatened to use more extensively, the previously dormant "hot goods" provision of the FLSA. This provision, which no previous secretary had invoked, allows the secretary of labor to seize or prevent the interstate sale of goods produced under conditions that violate the law (e.g., violating wages, hours, or child labor provisions) (*Houston Chronicle* 1994, Business 1). By September 1994, Reich put out the story that he had initiated five such "hot goods" charges against retailers. But ominously, the journalist to whom he gave the interview reflected the DOL worry about resources: "With only 800 federal inspectors nationwide and an estimated 22,000 small cutting and sewing establishments around the country, the Labor Department is hoping this approach will encourage retailers to aggressively monitor suppliers" (Lewis 1994, Economy 11). A small but steady flow of articles about sweatshops and enforcement strategies continued through 1994.

At some point between 1994, when the hot goods provision of the FLSA was held over the heads of retailers, and 1995–96, Reich, the DOL, and perhaps principals higher in the administration made a course correction.

The new variation of enforcement became known as "compliance monitoring." The stick became a carrot. The Department of Labor sought monitoring agreements from manufacturers whose contractors had been found to violate the law. The brand names or retailers would monitor their contractors for compliance with the FLSA and for other relevant health and safety laws. When the manufacturers publicly agreed to do so, they became eligible for a public list the Department of Labor published (Office of Public Affairs 1995). Although called the "Trendsetter List," newspapers rapidly came to call it the "good guy" list—with embarrassing long-run consequences.

The program of compliance monitoring rapidly turned away from the threat of the hot goods provision and toward the reward of public approval. An initial group of over thirty manufacturers was put on the "trendsetters' list." Among these were firms whose products have eventually shown up in one or another of every high-profile sweatshop scandal in the last seven years. Indeed, the first firm to sign such an agreement and attain list status was Guess?. Guess?, however, turned out chronically to use violator contractors, and the DOL suspended the firm from the list. When UNITE, the Department of Labor, and vocal segments of the Los Angeles intelligentsia turned the spotlight on their company, the Marciano brothers ran away, moving most of their contracts to Mexico.

From the outset, the DOL created the compliance monitoring program in the context of a shortage of strategic resources. The Ford Foundation and the Institute for Government Innovation at Harvard University's John F. Kennedy School of Government acknowledged this in its citation granting the WHD a 1996 Innovation in American Government Award:

> Rather than having its small corps of 800 investigators chasing tips on possible sweatshop activity—the old way of policing the industry—the division decided to pursue a new high-profile, two-part, top-down approach that hinges on cooperation and publicity. First, division investigators began working with the manufacturers and retailers who buy from sewing contractors and subcontractors to make them aware of the conditions under which some of their clothes were being sewn, even preventing shipments under the federal "hot goods" law to force accountability. Second, the Department of Labor decided to publish lists of manufacturers and retailers who insist on legal and ethical practices among their contractors and subcontractors—and those who do not.
>
> The tactic was effective. (Institute for Government Innovation 1996)

The question of effectiveness—as always, when numbers count—is trickier than the self-congratulatory summary. Somewhat less brief than a Ford Foundation or DOL press release, it would be more accurate to say that private monitoring increases the rate of compliance with labor law. But most private monitoring is superficial, violation rates are still high, and the most recent data are not encouraging.

Table 12 is taken directly from Jill Esbenshade's 2001 published study of Department of Labor documents. The data show that, as of 2000, contractor firms that were subject to private monitoring by the manufacturers had much lower rates of labor law violation than those that were not monitored. The monitored firms broke the law "only" 56 percent of the time (with a compliance rate of 44 percent), compared to unmonitored firms that broke the law 89 percent of the time with a compliance rate of 11 percent. However, as many firms were unmonitored (30 percent) as were "effectively monitored" (29 percent) (Esbenshade's term; see note to table 12).

Under the Department of Labor monitoring policy, the firms hire auditors—private monitors—to do compliance inspections for them. Initially, in the early 1990s, as the DOL program started, among the first firms to offer services in this area were those with prior factory inspection expertise, for example, those doing workmen's compensation safety inspections for insurance companies. Later, at the end of the 1990s, as the monitoring industry began to be large and global, the large international accounting firms—sensing a new market—entered the business.

Esbenshade reports that many visits are announced beforehand. The atmosphere of these visits is rather different from that of regulatory enforcement. The job of the private monitors, we may infer, is to protect the interests of the manufacturer, which implies good relations with the contractor. The monitoring firms understand quite well that they are an alternative to two options, each more repugnant to the principals who hire them. Esbenshade quotes a lawyer who works for a monitoring firm:

> Through self-policing, my monitoring, the workers are able to improve their standard of living, increase their wage level without organizing, in effect. . . . So what's happened here is that through people like Cal-Safety, hired by people like Kellwood[9] who are socially responsible, minimum wage and overtime is guaran-

TABLE 12. Fair Labor Standards Act Compliance Rates for Los Angeles–Area Garment Shops, 1994–2000

	1994 (a)	1996 (a)	1996 (b)	1996 (c)	1998 (a)	1998 (b)	1998 (c)	1998 (d)	2000 (a)	2000 (b)	2000 (c)	2000 (d)
Overall compliance (%)	22	39	22	58	9	20	40	56	33	11	44	44
Minimum wage (%)	39	57	36	73	52	33	56	72	46	11	55	61
Overtime (%)	22	45	25	61	6	40	48	56	40	21	36	44
Average back wages per shop ($)[a]	7,284	3,235	4,872	1,972	3,631	5,324	2,955	1,413	4,062	3,924	4,502	2,819
% of shops surveyed	100	100	52	48	100	23	77	28	100	30	70	29

Source: Data from Esbenshade 2001.

Note: (a) = overall; (b) = nonmonitored; (c) = monitored; (d) = effectively monitored. The 2000 survey included 67 shops. Each of the previous surveys included approximately 70 shops.

[a]Back wages are the amounts of money that employees are owed for nonpayment of overtime and minimum wage. Although by state law workers are entitled to up to two years of back wage payments, the amount given covers only a 90-day investigation period conducted by the federal Department of Labor. The amount of back wages owed is one indication of the extent of the violations.

teed to be paid and the workers don't need to organize, they don't need to pay dues to Jay Mazur [then president of UNITE] in order to obtain the benefit because they have stronger forces than even the union in order to compel payment in accordance with the law. (Esbenshade 2001)

If compliance monitoring is an alternative to unionization, from the point of view of the Department of Labor and the evolution of public policy, it is an alternative to effective regulation by the government. The principals know this too. Esbenshade's interviewee is refreshingly straightforward: "What this is is a privatization of a government function" (Esbenshade 2001, n. 12).

Consider the following thought experiment.[10] A law is passed with particular penalties and conditions forbidding stealing from people under certain circumstances, for example, between 7:00 A.M. and 7:00 P.M. and while they are doing something, for example, sewing dresses. In a random survey of sixty-seven potential places where people might be victimized, in 56 percent of the places, people have suffered losses by theft. The thefts average $4,062 in each place in one ninety-day period. Extrapolating to an annual rate for all sixty-seven places, total annual theft losses for this random sample are $1,088,616.

It is not likely that average annual thefts of $16,000 per small establishment would be seen as a situation of effective law enforcement, *even if* the potential rate of loss, with a higher level of effective private monitoring, was only three-quarters as high (date from table 12). This is especially so, since the more typical level of private monitoring is associated with even higher levels of loss (see column c in table 12). If we estimate the number of individual workers per contractor shop at seventeen (the national average), the average individual loss per worker is $956 each year. If this is extrapolated to the Los Angeles garment workforce, estimated at a low 100,000, the losses in wages are over $95 million annually. Were this the case in ordinary law or if it happened to citizens with typical access to politics or communications media, it would be a total scandal. A society where thieves took $1,000 per year from each person would be considered lawless.

Few believe that Secretary Reich was anything but sincere in his efforts to protect apparel workers from the sweatshop conditions of the late twentieth century. Certainly, his time in office stands in contrast to his Republican predecessors and both his Democratic successor, Alexis Herman, and his Republican successor, Elaine Chao. None of them gave similar prominence to the sweatshop issue as Reich did.[11] Yet, as they have in many other areas, the policies of deregulation and privatization have not been strong supports for workers, especially the most vulnerable among them.

Nevertheless, de facto deregulation by enforcement disarmament was in place by 1996. Just as Congresswoman Velazquez had succeeded in restoring a bit of muscle to the WHD, the kernel of privatization became the administration's response to sweatshops on a global scale.

A Brief History of the Fair Labor Association: Global Privatization

The discovery in August 1995 of a slave workshop in El Monte, California, showed that the clothes were made for mainstream labels and retailers. Secretary Reich's initiative on sweatshops became more urgent among those with a professional interest in the industry—and it began the process of public education on the West Coast. Nevertheless, it was the Kathie Lee Gifford affair that gave Reich's campaign and the issue enough public visibility to reach for presidential involvement. In June 1996 Reich, with Gifford, announced a "Fashion Industry Forum" for July 16. Representatives of labor, public interest groups, government, and apparel and retail firms attended.

The forum was held at Marymount University in Arlington, Virginia. Besides model Cheryl Tiegs, joining Gifford as a repentant celebrity endorser, the forum heard somewhat predictable calls for reform—which was actually quite important, for they implied that the industry was acknowledging it had a problem. The forum also heard from a sewing machine operator from Manhattan, Nancy Penaloza, who described her factory in the garment center in vivid terms:

> My boss doesn't pay any tax or social security. I work at least 56 hours a week, Monday to Saturday. Sometimes I go 66 hours a week. I make $200.07 a week. If there is a lot more I have to work on Sundays. I never get vacation. I never even

get a whole weekend off. Sometimes I have to work on Easter, Thanksgiving and Christmas. The conditions are very bad. My factory is very hot in summer and very cold in winter. My boss is screaming to me all the time. He is always very angry. I can't ask him any questions because I'm afraid he's going to hit me. All the time he hits me working, like that (she gestures hitting her head with her fist). The factory is very dirty. When I am working I'm afraid because there is big rats and mice crawl on my feet. (Penaloza 1996)

Participants, prompted no doubt by administration policy specialists, indicated that a "sweat free" label could guide consumers to an ethical choice and elevate labor standards (Thomas 1996).

Shortly after the forum, on August 2, President Clinton announced the formation of what came to be known as the Apparel Industry Partnership (AIP) at a White House press conference. A presidential announcement focuses attention on a problem. The media coverage given to a presidential press announcement is de facto a process of anointing a problem—which may have previously been a "special interest" or a technical matter—with the status of an item on the public's—that is, the nation's—agenda. The president articulated then what would continue to be the poles of the problem and the public discussion. He said that he had met with a number of companies and

They have agreed to do two things. First, they will take additional steps to ensure that the products they make and sell are manufactured under decent and humane working conditions. Second, they will develop options to inform consumers that the products they buy are not produced under those exploitative conditions. They have agreed to report back to me within a maximum of 6 months about their progress. (Clinton 1996, 1244)

The original and charter members of the AIP task force of the Fair Labor Association, from 1996 to 1998, are on the following page.

Accomplishing both higher labor standards and agreement among stakeholders over an ethical choice label would prove difficult. Six months after the formation of the AIP, it had not yet made its report. The firms were highly resistant to the principle of independent monitors checking their adherence to the developing code of conduct for labor standards. The unions pushed for a wage standard that would provide for basic needs—a "living wage"—which is distinct from the legal minimum in many nations (Ramey 1997a).

Companies Represented
Liz Claiborne, Inc.
Nicole Miller, Inc.
Nike, Inc.
Patagonia
Phillips Van Heusen
Reebok International, Ltd.

Joined after 1996

Karen Kane, Inc.

Left over monitoring issue, June 1997

Tweeds, Inc.
LL Bean, Inc.
Warnaco
Karen Kane

Left over monitoring issue, April 1997

Kathie Lee Gifford

Citizen, Labor and Consumer Groups:
National Consumers League
Business for Social Responsibility
International Labor Rights Fund
Robert F. Kennedy Memorial
    Center for Human Rights
Lawyers Committee for Human
    Rights

Did not sign Fair Labor Association Charter, November, 1998
Interfaith Center on Corporate
    Responsibility
Retail Wholesale Department Store
    Union, AFL CIO
Union of Needletrades, Industrial
    and Textile Employees (UNITE),
    AFL-CIO

After a period of intense cajoling by the administration, the AIP task force approached a tentative agreement. Firms agreed to the principle of independent monitoring; UNITE, the apparel workers union, agreed that this did not have to be performed by human rights groups, although the language of the document called for consultation with them. The union, apparently compromising for the sake of the draft document, gave up a clear statement of the wage standard as a living wage. Even as the wage standard was announced as the higher of the "legal minimum" or the industry-prevailing wage in each country, it also included the rhetorical concession that the "Employers recognize that wages are essential to meeting employees' basic needs" (FLA 2003a)

One of the largest U.S. apparel producers—Warnaco—left the task force a few days before it published its draft report. Warnaco said it had adequate monitors of its own (Ramey 1997b). Weeks later, women's apparel manufacturer Karen Kane, Inc., departed for much the same reason (Ramey 1997c).

On April 14, 1997, the AIP published the draft "Workplace Code of Conduct and Principles of Independent Monitoring." The labor standards, which were to remain unchanged in the final document released nineteen months later, ban forced labor, child labor (fourteen years of age in poor countries, fifteen elsewhere), harassment, and discrimination. It calls for adequate health and safety, freedom of association and collective bargaining, and payment of the legal minimum wage or prevailing wage if it is higher, and it sets a forty-eight-hour workweek as standard (except where lower by law) and twelve hours of overtime as permissible. It calls for one day off in seven. Overtime pay should adhere to local law, which does not always provide for premium pay—but it should be paid (Fair Labor Association 2001).

Labor and human rights groups heavily criticized the April 1997 document. Their dissent focused on the code's use of the legal minimum wage as the standard in many countries. This is often inadequate, as the U.S. State Department's human rights report noted at the time (U.S. Department of State 1999):

> *Bangladesh:* "There is no national minimum wage. Instead, the wage commission, which convenes every several years, sets wages and benefits industry by industry. In most cases, private sector employers ignore this wage structure."
> *Nicaragua:* "The minimum wage does not provide a decent standard of living for a worker and family. It falls far below government estimates of what an urban family must spend each month for a basic basket of goods ($129.51, or 1,400 cordobas)."
> *Mexico:* "The minimum wage does not provide a decent standard of living for a worker and family."
> *El Salvador:* "The minimum wage with benefits does not provide a decent standard of living for a worker and family."
> *Indonesia:* "After the latest minimum wage increases in August, which averaged 15 percent nationwide, the average minimum wage was equal to 76 percent of the government-determined 'minimum living need,' down from 95 percent in 1997. In Jakarta the monthly minimum wage is about $17 (Rp 198,500). There are no reliable statistics on the number of employers paying at least the minimum wage. Independent observers' estimates range between 30 and 60 percent. Enforcement of minimum wage and other labor regulations remains inadequate, and sanctions are light."

Another major point of contention in the formation of the original (and final) report of the AIP was the monitoring procedure. The labor and advocacy communities contended that the monitoring of labor standards was best performed by groups that workers would trust. They envisioned the major accountancy or insurance consultants—dressed apocryphally in suits, approaching fearful workers and being treated like agents of the employers—with silence. By contrast, many pointed to the precedent of the Mandarin factory, a contractor to Gap in El Salvador.

After Salvadoran workers at the Mandarin firm began a campaign against labor abuses, they received active support from the NLC, whose lead staffer is Charles Kernaghan. Kernaghan organized U.S. consumer action and media coverage targeting Gap. Eventually, the firm and its contractor agreed to the first ever independent monitoring of labor conditions in 1995. More relevant to the future history of the Fair Labor Association, the monitors were local organizations, including the human rights office of Jesuit University and the Catholic Archdiocese. The NLC considered this a major success (Krupat 1997).[12]

Wary as they were about the principle of monitoring, however, the apparel firms would not consider making human rights groups a major part of the monitoring protocol. Even the mention of consultation with such groups was part of the reason Karen Kane, Inc., left the AIP in June 1997.

In agreeing to the April 1997 AIP draft, UNITE was apparently hoping that progressive forces would create enough criticism and momentum that the administration would pressure the firms to make concessions on the wage and monitoring issues. In any case, UNITE signed the 1997 agreement with the understanding that there would be a period of consideration of both the details and the substance of the points. This calculation put the union in the occasionally embarrassing position of having prolabor advocacy groups vehemently attacking a draft agreement to which they had lent their name. UNITE president Jay Mazur joined in the April 1997 presidential announcement:

> I do not think it is an exaggeration to say that we have taken a very historic step forward. All of us with a stake in this industry, a stake in this new global economy, a stake in our democratic way of life have found common ground and mapped out a route to dignity and respect for workers in the industry throughout the world. (Mazur 1997)

"It's a historic and significant beginning," Mazur told *New York Times* columnist Bob Herbert (Herbert 1997, 15). But Elaine Bernard, Harvard Labor Program director and frequently requested speaker, called it a plan for a "kinder, gentler sweatshop" (Bernard 1998). Global Exchange director Medea Benjamin said, "Unless we talk about a living wage and start to define it, a sweatshop will always be a sweatshop" (Greenhouse 1997, A1). Benjamin went further in talking to *Washington Post* writer William Branigin: "I think it's business as usual, while giving the consumer the impression that the issue has been taken care of. . . . It's not good enough to be the best plantation owner on the block," she told the *Post,* and charged that the accord's recognition of workers' right to form unions is "pure hypocrisy." "Why, then, do the companies manufacture in countries where it is illegal to organize?" (Branigin 1997b, A10).

In the months after April 1997, activists and observers outside of insider policy circles assumed a consensus sweat-free label was in the making. However, a long period of stalemate began. In a May 1998 interview, an industry insider fully knowledgeable about the business perspective on the AIP task force said that the companies did not think they could work with the union. Confirming this view, a prominent activist privy to union views on the task force in that mid-May 1998 period was grimly pessimistic about the outcome—and, in fact, predicted the collapse of the AIP. This same person, a Washington operative, had told me in April 1997, at the time of the original announcement, "We've got a deal we can live with, a start."[13]

In July 1998 Steven Greenhouse of the *New York Times* was the recipient of a leaked document stating the union/human rights position—a leak intended to develop pressure on the firms. Roberta Karp, cochair of the AIP and general counsel to Liz Claiborne Inc., told Greenhouse it was "regrettable that someone chose to try to leverage through the press a proposal that would impede the mission of the Apparel Industry Task Force" (Greenhouse 1998a, A16). The union position document addressed two major concerns it had—and would continue to have—about the labor standards of the new Fair Labor Association. Greenhouse's July 3 report parallels exactly what the union would say four months later upon its refusal to sign the final agreement.[14] As Greenhouse reported it, UNITE was troubled by the monitoring provision, which allowed but 10 percent of a firm's contractors to be monitored in a given year and 30 percent in the first three years of the agreement. The union wanted 30 percent of a firm's contractors' factories to be inspected each year if the firms were to continue to have the right to sew inside each garment a certified version of a sweat-free label. Furthermore, the union articulated its concern about union rights in repressive countries. The companies were willing to assure that they would not punish or seek to have punished union-minded workers. UNITE's position, though, was that, after a company had made a good faith effort to preserve the right to association and collective bargaining of its workers, if this was impossible in a given country, then no clothing originating in that country should be able to earn the certification label. The main target of this concern was China.

China, as we have seen, was then and is now the world's largest exporter of clothing and is roughly tied with Mexico as the largest apparel exporter to the United States. The wholesale value of Chinese apparel exports to the United States in 1997 was $6.02 billion ($10.9 billion in 2002); Mexico's was $5.92 billion ($9.2 billion in 2002). These were the top two. Advocates of labor rights the world over believe that independent unions or persons trying to organize them are in constant danger of imprisonment in China.

The union position is that after good faith efforts at remediation, there should be a clear process that could result in decertifying all clothing originating in any place where the right to association and collective bargaining cannot be asserted. Given the size of their stake in China, and the extraordinary low level of wages there, the brands would not relent on this point.

In his article Greenhouse (1998a) also previewed the wage issue as it appeared to the apparel union and its human rights allies. It appeared to Greenhouse then that the union was willing to accept the minimum wage/prevailing wage standard provisionally but that it wanted the Department of Labor to perform living wage studies in each country and explicitly to compare these to the wages paid in apparel contracting. At some future time the code envisioned by the union and human rights grouping would include this living wage in its certification standard. The companies, by contrast, were willing to have a wage study done, but not to apply the living wage as a standard for certification.[15]

By October 1998 the rift was irremediable. In an October 10 interview, a prominent and knowledgeable labor rights advocate said that UNITE and others would split from the task force but that the task force would make its final report without them. The issues were described essentially as the May 1998 informants had described them and as the July *New York Times* (Greenhouse 1998a) story had related them.

On November 2, 1998, the final report of the AIP task force was released, in the form of a charter document for the FLA. UNITE, the United Food and Commercial Workers (UFCW),[16] and the Interfaith Center on Corporate Responsibility (ICCR) declined to become members of the FLA. Breaking ranks, however, the International Labor Rights Fund (ILRF), headed by the prominent spokesman Pharis Harvey, signed the charter, as did the Lawyers Committee for Human Rights.[17] The latter's spokesman, Michael Posner, had taken a "point man" role throughout the life of the task force and was frequently quoted in an optimistic mode.[18]

The defection of the ILRF must have been particularly hard for UNITE. The ILRF's board is widely thought of as friendly to organized labor, including, for example, Ray Marshall, a secretary of labor in the Carter administration. The ILRF has, before then and since, been seen as a defender of organized labor's position on trade and other issues. Its defection was notable. Therein lies a tale.

In a little-known letter to Pharis Harvey,[19] Lenore Miller, president emeritus of the UFCW, a member of the task force that quit in solidarity with UNITE, praised the ILRF for staying in the FLA. Miller says she signed the AFL-CIO statement of nonparticipation in "the interest of preventing a split position in the labor movement becoming the main focus of the press." Despite this solidarity position, Miller told Harvey in her letter that she thought the "less than perfect document . . . is a step in the right direction toward helping the most exploited workers in the world." Miller says that though she signed the labor statement, she did it knowing "that the labor movement" might "come back in at any time." The critical phrase in her letter follows immediately: "I did that knowing that organizations such as yours would be the watchdog" (L. Miller 1998).

The immediate result of the AIP-FLA report was moral confusion. If a consensus report on the standards for a sweat-free label had succeeded by including business, human rights advocates, and labor unions, the Clinton administration's and Secretary of Labor Reich's hope for a consumer-friendly label would have been achieved. But dissensus among the stakeholders threatens the worst of all possible consumer outcomes: labels *claiming* ethical standards, with public relations "reach," but ones that are repugnant to the key laborers' representatives in the industry.

Shortly after the publication of the final report founding the FLA, the Collegiate Licensing Company (CLC) adopted a code (on November 30, 1998) that closely parallels the FLA code.[20] The CLC acts as a broker for 160 colleges and universities that sell the right to use their names on clothing and other paraphernalia. The collegiate licensing business is estimated at $2.5 billion annually in retail sales. The CLC proposed that licensees who pay royalties to universities for the right to sell clothing with university insignia should require that their own contractors—the actual garment factories—meet at least the labor standards of the AIP-FLA. The code adopted on November 30 was clearly related to the student movement then becoming discernable on the horizon. The new student movement for a sweat-free campus forced the terms of the FLA standards into visible, public debate. In its weakened state, UNITE could not have made the FLA a broadly public issue. Given the status-driven nature of mass media news coverage, campus protest at elite colleges and flagship state universities provided public exposure for UNITE's position that it could not—or did not—gain on its own.

Having already been activated in a "sweat-free campus" campaign, students at an initially small number of campuses were ready to challenge the proposed CLC-FLA code at each institution. By the fall of 1998, United Students Against Sweatshops (USAS) had been formed, with about fifty campus groups involved.

In January and February 1999, groups loosely affiliated with USAS held sit-ins at Duke, Georgetown, Wisconsin, Michigan, and Arizona Universities and had had large rallies for campus codes of conduct at many other campuses, including Princeton, Harvard, and Boston Universities. The new student movement and its sit-ins adopted the labor critique of the FLA charter. They demanded that their local administrations require labor standards of their licensees that were more rigorous than those of the CLC, AIP, and FLA. The most prominent student position in the sweat-free campus movement has been a rejection of the FLA standards and pressure for a living wage standard. Under pressure—directly or prospectively—some fifty-seven universities became affiliated with the FLA only to have this new standard of decency challenged.

The student movement added an item to its list of concerns that had been outside the central discourse of the old task force, but one particularly suited to a movement of ethical consumers. The sweat-free campus movement of the spring of 1999 adopted a position pioneered by Charles Kernaghan and the NLC: "public disclosure." Kernaghan had launched the public disclosure idea in relation to Wal-Mart and its contractors in 1998. The NLC encouraged local groups to adopt the public disclosure idea to local circumstances from its beginning (Briggs 1998).

The public disclosure position requires that manufacturers reveal to the public the complete list of their own and their contractors' factory locations. Jeffrey Ballinger—a former AFL-CIO representative in Indonesia and perhaps the United States' most knowledgeable critic of the Nike corporation, in Indonesia in particular—put the position this way at a forum at Brown University: "Tell us where the factories are, and the NGOs will find out about human rights abuses" (Ballinger 1999).

The next step for the student movement was the creation of a Workers' Rights Consortium (WRC) in 1999. In their eyes, the WRC was superior to the emerging FLA because it stood for public disclosure, a living wage, and independence from corporate governance. In a ferocious six months, with sit-ins on dozens of campuses, the young USAS movement was able to attract over fifty campus affiliations by April 2000, when they held their official founding meeting. By March 13, 2002, this number had grown to ninety-four affiliates; by the summer of 2003, it was over one hundred. The WRC does not require a particular code of conduct from its affiliates, though it publishes a model code and requires from affiliates some code that covers the similar topics (see chapter 1). It does not provide regular or random inspections of workplaces. Instead, the WRC has used a complaint-driven model and auditing teams of NGOs and experts. In some notable cases—for example, the Kukdong/Mexmode factory in Mexico, the BJ&B plant in the Dominican Republic, and the New Era cap company in New York State—the WRC was able to bring attention to bear on a group of workers who had been abused and frustrated in their attempts to form independent unions. Eventually the workers were successful (see chap. 11).

Born in the heart of embarrassed scandal, the FLA was once the hoped-for moral savior of the apparel industry. Mired in controversy, however, the FLA became the target of the antisweatshop movement, symbolizing co-optation and evasion. The paradox and irony do not end there. A vigorous movement of young adults created in its stead another form of privatized standards enforcement. The WRC is, to be sure, independent, but it attempts to raise the global standards of apparel workers, with a budget of $500,000–$800,000, one factory at a time.

Another Shot at Law Enforcement

In the meantime, with social activists, Clinton administration officials, and NGOs focusing on contested types of privatized rule enforcement, the economy continued to grow, but there was no follow-through on Congresswoman Velazquez's attempt to put more cops on the fair labor standards beat. As a result, from 1997 to 2002 the ratio of cops to the size of their beat once again deteriorated. From its peak of 1:153,000, the ratio of investigators to jobholders dropped to 1:130,000 in 1997; but by the end of 2001 the ratio was back to 1:140,000 (see table 11).

Department of Labor budgets under Secretary of Labor Elaine Chao drastically cut funding for wage and hour enforcement. President Bush's initial fiscal year 2002 budget proposal called for a tiny increase in spending for enforcement of the FLSA—from $166 million to $169 million, 1.8 percent. Since the authoritative economic forecasts had predicted price increases between 2.6 percent and 2.8 percent, the president's budget actually implied a relative *loss* of enforcement ability.[21] The eventual result was even worse: In fiscal year 2002 actual enforcement spending sank to $165.2 million, and it was barely higher in fiscal year 2003 (U.S. DOL 2003).

Given that as many as 265,000 apparel workers work for less than the minimum wage; that it is likely that even larger numbers of restaurant workers are not paid for overtime; that this is an area of law enforcement that really *is* about the administration of *justice,* one is forced to conclude that there is a deep class bias in the law-and-order rhetoric in Washington. No one wants a government that is too large; but right now, when it comes to fair labor standards, we do not have one large enough to do the job. Deregulation is not the way to end labor abuse.

8 Immigrants and Imports

when most people think about sweatshops in the apparel business, they think of immigrants. Early in the twentieth century it was Jewish and Italian immigrants who toiled in tenements and dangerous factories and struggled to form unions to protect their livelihoods. Following the Jews and Italians in New York and Los Angeles, still in the period when union protection was meaningful, were Puerto Rican, Black, and Mexican workers, migrants and immigrants too.[1] Now, new immigrants from Central America, China, and other Asian countries join Mexican immigrants in the sweatshops of the rag trade. It is not surprising then that some see sweatshops as an issue for immigrants or as a problem created by the growth in immigration.

There are two broad approaches that researchers and journalists currently apply to understanding the reappearance of sweatshops in the United States. The first approach focuses on the appearance of a large immigrant labor force that has grown rapidly since the 1965 immigration reforms. The second approach, the one that forms the basis of this chapter, emphasizes the structure of the global political economy, especially the free trade process, as the necessary condition for the large-scale reappearance of substandard conditions of labor in the last twenty years. This chapter shows why researchers and journalists "reach" for the immigrant

172

explanation yet why it is only a small part of the whole picture compared to the broader structural factors we have already discussed. The implications of the evidence are that immigration is not the sufficient cause for sweatshops while low-wage imports are necessary. Immigration restriction would not solve the problem of substandard conditions of employment for American workers.

Analyses of the causes of the new sweatshops do have policy implications. If the supply of immigrants is at the heart of the problem, one might look to different solutions than if low-wage competition, inadequate law enforcement, the power of retailers, and the loss of union protection are necessary conditions for the repression of labor rights among new immigrants. As Ross and Staines argue (1972), distinctions between system- and person-blame attributions of a problem are likely to have a powerful effect on policy solutions. A group's or a person's political interests and preferences influence the constructions—definitions—of a problem that are congruent with their policy preference. The analysis of a problem strongly influences the solutions. The academic's search for causes has much to do with the political choices of policymakers.

Immigrant Labor Explanations

The immigration hypothesis explains the reemergence of apparel sweatshops in the context of cultural and economic factors at work within immigrant communities. It sees the simultaneous growth of both legal and illegal immigration as perhaps the most important reason for the reemergence of sweatshop conditions.

Legal immigration rose dramatically in the United States between 1965 and 1990, and it continues now. In 1960, 265,398 immigrants entered the United States. By 1985 the number was 570,000, and by 1990 it was 1.5 million (U.S. Census Bureau 1994, 10). The first decade of the twentieth century saw 8.8 million immigrants enter the United States. The last decade of the century was the only one to exceed the first, when 9.1 million new residents entered the United States (INS 2002).[2] The destination of new immigrants is consistent with the location of the greatest number of new sweatshops—at least those that have been noted in the apparel industry: the Mexican border, Los Angeles, New York, Miami, and Dallas (see, e.g., U.S. DOL 1996). These sites are often the global cities of our new economy, highly polarized in terms of class and wealth (Ross and Trachte, 1983, 1990).

The "new immigration" of the post-1965 era is different from the turn-of-the-century immigrant flow—just as it, in turn, was different from the one that preceded it. Immigrants in the era of the old sweatshops came in the greatest number from Eastern and Southern Europe, the Jews and Italians among them. Between 1890 and 1920, 87 percent of the 18.2 million immigrants came from Europe.[3] Most of these immigrants, in contrast to the Protestant Northern and Western Europeans who preceded them, were Catholic, Orthodox, or Jewish. While their levels of formal schooling were low compared to native-born Americans, education was less of a barrier to economic participation at that time than it is in our era. Today's immigrants have changed yet again. Only 14 percent of immigrants during the period 1970–2000 came from Europe. Western Hemisphere (48 percent), and particularly Mexican, immigrants are the largest group, while Asians (34 percent) also make up a major portion of this era's new Americans (INS 2002).

Today's immigrants have polarized levels of educational attainment. On average, they have completed college and attained graduate education at about the same rates as citizens born in America. However, immigrants of the last two decades are more than twice as likely than native-born residents to have less than a high school education (33 percent compared to 13 percent) (U.S. Census Bureau 2002b). Hispanic and particularly Mexican workers are more likely than others to be in this group: half of Latino-American immigrants have less than a high school diploma. Two-thirds of people over the age of twenty-five from Mexico have less than a high school diploma. On the other hand, about half (45 percent) of Asian immigrants have college degrees at least (compared with 25 percent for the native population) (U.S. Census Bureau 2002b). The Asian educational distribution is bimodal—for it is not a homogeneous group of nationalities. Immigrants from India and Korea, for example, have higher average levels of education than does the American population as a whole, while Cambodian and Laotian groups are lower in formal schooling. The mainland Chinese are, on average, lower in formal schooling than the Taiwanese—but both are higher than the U.S. average (Le 2003).

These characteristics suggest a structure of the labor force and roles in the apparel industry. In the first instance, immigrants with higher levels of education, business experience, or ambition may want to be business owners. They may come from linguistic communities where there are large numbers of women without language or professional skills that would give them entry to well-paid employment. In the 1980s, for example, Korean entrepreneurs and sewing machine operators populated firms in the Dallas–Fort Worth area (Um 1996).

The economic penalties of low levels of schooling have grown in recent years. Wages in the low-wage labor market have become relatively lower. The failure of blue-collar unskilled and semiskilled jobs to maintain purchasing power is among the forces driving the increases in inequality of the last generation. Immigrants arriving in America face a blue-collar labor market that is considerably weaker—looser—than in other parts of the skill and schooling distribution.

Immigrants go to places where they know people or where they have heard they can find housing and work. They seek those with whom they can converse, worship, and shop; they flow toward opportunity. Immigrants then create communities through the phenomenon of "chain migration." To a demographer or social geographer making maps of the concentrations of different groups, chain migration creates concentrated immigrant destinations. The simple process of heading toward a place your cousin went or where you have heard that someone from your village got a job has focused the 17.4 million entrants to the United States on only a handful of major destinations.

In March 2000, "70 percent of the foreign born population of the United States lived in six states: . . . California (8.8 million), New York (3.6 million), Florida (2.8 million), Texas (2.4 million), New Jersey (1.2 million), and Illinois (1.2 million)." The New York and Los Angeles metropolitan areas combined to hold one-third of the foreign-born population; 55 percent of the foreign born were in nine metro areas (Schmidley 2001, 2). What these data about concentration mean is that fairly dense community networks are being built. Within them there are enough people to sustain a life with very little contact with the host culture. The protective insularity of large immigrant communities is both a comfort and a penalty.

In some of the academic literature, immigrant entrepreneurs play a heroic role by bridging the gap between immigrant labor supply and gainful employment, by building capital in the immigrant communities, and by creating vital rungs in the ladder of immigrant success. The ethnic entrepreneurs in this view are specialists in finding the niches that match (low-wage) labor supply and demand. Small apparel subcontractor shops are used in such arguments as examples of this niche function of immigrant entrepreneurship (Waldinger 1986; Bonacich and Modell 1980).

So, in this version of the story, a Korean or Vietnamese or Chinese subcontractor scrambles to find a competitive niche by offering low-cost, quick turnaround to a larger, more established firm. The ethnic entrepreneur can do something the more established firm cannot accomplish in the context of American urban life: find and recruit the steady stream of willing women (and some men) who will work at all hours (that is the implication of the turnaround time requirement) for low—even illegally low—pay.

Subcontractors operate within the larger system of apparel production to reduce labor costs. Their small size and modest capital requirements make garment subcontracting shops an attractive way for immigrants to become members of the business class (Kwong 1987; Chow 1992). Low overhead costs are maintained by using substandard spaces and facilities.

The workplaces in American sweatshop districts are quite different from the factories of developing countries against which they compete. In Los Angeles, for example, the principal fashion district is clustered around the old (1920s) downtown office district (Bonacich and Appelbaum 2000). Many cutting and sewing shops take up spaces in deteriorating office buildings. For example, during a field visit in 2001, two offices were found that had been joined, but the hallway door to the second office—the "backdoor"—was locked as a security measure. So the vital—and legally required—second door was unavailable in case of fire. In New York's Chinatown little shops are found in the basements of residential or mixed commercial and residential buildings. By contrast, the export processing zones of Central America or the export factories in Asia are generally more modern and larger.

In any case, when one enters a sewing shop in the United States, one enters a world of immigrants. In a shop I visited in New York, for example, traditional Chinese music was playing on a radio, the wall calendars were in Chinese characters, and the only non-Chinese person in the shop of about thirty people was the Vietnamese owner.

The wages offered in such a setting, while they may be below the minimum set by the FLSA, may be paid partially in cash (avoiding taxes by both employee an employer) and in many cases may *seem* like good pay to people who come from poor countries. Such firms may not pay overtime, Social Security taxes, or unemployment insurance.[4] With their low investment and typically marginal returns, such shops often significantly violate the health and safety codes of federal and local government. When the violations are significant and frequent, the ethnic entrepreneur is operating illegally and has become a sweatshop operator.

The steady stream of recruits to the sweatshop are in some sense "willing"; it is rare that they are bonded or slavelike laborers.[5] This gives the laureates of the free market their license to justify sweatshops, both in the United States and most emphatically elsewhere. But freedom, contrary to Janis Joplin, is not nothing left to lose. Those with nothing have no choices. A choice to take bad work is not so free when structural or cultural obstacles prevent one from taking better work.

Gender and ethnicity combine to compose the barriers to decent employment for the women employed in apparel subcontracting firms. Cultural barriers to full participation in their new community often restrict immigrant women from alternative employment in better-paying segments of the labor force. Immigrant women, particularly those most newly arrived, typically find themselves in a strategically vulnerable position. Language deficit, lack of formal schooling (Stier 1991; Loo and Ong 1987),[6] or simply isolation from job-acquiring information networks are examples of the economic barriers they face. Transportation outside of their residential community or its well-known travel routes can be frightening for newly arrived immigrants unfamiliar with the cultural conventions of the United States. When these women look for jobs outside of ethnic neighborhoods they are competing with other unskilled workers for the lowest-paid jobs in the most depressed industries. The workers in these industries suffer from the constant threat of unemployment (Kwong and Lum 1988). This may mean that such women have little or no choice but to accept unsafe work that requires that they suffer illegal conditions.

Patriarchal constraints on women's work and family roles also compose barriers to more mainstream employment. In traditional families, husbands often require that wives and daughters engage in paid employment to help support the family (Rosen 1987). In addition, some informants report that, among traditional Chinese families, husbands may require that women have no contact with men who are not relatives or who are outside of the ethnic community (Chow 1992). For these and other reasons, my analysis of the data that Zhou (1992) reported from a survey of over four hundred Chinatown women workers finds that their *average* wage was below the legal minimum.

When women are mothers, the decision to work is often materially and emotionally difficult. In a 1979 study of women workers in San Francisco's Chinatown, Loo and Ong (1987) found that three-quarters of working mothers had sole responsibility for household chores. One result of this double burden of paid work and household and child care work is homework—work done at home and paid at piece rates. This work can be extremely exploitative, as it is seldom steady and employees can be pressured to work very long hours in bad conditions. For immigrant women employed in apparel sweatshops, the competition of homeworkers forces wages down; appeals for better pay can be met with threats that their work can be given to homeworkers (for whom the manufacturer incurs no overhead costs).

Another result of the double burden of economic responsibility and traditionally defined motherhood roles is a willingness to accept work and workplaces that make allowances for them. One report of New York's Chinatown operators indicated that their employers would allow them to break in mid-afternoon to pick their children up from school; they would then return and work late. Other informants indicated that employers would let little children accompany their mothers to the workshop (Chow 1992).

The ability to mobilize workers and to obtain their loyalty while they have very little choice gives the entrepreneur a relative advantage in the cutthroat world of subcontracting: he can function at a very low wage level.

These descriptions of the way immigrants and entrepreneurs meet in the apparel industry point to the thesis that *immigration is the key process, the dynamic requisite, for sweatshops in otherwise more affluent economies.* The presumption is the existence of a large pool of women immigrants available for work. Most anecdotal stories about sweatshops populate them with immigrants; studies of restaurant and apparel employment in New York show that, at the low end of *legal* employment in these fields, immigrant labor predominates. The same is true for Los Angeles. Thus, in favor of the immigration hypothesis is the presumptively accurate generalization that sweatshops are populated by immigrant minorities.

Critique of the Immigrant Thesis

There are problems with the labor supply thesis, however. One of these has to do with the advantages of co-ethnicity. When employers and employees are of the same ethnic background, the ethnic enclave or ethnic entrepreneur model suggests that the business owner is using his or her language skills and cultural familiarity to get access to a labor force that others could not mobilize. This allows the co-ethnic employer to hire at a lower wage or in environmental conditions that are less compliant with legal standards. The co-ethnic, who may be a distant relative but in any case is no distant stranger, is harder to oppose in a class-conscious way than a foreigner with whom one feels literally to have nothing in common.[7]

The co-ethnic model of labor mobilization/exploitation is apparently accurate in New York's Chinatown and in other locations where Chinese contractors hire Chinese immigrants. When Korean contractors hire Koreans, as in Dallas, or when Central American or Puerto Rican owners run shops with other Central American or Caribbean workers, other versions of the model are operative. For example, a Boston shop that later closed for persistent safety violations was owned by a Vietnamese immigrant and employed Vietnamese women as operators (Mallia 1997, 1 et seq.; Crittendon 1997, 7).

However, in large sections of the sweatshop world of cutting and sewing the contemporary reality is that people from some immigrant groups exploit people from other immigrant groups, including but not at all restricted to their own. The most frequent pairing of employers and employees in the Los Angeles fashion district is Korean owners and Mexican workers—this happens in about 40 percent of all shops (Bonacich and Appelbaum 2000). The ethnic entrepreneur thesis makes the immigrant sweatshop operator a hero of the Joseph Schumpeter saga of "creative destruction."[8] There is an alternative to this view, one that captures the gritty reality of little shops in grimy ghettos. In that alternative, one sees an immigrant petty bourgeois, striving to be a business owner, squeezed by price competition with other contractors, but without any leverage over the big gorillas of the retailers or brand name merchandisers. Immigrant entrepreneurs step into the niche because potential owners with more choices don't want the risky and ethically hazardous business.

Another problem with the immigrant labor supply thesis is historical—it does not distinguish between those periods in which vulnerable workers are paid low but *legal* wages and those periods in which their employment is below even the legal level. The labor supply thesis does not inquire as to why low wages become conditions that sink below the moral standards of the time. For the apparel industry, *the immigrant thesis is a simple female labor supply thesis.*[9]

With so many entrants to the labor force in a handful of big cities, there is ample labor at the low end of the labor market. Language and skill deficiencies and traditional patriarchal culture combine to create a huge reservoir of women workers for ethnic or other entrepreneurs.

The Global Capital Explanation

The alternative explanation—global capitalism—incorporates but supersedes the immigrant explanation. In this view, immigrant women, as particularly vulnerable participants in the labor market, find sweatshop jobs among the few they can get. However, the pressures that generate the low wages and substandard health and safety conditions that violate the law are located in the neoliberal trade regime and capital mobility of the recent global capitalist era (see Ross and Trachte 1990; Sassen 1988; Loucky et al. 1994).

The immigrant labor explanation focuses on the options of (women) *workers* and their decisions to accept the available work. It describes the pressures on these workers as opportunities for entrepreneurs. By contrast, the global capital approach examines the pressures on *entrepreneurs* and sees these pressures as stemming (largely) from economic globalization. This approach seeks to explain why the industry now offers so many jobs in sweatshops as opposed to work in firms where labor and health and safety regulations are sustained. Basically, this view of the problem asserts the primacy of the new global competition over immigrant labor supply as a source of the sweatshop conditions of the last twenty years.

Testing Competing Theories

Clearly, a fundamental difficulty of testing theories about causes of an illegal phenomenon is the absence of reliable data. If there were reliable annual data about the number of sweatshop employees, for example, powerful statistical techniques could use a variety of standard quantitative data as potential predictors of the number of sweatshop workers: immigration and imports would be among them, and their relative weight could be compared in an ordinary regression procedure. Absent such a procedure, problems grow, for it is clear that the timing of the new sweatshops coincides with the timing of the new immigration, which also coincides roughly with the increase in imports. Testing these claims requires a new empirical or logical procedure.

The issue can be explored because there is a period of high immigration and low imports. This case is framed by the interesting technical status of the Puerto Rican migration to the United States. As citizens of the Commonwealth of Puerto Rico, Puerto Rican people are citizens of the United States, so they are not recorded as immigrants when they migrate, for example, to New York City. Thus, conditions of high immigration and low competition are met in the United States in the period before 1965, a period in which there was extensive immigration to New York City from Puerto Rico. As discussed in chapter 1, there was very little evidence of sweatshops during this period. As shown in table 13, between 1940 and 1960, New York's Puerto Rican population grew dramatically, from 61,000 to 612,000.

Like more recent immigrant groups, Puerto Ricans were not fluent in English. They typically were poor and worked at the margins of the mainstream economy. Puerto Rican women, as generations of immigrants before and after them, became a mainstay of the New York City apparel industry. Table 14 shows the extremely high poverty rates of Puerto Ricans in New York in 1960 (51 percent) and selected other data.

What these two tables indicate is that Puerto Rican New Yorkers of the 1950s and 1960s were good fits to the model of today's Dominican or other migrants who populate the sewing sweatshops of New York (cf. Pessar 1987). They were poor and numerous; their community had high rates of unemployment; and they faced language and educational barriers, not to mention discrimination, in the labor force. Furthermore, Puerto Rican

TABLE 13. Puerto Rican Population of New York City, 1940–60

	Puerto Rican Born Population of New York City
1940	61,463
1950	187,420 (245,880)[a]
1960	612,574

Source: Puerto Rican Forum 1964. U.S. Census Bureau 1961, p. 233, tables P-1, P-4, P-5.

[a]The number in parentheses includes those born in New York City of Puerto Rican parents.

women had a strong ethnic concentration in the New York apparel industry of the 1950s and 1960s: some economists have asserted that their low-wage labor "saved" the industry in a period in which it was experiencing rapid geographic losses (Rodriguez 1979). From the ethnic enclave perspective, then, we should expect that sweatshops would have flourished during this period.

Puerto Ricans in the Garment Industry: Sweatshop Conditions?

In the context of the logical test ascertaining whether sweatshop conditions existed in the Puerto Rican garment industry, the history of Puerto Rican women in New York is highly relevant. In chapter 1 our investigations of the "new sweatshops" showed that journalists, scholars, and government investigators believe that sweatshops had more or less disappeared during the 1950s and 1960s as a result of labor legislation and union strength.[10] In chapter 4 we noted the views of Altagracia Ortiz, Herbert Hill, and Dan Wakefield, who dissented from this interpretation of this period in New York. A small hint from Wakefield's discussion allowed an estimate of a few hundred to a few thousand sweatshop workers for the late 1950s, a number insignificant by the standards of today's collapse of labor standards in the industry.

The presence of de facto immigrants in an economic context *without extensive foreign competition* did not lead to the growth of sweatshops in

TABLE 14. Poverty Rates and Social Indicators for Population Groups in New York City, circa 1960

	Percentage in Poverty, 1959	Percentage Employed as Operatives (female), 1960	Percentage Unemployed, 1960	Percentage > 25 Years Old with < 4 Years High School, 1960
Puerto Ricans	51.2	69.7	9.9	87.0
Non-whites	42.9	25.9	6.9	68.8
Other whites	13.2	15.8	4.3	59.9

Source: Puerto Rican Forum 1964; U.S. Census Bureau 1961, tables P-1, P-4, P-5.

the 1950s. While it is true that the economy was growing more rapidly in the 1950s than it did in the 1980–90 period (over 4 percent annually as distinct from 3 percent), nevertheless, the New York industry was under intense price competition to move out and was shrinking; and Puerto Rican unemployment rates were around 10 percent (see table 14). Growth was not creating a tight labor market in the garment industry that strongly favored the new Puerto Rican migrants. A simple contrast of growth rates does not explain the difference in labor conditions in the two periods.

However, increased low-wage competition from exporting countries, in the presence of exploitable workers in the United States, did generate the economic pressures on ethnic entrepreneurs that fueled the development of sweatshops in the late 1970s and 1980s. The immigrant thesis, a simple labor supply thesis about sweatshops, falls short in the context of the experience of Puerto Ricans in New York City.

Sweatshops and Citizen Status

The logical test of the immigrant issue using the Puerto Rican presence in the garment industry has a weakness of its own. Though American citizens, Puerto Ricans could be and were discriminated against because of their language or color. However, they could not be deported. By contrast, many of today's immigrants are undocumented. In 2003, the former Immigration and Naturalization Service (INS), now the Bureau of Citizenship and Immigration Services (BCIS), estimated that 7 million undocumented workers resided in the United States, over two-thirds of whom were from Mexico (U.S. INS 2003, 16–17). Notoriously, the immigration reforms of 1986, which made it illegal for an employer to hire an undocumented worker, have made the INS the perfect union buster. For example, when an undocumented worker approaches an employer for a job, the employer will instruct the worker on how to procure the proper identifications—or will knowingly fail to ask for them. Should that worker then begin to speak up for her rights or seem to be interested in a union, the employer has many strategic resources. He can simply call "*la migra*," as the INS is called in Spanish street slang, and "drop a dime" on the worker. Alternatively, the employer can fire the worker with little fear that he or she will complain.

The large pool of workers with few rights makes their individual employment vulnerability all the greater; this pool of workers without effective rights acts as well to weigh down labor standards for all immigrants.[11] In this regard, the immigration thesis is probably relevant to the decline of labor standards in the apparel industry—for workers are in practice often bereft of citizen rights.

At least one body of research supports the view that large-scale undocumented immigration reduces wages in the low-wage labor market. In a review of literature and a report on a modeling study, researchers at UCLA concluded that continuation of the current policies (NAFTA-based trade and restrictive immigration laws) would lead to more economic growth in both countries and additions to higher income groups' purchasing power. The study concluded, however, that these policies would also reduce wages of legal low-wage workers and would increase inequality among low- and high-wage workers in both the United States and Mexico (Hinojosa Ojeda 2001). Notably, the conclusions of Hinojosa Ojeda and his colleagues incorporated U.S. DOL findings about the effects of the 1986 immigration reforms that legalized many Mexican (and other) undocumented workers. Those findings showed that, from the time the workers first got jobs while they were undocumented to the week before they applied for legalization, their hourly wages were flat or declining. From application in 1987 to 1992, however, their wages rose 18 percent—while other U.S. workers' wages rose only 15 percent in that period. The conclusion was that their illegal status had depressed their earnings.

Before concluding that illegal immigration has now proven to be the decisive, necessary, and sufficient cause of sweatshops, one last qualification is necessary. Many sweatshop workers are legal. Most, but not all, Chinese sweatshop workers are legal entrants to the United States; many Central Americans are too. The famous Nancy Penaloza, who spoke so poignantly about sweatshop conditions in Washington in 1996, was a legal immigrant from El Salvador. When she returned to her shop in

Manhattan, the one that failed to pay her a minimum wage and worked her without respite, some of her sisters from El Salvador were deported—but not Nancy.

Immigration per se is not the key to the new sweatshops. The undocumented status of many workers does leave them without important protections in a time of great pressure on the low-wage labor market. Yet, even without their illegal status, that pressure would depress—and has already depressed—their wages and conditions. In the first half of the twentieth century the immigrant (and migrant) workers who staffed the apparel industry created institutions to protect and advance their interests—unions. In the era of the new sweatshops the loss of union protection at home and the weakness and absence of unions abroad have left garment workers vulnerable to the naked forces of the market.

The next chapter examines union decline and more of its consequences.

9 Union Busting and the Global Runaway Shop

If the commandment that instructs people to observe a day of rest for the Sabbath is the first labor law, employers' desire to evade organized workers is probably about as old. In our times, modern capitalism has, after all, at least an aspect of a brutally simple strategic game. The employer wants more work for less cost; the worker wants more pay, easier work, and safe and dignified conditions. A body of workers effectively and collectively able to bargain with their employer is not likely to tolerate low, no less illegal, wages; very long work hours; or unhealthy and dangerous working conditions. To this strategic situation, the players bring different resources.

Workers' main strategic resource is their ability to work—or not to work. Workers may augment the ultimate possibility of the strike, in certain instances, by their ability to mobilize sympathetic opinion from consumers or to use legal constraints (on the employer) that are administered by the state. The employer ultimately has the ability to deny work to the workers but also has a richer set of options.

Geography, Structure, and Union Evasion

Three broad possibilities offer themselves to an employer who does not want to deal with organized workers prepared to advance their interests through collective action. The employer can use all available means to inhibit or reverse union formation and to deter the workers' active use of legally enshrined rights. Alternatively, the employer may go to another location where unions are less likely to appear. The third possibility is one frequently taken in the history of ready-to-wear clothing: restructure the work process so that the direct employers of labor are weak in relation to the owners of the next link up the chain; shift more risk down the links to the direct employers; and insulate oneself from legal, political, and economic responsibility for the workers that one nevertheless causes to be employed. The structure that has resulted from this process is the contractor/subcontractor system. The rise of the new sweatshops is a product of the successful use of all the strategies—antiunion activity, geographic flight, and restructuring.

Early in the twentieth century, the seesaw of advantage between labor and employers in the garment industry pivoted on the same point: the concentration of dense immigrant neighborhoods in big cities. Because of this concentration, a large pool of labor was available to employers: the Lower East Side residential neighborhoods and garment production had a magnetic effect upon one another in New York. One worker—metaphorically "right off the boat"—could replace a discontented operator. There was no law that prohibited firing a worker for union sympathy.

Their immigrant status and the formation of communities of language and residence (Italian and Yiddish) were resources for those workers. Many brought experience and knowledge of the European workers' movements with them. Dense networks of residence, work, and communal organizations facilitated communication. If an employer fired a worker for her union views, she might get another job in the industry (computer blacklists were still in the future) or in another industry in the big city.

Almost from the beginning of unions in men's and women's clothing, employers sought to evade organized workers. In today's environment of global capital mobility, we tend to take for granted the international geography of the search for cheaper labor. The history of the apparel industry shows the multiple dimensions of this mobility—and the way it structures industrial organization.

Union Busting and the Global Runaway Shop

Before the era of the strikes of 1909–10 ("the Uprising of the Twenty Thousand" and "the Great Revolt") there had been a tendency for the relatively new ready-to-wear industry to centralize. Work was flowing from subcontractors and homeworkers toward growing factories. The downturn of 1913–14 subverted the agreements that had emerged from those strikes (the Protocols of Peace) and signaled a flow of work to "outside" contractors—that is, outside of the union agreements in the conventional factories. This was an early moment in the dialectic of union advance and manufacturer decentralization. Gradually, with the waxing and waning of the business cycle and the union's strength, the strategy of union evasion took on both a structural and geographic dimension.

Structurally, advances by the union caused manufacturers to move work out of their own factories and into the hands of contractors (cutting and sewing shops) and submanufacturers (sewing shops). There was a wavelike movement here through the 1950s and beyond: union strength caused industrial decentralization; the union recovered; employers invented new forms of decentralization.

Even in the big Triangle Factory at the time of the 1911 fire, there was a form of decentralization inside the 800–1,000 person workforce. On the main production floor, the ninth, where the sewing machine operators toiled and then died, the historian Leon Stein could find only a handful of listed employees where over 250 actually worked. The listed persons were "contractors," who, in turn, directly hired workers. Stein, in a 1986 interview, called it a *padrone* system.[1] Blanck and Harris, the Triangle owners, attempted the fiction that they were not really the employers of the sewing machine operators in their factory.

During the 1920s gradual though uneven progress in working conditions was made in the New York industry, and it was paralleled elsewhere. In Chicago, for example, the Amalgamated Clothing Workers of American (ACWA—the "Amalgamated"[2]) was able to achieve unemployment payments for workers in the men's clothing industry. In New York, the contracted workweek in women's clothing declined from between fifty-six and sixty hours at the turn of the century, to fifty after the Protocol of Peace, to what Nancy Green (1997) calls a "theoretical" forty hours in 1928. The contracts, however, did not cover as much of the workforce as they had previously. The submanufacturer system was widely used to evade union contracts.

Internal fights, structural decentralization, and then the Depression set both the ILGWU and the Amalgamated back (N. Green 1997, 62). From a World War I peak of 129,000 members, the ILGWU had but 23,800 members in 1931. Then, "the ILG" rebounded from the fierce sectarian, internal struggles and the depths of the Depression with vigorous growth. By 1940 the ILG had 250,000 members (N. Green 1997, 64). War contracts further centralized production and strengthened the union's hand in the industry.

As noted in chapter 4, among the key strategies that controlled the dispersion strategy of the employers was the joint liability contract that Howard says "struck at the heart of the sweatshop system by cutting through the fiction of the contractor as an independent entity" (1997, 155). According to Schlesinger:

> Jobbers would pit contractor and sub-manufacturer against contractor and sub-manufacturer by giving work to the one who bid the lowest, only to discontinue further dealing with him when another contractor or sub-manufacturer came along with an even lower bid, only to discontinue further dealings with him and return to the first or go to another contractor or sub-manufacturer if they made a still lower bid. (1951, 16)

Control by Contract

Working conditions in the industry improved when manufacturers were held, by contract, liable for wages and benefits in the commodity chain below them. The contracts also caused the top-down organizing strategy discussed earlier: manufacturers were obliged to send work only to union contractors. Schlesinger thought that through these contracts the "basis of competition between contractors and submanufacturers rests on their work performance, promptness, skill and integrity, not on their ability to drive down wages and impair working conditions" (Schlesinger 1951, 91).

When Hegel famously said, "The owl of Minerva spreads its wings only with the falling of dusk," he meant that we learn or understand things (the owl of Minerva symbolizes knowledge) as they are about to ebb away. He somewhat less famously prefaced (and explained) his comment by lamenting, "One more word about giving instruction as to what the world ought to be. Philosophy in any case always comes on the scene too late to give it" (Hegel 1942, 12–13).

At the very moment that Schlesinger was reflecting on the components of the union's success in controlling the subversion of working conditions through subcontracting, the industry was in the midst of significant geographic and further structural decentralization. The first movements were eastward—to the far shores of New Jersey and Pennsylvania. The hop to New Jersey stayed within a short truck drive of the fashion center but out from under the close observation of Manhattan's union business agents. The second jump to small towns in Pennsylvania took advantage of rural women attempting to shore up family purchasing power in the metropolitan age. As the 1950s wore on, job loss in New York City's garment industry was barely balanced by gains elsewhere in the metropolitan region (N. Green 1997, 69–70). Barely holding on, however, was a signal of later decline. The industry was moving south and west.

Flight

The Los Angeles area was among the key growth centers of the clothing industry from the 1950s onward. Figure 11 shows the steady rise of employment in the Los Angeles apparel industry since 1972 and the plummeting employment in New York. Although the ILGWU had made some progress in Los Angeles in the 1940s, it did not maintain that momentum (Laslett and Tyler 1989). The generally antiunion atmosphere of the region is particularly strong among garment industry employers (Ellis 1997b). By 2001 Los Angeles had grown to a garment employment center of about 100,000, with no significant union contracts among clothing producers.[3] A mid-1990s estimate of Los Angeles apparel union membership was in the hundreds. In 2001 New York employment had shrunk to about 50,000 (from a postwar high of 354,000). Estimated New York union membership, Ellis reported in the mid-1990s, was roughly half of the industry (Ellis 1997b).

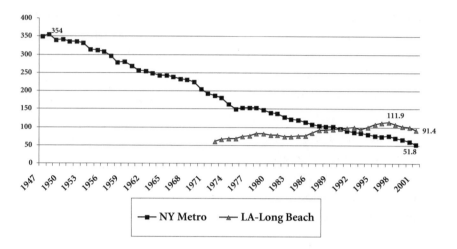

Fig. 11. Evading the union: Apparel employment (in thousands) in the New York and Los Angeles areas, 1947–2001

The well-known hatred of unions by the garment makers was one large part of the exodus from New York's garment center. Other reasons were similar to those that chased manufacturing from central cities in the same long generation that had weakened the apparel unions—high rents in central cities and congested streets unsympathetic to trucks. Los Angeles was a package that helped with these—its old office district offered rents lower than Manhattan, and its lower density was more friendly to trucks. In addition, Los Angeles had a weaker union tradition and a large pool of vulnerable—illegal—immigrants.

The apparel industry also moved to geographies even more hostile to workers' rights than California. The industry dispersed to many of the places to which the textile industry had migrated: the union-hostile Southeast and Southwest, where minority workers—Latinos and African-American workers—were available and relatively disempowered. Between the early 1970s and the 1980s, for example, North Carolina ranked among the very lowest of all the states in manufacturing wages and union density, and it rose from 6 percent to 8 percent of national apparel employment.

Union Decline in the Nation

The story of the apparel unions is part of the story of organized labor in the United States—an early, noble, and ignoble part of that story. Many of the demographic and political factors that supported union growth in general aided the apparel unions; when these supports eroded, so did the ability of the unions to represent and protect apparel workers. The dispersion of worker communities—first by subway (N. Green 1992) and then by automobile—disrupted the communal basis of worker support and communication.

At least one school of thought has argued that the consumer-oriented culture of the late twentieth century subverted a "culture of solidarity" and distracted contemporary workers through the atomized and solitary practice of TV watching (Fantasia 1988).[4] The argument that social theorists make is that the stay-at-home TV watcher does not participate in community- and job-related voluntary activity—does not learn about or actively discuss public affairs in a social, peer-like give-and-take setting but, rather, in a passive armchair, condensed form. In addition, the advertising messages that bombard the mass media watcher constantly emphasize individual consumption rather than communal participation. The result saps the ability of workers (and other citizens) to engage in collective action to attain group goals.

In accounting for the general decline of union membership, at least as powerful as the sociological factors that may have weakened community connectedness have been geographic shifts, legal and political assaults, and the combination of these with ever more resolute employer determination.

The geographic shifts are similar to those that saw the apparel industry migrate from New York to California and to the Southeast. Employment has flowed to places with lower union density and to branches of industry where unions have had less of a base. The deindustrialization of the United States has been particularly important in union decline. The very jobs that have migrated abroad have been in industries with higher rates of unionization.

Right-to-Work Laws and the Taft-Hartley Act

Part of the internal shift in the geography of American industry has involved a legal difference among the states. In 1947 Congress amended the NLRA (known as the Wagner Act) with a series of provisions frankly aimed at weakening the labor movement. They were successful. Known as the Taft-Hartley Act, these provisions of labor law include prominently an option for states to outlaw the union shop. These are known as "right-to-work" laws. Briefly, the union shop is an agreement between workers represented by a union and their employer stating that people hired into the collective bargaining unit must join the union.[5] Because normal turnover can bring a whole new (nonunion) cohort into a shop that has had a union majority, states that ban union shop agreements—"right-to-work" states—have lower average union rates than the nation. In 2000, for example, the average rate of union membership ("union density") of states with right-to-work laws was 60 percent lower than it was in those states without such restrictions on unions (10.5 percent compared to 16.8 percent) (calculated from U.S. Census Bureau 2001d, table 639). In addition to reinforcing the antiunion cultures of many southern states, the Taft-Hartley Act weakened unions by restricting their ability to use boycotts and strikes to bring employers to the bargaining table.[6]

Even with this change in direction of national policy, unions maintained their stature for a few years after the passage of Taft-Hartley. The high tide of union membership (as a proportion of the private labor force) occurred in 1953. In that year, 35.7 percent of the private workforce were members of unions and the union density of manufacturing was even higher (Labor Research Associates 2001). Figure 12 records the alarming story of the near destruction of trade union strength in the private workplace. Over time, the law—as well as the accumulated case-by-case interpretation of the law—turned against unions. Now with only 9 percent of the private workforce, aggregate union strength is but a memory of the past. In manufacturing, union density has gone from a weak 28 percent in 1983 to a paltry 15 percent in 2000 (U.S. Census Bureau 2001d, table 639). Knowledgeable observers consider the rights to form a union and to bargain collectively among those that are deemed "core labor

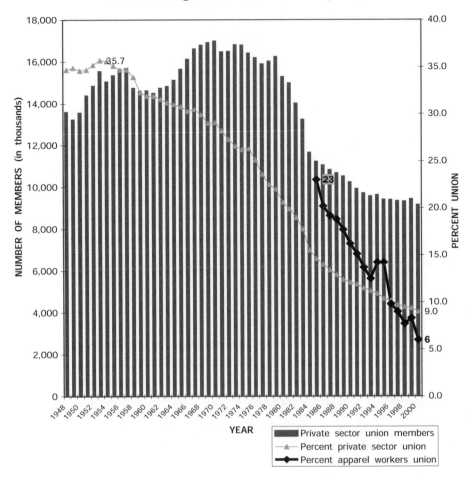

Union Busting and the Global Runaway Shop

Fig. 12. Private sector union membership in the United States, 1948–2000

rights" and human rights, by international consensus, to be in serious jeopardy in the United States.

Rothstein (1997b) cites the 1981 decision by President Ronald Reagan, when he simply replaced all the striking air controllers, as the decisive end of the effective strike—this despite what Rothstein says was a unique event when the teamsters won a highly publicized strike at UPS in 1997. The widespread use of replacement workers removes, he says, the strike from labor's strategic resource. Even if a bit overstated, Rothstein mentions numerous other features of law and practice that now restrict union strength. These include restrictions on picketing and the employer's ability to call "captive meetings" to intimidate workers into opposing union drives.

Rolling Back Labor Rights

In addition to defects in the U.S. legal framework, Theodore St. Antoine, dean of the University of Michigan Law School and president of the National Academy of Arbitrators, notes that "[t]he intensity of opposition to unionization which is exhibited by American employers has no parallel in the western industrial world" (cited in Compa 2000). Anti-union sentiment leads employers flagrantly and frequently to break the law that nominally establishes union rights. Compa notes that the NLRB devoted 40 percent of its work to unfair labor practices in 1948 and 80 percent of it in 1998 (Compa 2000, chapter 5, n. 128). He cites research that shows that thousands of workers are fired annually for exercising union rights of association. The NLRB between 1992 and 1997 awarded 125,000 workers back pay—186,000 between 1990 and 1998. Charles Morris concluded that "a substantial number of employers involved in union organizational campaigns deliberately use employment discrimination against employees as a device to remove union activists and thereby inject an element of fear in the process of selecting or rejecting union representation" (Compa 2000, citing Morris 1998, 331).

The combination of globalization and employer lawlessness produces a particular form of intimidation: the threat to close or move a work site if employees choose union representation. More than half of all employers whose facilities are engaged in a collective bargaining campaign threaten to close or move a work site; over two-thirds make the threat "in mobile industries such as manufacturing, communications, and wholesale distribution":

> not only are threats of plant closing an extremely pervasive part of employer campaigns, they are also very effective. The election win rate associated with campaigns where the employer made plant closing threats is, at 38 percent, significantly lower than the 51 percent win rate found in units where no threats

occurred. Win rates were lowest, averaging only 32 percent, in campaigns with threats in mobile industries such as manufacturing, communications, and wholesale distribution where the threats are more credible. In contrast, threats had much less of an impact in less mobile industries such as health care or passenger transportation, where win rates, even in campaigns with threats, averaged close to 60 percent. (Bronfenbrenner 2000, v–vi)

The erosion of union rights and the consequent decline of union membership relative to the size of the economy have multiplying effects. As union members decrease in visibility, the ability of the labor movement to defend itself politically also declines. One decisive moment was during the administration of Jimmy Carter, when, with a robust agenda of labor law reform, the AFL-CIO and its supporters could not muster the sixty votes needed to close debate and force a vote in the Senate. Similar initiatives were stalled during President Clinton's incumbency.

Indeed, after the Republican victory of 1994 the DOL leadership drew away from its antisweatshop work and engaged in defensive tasks. The DOL's leadership had to defend against the "Contract with America"[7] attack on the prevailing wage rules that oblige the federal government to pay union scale on construction projects. The WHD, headed by Maria Echaveste, also confronted an attempt to weaken the overtime pay provisions of the FLSA (by allowing employers to give compensatory time off for hours worked past the eight hour per day/forty hour per week provisions of the act). In that context, Echaveste could only dimly recall a bill that would hold manufacturers liable for contractor's labor law violations (the "Antisweatshop Bill," or the manufacturers' liability bill—introduced by Representative Clay of Missouri and Senator Kennedy of Massachusetts) (Echaveste 2002).

The apparel workers were harmed more than others by the forces converging to weaken their unions. Employers were moving to nonunion and antiunion political environments; the workers themselves were composed of increasingly vulnerable immigrants; and their industry was decentralizing, splintering really, into about twenty-five thousand small contractor shops. The big store chains dictated prices, and their dictates were based on international calculations pegged to the levels of living and of cost in poor countries, whose workers had even less legal protection than did they. Figure 12 records the sad result: by 2001 only six out of every one hundred apparel workers were members of a union.[8]

The combination of job loss in the apparel industry and the decline in union density has created a crisis for the apparel workers' union, UNITE. UNITE is the result of a 1995 merger between the Amalgamated Clothing and Textile Workers Union (ACTWU)—still known "the Amalgamated"[9]—and the ILGWU. The Amalgamated had been "present at the creation" when its president, Sidney Hillman, was a leader in the founding of the CIO. Even as late as the 1990s, the ACTWU had a reputation as a union that did aggressive organizing. After the merger, UNITE was led by Jay Mazur, who was a successor to a long line of ILGWU presidents. Upon Mazur's retirement many in the labor movement thought that Bruce Raynor, who had been a vice president of the Amalgamated, a veteran of tough campaigns in the South, would take an aggressive organizing strategy and remake a union that had been on the defensive. Subsequent events have shown that even tough guys can get beat up.

From 1998 to 2001, the combined union membership of UNITE (which represented only 6 percent of all apparel workers; it had members in other industrial categories, including textile and laundry workers) fell from 281,000 to 215,000—a drop of almost one-quarter of its membership (Gifford 1998, 2001). When friendly outsiders criticized the union's leadership of the burgeoning student and consumer antisweatshop movement, a union staffer replied, "When the ship is sinking it's hard to do long range planning."

Largely bereft of union representation, apparel workers became much more vulnerable—to the kind of extreme abuse we call sweatshops and also to the steady grind of inadequate though legal pay. We can get some insight into this by examining the situation of sewing machine operators.

The DOL and the Census Bureau cooperate in what may be the most exhaustive, accurate, and ambitious continuing sample survey in the world: the Current Population Survey (CPS). This survey is the source, for example, of the unemployment statistics that are regularly reported in the news media. The CPS produces data that others use to estimate the union density of occupations and industries. Among the occupations for which researchers use the CPS to estimate union membership and wages

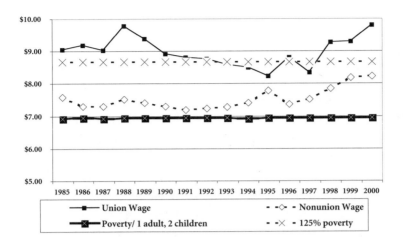

Fig. 13. Sewing machine operators' *official* hourly wages and poverty, 1985–2000 (inflation corrected to year 2000 $). Sources: Calculated from Hirsch and Macpherson 1996–2001; U.S. Census Bureau 2001c.

is sewing machine operators. This category is not restricted to garment sewing machine operators; the garment operators make up most of the category, though, and they earn less than the larger category in those reports that make the distinction. In the period for which data are available (1985–2000), sewing machine operators' union membership has tracked apparel union membership very closely, declining from 23.4 percent to 9.5 percent (Hirsch and Macpherson 2001).

Figure 13 shows the hourly wages of sewing machine operators, union and nonunion, comparing them to the hourly wage required to reach the poverty level for one adult and two children. It shows that nonunion operators—90 percent of all operators—were just above the poverty level until the full employment of the late 1990s gave them, as it did others, a bit of a boost.

At less than ten dollars an hour for the entire period, these data register no marked progress for workers in this occupation and specialty. That union workers earn a small premium is expected and welcome—but, as noted earlier, in this same period the unionized proportion of all operators sank from 23 percent to 9.5 percent.

Lamentably, these grim numbers mask a situation that is worse than it appears to be. Recall the DOL's early 1990s baseline studies of New York, Los Angeles, New Jersey, and San Francisco. Except for the latter, these studies showed that about 60 percent of apparel contractors fail to pay either the minimum wage and/or overtime premiums. This means that widespread employer deception corrupts official earnings data by over-stating it. Figure 13 depicts an occupation of women struggling to make ends meet; the underlying reality is one in which the working poor are stripped of the protections of unions and of the law.

Prof. Edna Bonacich of the University of California at Riverside argues that a signal moment for UNITE came at the transition time when the ILG was joining with ACTWU to became UNITE. Then, in the mid-1990s, the ILG had launched an ambitious campaign to organize Guess? Inc. in Los Angeles. Guess? is a story itself (Bonacich 2002).

The Guess? Campaign

Guess? Inc., the California fashion jeanswear firm, was the creation of the Marciano brothers. Immigrants from France (originally French-Algerian), the Marciano brothers are among the key figures in making denim jeans a matter of high fashion in the United States. Emblemati-cally, their billboard aids depict anorexic models, half-dressed, in sultry black and white. They are never shown working, are often reclining, and frequently look as if sex acts are imminent or recent. Jeans are trans-muted from clothes for miners and cowboys to sexy lay-abouts. The Marcianos were among the creators of a new fashion item—dress jeans for the hip set. Anecdotally, their boutique for jeans and accessories in Boston's Back Bay attracts a higher than Boston average ratio of well-coiffed European and Asian tourists coming to shop the chic Newbury Street for stylish clothes.

Guess? rose to great heights by the 1990s, and the Marcianos became wealthy members of the Los Angeles Jewish community. As distinct from other big-name manufacturers, most of their production—97 percent in 1994—was in the Los Angeles area in a scattering of forty-five to fifty con-tractor shops employing four thousand to five thousand workers (Hornblower 1997). The hip- and gluteal-hugging jeans commanded a premium price—fifty to seventy dollars—but Guess? made headway as more casual and traditional jeans, for example, Levis, lost market share. The Marciano brothers took their firm public, and though the stock did not do as well as they had hoped, they became even more wealthy. By 2002 the three brothers running Guess? Inc. held stock from their company worth more than $115 million (Maurice), $92 million (Paul), and $46 million (Armand). Brother George had parted ways from the other brothers earlier—and had taken over $200 million with him (Behar 1996a; holdings calculated from Guess? Inc. 2002 and stock price on May 10, 2002). Corporate revenue in the fiscal year 2000 was $779.2 million, and net earnings were $16.5 million (Guess? Inc. 2001).

There was, however, another side to the tale. As early as 1992, Guess? had to pay $573,000 in back pay to contractors' workers who had been cheated. Guess? has the distinction of being the first firm against which the WHD of the DOL used the "hot goods" provision of the FLSA. Guess? was the first firm to sign an agreement to "monitor" its own contractors, thus becoming the first member of what Robert Reich and Maria Echaveste would soon call the Trendsetter ("good guy") List (Ramey 1992). Masters of image advertising, the Marcianos agreed to become Secretary Reich's poster boys of the corporate compliance effort. The Marcianos nevertheless continued to work with vendors, now more numerous, who abused their workers (Behar 1996b).

The Marciano brothers were becoming very rich men by garnering a commanding position in a $1 billion market—designer jeans. By elevating the status signature of their product they were able to make sales at price points considerably above their costs—at one point they were earning 20 percent (before taxes) on sales (Behar 1996b; Guess? Inc. 1996).

Competitive pressure—from makers with offshore production—eroded the Guess? position. Calvin Klein surged ahead in market share, charging less than Guess? for the CK brand of fashionably tight denims. Then Tommy Hilfiger and Ralph Lauren came into the market—at the forty-eight-dollar price point, beating Guess?.

Tough-guy style was part of the Marciano culture, dating back to their days of tax evasion and copyright infringement in Paris and the use of favors and money to influence tax and criminal officials in the United States. DOL or not, "One way to boost profits is to keep labor costs very low" (Behar 1996b).

As the DOL attempted to turn up the pressure in southern California, Guess? forced even more contractors to compete for the work. Their own monitor, Connie Meza, told *Fortune* magazine, "Many of the shops were filthy, cramped, overheated. Most of the workers were Latinos like [my]self, but they were afraid to open their mouths" (Behar 1996b). Contractors repeatedly were found using illegal homeworkers, paying below minimum wage, and ignoring overtime rules. Kickback gifts from contractors to Guess? executives were part of the culture that produced seventy-dollar jeans made by women earning under four dollars per hour.

In this context, the ILG decided to target Guess?'s production network in the period leading up to the union merger. Aiming at the cutting shop and warehouse and attempting to make contacts through the network of contractor shops, the ILG began an organizing campaign. The campaign was unique—since the 1960s—since it also involved outreach to students, to nonprofit advocacy organizations, and to LA intellectuals—professors, artists, poets, and writers. In retrospect, some union staff believe the campaign went public too early, calling for support and boycotts before the union had developed sufficiently deep support among the groups of workers. If the Nike brand came to symbolize for a time ruthless exploitation by contractor factories abroad, the ILG/UNITE campaign cast Guess? as the symbol of the exploitation of Latino workers in the United States.

Bonacich (2002) speculates that by 1996, with the union merger formally accomplished but actually still in process, the Guess? campaign was the victim of loss of attention and also of different organizational cultures in the two unions.

Many observers think the former ACTWU (whose principal components were the older men's clothing union and the textile workers' union) had a more aggressive organizing style and was more willing to confront employers. The ACTWU was more active in the South, to which its textile base had moved in the course of the twentieth century. By contrast, the ILG was widely believed to have depended too heavily on the top-down strategy of getting manufacturers (brand names or jobbers) to pick union contractors—and to have lost the ability to aggressively organize new shops. Among the tasks of the merger was to successfully merge the two organizations, and outsiders concerned with the sweatshop issue hoped that ACTWU's aggressiveness would reinvigorate organizing in the women's clothing industry. UNITE did take on new tasks—but not in time to make the Guess? campaign a success.

The DOL continued to find violations at Guess? contractor shops, and eventually Guess? was taken off the Trendsetter List. UNITE's campaign led to unfair labor practices charges, and Guess? was under scrutiny by the NLRB (Ellis 1996, 1997a; Behar 1996a). Yet the union was not succeeding in developing enough support among the workers to make incursions on the firm's day-to-day functioning. Then, in January 1997, came the key and negative turning point.

Guess? faced a successful campaign by Los Angeles movement support-ers—the intellectuals mentioned earlier, politicians, and groups of stu-dents—to "dirty up" their otherwise hip image. Their supply chain was the object of attention by a DOL that had incurred the wrath of labor unions over NAFTA and in this instance was (in compensation?) acting as an ally. A union inspired-boycott threat, among hip young adults whose hips they yearned most to cover, was beginning, fueled by the stream of negative news from Los Angeles. Guess? did what rational investors have been doing for a generation: they ran.

In January 1997 Guess? announced they were moving 40 percent of their production contracts to Mexico (Hornblower 1997). Union strate-gists had thought this might occur, but they had hoped that, in the face of a strike or an organizing campaign, the NLRB would find the move an unfair labor practice. No strike was ever organized; the devolution to a legal strategy left the mobilized campus, intellectual, and worker con-stituencies without a role. The campaign bled away; the union had sunk millions into it; it had lost (Bonacich 2002).

Sometime at the end of the Guess? campaign, those involved in research and the organizing of labor abuse among U.S. garment workers sensed a sea change in UNITE. It is hard for outsiders to isolate the moment of decision. Perhaps within the leadership of the union it would also be hard to say when their future course became clear. By 2000, though, it was apparent that UNITE no longer thought it could organize new immigrant workers at sewing contractors. It had a base of contracts in New York, where employment was plummeting, but it was frozen out of the clothing industry in LA. UNITE decided to move on.

By 2001 observers noted that UNITE was doing hardly any new organizing in clothing shops. The union's strategic focus for new organizing seemed to be on uniforms, laundries, and warehouses. The uniform and laundry segments of the industry are related. Uniform "manufacturers" are often renters and launderers of uniforms. Much to UNITE's interest, large consumer groups include unionized municipal personnel, such as police, firefighters, and hospital employees.

So UNITE has begun, somewhat erratically, to lead campaigns for local ordinances to make sweat-free or union label uniform purchases. How to guarantee this is not so easy, though many city councils—about thirty—seem quite willing to vote for the aspiration.

In the meantime, in an industry where workers once earned near the average for manufacturing workers, wages have fallen to about 55 percent of the average manufacturing wage. Barely above the official poverty line, wages of today's sewing machine operators, 90 percent of them bereft of union protection, fall below the line of 125 percent of official poverty—considered by many the borderline of decency (see fig. 13). Their union sisters manage to tiptoe above that line under the full employment conditions of the turn of the century. The new century, ushered in with a recession, may not be so kind.

In an interview about the DOL's struggles against sweatshops, Maria Echaveste, who headed the WHD during Robert Reich's period as the head of the DOL, explained their emphasis on getting firms to monitor their own contractors, including those overseas: "If we had problems convincing our Congress to increase spending on investigators and staff, imagine what depending on law enforcement would be like in a poor country like Bangladesh" (Echaveste 2002). Assume, nevertheless, a staff relatively as large as Eisenhower's—when the earlier estimate showed there might be 2,700 Wage and Hour investigators instead of the current 940. Under the pressure of low-wage imports, with a vulnerable labor force abundantly available, it is hard to imagine sole dependence on law enforcement as an adequate solution to labor abuse in the domestic economy.

On the other hand, every clothing workplace has workers in it—individuals who know *exactly* what their conditions are. Any given group of workers does not always know what its rights are or what others who have had more success in bargaining with employers have experienced. A union, not even at its best, merely when it is ordinary, is a classroom for workers. It teaches them about those things that their peers elsewhere experience and thus what they can aspire to; it teaches, de facto, about empowerment. When just a little better than ordinary, a union teaches members to be their own inspectors. Grievance committee persons learn about safety; bargaining committee members learn about productivity issues. Hidden from the view of our hyper-credentialed society, where degrees are mistaken for competencies, is the concrete process by which people acquire the means to defend their interests in an industrial system in which they are considered mere inputs. There is no greater school of self-defense than a democratic union.

Workers who made women's clothing produced it, in 1999, at 83 percent of the unit cost of 1988 (calculated from Bureau of Labor Statistics 2001b). Their output per hour was 72 percent greater in 1999 than it was in 1990 (calculated from Bureau of Labor Statistics 2004b). On average, though, apparel workers brought home less than 4 percent more in real purchasing power from 1988 to 2000. In the context of an industry rocked by globalization and left without protection of law enforcement, even union workers only increased their hourly wage by three cents an hour from 1988 to 2000. When the history of these times is written, the destruction of union power in the apparel industry will be recorded as one of the reasons why the beginning of the twenty-first century looked a lot like the beginning of the twentieth.

10 Framing Immigrants, Humiliating Big Shots

Mass Media and the Sweatshop Issue

Introduction

The reemergence of sweatshops in the American apparel industry was—eventually—accompanied by high-profile mass media coverage of the extreme exploitation of workers. The main subjects of print media stories have been contractors for American firms abroad. Domestic sweatshop reporting has also had an "externalizing" tendency by focusing on the immigrant status of the exploited workers. Reporting of the sweatshop issue was measurably increased by the embarrassment of Kathie Lee Gifford in 1996, and there are regular story cycles in which attention is fitfully focused on celebrity apparel endorsers. Thematically similar to the generic story line "Celebrity X Clothing Found Made by Children (or Slaves or Poisoned Workers)" is the "Big Company Caught Again" angle such as this: "Nike Workers Report Abuse by Supervisors" (Chandrasekaran 2001).[1]

The aggressive consumer, and latterly, student movement (Greenhouse 1999; Zernike 1999; Krupa 1999; Featherstone 2002) were also the subjects

Labor law violator shop (for minimum wage and nonpayment violations) in Manhattan garment district. Photographer: Robert J. S. Ross.

of a high-volume print reportage. Among the themes of student anti-sweatshop reporting has been the awakening of students "out of apathy" and the rebirth of idealism—a theme very familiar to students of the 1960s movements. After the 1999 Seattle demonstrations against the World Trade Organization (WTO), which were accompanied by some street vandalism, one might have expected the major themes of media coverage to be the absence or presence of violence. This was the track of reportage on the anti–Vietnam War movement as it developed on the New Left: from idealistic antipoverty and civil rights campaigners to violent subversive allies of the enemy (Gitlin 1980). Quantitative results do not sustain the expectation that the print media took this turn on the post–Seattle sweatshop campaigners. Instead, on the editorial pages of leading newspapers, the critique of the movement for global justice has focused on the allegedly "protectionist" nature of its appeal and the provocative proposition that the antisweatshop campaign was harmful to poor people around the world.

This chapter discusses these media frames—the external frames (foreign and immigrant workers); the celebrity frame; and the "movement as stupid" frame—and it will reflect on their possible and probable consequences. The examination of the immigrant-ethnic frame reports a study of college students drawn from four campuses. The analysis begins with an overview of newspaper coverage of the sweatshop issue in the 1990s and the beginning of this decade.

Sweatshops as a Media Issue since 1990

As early as 1979 the first major journalistic exposé of the new sweatshops had been published in *New York* magazine (Buck 1979); NBC and CBS broadcast brief reports in 1980 and 1981, respectively. The earliest academic discussion began around 1983 (Weingarten 1981; Ross and Trachte 1983; Wong 1983). A courageous New York state senator, Franz Leichter, pioneered investigations (Leichter 1982; Leichter, von Nostitz, and Gonzalez 1981). By 1990 the level of reporting on the issue was still quite low—although the crisis was already devastating membership of the apparel workers' unions and labor standards in the apparel industry.

As we have seen, at the tail end of the Bush administration in 1992, DOL professional staff began to consider a new set of tools to obtain compliance with the FLSA (see chapter 7). Shortly thereafter, when Robert Reich became secretary of labor under President Clinton, he and his senior staff decided to make a concerted effort against sweatshops in the apparel industry. This partly explains the coverage of the issue in the years from 1992 to 1995. On the one hand, the sweatshop story is usually a feature rather than an event-reporting story, and it is about or refers to conditions elsewhere—for example, Bob Herbert's *New York Times* (1994) article of December 18, 1994, on a report that analyzes the 1993 fire in a Thai garment factory, which killed more workers (188) than the infamous Triangle fire.

In the early period, 1992–94, when a story was about U.S. conditions, it concerned enforcement and was driven by events about which the newspapers learned through the activity of government press relations—for example, the *Houston Chronicle*'s article on October 27, 1994—"Sweatshops to Pay Workers Millions Owed in Back Wages"—which reported on DOL enforcement actions (Smith 1994).

Despite Reich's efforts, though, the "sweatshop story," like many other stories concerned with the day-to-day conditions of working Americans, was not yet prime time. In 1993 and 1994 the *New York Times* ran 15 and then 9 stories with the word *sweatshop* in the headline or lead; the *Los Angeles Times* mentioned the word *sweatshop* in 124 stories in that period.[2]

Two events propelled the issue into mainstream view: the August 1995 El Monte case and the May 1996 Kathie Lee Gifford affair. Press coverage focused heavily on these events. But they are the products of different dynamics. The El Monte coverage was a result of event coverage and governmental press releases. Charles Kernaghan and his NLC created the Gifford affair—the coverage, though it at first surprised Kernaghan, was a product of movement enterprise.

The El Monte slave labor case had a tremendous impact on coverage nationally and internationally, but it was most sharp in Los Angeles—where stories tripled. The Gifford affair had little impact on the quantity of stories in the *Los Angeles Times,* but it continued to produce additional coverage in the *New York Times.* It also made an impact on TV. CBS, for example, broadcast items about sweatshops forty-four times in the thirteen years from 1990 through 2002; fourteen of these were in the seven months after Kathie Lee first cried on her television show.

Shortly after the 1996 events the student movement against sweatshop conditions in the production of campus logo clothing came into existence, and the coalition against corporate globalization in Seattle in 1999 generated a large volume of news coverage. The 1999 and 2000 story counts reflect the campus sit-ins and agitation of the period. The level of press, however, did not reach that inspired by El Monte and Kathie Lee.

Figure 14 shows the story count data during the period 1990–2002. In 2001 and 2002, the sweatshop issue was "chased off" the front page by the post–September 11 wars on terrorism and Iraq. At a deeper level, however, we can discern the structure of the news coverage—one that continues.

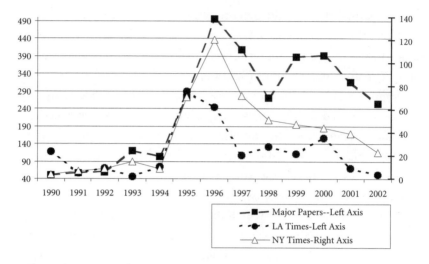

Slaves to Fashion

Fig. 14. Story counts for major newspapers, the *Los Angeles Times*, and the *New York Times*, 1990–2002

Media Frames and Frame Effects: What Is at Stake

A media frame is the context chosen by a writer or producer that explicitly or implicitly directs attention to causes of the subject matter or attributions of moral or empirical responsibility. A story frame may call special attention to certain characteristics of actors or environments, implying that they are key to understanding the story. Not all frames, or even most, are intentional. Editors always ask reporters, "what's the story?"—meaning what is the "angle" or "spin" that at once makes a set of facts both novel—so that it is "news" and not merely a rehash of something familiar—and familiar enough so that readers or viewers are known to be interested in it (see, by comparison, Gitlin 1980). Frames, therefore, appear to editors and writers as "natural" aspects of news judgment.

Gamson and Modigliani define a news frame as a "central organizing idea or story line that provides meaning to an unfolding strip of events, weaving a connection among them. The frame suggests what the contro- versy is about, the essence of the issue" (1987, 143). Entman goes further, claiming that a frame "promote[s] a particular problem definition, causal interpretation, moral evaluation, and/or treatment recommendation for the item described" (1993, 52).

Changes in the way publics or officials see events, and the policy pref- erences they have as a result, are called "framing effects." There have been many studies that document framing effects (Iyengar 1991, 11; Yows 1994; Capella and Jamieson 1996; Nelson, Clawson, and Oxley 1997; Domke, Shah, and Wackman 1998).[3]

Iyengar's study *Is Anyone Responsible?* (1991), for example, examines framing in broadcast news stories. Iyengar observed that stories about poverty were framed as an individual's problem rather than a social prob- lem affected by government policies or corporate business. Crime was the problem of inner cities or, more specifically, minorities rather than some- thing caused by our social system or inequalities between groups; and racial inequality was caused by certain discriminatory individuals rather than by the social structure as a whole. These frames influenced the audi- ence's views on issues of poverty and crime.

Iyengar's work establishes empirically a conceptual claim made by Ross and Staines in 1972. Ross and Staines argue that there is a "politics of definition" in social issues, and these concern the "attribution" structure of a social issue definition: what caused the phenomenon that is defined as a problem. Their major point was that the definition predisposes the pol- icy. For example, Ross and Staines noted, if unemployment is an individ- ual problem of work habits, the logically appropriate policy is not apt to be macroeconomic stimulation—for example, government spending on a jobs program. Similarly, if the problem of sweatshop labor abuses is immigration, the solution is not apt to be change in trade agreements or wages and hours regulatory policy.

Consider the report of a tragic factory fire in Hamlet, North Carolina, on September 3, 1991. The September 4 headline in the *Washington Post* read: "25 Die as Fire Hits N.C. Poultry Plant; Locked Doors Are Said to Add to Toll" (Taylor 1991a). The story continued:

Fire broke out near a deep-fat fryer fueled by natural gas at a chicken-processing plant in this rural community, killing at least 25 people and injuring at least 49 others this morning, authorities said.

Friends, relatives and coworkers of victims at the Imperial Food Products plant said locked doors at the one-story brick and cinderblock building contributed to the death toll. Most of the victims suffered from smoke inhalation, not burns, fire officials reported.

"I don't see how people can lock doors in a plant where you know something like this can happen," said Thomas Brown, 25, whose cousin was flown to a hospital in Durham, about 100 miles north, to be treated for smoke inhalation. (A1)

The twelfth paragraph of this, the first day, story was composed of this sentence: "'You couldn't tell if the bodies were black or white, because everybody was black from the smoke,' [Hamlet Police Lt.] Downer said" (Taylor 1991a, A1). It was not until the second day of the story cycle that readers of the *Washington Post* learned that "Imperial employees are non-union, and most work for near-minimum wages of between $4.90 and $5.60 an hour. Most are black, and an even larger majority are women" (Taylor 1991b, A1). This information came in the twenty-fourth of a thirty-four-paragraph story.

These stories created a context for their readers. In this context the fire caused the tragic death of twenty-one workers; the workers were jeopardized by bad conditions, and their deaths were in some sense caused by a locked back door and, thus, by the negligence of the owners. The race of the workers is not a central part of the story.

The story of the locked exits that contributed to the twenty-one deaths in Hamlet stirs, in any human who recalls the Triangle Factory fire, a heavy-hearted sense of déjà vu. Exploited workers, a locked door, negligent conditions, death by smoke and fire. Do things ever change?

Indeed things do change, some for better and some for worse. The owners of the Triangle Shirtwaist Factory were acquitted of manslaughter; the owner of the Hamlet factory was jailed (*Washington Post* 1992). One thing that did not change in reporting these fires is the relative insignificance of the ethnic or racial attributes of the victims.

The *New York Times* story of March 26, 1911, had the following headline and lead:

Framing Immigrants, Humiliating Big Shots

"141 MEN AND GIRLS DIE IN WAIST FACTORY
FIRE; TRAPPED HIGH UP IN WASHINGTON
PLACE BUILDING; STREET STREWN WITH
BODIES; PILES OF DEAD INSIDE"

Three stories of a ten-floor building at the corner of Greene Street and Washington Place were burned yesterday, and while the fire was going on 141 young men and women at least 125 of them mere girls were burned to death or killed by jumping to the pavement below. (*New York Times* 1911, 1)

In the fifth paragraph of the story, readers were told:

The victims who are now lying at the Morgue waiting for some one to identify them by a tooth or the remains of a burned shoe were mostly girls from 16 to 23 years of age. They were employed at making shirtwaist by the Triangle Waist Company, the principal owners of which are Isaac Harris and Max Blanck. Most of them could barely speak English. Many of them came from Brooklyn. Almost all were the main support of their hard-working families. (1)

In the twenty-sixth paragraph of the story readers were told:

The victims mostly Italians, Russians, Hungarians, and Germans were girls and men who had been employed by the firm of Harris & Blanck, owners of the Triangle Waist Company, after the strike in which the Jewish girls, formerly employed, had been become unionized and had demanded better working conditions. (1)

So, back in 1911 the immigrant character of the victimized workforce was not in the lead paragraph, and when the reader was informed of the ethnicity of the "girls," he or she learns, literally in the same sentence, that employees of the Triangle firm had led the famous strike of the year before.

In these stories the frame is about working conditions and owners' accountability. Consider, by contrast, the headline and lead paragraph of the first-day story in the *Los Angeles Times* on the El Monte slave labor workshop. After the shop was raided at dawn on August 2, 1995, the story ran on August 3.

"WORKERS HELD IN NEAR-SLAVERY,
OFFICIALS SAY"

State and federal agents raided a garment factory in El Monte early Wednesday that allegedly held dozens of Thai immigrants in virtual slavery behind barbed wire for years, forcing them to labor in servitude to supposedly pay off creditors.

The pre-dawn raid by a multi-agency team headed by the California Depart-ment of Industrial Relations discovered more than 60 Thai nationals living and working at a gated apartment complex ringed with barbed wire and spiked fences. The raid exposed conditions that seemed to belong to an earlier era.

Workers told government agents and The Times that they had been held against their will and that they were forced to toil day and night for less than $2 an hour. Some said they were told they must repay the cost of transporting them from Thailand, yet the detention continued after the "debt" was repaid. One worker—who provided only her nickname, "Yat"—said she has not been allowed to leave the complex in the 2 1/2 years she has lived there, even though her debt was repaid long ago. (White 1995, A1)

In three of the first four paragraphs of this story, the *Los Angeles Times* told its readers that the El Monte workers were Thai and were immi-grants. The *San Francisco Chronicle* did not wait for the lead paragraph: its headline was "70 Immigrants Found in Raid on Sweatshop; Thai Workers Tell Horror Stories of Captivity" (Wallace 1995). In second-day coverage, the *Los Angeles Times* ran three stories. One headlined Thais; the other two were framed about Thai immigrants in the first sentence (see *Los Angeles Times*, August 5, 1995).

The reporting of the El Monte case was sensational, but it shaped pub-lic opinion by telling people that the case was about immigrants. Others too have found that the kind and context of information an audience receives helps shape public opinion (Pritchard 1994; Salmon and Moh 1994). Research has shown that slight alteration in the context within which an issue is presented can lead to different impacts on audiences (Capella and Jamieson 1996; Nelson, Clawson, and Oxley 1997; Domke, Shah, and Wackman 1998). The way media attention is focused on events may spark policy decisions by officials (Dopplet 1994, Pritchard 1994).

These ideas suggest the potential impact—the stakes—in framing sweatshops in an immigrant context. The framing of stories on submini-mum working conditions may deflect the attribution of these conditions onto the ethnic or immigrant groups or individuals described rather than onto other factors such as employer greed, industrial structure and power, the trade structure of global capitalism, or the lack of government regulation. This is the distinction Ross and Staines (1972) called "person

"Welcome to El Monte": The site of the slave workshop discovered in 1995. Courtesy of the Smithsonian Institution.

At the rear of the complex is barbed wire to keep the captives in place. Courtesy of the Smithsonian Institution.

blame" versus "system blame," widely used by sociologists in the form of individual versus social attribution.

Simon and Alexander (1993) examined the portrayal of immigrants in newsmagazines since 1880, concluding that it led to attitudes in favor of immigration restriction on the grounds of job displacement and an unwanted addition to the "culture of poverty."

The Immigrant-Ethnic Frame

It is—especially given the media treatment of the issue—"natural" for people to ask whether the workers in American sweatshops are immigrants. Of course, the answer to this question, as we have seen empirically, is *yes*. It seems logical to assume that, if a story on sweatshops is framed in an immigrant context, audience members may blame these apparel conditions on the immigrant status of the workers. For example, a person might reason that, after all, an immigrant has got a hard time anyhow and these conditions are just part of the hard time of adjustment. Or, in a longer time horizon, today's hard time might become a success for an immigrant's granddaughter. In this version, today's exploitation and suffering are mitigated and even justified by tomorrow's decency.

If the implicit causal attribution of a large fraction of sweatshop stories points toward the large labor reserve of immigrant workers, improvement would be logically oriented to immigration restriction, employer sanctions, or similar remedies. By contrast, the policy options less likely to stem from an immigrant-ethnic frame are those aimed at poor labor conditions, the lack of governmental regulation in the apparel industry, exploitive apparel manufacturers, unethical employers, or the problem of import competition from nations with low levels of labor rights.

An immigrant frame print article is one that may talk about the exploitation of workers but mentions immigration early on, either in the title, lead line, or the first paragraph, with this theme most likely continuing throughout the story. An article about sweatshops that does not contain an immigrant frame might, by contrast, discuss poor working conditions in terms of the workers but would not highlight the nationality, ethnicity, or immigrant status of these employees.

Immigrant Frame Incidence

How frequent is the immigrant-ethnic frame? The May 1997–May 1998 time interval is a good candidate for study to answer this question because it fell *after* the extensively covered August 1995 El Monte incident, where the Thai origin of the enslaved workers and their smuggler-captors was a universally noted aspect of almost every story. By mid-year 1997, too, the May 1996 Kathie Lee Gifford story had subsided substantially. By cutting off before the fall of 1998 or the beginning of 1999, this time period also avoided the developing story of the student movement focused on labor standards of collegiate apparel licensees. The Lexis-Nexis database was searched to establish the data in table 15.[4]

TABLE 15. Sweatshop Newspaper Stories, May 5, 1997, to May 5, 1998

	Number of SS Stories[a]	Number of SS + IM Stories[b]	Percentage of Sweatshop Stories That Mention Immigration
Lexis-Nexis database of major newspapers	400	145	36.2
New York Times	37	19	51
Los Angeles Times	29	12	41

Note: The source of the major newspaper and *New York Times* data is the Lexis-Nexis on-line database; it counts the use of *sweatshop* in a headline or lead paragraph of a story. After the analysis of the Kathie Lee Gifford material reported in this chapter, that database changed, and the *Los Angeles Times* archive was no longer available. The *Los Angeles Times* count in this chart is therefore a count of the occurrence of *sweatshop* anywhere in a story. The data reported in this table are raw numbers that do not correct for the fact that the Lexis-Nexis "major newspaper" database includes numerous non-U.S. newspapers. Also, duplicates of stories appear when they are carried in separate editions of metropolitan papers: for example, the *Los Angeles Times* "home" and its "final sports edition" may both carry slightly reedited versions of the same story and may both be listed in the story count.

[a]SS = "sweatshop" in headline or lead paragraphs.

[b]SS + IM = "sweatshop" in headline or lead paragraphs and any of the following in headline or lead paragraphs: "immigrant," "immigrants," "undocumented," "Mexican," "Mexico," "China," "Chinese," "Philippino," "Philippines," "Thai," "Thailand," "Korean," "Korea," "Dominican," "Haitian," "Haiti," "Vietnamese," or "Vietnam."

The immigrant-ethnic frame is dominant in a newspaper story if the word *sweatshop* appeared in the headline or lead paragraphs *and* if the headline or lead also referred to the immigration status of the workers or the ethnicity of the workers or their employers. By these criteria over 50 percent of the stories in the *New York Times* and 40 percent of the *Los Angeles Times* stories used the immigrant-ethnic frame as the dominant frame. The Lexis-Nexis database of major newspapers reveals its use among the larger sample of a bit over one-third of the time. Immigration status or ethnic identifiers were seldom used in sweatshop stories when they were not used in the leads—indicating that when it is used the immigrant-ethnic frame tends to be prominent.[5]

Thus, in terms of incidence, we find the immigrant-ethnic frame to be quite common, occurring in roughly one-third to one-half of the sweatshop stories examined. We will analyze the celebrity frame later.

Does the Immigrant Frame Make a Difference?

To determine whether the immigrant-ethnic frame on sweatshop stories might have an impact on public attitudes, we chose a news article by William Branigin that originally appeared in the *Washington Post* on February 16, 1997, a sympathetic feature that nevertheless illustrates the tendency to "lead with immigration." The headline was "Reaping Abuse for What They Sew." The lead of this article strongly establishes the frame:

> After an arduous trek across the border from her native Mexico, Aurora Blancas made her way to New York City and took the first job she could find: sweeping floors and packaging clothes sewn by other illegal immigrants at a sweatshop in the garment district.
>
> No experience—or documents—necessary. (Branigin 1997a, A.01)

To determine if this immigrant frame has an impact on readers, an undergraduate research assistant presented two versions of the Branigin article to groups of college students. One version contained verbatim excerpts from the Branigin article with the immigrant references intact. The other contained the same excerpts with all ethnic and immigration references removed, including ethnic-sounding names. Accordingly, the lead line of the edited version reads,

> After an arduous search for work, Aurora Blanchard made her way to New York City and took the first job she could find: sweeping floors and packaging clothes sewn by other women at a sweatshop in the garment district.
> No experience necessary.

In this way, what the study termed version 1 is framed as a struggling worker encountering unsavory labor conditions.

The respondents of the two versions were undergraduate students at Clark University in Worcester, Massachusetts; Keene State College in New Hampshire; Boston College in Chestnut Hill, Massachusetts; and Wheaton College in Norton, Massachusetts. The students were enrolled in classes where instructors had agreed to assist us: biology and sociology at Clark; sociology at Boston College; sociology at Wheaton; and English at Keene State. In each class students were randomly assigned (roughly every other packet, presorted before distribution in classes) version 1 or version 2 of the Branigin article. After reading the brief article, 233 students completed usable identical questionnaires, which included questions on their political attitudes and personal characteristics. More importantly, the questionnaire contained scaled questions about responsibility for subminimum conditions in sweatshops. One index we developed measured respondents' adherence to an immigrant blame thesis for the causes of sweatshops in the United States.[6]

The immigrant blame thesis holds that the ready supply of immigrant labor is the cause of the abuse of immigrant laborers. Technically, immigrant blame is a *labor supply theory* of the problem (see Ross 1997a). It may be contrasted to (or blended with) hypotheses about insufficient government regulation; imports from low-wage platforms (globalization); union weakness; or the developmental justification of low-wage industry (or jobs) for nations or immigrants.

The statistical analysis of the results (see table 16) showed that readers of sweatshop articles framed in an immigrant context—regardless of the readers' gender, class, and parental or own immigration status—were more likely to blame immigrants for sweatshop labor conditions. They were more likely to agree with immigration restriction as a solution and less likely to take a pro-labor view of the matter.[7]

In a broader sense, there is much to be said about the social significance of framing sweatshop stories in terms of immigration, since this frame, indeed, has a tendency to impact readers' views so considerably. That the *New York Times* and the *Los Angeles Times* frame the sweatshop story in an immigrant context about 47 percent of the time (combined), and the broader Lexis-Nexis sample one-third of the time, our findings suggest that the normal routines of reportage on this issue may have a profound impact on public opinion. Specifically, potential public outrage about extreme labor abuse as a normal part of apparel making in the United States may be deflected toward a view that it is immigrants who are subject to high levels of immigration that cause the problem. In turn, this may result in either hostility toward immigrants or (more likely in terms of this issue) passivity toward the legislative or action alternatives for domestic sweatshop control.

As Dopplet (1994) and Pritchard (1994) suggest, if a topic is deemed irrelevant to a larger public, then actions will not be taken to correct the problem. To the extent that immigrants' problems are considered specific to them or to the members of the affected ethnic groups and are not relevant to workers as a class, the broader "public" may choose to address

TABLE 16.   Regression of Immigrant Blame on Version of Experiment and Selected Control Variables

Independent Variable	Model 1	Model 2	Model 3
Version	.24[a]	.24[a]	.22[a]
Gender	−.20[a]	−.18[a]	−.18[a]
Parental occupation	−.03	−.02	.06
Immigrant background	−.04	−.01	.01
Political ideology		.21[a]	.26[a]
Union background			.08
R-squared	.094	.144	.160
Adj. R-squared	.075	.120	.125

Note: Reported coefficients are betas.

[a]Beta is at least two times its standard error.

policy about immigration rather than about working conditions as a corrective. Additionally, public sentiment against immigration and immigrants may develop as new Americans are viewed as the active agents in undermining labor standards and driving down wages. The frame influences attribution, and attribution of cause influences policy.

The atmosphere after the attacks on the World Trade Center on September 11, 2001, appears to have created an uneasy attitude toward America's immigrants. Much rhetoric defends the traditional principled stance of George Washington, who noted that the new American state did not "tolerate" difference but rather that religious (and by implication) ethnic difference was a matter of *right* in the new republic.[8] Despite these "sentimental" affirmations, the policy direction of the government is toward a hardening in relation to immigrant rights. Perhaps coincidentally, the Supreme Court ruled in March 2002 that undocumented immigrants could not collect back pay from employers who violate the NLRA—a major setback for immigrant workers (Savage and Cleeland 2002).

These possibilities for the general public are implicit in our data. Somewhat more speculative is the possibility that the effects we observed were relevant to understanding the lack of focus on domestic apparel workers by the activists of 1999. The immigrant-ethnic frame may raise, for these students, the unhappy choice of restricting immigration or tolerating sweatshops. Better, perhaps, to ignore the domestic problem.

It may be, then, that journalists' and editors' practices are factors in the process of reform and change in this and other social movements. In contrast to the immigrant-ethnic frame, after the Triangle Fire of 1911, the factory reform movement took another course: it ignored, for policy purposes, the ethnicity of sewing machine operators and store clerks who were the victims of abuse. They addressed instead the regulatory regime necessary to change the terrain of competition, leveling up the conditions of all workers. Consider the headline that was never written: "Workers Found Held Slave by Garment Contractors: Major Chains Bought from Slave Labor Factory."

That the workers enslaved in El Monte were from Thailand is indeed a significant part of the story. It may have led readers to believe that tighter borders would end labor abuse.

The Celebrity Frame: Kathie Lee Makes a Difference

After the election of President Clinton in 1992, his first secretary of labor, Robert Reich, made, as we have seen, a special project of combating violations of the FLSA of 1938. In southern California, the discovery on August 2, 1995, of the seventy-two garment workers held in semi-slavery in El Monte focused a great deal of local attention on the issue, but the sweatshop story was still restricted by both region and constituency (White 1996).

Then, on April 29, 1996, labor rights activist Charles Kernaghan told a hearing held in Washington, D.C., and organized by the Democratic Policy Committee on Child Labor—the Democratic congressmen on the House Labor Committee[9]—that clothing made by child laborers in Honduras was sold with the Kathie Lee Gifford label at Wal-Mart stores. Shortly thereafter, Kathie Lee labels were brought by workers to a Manhattan Workers' Center staffed by UNITE. The labels were being put on clothing made in sweatshop conditions in Manhattan's venerable garment center.

At first, Gifford resisted responsibility for the problem, indignantly proclaiming her commitment to children's causes. Then she became convinced, apparently, that she bore some responsibility for the matter. She eventually became a public supporter of a type of independent monitoring of contractor compliance with labor laws. The detailed story of the Kathie Lee Gifford affair demonstrates a celebrity's particular ability to command widespread attention to this issue. What follows is a measurement of that effect.

Celebrity Endorsers and the Commodity Chain

At the top of the clothing commodity chain,[10] along with the famous name merchandisers and labelers, are the big retailers who commission production for their house labels. Often these are not intrinsically prestigious stores, though they may range from mass market, such as Wal-Mart or Sears, to midline, such as Filene's. One strategy used by mass-market firms to move their house brands is to create "designer" lines endorsed by a celebrity thought to appeal to women and men in the target audience.

Famous models and TV personalities typify this approach, as do athletes' endorsements for athletic shoes and other garb. Wal-Mart, the largest retailer in the world and the largest employer in the United States, carried the Kathie Lee Gifford line of women's sporty clothes. Martha Stewart, for a time, embellished household goods for Kmart, and, of course, Michael Jordan sells shoes for Nike.

The endorsers are much like university logo licensors: they sign contracts for the use of their names and may directly supervise or inspect the contractors who make the goods that bear their names—which they didn't do until Kathie Lee's ordeal. If the merchandiser is big enough and the celebrity name has enough reach, these contracts can be a fortune in themselves. When Kathie Lee's line was introduced it zoomed toward the top of fashion sales at $200 million gross in its first year (1995) (see *Women's Wear Daily* 1995, 40). As of mid-1996 Gifford had earned an estimated $9 million (since 1995) from her endorsement (Howe et al. 1996). By 1999 the line had sold over $660 million (Meyer 2000).

The brokering of contract production and endorsements can create a maze of relationships. In the course of her difficulties, some of Gifford's lines of blouses were being made in a shop in New York City that failed to pay its workers. Stephanie Strom of the *New York Times* discovered the following chain of the Gifford blouses:

> Robert W. Adler [is] president and chief executive of Halmode Apparel Inc., the Kellwood Company unit that holds the license to use her name on clothing . . . [which has a] Wal-Mart . . . contract for the blouses. . . .
>
> "The contract for those blouses said the goods were supposed to be manufactured by a company in New York called Bonewco, which would subcontract some of the work to a manufacturer in Alabama," Mr. Adler said.
>
> What [the contract] did not say was that the Alabama company then "sub-subcontracted" part of the order to New Jersey-based Universal Apparel, which in turn sub-sub-subcontracted to Seo [the sweatshop in Manhattan]—both typical transactions in the garment business. (Strom 1996)

The Fall and Rise of Kathie Lee Gifford

Early in 1996 Kernaghan traveled to El Salvador and Honduras, as he does periodically, to investigate abuses of workers' rights for his small organization, the NLC. Across the road from a factory called Global Fashions, he met at a food stand with a number of women and girls who worked at Global. He had previously been told of all-night, forced shifts, extremely low pay, sixty-five-hour workweeks, brutal discipline, and child labor. On this day, fearful that a company spy was in their midst, the women did not speak very much. But one of the workers handed Kernaghan a label of the type that they were sewing onto the blouses they were making. It said "Kathie Lee." Kernaghan, not a daytime television watcher, did not realize the potential of what he had in hand until he returned to the United States (Kernaghan 1996).

Kathie Lee Gifford was the cohost with Regis Philbin of a mid-morning interview and chat show called *Live with Regis and Kathie Lee.* A former model, Kathie Lee presented an extremely pretty and wholesome appearance, and, quite relevant to this story, presented herself as particularly concerned about children. Her own family was a frequent referent in her discussion on screen, and they appeared in advertisements she made endorsing products.

Kathie Lee endorsed a line of clothing sold in Wal-Mart stores. She claimed, and this is on her labels, that some of the profit from her endorsement was devoted to children's charities. In this sense, Kathie Lee has "standing" in regard to children's issues but also vulnerability (Meyer and Gamson 1995, 190).

On March 15 Kernaghan hand-delivered to Gifford a letter telling her of the terrible conditions in the Global Fashions plant. Another letter followed two weeks later (Bearak 1996). There was no response from Gifford.

On April 29 Kernaghan spoke to an informal hearing composed of the Democratic members of the House Committee on Labor. Meeting as the Democratic Policy Committee on Child Labor, members of Congress heard testimony from a young Canadian activist involved with child labor issues and from Kernaghan. According to Kernaghan, the ample television coverage of the event was largely focused on the young man from Canada. That afternoon Kernaghan returned home with no inkling of the tumult to come. The next day's *New York Times* carried a story about $1 million in back pay awarded to workers in California, including those Thai immigrants discovered in August 1995 who had been held as semi-slaves in El Monte. There was no story about Kernaghan's charges about Kathie Lee's line of clothing, nor was there one on May 1. By contrast, the *Los Angeles Times* did carry a business section story on April 30 about the charges (Salem 1996).

On May 1, Kathie Lee Gifford responded to Kernaghan's charges on her television show. According to the *New York Times* (May 2, 1996), Gifford "held back tears" denying that her clothes were made in sweatshop conditions. *People* magazine described her as quaking with teary rage as she denied the story. This is Kathie Lee as quoted and sanitized by *People:* "You can say I'm not talented . . . but when you say that I don't care about children. . . . How dare you?" (Howe et al. 1996, 60). Her comments included a threat, reported more fully by the *Los Angeles Times:* "But when you say I don't care about children . . . mister, you better answer your phone because my lawyer is calling you today. How dare you?" (Bearak 1996, 1). Kernaghan reports this quite jovially, convinced it was the making of his ability to gain media attention for his views about the issue: Kathie Lee made *him* an object of attention (Kernaghan 1996).

Gifford's defensive stance about child labor attracted a great deal of attention, for Kathie Lee labels promise that a share of the proceeds will benefit children. *People* reported that she donated about $1 million of the $9 million that her endorsement netted to the Association to Benefit Children (ABC) (Howe et al. 1996, 60). ABC then opened shelters in New York for crack-addicted and HIV-infected children—named for Kathie Lee and Frank's own children, Cody and Cassidy (Strom 1996). Kathie Lee told *People* that her line sold $300 million its first year (Howe et al. 1996, 65).

Kernaghan arranged for one of the Global Fashions workers, Wendy Diaz, age fifteen, to come to the United States to be a witness to the truth of his contentions. Then, on May 22 Gifford and her husband, Frank, a famous former football star and broadcaster, taped an interview for broadcast that night on ABC's prime time television magazine show *Prime Time.* On the taped show Gifford said she wanted to finance inspections of places where her line of clothing is made (Bearak 1996). As they awaited air time of the taped show, Frank and Kathie Lee learned that the Kathie Lee line was also produced in a Manhattan shop where workers had not been paid for at least a week of work. The DOL had launched an investigation of Seo Fashions on West 38th in the heart of New York's garment district. Eventually Seo was found to have cheated twenty-five men and women of two to four weeks of pay in the production of fifty thousand Kathie Lee blouses (Howe et al. 1996, 58), and the place had a list of grossly unsanitary conditions that filled out the sweatshop description.

Some time before May 22, UNITE had been alerted to the situation at Seo when a worker came into their Garment District Justice Center with a complaint about back pay and conditions—and a Kathie Lee label in hand. UNITE then worked with the DOL and with Kernaghan to use the discovery to maximum advantage.

On May 23 Frank Gifford went to Seo Fashions with seventy-five hundred dollars in hand, according to the *New York Times* (Greenhouse 1996), but nine thousand dollars according to the CNN Web site. His intention was to give the money to the workers in three-hundred-dollar packets. The firm had closed, so only a handful of former employees were present at the Justice Center to receive the money. Once again, Gifford tearfully denied knowledge of these conditions on her show. When he brought the money, Frank Gifford said, "I apologize for our country" (Howe et al. 1996, 58). He also had with him a public relations consultant, Howard Rubenstein, who had been engaged by the Giffords.

While the ABC *Prime Time* tape is sympathetic (ABC 1996), it should be noted that *Live with Regis and Kathie Lee* is also an ABC property— they had a mutual interest in her successful defense of her benign image. There is another but less obvious institutional connection relevant to this issue. The connection is more redolent of irony than proof of influence. ABC is owned by the Disney Corporation, and Disney in turn was also under attack from Kernaghan and the NLC. Kernaghan and others had collected information demonstrating the extremely exploitative conditions under which its T-shirts are made in Haiti; and he claims that Disney's relationship to the contractor has been maintained for twenty years (Kernaghan 1996). This is more a matter of paradox than conspiracy: the logical thing for Disney to instigate would be to bury the issue, not continue to give Kathie Lee free rein to condemn the conditions and defend her honor.

A few days later, on May 29, Kernaghan introduced Wendy Diaz, the

Honduran employee of Global Fashions, to the Washington Press Corps. On May 30 Kathie Lee Gifford appeared with Governor Pataki of New York as he announced plans for New York State legislation that would outlaw the sale of sweatshop-produced clothing. That day, Secretary of Labor Reich met with the Giffords to discuss the sweatshop problem. On June 1 the *Los Angeles Times* reported that Kathie Lee would help Secretary Reich organize a public forum for the fashion industry to deal with the sweatshop issue.

In the meantime, Kernaghan was arranging a meeting between Gifford and Wendy Diaz: at issue were place, auspices, and attendees. Finally agreed on was the date of June 5, at the residence of Archbishop John Cardinal O'Connor of New York—St. Patrick's Cathedral in New York. Present were Kernaghan; Esperanza Reyes of the Committee for the Defense of Human Rights in Honduras; Rev. David Dyson of the People of Faith Coalition; Jay Mazur, president of UNITE; Kathie Lee; and Wendy Diaz. Kernaghan describes this as a moment of high emotion. Wendy Diaz, he says, was strong and articulate beyond the expectation of her years.

The attentive listener to Kernaghan hears an experienced political operative—a breed not naturally credulous—finally persuaded of another person's sincerity as he recounts Gifford's response to Wendy. Afterward Kathie Lee would advocate independent (third-party) monitoring of working conditions at contractor sites but a desire to continue to send work to Global Fashions. One can see in this result Kernaghan's striving to protect the Global workers from losing their jobs (through withdrawal of Wal-Mart contracts) as a result of speaking out. The model of third-party monitoring was adopted at this meeting for domestic work sites as well (Kernaghan 1996; Bearak 1996).

On July 2 Gifford appeared at Governor Pataki's press conference as he signed the New York antisweatshop bill barring the sale of clothing made under conditions violating labor law. On July 16 Reich hosted a Fashion Industry Forum at which Gifford—as well as three hundred other leading spokespersons of the fashion and entertainment industry—appeared. The day before that event, Gifford went to Capitol Hill to urge the passage of further child labor protections. Also in Washington, Gifford met on August 2 with the president, the vice president, Secretary of Labor Reich, and Senate Minority Leader Tom Harkin to discuss child labor issues.

On August 23 the *Los Angeles Times* and the *New York Times* reported once again on DOL raids on sweatshops found producing Kathie Lee clothing, and in September there were reports of raids on firms making supermodel Kathy Ireland's line sold at Kmart stores.

By early fall 1996 stories about Gifford's troubles continued to appear in newspapers and magazines, but a discerning observer would have noted that, while she had become a spokesperson for reform, others, for example, Michael Jordan, had eschewed responsibility for the conditions of production of clothing that bore their names. "I don't know the complete situation," Jordan told the Associated Press. "Why should I? I'm trying to do my job. Hopefully, Nike will do the right thing" (Strom 1996).

Gifford had moved into another realm: whatever one thought of her talent—and, indeed, even if one had this or that quibble with the solutions she advocated—nevertheless Kathie Lee Gifford had become a responsible moral agent. However much Gifford may have grown personally, it is the impact of her celebrity on the visibility of the sweatshop issue that explains the repeated return of movement activists to the Gifford well.

The Media Impact of Kathie Lee

One measure of the impact of the Kathie Lee affair is very simple.[11] When people do not understand the sweatshop issue or do not know who Charles Kernaghan is, one need only say, "the stuff Kathie Lee got caught about" or "the guy who made Kathie Lee cry." The media impact of the Kathie Lee Gifford affair can be measured more formally by counting stories with the word *sweatshop* in them during the six months before the April 29 hearing at which Charles Kernaghan spoke about child labor in the production of the Kathie Lee line of clothing and then by comparing that to the number of stories appearing during the six months after the hearing. A pilot examination of the *New York Times* and the *Los Angeles Times* stories found that a number of stories contain the word as incidental references, as in the general form "Madame X, a Vietnamese immigrant, worked in garment sweatshops before opening her own restaurant." Still other stories contained basically irrelevant references in the form of historical subjects, for example, an obituary of a veteran of the struggle against sweatshops earlier in the century. Yet other stories used the word as a metaphor, as in a story on "new sweatshop jobs" reviewing Internet Web sites for low pay. However, the before/after ratio of the total number of stories (including the irrelevant ones) was not markedly different from a winnowed list of those strictly about apparel sweatshops with illegal conditions of work.

Besides determining that no major difference in effect would result from a finer-grained story count, a broader net has a certain virtue in defining a turning point in public language. Among the effects of renewed *attention to sweatshops as a social issue,* I contend, is its renewed use as a pejorative applied to a variety of circumstances—including those not so very horrible. An increased story count indicates both an increase in public attention to an issue and an increase in the public currency of a particular adjectival usage.

Story Count Findings

The number of stories about apparel sweatshops or that used the word *sweatshop* rose markedly in the period after Kathie Lee's embarrassment (see table 17). The six regional Knight-Ridder papers, those in cities with a garment industry base (e.g., Philadelphia and Miami) and/or a large number of Mexican or Latino workers (e.g., San Jose), start with a moderately high base of stories and then *triple* them. The ratio is higher in Detroit, but the base in this heavy industry town is lower. The story count for the *Los Angeles Times* more than doubles, as does the *New York Times.* It is interesting to note that, although New York is the venerable center of the nation's garment industry and the symbolic home of the struggle against the sweatshops, the *Los Angeles Times* has paid much more attention to the sweatshop issue. In fact, the *Los Angeles Times* carried more sweatshop stories *before* Kathie Lee than the *New York Times* did *after.*

The surge in attention devoted to the sweatshop issue may have been caused by the media magnetism of celebrities, but the effect was to move the issue itself into the spotlight. The increase in the number of stories about sweatshops is marked, even if all the stories in the six-month period that mention her name are subtracted. The total number of sweatshop stories carried in the Lexis-Nexis database in 1996 zoomed to 496—about one-quarter of these (131) mentioned Kathie Lee prominently.

As with El Monte, the celebrity effect put the issue on the minds of editors and reporters; not every story had this "spin," but it was the celebrity hook that gave the other stories their "legs."

The attention that focused on Gifford's discomfort apparently had the effect of boosting or hastening a number of political developments. During the summer of 1996, after the revelations about Gifford's clothing line, conservative New York governor George Pataki, not previously known as a labor reformer, proposed that New York pass a law to "bar the sale or distribution of clothing produced in so-called sweatshops. In addition, authorities could confiscate merchandise produced in any shop that pays workers less than the minimum wage and provides substandard working conditions" (Moody 1996). This is, at the state level, the equivalent of the "hot goods" provision of the federal government's FLSA. The law was passed by the New York legislature and signed by Pataki with Gifford at his side.

TABLE 17. Sweatshop Stories in Newspapers before and after the Kathie Lee Affair

	6 Months before the Hearing (11/1/95–4/30/96)	6 Months after the Hearing (5/1/96–10/30/96)
Knight-Ridder newspaper group		
Miami Herald	9	35
Philadelphia Inquirer	9	39
Detroit Free Press	2	26
San Jose Mercury News	24	42
Total	44	142
New York Times	4	29
Los Angeles Times	44	81
Boston Globe	4	22
Total	52	132
Grand total	96	274

"'In no small measure, this bill is going to be signed this afternoon because Kathie Lee Gifford and Frank Gifford made this a personal crusade, to take these steps to put sweatshops out of business in New York State,' said Pataki before signing the bill into law" (Moody 1996). While only a state, not a federal, law, the celebrity attention effect was clear in this case.

In the fall of 1996, Representative Clay and Senator Kennedy, the ranking minority members of the House and Senate Labor Committees, symbolically introduced federal legislation calling for "manufacturer's liability"—announcing the Democrats' intention to pass it if they were returned to a majority in the Congress.

The Gifford affair contributed to the atmosphere that made possible a highly important policy change in Washington. As discussed in chapter 7, after a long period of decline in the number of investigators available to the WHD of the DOL, in the summer of 1996, at the initiation of Congresswoman Velazquez, money was appropriated that made possible an increase from under eight hundred to just under a thousand investigators at the start of the next fiscal year. Interviews at both the DOL and among lobbyists and legislative staff (e.g., S. Green 1997) confirmed the importance of the Gifford episode to this advance. Congresswoman Velazquez put it this way on the floor of the House on July 10, 1996:

> Mr. Chairman, we cannot pick up a newspaper, turn on the radio or television without seeing the names and faces of celebrities caught using sweatshop labor to produce their signature line of goods. Last month it was Kathie Lee Gifford; then it was Michael Jordan; and next week, it will be someone else. The fact of the matter is, sweatshops are a very serious problem throughout the United States. (Velazquez 1996, H7234)

I record these policy initiatives to counter the notion that celebrity-inspired attention to this issue was as trivial as the basis for the individual's celebrity. Serious consequences arose from the Kathie Lee Gifford affair.

Reflections on Celebrities and Social Issues

The Kathie Lee Gifford affair is somewhat different from other instances of celebrity involvement with social issues because it begins with a negative. The archetypical case occurs when a famous person uses his or her renown to give voice to a cause. In Meyer and Gamson's (1995) discussion of celebrities and social movements, for example, this relationship is assumed: the celebrity is the willing advocate. In their work, what is at issue is the role of celebrities in mobilizing resources and constructing collective identity (183). Their aim is to understand the influence of celebrities on movements—the movements they join.

The Kathie Lee problem is a bit different from that set by Meyer and Gamson. Gifford didn't join; she was drafted by embarrassment but then lent her support to policy changes. The impact of her celebrity was—initially—to give the issue *exposure.*

Citing many other writers, Meyer and Gamson note that in contemporary society celebrity is manufactured—often deliberately manufactured—thus "the famous are not necessarily the deserving" (183) and influence is not necessarily based on formal institutional power. Gifford sat atop no commanding heights of the economy, ordering minions here and there over the globe. Yet, surely she has formal institutional sponsorship and dependence. Should Wal-Mart or ABC or other corporate advertisers decide she is not an asset, her name would disappear in weeks (from all but the supermarket tabloids)—as it did when she left her television show in 2000. Her celebrity is manufactured but not self-made.

Still, the ability of the celebrity's name to command attention, the very circularity of the definition, is important to this story. Prior to the spring of 1996, Kathie Lee had no staff person in charge of her endorsement relations to Wal-Mart (Kernaghan 1996). She had no institution to process or oversee her millions of dollars of revenue based on her label in the clothing. When the NLC and then UNITE challenged her, it was her name and her relation to Wal-Mart that were potential resources—for her and for them. Her command ability—that is, bureaucratic authority to order resources—was not important. Hers was media-based ability, not an organizational one.

"Their notoriety has less to do with what they *do* or with how they can directly affect lives, than with what and who they *are*" (Meyer and Gamson 1995, 184). When celebrities enter social movements they bring the concerns of "the notoriety industry," which is untidily made up of public relations, entertainment law, and entertainment production companies. The activity of this industry is visible in the (mass) media. So motive and authenticity are questionable at all times. Kathie Lee Gifford had notoriously defined her own self as the subject of her story. That story was importantly one involving family, children, and her sympathy for children. By virtue of her gigantic daily audience and mass-marketing success Kathie Lee herself was news. When the large media space that her "self" occupied was threatened with the obvious charge of hypocrisy, a dramatic dynamic was created.

Kathie Lee's particular influence on the framing of the issue of sweatshops tended to create a privileged status to the issue of child labor. The highlighting of child labor during and after the Kathie Lee episode was the product of the antisweatshop movement's conscious exploitation of Gifford's vulnerabilities and the media's sense of "standing" (legitimacy to engage publicly in a particular issue; see the next section). Gifford had claimed the role of child advocate. It was fair game to challenge her on issues of child welfare. By contrast, Michael Jordan and Tiger Woods are careful not to claim intense interest in or expertise about labor, racial, or child welfare issues: when they disclaim responsibility for Nike's labor problems, they are not vulnerable to charges of hypocrisy.

Social Movements and Celebrities

"Celebrities bring the spotlight with them," explain Meyer and Gamson. "The presence of a media-certified celebrity makes an event inherently newsworthy. Depending on the magnitude of her . . . star, by virtue of presence the celebrity can bring media and public attention to a cause that would otherwise be neglected" (1995, 185). This may draw in other participants—extending, as Schattschneider (1975 [1960]) suggested, the boundaries of the audience and the actors in conflict. If one considers the resources mass-based social movements need to make social change in developed political economies, the ability to achieve media attention would be early on the list.

Participation of a celebrity in an event gives the media a "hook"—that is, the news value for an event. And the appearance of a celebrity is a "selective incentive"[12] to attend a movement event (Meyer and Gamson 1995, 185–86). Celebrities are also fund-raising assets (186). Attention yields funds, and funds yield more funds.

Politicians and policymakers are more likely to meet with celebrities; this may allow the celebrity to bring issue activists in contact with decision makers. These advantages and possibilities "significantly improve the prospects for a challenging social movement to reach and mobilize its activist constituencies, to gain mass media attention, to raise money and to win access to political decision-makers" (Meyer and Gamson 1995, 187).

All these characteristics bring risks and costs to a movement and to the way a movement might wish to see its cause framed as a social issue. Meyer and Gamson note that the "spotlight of notoriety" may "drown out" aspects of a movement's cause. Celebrities may have less to say, but more of what they say will be covered (187). Gifford's notoriety as a child advocate played a dual role in this case. Her previous profile as a child advocate gave the media a hook for their stories. The sweatshop issue veered toward becoming a child labor issue. Worse things could occur to obscure activists working in the shadows of a conservative political climate. But there is always a cost.

A September 1996 field trip with a UNITE organizer in search of sweatshop locations in eastern Massachusetts illustrates the problem of the selective frame on child labor. The organizer came upon a shop called Modern Dress in Boston located in a storefront at street level, a former retail corner store. The old plate-glass windows were covered with steel shutters. The door, recessed from the street, had a steel security grate in front, and at two o'clock in the afternoon it was lowered two-thirds of the way down. One had to enter (or, significantly, exit) on hands and knees (see the following photo). Inside, the clean and well-lit store had three rows of sewing machines, perhaps twenty of them. The aisles between them, however, were adrift with high piles of fleece wear being prepared for the winter season. Access over the floor at Modern Dress was extremely slow, and at the door there was, after all, the steel grate. The union organizer had been told by workers that Modern Dress did not pay

Boston sewing shop, Modern Dress, in "Little Saigon," 1996. Note the grate blocking the door. Photographer: Robert J. S. Ross.

overtime and that workers often did not get up to minimum wage at the going piece rate. This seemed like a mini–Triangle Shirtwaist fire waiting to happen. The union staffer described the time he had called the DOL about the place in the spring of 1996: "I called Labor about this place," he said, "and they came. The inspector walked in, looked around, and came out. She said, 'No kids in there; I don't see a child labor issue'" (Fishbein 1996).

In a world of limited resources, issue framing does count because it creates priorities. There are now only about one thousand Wage and Hour investigators for over 7 million workplaces (see chapter 7).[13]

The key concept for Meyer and Gamson's analysis of celebrity leverage is *standing*, an idea derived from legal theory and defined by them as "socially constructed legitimacy to engage publicly in a particular issue" (190). From the perspective of activists, they suggest, the problem is that celebrities, who after all have the "ear" of the media, may redefine movements in order to facilitate their own standing in it. In this case the matter is actually reversed: Kathie Lee's preexisting claim for public legitimacy as something more than just a pretty face gave the social movement advocates a place to stand in their moral demands on her.

The issue of sweatshops is broader than child labor, however. It is both domestic and foreign; and it is about pay for adults, not just childhood status. The Kathie Lee Gifford episode joins a broader type of dramaturgy in which the innocence of children is used by advocates as a prelude to larger issues. Homelessness is another of these: family homelessness occupies the moral and media drama while single men dominate the statistics. Of course, access to public concern through the issue of child labor makes difficult confrontation with more complex issues of justice. Adults are responsible parties; unlike children, when they work for illegally low wages some may say this is voluntary, an agreement undertaken by responsible parties. It is a somewhat sophisticated argument to say that such conditions of employment should be illegal even if entered into voluntarily. The emphasis on the child labor issue avoids this difficulty. Similarly, the emphasis on sweatshops abroad, though not the only part of the Kathie Lee story, evades the trends of inequality, union busting, and cutthroat competition in contemporary low-wage markets.

These cautions should not detract from a clear finding. Kathie Lee made a difference. If the El Monte slave labor case brought the sweatshop issue into the mainstream on the West Coast, Kathie Lee made it a national story. The enterprise of the NLC and its two key staff members—Barbara Briggs and Charles Kernaghan—has thus had a very largely amplified effect on the public perception of the sweatshop issue.

The Student Movement and the Print Media

The wave of sit-ins led by United Students Against Sweatshops (USAS) in 1999 and 2000 had the effect of buoying flagging newspaper interest in the story (see figure 14). In 1997 and 1998 media coverage of the sweatshop story fell from its heights of 1995–96. Then, as USAS got organized and the sit-ins took place, coverage increased again. About 30 percent of all stories in major newspapers featured students and their activities. About 15 percent of these stories mentioned sit-ins.

The new student movement had a number of resources that helped it generate largely friendly reports of its activity. The nonviolent nature of the actions and the unselfish motives of the students combined with a relatively accessible, nonsectarian rhetoric. They were easy to like.

On the other hand, the older generation of NGOs created an infrastructure that eagerly helped publicize the issues. Unions helped fund USAS; the labor rights NGOs lent expertise and legitimacy to their contentions. In the heat of the 1999–2000 controversy about the WRC and the FLA, for example, Kernaghan traveled to campuses throughout the country, speaking to full houses. In turn, his press work was done by accomplished professionals with long experience of issue publicity.

The news reporting contrasted to some of the op-ed commentary. After the World Trade Organization (WTO) demonstrations in Seattle in November 1999, elite commentators such as Thomas Friedman (1999) and Nicholas Kristof (Kristof and WuDunn 2000) found new virtues in third world sweatshops and protectionist ignorance in the student movement. They were joined by a group of economists—the Academic Consortium on International Trade (ACIT)—who petitioned their college presidents not to heed the new movement (ACIT 2000). Countered by a distinguished group of economists and social scientists (Scholars Against Sweatshop Labor 2001), it is not clear that the ACIT influenced campus dynamics very much: but their statement apparently buoyed the aggressiveness of the editorial and op-ed writers at the *New York Times* and the *Wall Street Journal* (Kristof and WuDunn 2000; *Wall Street Journal* 2000). While the discussion of the sweatshop issue in politics and on campuses continues to grapple with ethical issues and economic development, the discussion among the defenders of corporate globalization and the bulk of the economics profession has tended to depict the antisweatshop campaigners as "senseless" (*Boston Globe* 1999; Friedman 1999).

After USAS succeeded in founding the Workers Rights Consortium and the wave of sit-ins subsided, the frequency of sweatshop stories dropped drastically. There are stories that follow up on reports the WRC and FLA make about abuses highlighted by the student movement. The Kukdong/Mexmode campaign is an example, as is the BJ&B campaign. In an unusual convergence of circumstance, the student movement's preoccupation with post–September 11 war and foreign policy issues and the Bush administration's withdrawal from FLSA enforcement activities means that there are hardly any news stories about domestic sweatshop abuses. News stories are the product of someone's action: a government report or press release; an interest group's report or press conference; an editor's or writer's decision about a good feature. The *New York Times* and the *Los Angeles Times* covered the Mexmode and BJ&B campaigns, and they gave the student movement due credit: "Latin Sweatshops Pressed by U.S. Campus Power" ran the headline of a story from the Dominican Republic (Gonzalez 2003). As 2003 wore on, however, the domestic sweatshop story—like many domestic issues of working-class life—appeared to be dropping in priority on the public agenda. The prospect of a presidential campaign that would renew the salience of domestic issues gave advocates some reason for hope.

Appendix 2: Details of the Immigrant Blame Analysis

The Immigrant Blame Index

#4. Sweatshops in the United States are caused by excessive immigration.

#7. With all the unskilled immigrants in the country these days, it is natural there should be a lot of low-paying jobs in sweatshops.

#8. To control or eliminate sweatshops the United States should rigorously restrict immigration.

Pro-labor

#3. Sweatshops in the United States are caused by unethical employers.

#15. It's an outrage that garment workers are treated in 1998 about as badly as they were in 1900.

#27. Workers need strong trade unions to protect their interests.

The indices were an average of respondents' three answers coded by a Likert scale:

1. Strongly Disagree
2. Disagree
3. Neither Agree nor Disagree
4. Agree

5. Strongly Agree

The Independent Variables (Codes indicated)

Gender

1. Male
2. Female

Parent's Occupation

Here is a list of different types of jobs. Which type was held by the parent who earned the most money last year?

1. Professional or technical
2. Higher administration
3. Clerical
4. Sales
5. Service
6. Skilled worker
7. Semi-skilled worker
8. Unskilled worker
9. Farm
10. Unemployed

Immigrant Background

Were you or members of your family immigrants (legal or illegal) to the United States?

1. Great-grandparent
2. Grandparent
3. Parent
4. Self
5. Not for many generations
6. I am not a U.S. citizen

Union Background

Is any member of your immediate family a member of a labor union?

1. Yes
2. No

Political Ideology

Regardless of the party you might prefer, in politics today, do you consider yourself more liberal, more conservative, or somewhere in between?

1. Very liberal
2. Liberal
3. In between
4. Conservative
5. Very conservative
6. Neither

One of our steps was a simple analysis of the impact of the immigrant-ethnic frame. Initially we examined the mean scores on each of the indices, comparing the scores of those who read the edited version 1 with those who read the original (immigrant-ethnic) version 2.

The mean differences between version 1 and version 2 on the critical immigrant blame and pro-labor indices were small but statistically significant—that is, the result showed a weak association but the association was not caused by random chance. Those had higher scores on the immigrant blame index and lower scores on the pro-labor index.

Other factors beyond the simple reading of the Branigin (1997a) article might influence participants' views of immigrants and sweatshops. To assess this possibility, we conducted a regression analysis that specified the immigrant blame index as dependent variable and controlled for the effects of the following independent variables: the version of the experiment (original or edited), gender, family immigration background, parental occupation (as a proxy for social class), political ideology (i.e., liberal versus conservative), and parent's union background.[14]

Since each of these variables might influence a respondent's view of immigrants (e.g., a member of a family who recently immigrated to the United States might well be less likely to "blame" immigrants), holding them constant in a multiple regression analysis enabled us to assess the effect of our key framing variable (the version of the Branigin article) with more precision and confidence. The results of the regression analysis are presented in table 16. We use a hierarchical regression strategy that enables us to assess the degree to which the version effects changes across sequentially more complex models. First, immigrant blame is regressed on our most basic model, controlling for gender, parental occupation, and immigrant background (Model 1). Then, political ideology (Model 2) and union background (Model 3) are added to this basic model.

Table 16 shows, regardless of the complexity of the model examined, that the effect of the version of the article read (that is, the framing effect) was consistent, strong, and statistically significant across all three models. In other words, all else being equal, those who read the original version of the Branigin article were more likely to blame immigrants for sweatshop problems than were those who read the edited version of the article.[15] Simply put, there are measurable effects of the immigrant-ethnic frame.

Conclusion to Part 2

Producing Sweatshops in the United States

High, legal immigration is neither necessary nor sufficient for sweatshop appearance. This is shown by the period of the 1950s and 1960s in New York City. First, Puerto Ricans rapidly replaced Jews, Italians, and Blacks in the apparel industry, but though they filled the lower-wage sections of the business, standards did not drop below legal levels. Average wages in the industry were still comparable to manufacturing averages. Second, although import competition—globalization without enforceable labor standards—was not a necessary component of sweatshop appearance in the early part of the century nor during the brief resurgence of very bad conditions in the Depression, it is central to the modern period.

Consider the comparison between the 1950s and the turn of the nineteenth century. In both eras, immigrants influenced the New York garment industry but imports were low. The 1950s were the midpoint of the period of decency for the industry's workers. The earlier period is symbolic of all that has been wrong with labor conditions in the cities. Upon inspection, one very important difference is that the apparel unions—the ILGWU and the ACTWU—were at the height of their power during the years of relative decency.

A second factor deserves formal consideration. The period of high immigration and low sweatshop prevalence was one in which the immigrants were actually citizens—Puerto Rican migrants. The legal status of immigrants is another critical factor in the making of the new sweatshops.

Table 18 gives the summary:

TABLE 18.   Summary of Factors Supporting and Deterring Labor Abuse in the Apparel Industry

Deterring factors	• Union strength
	• Law enforcement of labor standards legislation
	• Legalization of immigrants
Supporting factors	• Low wage import competition: globalization without labor standards
	• Union weakness
	• National/local labor market niche surplus
	• Undocumented status of immigrants

Now we have made the long journey through the "causes" of the new sweatshops. Chief among these is the rise of global capitalism and the competitive race to the bottom that unrestricted capital mobility and trade without labor standards encourage. On a world scale the unrestrained power of the retail oligarchs of the rich countries allows them to command the lion's share of profits and value—and the power to dictate prices—in the worldwide clothing commodity chain. In the United States, the de facto deregulation of labor standards erodes the political and regulatory protections attained in the first half of the century. The confluence of global changes and U.S. immigration policy has created a large pool of disempowered workers who have few legal rights and an industry in which union protection is disappearing.

Approximately 250,000 workers toil under working conditions our grandparents and parents thought they had banished. That apparel sweatshops are widely perceived as external to our country, or a matter "only" of immigration, or an occasion to snicker at the moral failures of celebrities—these are in part a consequence of the kind of media attention attracted by the sweatshop issue. Part 3 explores the policies and movements addressing the problem directly.

Part 3 Movements and Policies

Introduction: The Variety of Antisweatshop Initiatives

The rise of the new sweatshops in the United States paralleled the rise of global commodity chains supplying the rich countries with apparel. In part this was the result of other aspects of U.S. foreign policy. For example, the Reagan administration's commitment to suppressing leftist movements and left-wing elected governments in the Western Hemisphere in the 1980s caused it to facilitate the planting of apparel suppliers in Central America. Ellen Rosen called this "making sweatshops" (2002) as an aspect of foreign policy. The connection between U.S. foreign policy and the sweatshop issue has added to the number and kinds of antisweatshop organizations in the United States. Other similar groups have sprung up in Europe, Australia, and Canada and in developing countries as well.

The most important force for defending workers against labor abuse is always their own collective ability. UNITE has found it difficult to maintain high "density," that is, high proportions of the labor force, in the U.S. apparel sector. The policy and legislative changes that would enable unions to more successfully organize in North America (and elsewhere) are part of any comprehensive antisweatshop perspective.

On a global scale the loose confederation of workers in this sector is the ITGLWF—the International Federation of Textile, Leather, and Garment Workers—headquartered in Brussels. While some U.S.-based antisweatshop activists interviewed for this study privately express skepticism about or criticism of the Brussels-based international confederations in general and the ITGLWF in particular, it is also true that the federation supports organizing and training projects in the developing countries and that its head, Neil Kearney, is an articulate defender of textile and apparel workers' right to a dignified existence in the global economy (see, for example, Kearney 2000, 2002).

Two of the three pillars of decency for working-class conditions are workers' self-defense (usually independent unions) and public and governmental policy that aids union growth and protects workers—for example, their health and safety—from employer abuse. The third historic pillar of decency has in the past been reformers—often middle class—but, in any case, outside the ambit of workplace or typically political organizations. Nowadays such groups are often referred to as NGOs.

There are numerous examples of active NGOs combating sweatshop conditions in the apparel industry specifically and labor abuse more generally.[1] While there are literally dozens (if not hundreds, including freestanding local groups) of NGOs, a few are particularly prominent.

The National Labor Committe in Support of Worker and Human Rights (NLC) is a New York–based group that tends to focus, although not exclusively, on Central America.[2] It was formed in 1981 to oppose U.S. intervention in Central America, but by the early 1990s it was focused on the apparel industry. Headed by Charles Kernaghan, the NLC produces closely documented research on working conditions around the world but is best known for the discovery of child labor and sweatshop conditions in the production of Wal-Mart's Kathie Lee Gifford line of clothes. (Kernaghan is often referred to as "the man who made Kathie Lee cry.") In 2003 the NLC returned to a focus on Disney and, in particular, on conditions in contractor factories in Bangladesh. Kernaghan and the NLC are associated with campaigns for third-party independent monitoring of codes of conduct: a policy innovation for which the NLC campaigned in relation to Gap, Inc., in the mid-1990s. Kernaghan and his associate, Barbara Briggs, have particularly close ties with labor unions (as with many close relationships these are not always without friction) and also religious activists. Their campaigns make use of these networks.

Global Exchange is a San Francisco–based organization that has taken the lead in Nike campaigns and also in combating the abuse of workers in Saipan.[3] It has many branches, including a "reality tour" business that takes North Americans to visit sites of controversy to experience global justice issues people-to-people; it also has a fair-trade retail division that sells goods (coffee, clothing, etc.) purchased from cooperatives in developing countries at fair prices. Its leader, Medea Benjamin, was a Green Party candidate for the U.S. Senate in California; her associate, Kevin Danaher, is the author of numerous popular books that criticize global capitalism.

Founded in 1995, the Toronto-based Maquila Solidarity Network (MSN) describes itself as "a Canadian network promoting solidarity with groups in Mexico, Central America, and Asia organizing in maquiladora factories and export processing zones to improve conditions and win a living wage."[4] Like the NLC in New York, religious and labor activists support the MSN; and also like the NLC, the group produces high-quality research and reportage. It also produces thoughtful work on public policy and tries to deal with a problem that is quite different in Canada than in the United States. In Canada, homework is legal, and worker advocates attempt to find ways to regulate or deter the exploitation of sewing machine operators. In the United States it is not legal, so the public policy problem is enforcement.

Among the leaders in the worldwide struggle against labor abuse in the apparel industry is the Clean Clothes Campaign, based in Amsterdam but actually a network of like-minded campaigns throughout Europe.[5] The CCC has close relations to a companion research center and produces highly documented research reports and policy proposals. It took the lead in producing a code of conduct for European retailers and producers and, distinctively, organizes European consumers to send postcards to targeted firms questioning their labor practices. They claim that up to 100,000 have been sent in a campaign. The base of support is labor organizations, fair trade shops, religious solidarity groups, and consumer organizations.

Returning to the United States, over the last fifteen years a new form of labor-community partnership has emerged in over forty metropolitan areas. Founded in 1987 these coalitions are called Jobs with Justice (JwJ).[6] The main stems of membership are locals of the larger unions. In addition, community groups and often individuals sympathetic to labor issues, including those who are part of church social action committees, are formal members. JwJ emphasizes labor union struggles, and its strategy is to get local labor activists, and its supporters, to join in a given labor struggle in solidarity. It is distinctive in its outreach and mobilization of nonunion constituencies to aid in union struggles. This led the local JwJ in Boston, for example, to effective support work for the Harvard living wage sit-in and in support of textile workers in 1998.

JwJ has a close strategic relationship to the Student Labor Action Project (SLAP). SLAP, in turn, is often part of local USAS projects and chapters on local campuses.

Most of these NGOs depend on publicity to pressure firms to improve labor conditions and/or to respect workers' rights to agitate for those improvements. USAS brought a new concept to these campaigns and inspired a new and very large wave of student activism when, in 1998, it began to use the power of university contracts to implement these goals.

In part 3 we will explore the student movement and some of its campaigns and then turn to global and national policy ideas that aim to end sweatshop abuses.

11 Combating Sweatshops from the Grass Roots

Introduction: Same Plot, Different Story

In January 1999 a new student movement announced itself on the campuses of American universities. It began a campaign for a "sweat-free campus" and announced itself in dramatic fashion—by occupying over the next four months administration buildings on seven campuses—Duke (January 29), Georgetown (February 5), Wisconsin (February 8), Michigan (March 17), Fairfield (April 15), and North Carolina and Arizona (April 21). In each case, the students' demands were focused on the apparel sweatshop problem. The workers evoked in the students' rhetoric were usually distant from them in space both geographic and social. The objects of the students' sympathy were at the base of a pyramid whose top includes big American and European corporations. The sit-ins were not all quick, nor were they intended to be merely symbolic, so some took on a kind of siege structure and logic.

A person old enough to remember or to have participated in the movements of the 1960s might be tempted to nod with familiarity, cynical or not, secure in the perception that the story line was familiar and the outcomes predictable. The sit-ins would be ended by police arresting the demonstrators, followed by an outburst of revolutionary rhetoric, followed then by a big demonstration for amnesty for the militants now in jeopardy for their college careers. At the end the movement might have grown, but few measurable gains would be made.

There is a strong contrast between the familiar (or stereotyped) 1960s-based story line and the actual course of events. During this first round of sit-ins, in none of these places did administrations call in police; nor did they seek to punish the students or their leaders. In each of these institutions, the students appeared to have won the major portion of their program. None of these results was characteristic of any of the waves of campus sit-ins or demonstrations during the 1960s.[1]

Later, in the spring of 2000, there were arrests in six out of the ten sit-in or occupation actions that focused on the campus apparel issue (see table 19). It is more than symbolically relevant, though, that at the University of Wisconsin, where the largest number of students were arrested (fifty-four), the result was still what has to be a resounding policy advance for the students: the university joined the WRC, which was their main demand, and the president who called in the police resigned.

By the end of 1999 the campus-based antisweatshop movement had joined with other populist student groups to protest the current—neoliberal—form of global capitalism. The widely noted Seattle demonstrations of November 28–December 3, 1999, united environmental organizations, campus-based sweatshop campaigners, and labor unions. Approximately this same coalition also demonstrated in Washington, D.C., on April 15–17, 2000, at the World Bank/International Monetary Fund (IMF) meetings, although the youthful global justice demonstrators were not as closely integrated with the AFL-CIO rally as previously. That pattern continued as a few thousand North American activists converged on the April 2001 Quebec meeting of thirty-four Western Hemisphere governments planning a Free Trade Area of the Americas (FTAA). In another general post-Seattle pattern, issues of vandalism, police response, and decorum rather than free trade, labor, or environmental standards dominated some reports of the demonstrations. While the young demonstrators label themselves a global justice movement against "corporate globalization," their mass media critics framed them as "antiglobalizers" (Ford 2001).

The new movement staged a smaller, more muted post–September 11 demonstration in Ottawa in November 2001 at meetings of the finance ministers of the leading economies (the "G20"). Then, on April 20, 2002, the "global justice" movement had as many as seventy thousand (estimated at between fifty thousand and eighty thousand) demonstrators in Washington, D.C., declaring their continuing rejection of corporate globalization and now opposition to the Bush administration's "war on terrorism" (see Featherstone 2002).

As a cohort of activists broadens its concerns, it can also have difficulty in communicating the ways in which its once focused agenda has led it to its new agenda. A large part of the activities on April 20, 2002, included demonstrations critical of the Israeli occupation of the West Bank and in favor of Palestinian statehood. The broader agenda of the many global action networks was perceptually drowned out by the novelty of a large pro-Palestinian manifestation. This is how the *New York Times* lead sentence framed the story:

> Tens of thousands of Arab-Americans blended with demonstrators against the military campaign in Afghanistan and those criticizing international financial institutions during protests today in Washington, with the cause of the Palestinians and criticism of Israel turning into the main message of the multifaceted crowd. (Labaton 2002)

The global justice issues were seen, by the nation's newspaper of record, as unimportant in the context of post–September 11 politics.

The events of September 11, 2001, have had a profound impact on the young left, and its future course is very hard to predict. This chapter shows the ways in which this youth movement, whose first manifestations were as an antisweatshop campaign, has evolved into a global justice movement. It will answer by way of two case studies the provocative question often implicit in the criticism of its stance: Has this movement done any good for any workers anywhere? Along the way the chapter will also reflect on some startling ways this movement is similar and different from the last great upsurge in young adult activism, that of the New Left of the 1960s.

TABLE 19. Sit-ins on the Campus Logo/Sweatshop Issue, 1999–2000

	Arrests	Outcome	Source
1999			
1/29	Duke University	code of conduct adopted; public disclosure of contractor sites	Kreider 2000, 2001
2/5–2/8	Georgetown University	public disclosure of contractor sites	SP
2/8	University of Wisconsin	public disclosure of contractor sites; living wage research; women's rights	Kreider 200, 2001; PR
3/17	University of Michigan	public disclosure of contractor sites; living wage research; women's rights	PR
4/15	Fairfield University	janitors' union formed; university dropped janitorial contract	*New York Times*
4/21–4/30	University of Arizona	public disclosure of contractor sites; living wage research; women's rights	SP; PR
4/21	University of North Carolina	public disclosure of contractor sites; living wage research; women's rights	PR

2/7–2/15	University of Pennsylvania		joined WRC	*New York Times*
2/16–2/18	University of Michigan		joined WRC	Associated Press
2/17–2/20	University of Wisconsin	54	withdrew from FLA; joined WRC	*Milwaukee Journal*
3/6–3/17	Macalester University		withdrew from FLA	Associated Press, SP
3/15–3/25	University of Toronto		adopted code of conduct	*Toronto Star*
3/27–4/7 (hunger strike)	Purdue University		joined WRC	SP
3/29–4/9	Tulane University		withdrew from FLA and WRC	*Times Picayune*
4/4	University of Kentucky	12		*Lexington Herald*
4/5–4/8	University of Iowa	16	joined WRC; remained in FLA	SP
4/4–4/6	University of Oregon	14	temporarily joined WRC (later rescinded)	Associated Press; SP
4/4	State University of New York at Albany	11		Associated Press

Note: FLA = Fair Labor Association; WRC = Workers Rights Consortium; PR = university public affairs Web site; SP = student college newspaper Web site. Women's rights include protection of reproductive health, protection against firing for pregnancy, and protection against sexual harassment.

[a] Other labor-related sit-ins occurred at Johns Hopkins, Ohio State University, Pitzer College, Pomona College, and Wesleyan College in the year 2000.

The Formation of USAS

The campus-based antisweatshop effort has its origins in changes in the AFL-CIO that were signaled by John Sweeney's election to the federation's presidency in 1995. The new Sweeney administration created two programs aimed at reviving organizing activity in the labor movement—an effort whose need we analyzed in discussing the way union decline contributed to an increase in sweatshops in the United States. The AFL-CIO created an Organizing Institute (OI) to train new organizers. The OI engaged in aggressive outreach, which included recruitment among college students and recent graduates. Associated with the OI is a program called Union Summer.

Explicitly recalling the idealism of the Mississippi Freedom Summer of 1964, Union Summer recruited young adults to "try out" the labor movement by way of summer internships as organizers. In the summer of 1997, a group of Union Summer interns at the old ILGWU offices in New York, now the headquarters of the merged UNITE, began to develop the idea of a sweat-free campus. Their supervisor, Ginny Coughlin, a staffer with experience as a youth organizer for the Democratic Socialists of America (DSA), helped them elaborate the idea. One of these interns was Tico Almeida, a student at Duke University (Coughlin 1997, 2001).

Aimed at a bit over 1 percent of the U.S. apparel market, the campaign for sweat-free campus clothing nevertheless targets an approximately $2.5 billion market in clothing that bears university and college insignia or logos. This market is structured largely through licensing contracts. A university licenses a company—for example, Champion, a maker of premium sweatshirts—to use its logo and name on clothing. In turn, the company pays the university or college about 7.5–8 percent of revenue for that right. Clearly, some schools have national markets (the top three licensors in 2001–2002 were North Carolina, Michigan, and Tennessee); others have regional markets; and still others have only campus sales. Some small schools are nonlicensors—generally their campus bookstore contract calls for the store to have the right to sell logo apparel, and the store's rent or fee to the university includes consideration for this right.

The licensees—in another example, VF Corporation, the largest apparel maker in the world—behave as clothing manufacturers do: they find contractor factories to make the gear.[2] VF (and its label Lee Sport) contracted for a variety of products for Michigan, North Carolina, Northwestern, Arizona State, and other universities with Sinha Apparel in Dhaka, Bangladesh.

About 180 of the largest schools use the CLC to broker and manage their licensing deals. Much of the initial round of actions in the sweat-free campus campaign was directed at the CLC. In the fall of 1998 it adopted de facto the code of conduct that the AIP (later the FLA) announced. Criticism of that code led students into conflict with universities who made use of CLC services.

When he returned to Duke in the fall of 1997, Tico Almeida organized a letter from student leaders to Duke president Nannerl Keohane, urging that Duke adopt a code of conduct governing conditions under which Duke licensees might produce Duke logo clothing.[3] Duke agreed.

During the next year Duke did adopt a code, but as it turned out the Duke administration's initial agreement to Almeida's initiative did not include an item that the student movement soon came to believe was critical to the overall effort to monitor labor standards—full disclosure of licensees' contractor sites. This was a critical matter—for campus logo apparel as it is for retail chain store brands.

If a university licenses a firm to make T-shirts and sweatshirts, that firm will then contract with (potentially) hundreds of factories to make the garments in question. For the very large manufacturers and licensors, a staggering number of contractors is involved in the commodity chain of their licensees. There are almost fifty-seven hundred entries in the University of Michigan database of factory locations; of these my estimate is that there are about fourteen hundred to nineteen hundred discrete factories that produce everything from glasses to coolers to T-shirts to T-shirt printing (WRC factory database). Realizing that no particular monitoring protocol could necessarily guarantee 100 percent coverage, the students wanted to have full disclosure of the list of contractor factories (vendors) that made the logo clothing. The demand for disclosure of contractor sites parallels two broader concepts that now have currency in both conservative and liberal criteria for public policy: transparency (that is, visibility of transactions and openness to scrutiny) and accountability (that is, the means by which an actor can be made to accept responsibility for its actions).[4]

In support of their demand that the Duke administration include disclosure, the students held a sit-in at the administration building. It lasted but one day, and by the time the sit-in ended on January 29, 1999, Duke had agreed to the demand.

In an interesting regional convergence, a group of students at the University of North Carolina, twenty minutes down the road from Duke, among whom Marion Traub-Werner was an active leader, had been actively addressing the major contract that Nike was in the process of signing with their own major college athletic teams. They too demanded a code of conduct (Traub-Werner 1999).

While these two spearhead campuses were working on their local versions of the issues, in the summer of 1998 students from thirty campuses had met in New York

> as an informal but cohesive international coalition of campuses and individual students working on anti-sweatshop and Code of Conduct campaigns. The general goals of the group were: 1) to provide coordination and communication between the many campus campaigns and 2) to coordinate student participation and action around the national, intercollegiate debate around Codes of Conduct and monitoring systems. (USAS 2002)

During the spring of 1998 UNITE had sponsored a campus tour of workers from the BJ&B factory in the Dominican Republic. Manufacturing college logo hats under oppressive conditions, these workers had dramatized and personalized the issues for the founding cohort of USAS leaders.

By early 1999 USAS had been formed, and about fifty campus groups were involved. In January and then through April groups loosely affiliated with USAS held sit-ins in seven places and had large rallies for campus codes of conduct at many others. In the course of 1999, a new activist movement was clearly in evidence on American campuses.

Through the academic year 1999–2000 USAS continued to grow, but it added a startling new dimension to its activity. In the fall of 1999, reacting to UNITE's criticism of what was now called the FLA, a group within

USAS, centered at Brown University, devised an alternative plan for ensuring that university-licensed apparel would be sweat-free. Calling their proposal a "Worker Rights Consortium" the USAS chapters around the country worked on their various campuses to get their universities to join the WRC and to reject or leave the FLA.

The campaign for the WRC was most intense as the deadline for its first national founding convention in April 2000 approached. Against many predictions, USAS was successful in getting over fifty universities and colleges to join the WRC, many of these leaving FLA. By May 2002, 100 institutions had joined the WRC; as of January 2003 it had 112 members (see WRC 2003).

Whether the WRC can fulfill the students' hope for important change in the apparel supply chain is a matter for both skepticism and patience. The college apparel market is but 1–2 percent of the entire apparel market. As such it is a niche market that may be exploited in a specialized way. Many of the largest suppliers to this market are part of very much larger firms. College and licensed apparel are but small fractions of the sales of these firms and a similar fraction of profits. The leverage of university licensors in relation to the largest suppliers in the market is only moderate. On the other hand, the market is large enough to sustain some sizeable enterprises. This may be the logic behind SWEATX, a new unionized T-shirt maker funded by Ben of Ben and Jerry's famous ice cream (Haefele and Pelisek 2002).

Other aspects of the nature of the apparel commodity chain multiply the potential effects of student influence on the collegiate market. While the university licenses may be but small parts of some of the firms who supply the market—Nike or VF, for example—these firms are sensitive to the image of their brands, especially among the age groups that students represent. In turn, the factories with which the firms contract for production usually supply other, nonuniversity market segments. So if, for example, worker and student pressure gets a cap factory to sign a union contract with its workers, they have won a bridgehead that supplies the rest of the factory's clients—not just the university segment.

The creation of the WRC and subsequent affiliations with it is a major victory for the new student movement, and as of the summer of 2003

USAS claimed over two hundred campus groups.[5] This rate of growth is equivalent to or greater than that of Students for a Democratic Society (SDS) in the mid-1960s or of the White and/or Northern support groups for the Southern civil rights movement in the early 1960s.

The old New Left witnessed a progression from larger and/or more selective elite institutions outward to more broad-based institutions. From Michigan, Swarthmore, and Harvard early on, for example, chapters of SDS later developed at places such as Indiana, St. Cloud State, and Roosevelt University in Chicago. This process took five years and was, of course, speeded up after SDS was discovered by the national press around the time of the (first) March on Washington to End the War in Vietnam in April 1965. By the late 1960s community colleges had chapters of SDS or other New Left groups (for material on SDS chapter growth, see Sale 1973; Gitlin 1980).

The current pattern of outward diffusion has some, though highly compressed, similarity to the 1960s. Supplementing work first done by Aaron Kreider of Notre Dame University, who summarized the institutional rankings of campuses where major USAS actions occurred between 1999 and 2000, table 20 shows that during the period 1999–2000 there was marked outward movement from more to less elite campuses. The first wave of sit-ins in 1999 was at relatively elite or flagship state universities. Initiating movement groups among young adults with higher income and/or family education backgrounds is similar in both generations (see Elliot and Freeman 2000 for some family income data on the current activists).

During the spring of 2000, when students were intent on meeting an April deadline for the founding of the WRC, sit-ins were at places much more representative of the national student body (see table 20). The speed with which chapter construction moved to non-elite places was faster than SDS before the Vietnam War. Already by the fall of 1999 campuses in Alabama, Arkansas, and Georgia were involved and active. There were contacts at South Carolina and a few community colleges. Acting in response to local demonstrations, to fear of them, or even a desire to do the right thing, 122 universities had joined the FLA by June 1999 and 150 had joined by the spring of 2000. Then when USAS initiated WRC and campaigned against the FLA, FLA membership growth slowed drastically. Currently there are 170 college and university members of the FLA, a growth of only twenty in two years. In the meantime, WRC membership is now at 112, having grown by twenty-five each year in the same period.

A simple hypothesis about participation among "conscience" (as distinct from beneficiary) constituencies of movements like the antisweat-

TABLE 20.   Institutional Status and Antisweatshop Sit-ins, 1999–2000

(a) Universities

	Ranking (among national universities)
Spring 1999 USAS Sit-ins—Chronological Order	
Duke University	7
Georgetown University	23
University of Wisconsin at Madison	34
University of Michigan	25
Fairfield[a]	
University of North Carolina	27
University of Arizona	2d tier[b]
Spring 2000 USAS Sit-ins—Not in Chronological Order	
University of Toronto	1 (in Canada)
University of Pennsylvania	7
Johns Hopkins	7
University of Michigan	25
University of Wisconsin at Madison	34
Tulane University	44
State University of New York at Albany	2d tier
University of Oregon	2d tier
Purdue University	2d tier
University of Iowa	2d tier
University of Kentucky	2d tier
Ohio State University	2d tier

(b) Liberal Arts Colleges

	Ranking (among liberal arts colleges)
Spring 2000 USAS Sit-ins—Not in Chronological Order	
Pomona College	7
Wesleyan College	10
Macalester College	24
Pitzer College	2d tier

Source: Kreider 2000, 2001; *U.S. News and World Report;* and sources in table 19.
[a]Fairfield University ranks fourth among the "master's universities" of the northern United States.
[b]"2d tier" refers to those institutions ranked 51–120.

shop movement would predict concentration among affluent and professional families. Attention to international issues—and activism about them—tends to be higher among the more highly educated population. Even more than during the Vietnam War—which touched students' lives through conscription—current movement participants have little personal stake in the issue. Countering that, however, is the possibility that new cohorts of students among sons and daughters of blue-collar workers may be more empathic with sweatshop workers and may have a more positive sense of unions. The growing number of children of immigrants in higher education may make this issue more accessible to nonelite students.

About these possibilities there is only indirect information, and it conflicts. The institutional data mentioned earlier suggest, indirectly, that this movement has the same elite initiation with more broad-based recruitment subsequently—just as did the White New Left, albeit with more rapid change. On the other hand, a study of a sample of 233 students from four campuses discussed in Chapter 10 showed that immigrant background makes no very large difference in their general attitudes toward sweatshop issues.[6]

Strategy and Tactics: Direct Action

The 1999–2000 sit-ins of USAS focused on discrete behaviors or policies: adopt a code of conduct; join the WRC. This contrasts with the more diffuse agenda that emerged among some young activists as the movement became more oriented to the post–September 11 war on terrorism, American policy in the Middle East, and the war in Iraq (see Featherstone 2002).

In addition, there appears to be an important divide among the current activists. While some have committed themselves to campaigns for local fair labor purchasing ordinances by municipalities and others to living wage requirements for municipal contractors, most activists are uninterested in public policies in general. Opposition to the international financial institutions (IMF, World Bank, WTO) and to free trade agreements absorbs much activist energy, but not positive legislative agenda. This is associated with a widespread rejection of mainstream electoral action.[7]

Today's global justice movement has evolved from an antisweatshop movement to one whose leading cadres are more or less explicitly anticapitalist, certainly "anticorporate," in sentiment but who fear and recoil from the historically burdensome term "socialist." At their core the new young activists harbor a radical democratic impulse almost exactly similar to that of the young New Left of the early 1960s. The documents of today's campaigners attack the corporations and their greed; they talk of a new society built around new ethical principles—but they do not talk about a different mode of production.

Here is the opening paragraph from a mission statement from a local global action network.

> The people of WoGAN are feminist, partner preference supportive, anti-impe-rialist, anti-classist, anti-capitalist, anti-racist as well as being respectful toward all forms of life, all religions and the diversity of human experience. We believe that all should have equal access and equal voice in the global community. We view direct action as a viable method of decentralizing control and establishing autonomy. (WoGAN 2002)

At first glance one might think that this new movement was—as radical, labor oriented, and nonsocialist—the first authentically postsocialist left movement in American and even, given its equivalents abroad, world history. After all, movements built around community, race, or gender demands do not test whether the vision of a new economy is socialist or not. If radicals without a socialist vision led a movement for *economic* justice, that really would signal a shift in the paradigm of the left. As usual, reality is more subtle.

The vast majority of USAS activists interviewed for this study in the late 1990s said that in some personal way they were socialists or sympathetic to socialist vision. They did not, however, think that they could communicate this vision successfully to their peers or to other Americans; and their view of what social justice means is so communitarian and local, so close to the politics of race, gender and ethnicity, so close to identity politics, that the traditional meanings of socialism do not comprehend the totality of their consciousness. If the socialists of the 1960s were sociology students with economic ideas, this decade's radicals are international studies students with vegetarian anarchist culture.

This wave of activists began with sensitivity to the mass media and to the public discourse; they thought *socialism* was a losing phrase. Now, however, after September 11, 2001, and the Bush presidency, their mood is more culturally estranged and they embrace their own difference with more enthusiasm: there is hardly any ambivalence among them about their antiwar stance: if the United States is for it, they are against it.

Alliances: Relations to Labor

Until the fall of 2001, among the more striking characteristics of today's activists was their positive relation to the labor movement and to class issues.[8] In the 1990s the new movements, though not slavishly devoted to it, were influenced by the reformers in the AFL-CIO and, more strategically, related to working-class issues through workers in their production roles, not only or primarily in their community and consumption roles. Today's movement began not about the dependent poor but about those whose work is exploited.[9] This is poignantly expressed in the fact that sweatshop exploitation, not welfare reform, was the central founding issue of the new activists. The issue was made into a literally millennial vision when the Seattle 1999 demonstrations seemed to bring about a golden alliance of "turtles" (environmentalists, symbolizing young middle-class activists) and teamsters (symbolizing diverse unionists). This alliance with the labor movement, the most marked contrast between the old New Left and the beginning of the new New Left, was traceable to the emergence of global capitalism.

Although serious students of power rejected the notion of "big labor" by the 1960s, the desperate decline of the U.S. labor movement was not yet quite apparent. By 2000, though, union density in the private sector was one-third of what it was in the 1960s (see chap. 9, fig. 12). Blue-collar workers, who *seemed* to be riding the crest of American expansion in the 1960s, have been taking it on the chin for thirty years.

Decentralization and Organizational Structure

The continuing and dramatic attraction of a democratic vision produces among today's campaigners a goal of full participation by everyone, with little distinction between the responsibilities of leaders and others. It *prefers* consensus about decision making, and it reserves to local groups important decision making about policy and action. The resulting forms of organization are typically networks and only imperfectly unified or representative political organizations.

Local groups of the new global justice movement have elaborately formalized consensus decision-making procedures; they eschew representative forms almost entirely. Jo Freeman's famous caution about the "tyranny of structurelessness" is unknown (1972–73).

Perhaps as a result of the influence of a kind of seasoned feminism, USAS meetings are characterized by teaching and emulation of fairly sophisticated techniques of group discussion and leadership. As an example, the lead organizer from the Washington office at that time, Eric Brakken, led a New England regional group in a training exercise in resolving a community conflict. A rather detailed simulated problem was laid out, and elaborate role playing showed the different interests involved in a working-class community.

Observing USAS from the perspective of a campus at its periphery, one guess is that factional fights at its national center—at its annual conference, for example—has produced centrifugal force. Local groups are pretty much on their own, and the coordinating center has little authority. It has no real democratically empowered center; it runs locally on consensus, and it identifies strongly with life-style definitions of radicalism.

Life-Style Politics

Questions for every social movement include the following: Who is in? Who is out? Who are one's comrades, potential or actual? Who are one's adversaries?

Taken as a whole, the relation of the counterculture[10] to the political movement of the late 1960s and early 1970s had a paradoxical element. On the one hand, it is probable that without the ebullience of the counterculture the more focused political movement of young adults would have been much smaller. On the other hand, the counterculture and the associated "life-style politics" estranged the movement from most all subcultures and classes—not just "bourgeois" culture. It created a cultural ghetto within which political radicalism could flourish but beyond which it could not grow. If hostility to the nuclear family and contempt for the coping strategies of working-class families characterize a social movement, it is unlikely to make inroads to any class—no less the working class.

By comparison, today's young activists evince continuity with the cultural frontiers of the 1960s New Left, but with some differences. There is a high level of gender consciousness, and great care is taken to ensure gender equity. This is part of a broadly conceived identity consciousness in which inherited characteristics (e.g., race, ethnicity, gender, and religion, including the now fashionable "paganism")—what sociologists call *ascribed* attributes—are taken to be political building blocks.

Among the more obvious developments is the acute consciousness of sexual orientation in today's movement. Thus the litany of affirmations quoted previously from the local group Worcester Global Action Network (WoGAN):

> The people of WoGAN are feminist, partner preference supportive, anti-imperialist, anti-classist, anti-capitalist, anti-racist as well as being respectful toward all forms of life, all religions and the diversity of human experience. (WoGAN 2002)

Drug taking does not appear to be as central to identity and to cultural participation as it was earlier. On the other hand, vegetarianism has a strong and ostensibly political presence and privileged cultural position; animal rights—including a doctrine of species equality—are assumed and declared rather than debated.

International Context

The new student movement is sharply aware of the context of global capitalism. The opening years of the global justice movement had a different and vastly more positive relationship to workers and to unions at the cutting edge of international solidarity than did those of a generation ago. Even the war in Iraq did not cause an irreparable breach with the labor movement—for large sectors of the union leadership were skeptical about or opposed the war (Sweeney and Monks 2003; Sweeney 2002).

Nevertheless, the way this current cohort of activists addresses the sweatshop issue internationally has an apparently paradoxical quality. Despite its positive links to American labor, the movement activists emphasize the plight of sweatshop workers in other countries rather than domestic sweatshop workers.

When in the fall of 1999 activists at Brown University were asked in a group interview why they seemed to put forward issues in developing countries more frequently and with more fervor, the answer was that "It's more hard-core" to advocate for workers in a developing country (Brown University SLAC 1999). A rough translation: it is more chic to advocate for people in the Third World. In consequence, the quarter of a million sweatshop workers in the United States are rarely visible on their campaigns.

Examples of community involvement in North America are fewer—but not absent.

The Living Wage

The student sit-in for a living wage for Harvard University employees in the spring of 2001 is a noble example. In that campaign Harvard students supported a living wage standard (calculated at $10.68 per hour in Cambridge, Massachusetts) for university employees. In support of that demand the students occupied the administration building for three weeks. At the end, the university agreed to reopen discussions it had previously closed and to raise a group of cafeteria workers' wages.

Significantly, the contract discussions of those workers, under way during the sit-in, included the demand that the students be given amnesty for their action (Manners 2001; Kuttner 2001).

Reporting in 2001 Alexander Gourevitch observed that the living wage "movement has won ordinances in over 50 localities including Los Angeles County, Boston, Baltimore, San Francisco, Minneapolis, and Oakland. This parallels recent victories and partial victories on college campuses at Wesleyan, University of Connecticut (after a three day sit-in), Johns Hopkins, and Harvard" (Gourevitch 2001).

USAS activists know that workers in the United States have deep problems. And occasionally they make the connection between the poverty of workers in developing countries and poverty and poverty wages in Los Angeles. For whatever reasons, though, the most notable campaigns of the new antisweatshop movement on campuses have been on behalf of workers in developing countries.

A Tale of Two Factories

On August 31, 2001, a Mexican factory owned by a Korean investor, one that makes campus logo clothing for Nike and Reebok, recognized an independent union of its workers. The Mexmode (Kukdong)[11] management's recognition of the SITEMEX union followed a two-year struggle. On September 21, the independent union, representing more than 80 percent of the workers, signed a collective bargaining agreement with management (Burnett 2001; Centro de Apoyo al Trabajador 2001b, 4; Herzog 2001). With an officially recognized independent union, workers had, after a difficult and sometimes dangerous campaign, gained a means of voicing their grievances and negotiating their terms of employment.

On March 26, 2003, the Sindicato de Trabajadores de la Empresa BJ&B S.A., an independent union of workers at a factory in the company town of Villa Altagracia in the Dominican Republic, successfully negotiated a first contract with the BJ&B factory, owned by the Korean-based Yupoong Corporation (Hawley 2003). Included in the contract are promises by management to "neither encourage nor promote another union organization" and to "not exercise any form of discrimination against the union and its members" (Nova 2003a). Furthermore, the contract stipulates a 10 percent wage increase starting January 2004, ensures clean drinking water at the end of each production line, and promises an improved working environment with better lighting and more hygienic restroom facilities. The contract also guarantees an annual DR$500 Christmas bonus (Nova 2003a). This result culminated efforts of workers at BJ&B begun almost seven years earlier, in late 1996.

In both cases, antisweatshop campaigners in USAS had combined with U.S.-based unions to pressure firms based in the United States to respect workers' rights to organize unions. The institution they had created, the WRC, played a key investigative and negotiating role in both campaigns. Consumer-oriented advocacy groups—NGOs—had helped publicize the workers' cause. Taken together, the Mexmode and BJ&B cases show how much the new antisweatshop movement has accomplished and can accomplish and on reflection suggest the limitations of the factory-by-factory campaign approach to the global problem of labor abuse.

Mexmode (Kukdong)

Kukdong International de Mexico S.A. de C.V. is in many ways a typical maquila. Privately owned by a Korean man, Kyu Su Byun, eight hundred people are employed by Kukdong, 85 percent of whom are women. Most are single, between the ages of sixteen and twenty-three, and have a middle school education (Verité 2001, 2; Centro de Apoyo al Trabajador 2001a, 5–15). Kukdong has been producing sweatshirts and pants for Nike and Reebok since 2000. During that year, Kukdong produced approximately forty thousand pieces for Reebok and 1 million pieces for Nike (Verité 2001, 2). A significant percentage of the Nike and Reebok apparel produced in Kukdong is for American universities with which Nike and Reebok have licensing agreements. This was to prove vital for the workers' struggle to get union recognition and a decent contract.

Puebla State in Mexico has the largest apparel employment in the country. The town in which the Kukdong factory is located—Atlixco—

has another large factory as well—Matamoros Garment. Conditions there were so bad that Kukdong's initial recruitment in November 1999 found willing hands. Marcela Muñoz, a twenty-two-year-old single mother from Cheitla, a sewing supervisor at Kukdong and a former employee of Matamoros, said of Matamoros: "It was horrible there. The union that supposedly represented the workers was also CROC [Confederación Revolucionario de Obreros y Campesinos]. We were never paid on time and were forced to work overtime if we did not finish our daily quota. . . . The conditions got so bad I decided to leave and work at Kukdong" (Centro de Apoyo al Trabajador 2001a, 7). Juana Hernandez, a sixteen-year-old from San Juan Calmeca who worked in sewing line 1 at Kukdong, explained: "A group of Koreans that told us to work at Kukdong . . . said the salary at Kukdong was better, there was free transportation to and from work, and we would receive free breakfast and lunch" (Centro de Apoyo al Trabajador 2001a, 5).

The official union at Kukdong was the CROC.[12] The CROC was the trade union affiliate of the former ruling party in Mexico—the PRI. The PRI still has considerable local strength throughout Mexico, and it ruled so long and became so corrupt that its union affiliate, the CROC, became a series of company unions. The CROC is often a "protection union," with which employers write toothless "sweetheart contracts" in return for which CROC officials receive dues-supported jobs in the union bureaucracy. Local labor boards, which by Mexican law certify unions and union recognition, often have close and biased commitments to the CROC. The Kukdong workers did not know that management had signed a contract with the CROC in December 1999 for six months after it had been accomplished (Centro de Apoyo al Trabajador 2001a, 3).

At the Kukdong factory, workers suffered physical and verbal abuse from supervisors; rotten, infested food at the cafeteria; illegal withholding of bonuses; and mandatory overtime (Centro de Apoyo al Trabajador 2001a, 3; WRC 2001b; Verité 2001). Workers' concerns led them to try to form an independent union that would represent their collective interests. The heart of the struggle, one that engaged supporters and the public in the United States, was over their "associational rights"—their right to free association, to form a union, and to engage in collective bargaining. Firings of leaders and later members of their independent union and beatings by CROC thugs put the right of association in jeopardy.

During the first full year of operations factory conditions apparently worsened. Rotten food was the immediate cause of worker discussion and initial organization. On November 30, 2000, USAS planned a delegation to Mexico with the United Electrical Workers (UE). USAS activists Molly McGrath, Eric Brakken, and Evelyn Zepeda participated in the delegation, along with student and labor delegates from the UE. The delegation also included David Ernesto Alvarado, an employee of the AFL-CIO Solidarity Center in Mexico and a former USAS member (Mancini 2000; McGrath 2003; Williams 2000).[13] Alvarado had been building a relationship with Kukdong workers since he discovered the Kukdong factory on the WRC disclosure list and scheduled a visit with workers as part of the UE delegation. Molly McGrath, currently director of development in the USAS national office, recalls the workers stating that the situation at the factory was very bad and that it was time to do something about it (McGrath 2003).

On December 15, 2000, the workers boycotted the factory cafeteria. The CROC failed to represent them to the management (Centro de Apoyo al Trabajador 2001a, 3). After the holiday break, leaders and activists were fired. Workers confronted management to no avail, and on January 8 about six hundred workers held a two-hour strike demanding the reinstatement of the leaders. Management promised to explain themselves, but did not. On January 9 more than six hundred workers remained at the factory,[14] saying they would occupy the yard of the facility indefinitely until their demands were addressed. They voiced three demands: (1) the cafeteria food must be improved; (2) the company must replace the CROC; and (3) the fired supervisors must be reinstated (Centro de Apoyo al Trabajador 2001a, 4).

On January 11, after management had made official complaints and procured arrest warrants for the leadership of the workers occupation, two hundred police in riot gear violently broke up the demonstration and removed over six hundred employees, 85 percent of whom were women, from the facility (Boje, Rosile, and Alcantara Carrillo 2001; Burnett 2001; Centro de Apoyo al Trabajador 2001a, 14; Vickery 2001).[15]

Although the excessive police violence successfully evicted workers, it caused a backlash that mobilized U.S. activists. USAS immediately responded to workers' request for help by inundating the fax, phone, and e-mail lines of Kukdong management, Nike, and Mexican government officials in support of the workers' demands.[16]

The day following the police repression, USAS activist Evelyn Zepeda arrived in Atlixco to serve as a USAS-Kukdong liaison. The position was funded by the AFL-CIO Solidarity Center in Mexico to provide an international observer presence at the factory and to build the student-worker relationship. Zepeda lived with Kukdong organizer Marcela Muñoz and facilitated direct Internet-based communication between workers and USAS. Additionally, thousands of solidarity letters began pouring in to support workers, including letters from an independent union at a Nike subcontracted factory in Thailand and workers at another Kukdong-owned factory in Indonesia (Muchhala 2001; Joffe-Block 2001).[17]

With a USAS activist, supported by the AFL-CIO Solidarity Center, reporting events from the town of Atlixco, the workers then turned to the newly created WRC. On January 18, 2001, four Kukdong workers submitted a formal code of conduct violation complaint to the WRC. The workers were referred to the WRC via contacts at the local AFL-CIO Solidarity Center in Mexico. The WRC responded immediately by sending a fact-finding delegation to Puebla for the period of January 20–23 (Gourevitch 2001; WRC 2001a, 1). The day after the delegation returned, the WRC released its "Preliminary Findings and Recommendations," outlining the workers' complaints, the parties involved, the persons interviewed, and recommendations to Kukdong management. The document revealed thoroughly corroborated evidence of violations of Mexican labor law, the university Codes of Conduct, and ILO standards. The report stated that:

- Kukdong has employed children ages thirteen to fifteen for nine- to ten-hour workdays.
- Kukdong managers have committed acts of physical and verbal abuse against workers.
- Kukdong has denied maternity leaves and benefits and sick leaves to workers.
- Kukdong management does not pay the minimum wage as mandated by Mexican law for the occupation of seamstress.

- Poor quality of food served in the cafeteria has caused rashes, fevers, and gastrointestinal disorders for workers on more than one occasion.
- On January 3, 2001, Kukdong fired five supervisory workers for no credible reason other than their role in exercising their freedom of association.
- In response to a work stoppage supported by a broad majority of factory employees, Kukdong enterprise called in hundreds of riot police on January 9 and used excessive force to remove workers from the Kukdong compound.
- As of January 22, 2001, Kukdong has not honored its agreement to rehire hundreds of workers who were fired for their participation in the work stoppage. (WRC 2001a)

A final report, released on June 20, 2001, elaborated upon the delegation's findings.

The WRC disclosure list revealed that Kukdong produced apparel for almost twenty different U.S. universities.[18] Some of the universities with the largest licensing contracts and most leverage with Nike—University of Wisconsin at Madison, University of North Carolina at Chapel Hill, University of Michigan, University of Arizona, Indiana University, and University of Iowa—would be pivotal players in improving Kukdong labor practice (Nova 2003b). Students at these universities worked with the WRC to use the "Preliminary Findings and Recommendations" to pressure their administrations into action. The licensing contract between the universities and Nike and Reebok ultimately allowed the universities to hold the corporations accountable to the code of conduct agreement included in the university licensing agreement.

Over the first few weeks of 2001 students began demonstrations (including civil disobedience in Chicago and San Francisco) at Niketown stores demanding that Nike pressure Kukdong's management to respect workers' rights—and Nike declared it would do so (Manager 2001; Weaver 2001). In February, Verité, an independent social auditing firm hired by Nike and Reebok, performed a brief study and essentially verified the WRC findings.

Throughout the winter of 2001 the management at Kukdong made repeated pledges to rehire fired workers and to respect union rights; each time they failed to follow through, and Nike found itself repeatedly making public pledges to communicate its concerns to Kukdong. In March workers held a large assembly to initiate legal recognition as an independent union; also in March Nike pledged to support workers' right to do so; and Nike also criticized USAS for "inflaming" the local situation (Kidd and Morris 2001b).

Still Kukdong management used a variety of means to resist legally acknowledging the union.[19] The CROC harassed members and leaders—including bribery, threats, and beatings (Campaign for Labor Rights 2001; Centro de Apoyo al Trabajador 2001a, 16). The USAS response (recall that Evelyn Zepeda was on the scene) was once again to request letters, phone calls, faxes, and e-mails to Nike, Kukdong, and Mexican government officials.

During the summer of 2001 Nike, citing seasonal drop-off in demand for heavy sweatshirts, cut its orders with the factory. A U.S. student-based research team, coordinated by Zepeda, visited Atlixco and wrote a report on the workers' campaign for recognition (Centro de Apoyo al Trabajador 2001b). A team of students stayed in Atlixco for the summer. Their work and reports moved through the USAS list serve.

By August 2001 the Kukdong factory had insufficient orders and laid off hundreds of workers; 350 remained. The factory changed its name to Mexmode. On September 10 the independent union, renamed SITEMEX, presented a new petition, endorsed by 400 active and former workers of Mexmode, for recognition to the local labor board (Centro de Apoyo al Trabajador 2001b, 1). A week later, SITEMEX was granted registration by the Puebla labor board. In a vote of confidence called by SITEMEX leaders, only two workers voted against the union, while two-thirds voted in approval. On September 21 the Mexmode management signed an agreement with the workers.

In October the factory began to revive, but Nike had not yet renewed any order with it. A delegation of Mexmode workers visited U.S. universities, including the licensors who had contracts with Nike and Reebok. They thanked them for their efforts and encouraged them to communicate to Nike. On November 30, having received six thousand communications from seventeen countries (Maquila Solidarity Network 2001), Nike announced it would place new orders with Mexmode, explaining that it continued production at Mexmode[20] "to serve as both a successful incentive to the factory management to adopt changes and to stabilize the workforce" (Kidd and Morris 2001b).

Combating Sweatshops from the Grass Roots

On April 1, 2002, with the leadership of the independent union, Mex-mode workers won a wage increase. The settlement included a 10 percent increase in wages, a 5 percent increase in benefits, and an attendance bonus (Maquila Solidarity Network 2002). As of June 2003, wages have increased several other times since that date. The Centro de Apoyo al Trabajador, formed to support workers in the Kukdong struggle, subsequently became active supporting workers organizing for an independent union in Matamoros Garment.[21]

Components of Success I

This case history highlights a very few key resources and dynamics that underlay the workers' ability to secure union rights and improved conditions.

- Once the Mexmode (Kukdong) workers initiated action, they received support and assistance from two related northern allies: organized labor and the student movement.
- The AFL-CIO resources supported contacts and organizers among the workers.
- The USAS presence created a fast-acting communication and pressure network.
- The communication network was aimed at the top of the power pyramid—the big brands Nike and Reebok—upon whom pressure by publicity was exercised.
- The big brands in turn applied pressure to the contractor to change its behavior.
- The student movement had created an institution—the WRC (with the help and advice of UNITE)—that was able to respond quickly to worker complaints.
- The ability of the AFL-CIO's Solidarity Center staffer David Alvarado to target Kukdong, and for the WRC to bring pressure to bear on Nike and Reebok, was based on the disclosure requirement in WRC members' codes of conduct and the contractual agreements into which licensees entered with universities that imposed codes of conduct (including disclosure of sites of production).

Unexplained are the social, cultural, and psychological resources that enabled the workers to persevere despite intimidation and frustration over an extended period of time. There are two hints, however. Numerous among the Mexmode workers and activists were those who had worked in the United States—and at least one had been a UNITE activist in New York City. Josefina Morastitla Morales, for example, had participated in five organizing campaigns in Manhattan's sweatshops and attributed her deportation to owner vengeance. An estimated 75 percent of Mexicans in New York are from Puebla, and even while the struggle at Kukdong was going on, workers from that factory were migrating to the United States (Centro de Apoyo al Trabajador 2001a, 12). So there was direct and prior experience among these workers of the industry, of union activity in it, and of American companies and their ways. These are not totally naive rural migrants.

Another local resource developed during the course of the Kukdong struggle: Centro de Apoyo al Trabajador. It is staffed by students and professionals and aids in communications and research. Centro de Apoyo al Trabajador teamed with various delegations to produce research that revealed the Kukdong struggle to broader North American audiences.

The structure of this success is strikingly similar to that of the BJ&B campaign in the Dominican Republic. Though it was settled later than the Kukdong campaign, the BJ&B story started earlier, and it links vitally to the very founding of USAS.

Villa Altagracia, Dominican Republic: BJ&B

The Korean hat and cap manufacturer Yupoong Incorporated owns the BJ&B S.A. factory in the Zona Franca Industrial de Villa Altagracia (Yupoong Inc. 2002). Villa Altagracia is a town of approximately eighty-five thousand people located twenty miles northwest of the Dominican capital of Santo Domingo (Safa 1999). The BJ&B seven-plant industrial complex originally employed approximately 2,050 workers (as of spring 2003 the number was 1,500), 95 percent of whom were female, and is the main economic base for an area suffering from its decline as a sugar-processing center (UNITE 1998; Safa 1999).

Yupoong Inc. was established in 1974, and it is the second largest worldwide manufacturer of baseball caps (UNITE 1998; Yupoong Inc. 2002).

Yupoong's BJ&B factory produces ball caps for several major American universities, including Cornell, Purdue, Tulane, Louisiana State, San Diego State, and Northwestern University, as well as the universities of Arizona, Connecticut, Missouri, New Hampshire, North Carolina, and Washington (WRC 2001b). In addition, it has contracts with the four main American professional sports leagues—the MLB, NFL, NHL, and NBA—as well as with major brand names such as Nike, Champion, Gap, Disney, and Fila, among others. Between the BJ&B factory and the much smaller Moca factory, Yupoong Inc.'s subsidiaries in the Dominican Republic manufacture 14.4 million hats per year (UNITE 1998).

In late 1997, UNITE was contacted by the Federacion Nacional de Trabajadores de Zonas (Federation of Free Trade Zone workers, or FENATRAZONAS) to investigate BJ&B (Ordonez 2003). UNITE staff traveled to BJ&B and conducted an investigation of the factory from December 1997 to January 1998.

In April 1998, UNITE published a report on BJ&B conditions directed toward students at universities that licensed products produced at BJ&B. The report listed numerous labor rights violations by BJ&B management. It asserted that workers at BJ&B were physically abused by managers, with one two-year veteran of BJ&B reporting, "When you get in trouble, they will grab your face and smack you on the head" (UNITE 1998). Workers were sexually abused as well—managers often groped women with impunity. Workers also suffered verbal humiliation, with Korean managers yelling graphic racial and sexual insults at the employees.

The Dominican government itself acknowledged that the sixty-nine-cents-an-hour wage earned by BJ&B workers was approximately one-third of the wages needed to house, feed, and clothe the typical family. BJ&B's wages effectively forced lives of poverty upon its workforce. Most BJ&B workers live in small self-made houses of corrugated iron or wood. Many lack indoor plumbing; all are crowded (UNITE 1998). When told that the hats he makes sold for twenty dollars in the United States, one man asked, "Why do we get paid so little if these caps sell for so much? I'm working 56 hours a week and sometimes I can't afford clothes for my children" (Herbert 1998).

The factory itself was hazardous. Workers once found a mound of ringworms in the water that BJ&B provided; when a manager was shown, he laughed. There were documented incidents in which employees injured on the job were subsequently fired (UNITE 1998).

UNITE began its 1998 campaign in support of BJ&B workers at the very moment it was also supporting the initial stages of the organization of USAS. Just as the union was about to sponsor a delegation of BJ&B workers to visit American campuses where their hats were sold, the founding group of USAS activists at Duke, including Tico Almeida, were seeing the first code of conduct adopted.

During mid- to late April 1998, UNITE followed up on its report by bringing two BJ&B employees to the United States to tell their stories. The employees, nineteen-year-old Kenia Rodriquez and twenty-year-old Roselio Reyes, embarked on a tour of universities. These included Harvard, Brown, Georgetown, Cornell, Rutgers, and the University of Illinois (Herbert 1998). The goals for Rodriquez, Reyes, and UNITE were to inform students of the conditions under which their university's logo clothing was being produced and to pressure administrations to implement codes of conduct as Duke had done. Students held demonstrations to complement the speakers' message and to inform their classmates of the situation (*Business Wire* 1998). One Boston University student picked up on the new spirit of solidarity between students and workers: "A lot of people are being exploited. I feel that I need to do something" (Keppler and Shaw 1998).

The tour garnered major press coverage and the attention of public officials. Articles appeared in the *New York Times,* the *Irish Times,* the *Boston Globe,* the *Boston Herald,* and several college newspapers, as well as on *National Public Radio*'s "Weekend All Things Considered." On June 14 at a Northeastern University rally, Senator Edward M. Kennedy urged Massachusetts's schools to put into place codes of conduct requiring that merchandise suppliers pay workers a living wage (Wolfson 1998).

At the USAS founding conference in the summer of 1998, BJ&B came to highlight the issue of sweatshops for the group, and USAS began a close collaboration with UNITE on the issue (McGrath 2003).[22]

In the period after this initial tour, the factory management apparently made some changes:

Clean drinking water has replaced the ringworm infested cistern water that was provided for employees to drink; putrid bathrooms have been cleaned; and, students are now allowed to leave work on time in order to be able to attend night classes (factory managers allow them to leave earlier, unless production is high and deadlines need to be met). (behind the label.org, 2001)

Despite the initial movement, the 1998 attempt to form a union by BJ&B workers was not immediately successful. One of the speakers on the 1998 tour, Roselio Reyes, was a college student working at the factory. He eventually went to work for FENATRAZONAS. Reyes participated in the USAS actions that led to the formation of the WRC (Schwennesen 2000).

By the fall of 2001, the WRC had been founded and had started functioning—and once again BJ&B workers turned to their North American allies. Evelyn Zepeda, the former USAS member who had worked in the Kukdong campaign, moved to Villa Altagracia for nine months to aid the workers there. In December 2001 they filed a complaint with the WRC stating they had been prevented from exercising their right to form a union. The WRC, after consultations, determined there was cause for concern. Director Scott Nova contacted Nike (then the largest customer of the factory), but no action was taken before the holiday closure.

In January 2002 Nova traveled to Villa Altagracia. There he interviewed workers, union leaders, and the plant management. Nova attempted to persuade the factory management to rehire the twenty workers they had fired in retaliation for their union activity. Upon returning to the United States, Nova contacted Nike on January 14 and again urged the corporation to take action and put pressure on the plant owners. Nova also briefed the FLA's director, Auret van Heerden, on the situation. Nova and van Heerden agreed that the WRC and FLA should cooperate on the case (Nova 2003b). On January 16, Nike, joined by Reebok International Ltd. and adidas-Salomon, filed a third-party complaint with the FLA over the antiunion activity at BJ&B (FLA 2003a).[23] After talks and negotiations between the WRC, FLA, the union, BJ&B management, and Yupoong, an agreement was signed on January 28 to reinstate thirteen of the twenty fired union organizers. The remaining seven either had left the union and been reinstated or no longer sought to work at BJ&B (Nova 2003a).

By early February 2002 the workers filed a new petition for recognition of their union. This was granted (by the Dominican authorities). Yet another WRC delegation visited the plant in this period, and once again they found management intimidating workers to prevent them from joining the union. The WRC approached the brands, in particular Nike, and later in the month Nike wrote a letter to the plant management, saying that

> The workers of BJ&B should be allowed to freely decide if they want a workers' organization, and if so, which organization they want to have that role, free of any interference by factory management or any outside interested party, in accordance to the legal procedures established in the law of the Dominican Republic. (Kidd, cited in FLA 2002b, 7)

Reebok and adidas-Salomon also wrote letters of similar content in the course of the spring of 2002. The formal FLA delegation visited the plant in the first week of March. Nova accompanied as an observer. Although the FLA report is written in extremely bland and conditional language, it finds in effect that the management abridged the right of association (FLA 2002b). The FLA proposed a variety of remedial actions, including policy clarification, training for supervisors and workers on the right of association, and cessation of antiunion indoctrination of new hires.

The spring and summer of 2002 witnessed some progress in labor management relations, but there were spectacular failures. Resin fumes overcame fifty workers in early June, causing a three-day plant closure; the Dominican Department of Labor intervened and, with the help of the respected labor lawyer–mediator Dr. Rafael Albuquerque, saw to the formation of a safety and health committee.

Then, in mid-June, anonymous leaflets accused the union activists of being terrorists, saying their activity would cause BJ&B to close. The other Dominican factory owned by the firm and one in Bangladesh gave this threat credibility. As in other towns that have suffered loss of employment, many in Villa Altagracia were fearful that union activity might cause further capital flight: the race to the bottom in labor standards globally usually involves the mobilization of local opinion to deter worker aggressiveness—everywhere. The WRC made representations about the importance of workers' rights to organize to its member universities and their codes of conduct, to Yupoong in Seoul, and to its lawyers in Washington; and Director Nova met with the brands and the FLA to warn them of the latest threats to the workers' rights. On July 12, 2002, BJ&B's top managers announced that, as advised by Yupoong, they had met with all supervisors and ordered them to cease all antiunion activity (Nova 2003a).

Through the rest of 2002 the BJ&B management continued to fight each stage of the process and to harass the union activists between each stage. When the union filed with the labor board, declaring it represented a majority of the workers, management disputed its majority. Then management fired some union leaders (again). The WRC-FLA tandem subsequently persuaded the BJ&B management to accept the "neutral party" Dr. Albuquerque's count of the workers signing cards indicating their membership in the new union—and the union majority was once again official.

With official status secured by early 2003, the BJ&B workers received solidarity delegations from USAS in March, and USAS held actions and sent messages in support of the workers to the brands in March 2003 as well. Throughout this period Evelyn Zepeda, a former Pitzer College student and USAS member, lived in Villa Altagracia—from December 2001 to September 2003 (Zepeda 2003).

On March 26, 2003, the first contract was signed; Saturday, May 24, 2003, was the first day that dues were deducted from union workers' paychecks. Consequently, it was the first day that management had a complete list of all union members. Although the WRC had received assurances that no intimidation would ensue, a number of BJ&B supervisors took it upon themselves to personally deliver the unionized employees their paychecks, often with words of harassment. In some cases workers were threatened with termination in response to their union affiliation (Nova 2003).

The following week, Sindicato de Trabajadores de la Empresa BJ&B S.A. dealt with the situation without the aid of any of the watchdog NGOs. Management was made to apologize over the factory PA system and announce that no workers would be terminated for association with the union (Nova 2003b).

Today, Sindicato de Trabajadores de la Empresa BJ&B S.A. is the largest representative and democratic union in any free trade zone (USAS 2003b). According to the WRC's Scott Nova, although the primary emphasis of understanding this result should be on the years of struggle and hard work on the part of the workers at BJ&B, the student movement in the United States helped tremendously (Nova 2003b). As Nova explained it, the codes of conduct that so many students fought for, rallied for, and sat in for are what gave the WRC and other organizations the footing and teeth to launch their own campaigns to ensure compliance. Quite simply, "The outside intervention was made possible by codes of conduct" (Nova 2003b).

The general secretary of FENATRAZONAS, Ignacio Hernandez, said in the latest *New York Times* article on the case, "I never thought a group of students, thousands of them, could put so much pressure on these brands. We were determined to win, but without them it would have taken five more years" (Gonzalez 2003).

Components of Success II

Through an antisweatshop grant from the United States Agency for International Development (USAID), the AFL-CIO Solidarity Center provided support for training of union organizers, supported USAS delegate Evelyn Zepeda's stay in Villa Altagracia, gave general advice and counsel to the local organizers, and facilitated connections between the union on the ground and other organizations.

Jeff Hermanson, the head of the AFL-CIO Solidarity Center in Mexico and formerly a leader in UNITE's attempts to combat sweatshops in New York and Los Angeles, set down his thoughts about the BJ&B contract signing in a file memorandum in March 2003.

Noting that this was "the first time a free trade zone company has agreed to a contractual wage increase above the government-mandated minimum wage," Hermanson observed that "The organizing campaign saw fierce intimidation and threats of firings and plant closing, and many unlawful firings of union leaders and activists. Some union leaders were fired three times" (Hermanson 2003a).

Strategically, Hermanson said,

> the success of the BJ&B campaign is evidence that the multifaceted anti-sweat-
> shop strategy that has been developed in the past few years in campaigns such as
> Kukdong (Mexico) . . . is an effective means of combating the evils of the sweat-
> shop. By winning important and high-visibility victories in the *maquiladoras*
> and free trade zone factories of Asia, Africa and Latin America, drawing upon
> local resources and support organizations, linked with a network of global sup-
> port organizations, using all the levers of pressure in the home country and in
> the global marketplace, this strategy demonstrates to workers and their support-
> ers the road forward, and sets the stage for victories on a broader scale.

Hermanson, of course, honored the endurance and activism of the Dominican union federation and of the BJ&B workers themselves. He noted that Evelyn Zepeda, "also an important presence in the Kukdong campaign in Mexico in 2001, provided daily guidance, training and tech-nical assistance to the union activists, and provided assistance in main-taining direct communication between the organizing campaign and the student and NGO support movement in the US." He said that "the cam-paign could not have been successful without the broad and diverse net-work of organizations that provided information in support of the cam-paign to US consumers and the general public." Hermanson identified the WRC codes of conduct, its consultations with the brands, and with the FLA as essential to the union victory.

Hermanson's view of the components of the BJ&B success has a strik-ingly similar structure to the one we discovered in the Mexmode (Kuk-dong) case:

- Worker activism that persisted despite intimidation and firings and physical harassment.
- Critical resources supplied by U.S. unions.
- Activist support among consumers with leverage—the colleges with logo licenses and the student consumers.
- Institutional support in the form of the WRC's ability to act quickly and the WRC's willingness to turn to the FLA—its nominal competitor—for resources and leverage at the right moments.

The critics of the antisweatshop movement—and its own internal doubters—often wonder whether it actually has had any positive impact. Harvard hourly workers; Mexmode apparel workers; BJ&B cap makers—

they have little doubt as to the answer to this question. Yet, the apparel business engages tens of millions of workers around the world.

In addition to the elements common to both of these cases of grass roots "victories" was an obstacle: the inability or unwillingness of local governments to enforce their laws impartially and the absence of consistent policy favoring union organization of the workforce. Lurking beneath both cases, too, was the fierce resistance to workers' needs and union demands by the middleman contractor. While in the United States these contractors are typically small with but dozens of workers, in Central America and around the world, apparel sweatshops tend to be much larger, and the contractors are a new kind of multinational corporation: middleman employers of direct labor working on behalf of globally identifiable brands.

The Limits of the Campaign Approach

While the number of global retail chains and the number of brands that commission apparel production is small, the number of factories globally engaged in the rag trade is large indeed. The U.S.-based NLC once estimated that Wal-Mart contracted with one thousand factories in China alone (NLC 2000). Nike reported to the FLA that it contracted with about eleven hundred factories. If change efforts were to focus on one campaign per factory, the reform process could stretch through a millennium.

Instead, campaigners hope that their successes will restrain unscrupulous employers in succeeding rounds of organizing. Furthermore, they hope that big powers in the industry will become ever more sensitive to the demands for decent treatment and will impose conditions on their contractors earlier and with more force. These hopes might be but slender reeds when pushed up against the tides of global competition.

When Jeff Hermanson read a draft of these comments, however, his thoughtful reply provided a rationale for this campaign strategy:

> In my reading of the history of working class struggle, the major broad social gains (such as the Wagner Act and the Fair Labor Standards Act) were a product of broad class movements, but those movements were gestated in one factory

after another, quite often following epic, ground-breaking struggles in a single workplace . . . which precipitated many other . . . strikes. (Hermanson 2003b)

Hermanson continued, saying that the strategy is to find a vulnerable plant and win:

> Workers in the sector and/or region see the victory and begin to realize their own power to change conditions, and to be more receptive to the idea of organizing. Employers in the sector also see the victory, and begin to realize their vulnerability, and to think of ways to deal with it, among the ways being "making a deal to save the company from a damaging fight."
>
> If the situation is "ripe" enough, i.e. if conditions in the factories are generally bad, the workers are not completely defeated and hopeless, the state is not prepared to openly and violently repress every struggle, the employers are not able to shut down every factory where a campaign is begun, etc., then it is quite probable that a single important victory can lead to a broad movement in many factories.
>
> The "single plant organizing" is that only in appearance, as it is part of a broader strategy to organize the entire industry, starting with a single factory, and progressing as rapidly as possible to develop the forces capable of organizing many factories.

Hermanson's comments accurately reflect aspects of the (relevant) experience of the surge of industrial union organization in the United States during the mid-1930s. Nevertheless, the sense they have of the need for broader, systemic address to labor exploitation accounts for the gradual broadening of the antisweatshop movement within USAS itself but also among activists who move from USAS to other global justice formations. This broader agenda is a function of their perception that the key to global justice, including labor standards, is the regulation of global capital and trade.

12 Solidarity North and South

Reframing International Labor Rights

Prologue on May Day 2003

When the advocates of unrestrained global capitalism attack regulations against labor abuse, they usually refer to economic growth as the curative for long hours and low pay (e.g., Kristof and WuDunn 2000). Thinking about the history of May Day observances shows how closely it is related to the story of sweatshops and efforts to control the labor abuses they signify. The story of May Day begins with the struggle to make the eight-hour workday the legal and economic norm for wageworkers. In the older industrial countries this struggle was largely successful, though, as we have seen, the last twenty years of apparel work has brought old abuses back. It makes sense to think about this history carefully.

Had the task of regulating the workday been left only to market effects of economic growth, and not to social, political, and trade union action, how many more of us would be toiling the same ten- and twelve-hour days that our grandparents did or that sewing machine operators in New York, Los Angeles, and Guangdong Province do now?

Since late in the eighteenth century American workers have sought to protect their lives, families, and humanity by limiting the hours of the

284

workday. In 1844 John Cluers led a labor federation calling for July 4 of that year to be declared a Second Independence Day in support of the ten-hour day (Foner 1986, 17).

In the fall of 1885 the predecessor to the AFL decided upon May 1886 as the start of a series of strikes for the eight-hour workday.[1] They called for demonstrations declaring that after May 1 the working day would be de facto eight hours. Hundreds of thousands did demonstrate and strike that day, and tens of thousands won shorter hours (Foner 1986, 27). The most memorable and tragic events of the 1886 struggle occurred in the days directly after what Samuel Gompers, the first AFL president, also grandly called the Second Independence Day.

In Chicago the lumber shovers' union of ten thousand was on strike for the eight-hour day. They held a rally on May 3. The earlier May 1 rally in Chicago had been gigantic, and the city was tense. The May 3 rally took place very near the McCormick Harvester Works, then gripped in a bitter lockout and strike. As the workday ended at Harvester, strikebreakers came through the gates and some of the six thousand rallying workers protested against them. Police shot at the rallying lumber shovers and killed four.

On the next day, May 4, the leaders of the Chicago eight-hour movement, anarcho-syndicalists of exceptional leadership ability, called for a protest of the shootings and a demonstration of resolve. It was rainy, and there were numerous neighborhood rallies that day. The crowd was small. It dwindled from three thousand when the charismatic Albert Spies spoke, followed by his comrade Albert Parsons. By the time Samuel Fielden began his address the crowd had become only three hundred.

Then 180 armed police, who had been waiting in a side street, marched into Haymarket Square, surrounded the small throng, and ordered the crowd to disperse. Fielden defended his right to speak. The police approached the platform, and a bomb was thrown at them. One died there and six later. Later research showed that the police who later died were shot by friendly fire as a result of indiscriminate firing into the crowd (Foner 1986, 31, citing Paul Avrich).

Without any evidence at all, the leaders of the eight-hour movement were tried and convicted of the murder of one of the policemen. Four were eventually hanged in November 1887; years later a courageous governor of Illinois, John Peter Altgeld, pardoned three who were still in jail. One of the eight died in prison.

After the convictions of the Haymarket leaders, a worldwide movement in their defense spread through the labor and socialist camps. Thus, the American struggle for an eight-hour day was internationalized by the trial of the Haymarket martyrs. At home, the defense efforts were not successful—although three of the eight had their death sentences commuted. The Haymarket bombing sparked the first Red Scare. Police around the country hounded labor leaders and socialist and anarchist groups.

However, by 1888 Gompers and the AFL were ready to launch once again a militant movement for the eight-hour day. The AFL called for a series of demonstrations, including one on Washington's birthday, on July 4, 1889, and on May 1, 1890.

In the summer of 1889, the (Second) Socialist International was being refounded in Paris. A representative from the AFL read a letter from Gompers to the Socialist Congress asking for support for worldwide demonstrations in favor of the eight-hour day. The French representative LaVigne inserted into a prior resolution on the eight-hour day support for the American demonstrations on May 1, 1890.

And so, around the world on May 1, 1890, workers called for the eight-hour workday—and many struck and achieved it or shorter hours. In Vienna, the entire working class called for the day off. In the United States, the carpenters, leaders in the struggle, won shorter hours for seventy-five thousand workers. By the next year, 1891, it appeared that the May 1 demonstrations for a shorter workday had become an international and regular practice, becoming also a call for universal peace and a celebration of working-class power. Eventually, the conservative swing of the AFL would cause that labor federation to give up ownership of May Day and instead to preserve Labor Day as a more conventional American celebration.

Recently, though, our knowledge of working conditions in a world that has become de facto one large labor pool has or should have made us more sharply aware of the role of social regulation and the ways in which our current practices were earned. The laureates of the market would have us believe that those demonstrations and strikes—that blood and honor—were simply small absurd sideshows to history.

When trade and labor standards are discussed, the history of norms of decency for labor is often obscured. May Day—the international workers' day—began in the United States as a struggle for the eight-hour day. It is our obligation to understand where we have come from in order to discern where we might go.

Here it is from the "Eight-Hour Song":

We want to feel the sunshine,
we want to smell the flowers
We're sure that God has willed it,
And we mean to have eight hours.

Introduction

While demonstrators in the streets of Seattle in 1999 called on the WTO to include environmental and labor issues in its agenda of trade negotiations, governmental trade ministers were carrying on a battle of another sort. Representatives of low-income exporting nations, particularly those from Asia, strongly resisted a proposal by countries from the richer Global North, led by the United States, to link environmental and labor standards with trade by inserting a social clause into WTO agreements.[2] They argued that such a social clause is a protectionist ploy used by rich nations to protect their own workers' jobs from competition by developing countries.

There is in this juxtaposition a strange disjuncture. In the United States and elsewhere in developed country labor movement circles, critics of global capitalism and the neoliberal market regime associated with it tend to assume that social considerations, including labor and environmental standards, are part of the broad critique that makes the WTO and the other IFIs so controversial around the world. While there are points of contact in the worldwide critique of global capitalism, incorporating labor rights into trade agreements is not one of the consensual points. In fact, it is widely understood to be a basic divide between labor movements and people's movements in the Global North and Global South.[3]

This practical gulf between the developed and developing world dissident movements has been caused by and is part of a larger frame within which world issues are now perceived: that the global divide in competition in world trade is a North-South affair.

This chapter aims to provide a corrective to this image. It will show that the global competition in manufacturing export, especially of labor-intensive commodities, is not only a North-South matter—that competition is today as much South-South as it is North-South. With apparel manufacturing in China and Mexico as case studies, in the absence of some form of minimal labor standard setting, these two countries may be trapped in a negative competition that will erode wages and/or labor standards—a race to the bottom. The problem for the apparel industry drastically will worsen after the trade barriers for apparel are finally and fully dismantled. A potential cataclysm for labor standards looms in 2005 after the expiration of the last remnants of the Multi-Fiber Agreement (MFA). The MFA restricted the amount and rate of increase of imports of apparel and textiles from any given country; both the United States and the EU have versions of it. After the establishment of the WTO the MFA was replaced by an Agreement on Textiles and Clothing (ATC) (WTO 2002). The ATC scheduled the removal of quota restraints on trade in apparel and textiles over ten years that end in 2005. Right now, the MFA and its successors have the effect of "spreading" the producer countries. Upon the MFA's expiration, influential observers expect China—and therefore Chinese labor standards—to dominate world trade in apparel and textiles. William Greider, perhaps hyperbolically, put it this way:

> The "giant sucking sound" Ross Perot used to talk about is back, only this time it is not Mexico sucking away American jobs. It is China sucking away Mexico's jobs. And jobs from Taiwan and South Korea, Singapore and Thailand, Central and South America, and even from Japan. Globalization is entering a fateful new stage, in which the competitive perils intensify for the low-wage developing countries much like the continuing pressures on high-wage manufacturing workers in the United States and other advanced economies. In the "race to the bottom," China is defining the new bottom. (Greider 2001, 22)

Solidarity North and South

Let us begin at the beginning—the creation of a world made safe for capitalism, Anglo-American style.

The Social Clause and the WTO

Following World War II, a Euro-American vision of a world free of barriers to foreign—that is, developed country—investors gradually prevailed on the world stage. Europe created the European Coal and Steel Community and eventually the EU. Subsequent to the 1980s, both Europe and the United States moved from Keynesian and social democratic national regulation of economic life to neoliberal globalization.

In North America, NAFTA opened Mexico's economy to U.S. investment in dramatic ways, and it facilitated the (already large) entrance of Mexican manufactures to the United States and Canada. At the heart of these regional trade blocs and worldwide trade facilitating agreements is, as the supporters of the WTO put it, the idea and the growing reality of a "rules-based" regime for world trade.

President Bill Clinton expressed the liberal globalizers' view shortly after the 1999 protests in Seattle:

> I think we have got to reaffirm unambiguously that open markets and rules-based trade are the best engine we know of to lift living standards, reduce environmental destruction and build shared prosperity. This is true whether you're in Detroit, Davos, Dacca or Dakar. (Clinton 2000)

The usage—"rules-based"—refers to a standard that some entity can enforce. The WTO enforces its rules by a process that ultimately can result in trade sanctions. Such sanctions might allow, for example, the nations who have successfully claimed that a rule has been broken to invoke tariffs on the products of the rule breaker.

The General Agreement on Tariffs and Trade (GATT) of 1994 lowered tariffs on many goods, and the WTO agreement embodied in it furthers this process. The many pages of specific agreements each include different timetables for more and less developed countries. Among the more powerful of the rules in the 1994 agreement is that governing Trade Related Investment Measures (TRIMS). This article requires member states to extend "national" treatment to all investors; that is, there is to be no discrimination against foreign investors. Thus, Mexico or China must treat the Taiwanese or American electronics or clothing firm equally with firms of local origin in their jurisdictions.

The rules-based aspect of the WTO implies a global governance system—a constitution for law making and (economic) law enforcement at the international level. Within this emerging constitutional structure, there is a striking asymmetry. The WTO rules protect firms and their products (including, gradually, services) from discriminatory treatment as they move across international boundaries. Workers who engage in production for this system of international exchanges have no similar standing in the treaties. Indeed, the WTO explicitly rejects such standing.

"Currently, labor standards are not subject to WTO rules and disciplines" (WTO 1999). The official WTO position was articulated by then director General Ruggiero in 1998:

> At the WTO's first Ministerial Conference in Singapore, we emerged from a difficult debate with a clear and strong consensus on the issues of labor standards—a consensus first, that members were committed to the observance of core labor standards; second, that the ILO was the relevant body to address these issues; third, that standards are best promoted by growth and development, fostered by trade liberalization; and fourth, that labor standards should in no way be used for protectionist purposes or put into question the comparative advantage of countries. (Ruggiero 1998)

There is less in this statement, whose content WTO spokespersons frequently repeat, than meets the eye. From the outset, labor unions and labor advocates, especially in Europe and North America, criticized the WTO. They argued that countries that did not allow workers the rights necessary to defend themselves were gaining investment at the expense of workers who had such rights. The low cost of labor in low-income countries, the argument asserted, artificially was perpetuated by workers' lack of rights in law or practice.

Although American labor unions make this argument, they also realize that the effective labor rights of workers in the United States fall short of international standards. This may surprise some observers from developing countries. As Lance Compa explains:

Human rights cannot flourish where workers' rights are not enforced. Research-
ing workers' exercise of these rights in different industries, occupations, and
regions of the United States . . . Human Rights Watch found that freedom of
association is a right under severe, often buckling pressure when workers in the
United States try to exercise it. . . . Core labor rights are systematically violated
in the United States. (Compa 2000)

If a rules-based international regime including labor standards gave
governments and workers in other nations a right to complain about
labor laws and standards in the United States, they would have grounds
for action.

Returning to the WTO, when it is criticized about the lack of regard for
labor rights under the various GATT treaties, officials respond most usually by citing the affirmation, by member governments, of the ILO core
labor rights. These core labor rights, condensed from the eighty-six-year
history of labor standards conventions passed by this arm of the United
Nations, are:

- freedom of association and the effective recognition of the right to collective
  bargaining;
- the elimination of all forms of forced or compulsory labor;
- the effective abolition of child labor; and
- the elimination of discrimination in respect of employment and occupation.[4]
  (ILO 1998)

The ILO core labor rights are procedural, not substantive: workers might
exercise these formal rights and still earn only a wage below subsistence
with no social protection. It is also true that nations may affirm these
rights without enforcing them.

The WTO's foundational document on labor rights is the Singapore
Ministerial Declaration, where it was asserted that the ILO, not the WTO,
is the relevant body to which labor rights issues should be addressed.
Translated: we affirm these rights, but transgressions of them should be
addressed elsewhere.

The next assertion is that promotion of labor rights—that is, correction
of deficiencies in their enjoyment by workers—is to be left to economic
growth. This is the major argument of WTO defenders—and their journalist and academic defenders. It is based on a long-term and oft-repeated

simple association: welfare measures (social protections) and democratic constitutions that protect civil liberties are positively associated with higher per capita income.[5]

In the contemporary discourse about rights and development, the simple association between GNP and constitutional rights is used to negate the entire real history of the attainment of labor standards embodying, or approximating, these rights—the history of labor movements and labor parties, the arduous struggles for both procedural (legalization of unions) and substantive (social protections) rights by workers in both rich and poor countries, is made invisible by the proposition that economic growth takes care of everything. No need to have laws or unions: economic growth will magically lift the humble and restrain the haughty. With one swift rhetorical stroke the need for democracy is thus removed from the accomplishment of democracy. Leave the dictators and industrial tyrants alone: when they get richer some magic wand will give us democracy and will stay their hands from the whip of penury.

The heart of the WTO position is more narrow: "Labor standards should in no way be used for protectionist purposes or put into question the comparative advantage of countries" (WTO 1996). Translated: though we have agreed to rules that treat foreign investors as legal equals to local investors, and both shall have certain rights in trade and local consideration, and these shall be enforced by the possibility of trade sanctions, workers are affirmed to have certain procedural rights, but these shall not be enforceable.

The ILO is, as WTO officials and supporters claim, competent to inspect, and to train local governments to inspect, workplaces concerning compliance with labor rights. But the ILO has no enforcement powers whatsoever. Nine years after labor unions and human rights advocates complained to the ILO about forced labor in Myanmar, and four years after an ILO report found the charges to be merited, no concrete action has yet been taken to enforce the ILO convention against forced labor.[6]

Countries, as a matter of national policy, or enterprises within them, as a matter of practice, may abuse labor rights and thereby cheapen labor or make it more docile and attractive to investors. In this fashion, nations or firms may gain competitive, so-called comparative, advantages over others. The WTO paragraph in question seems to assert that comparative advantage, even if gained by abusing labor rights, is not to be hindered.

The Social Clause

The dramatic Seattle protests brought sharp focus on these matters. The position of the international trade union movements—led by Western, particularly European, trade union leadership—articulated a direct programmatic demand for the WTO. This position had two parts: First, and most controversially, access to the trade concessions embodied in the WTO should be ultimately conditional on respect for the core workers' rights. Second, the ILO should be the competent body to make determinations of the status of these rights in any given place. In Seattle, the AFL-CIO invested heavily in the issue itself and also, for the first time in over fifty years, in a broad-based coalition with youth, environmental, and other civil society groups.[7]

In a pronouncement that surprised many, President Bill Clinton appeared to support some such general approach to a social clause. As the demonstrations disrupted the WTO conference, Clinton remarked:

> I think what we ought to do, first of all, is to adopt the United States position on having a working group on labor within the WTO. And then that working group should develop these core labor standards, and then they ought to be a part of every trade agreement. And ultimately, I would favor a system in which sanctions would come for violating any provision of a trade agreement. But we've got to do this in steps. (Clinton 1999, 2182)

This declaration was surprising to some and repugnant to others. It was surprising to the dissident movements in the United States and to journalists who had not been paying attention. It was repugnant to many corporate interests and to third world governments intent upon penetrating rich country markets without reforming their domestic practices.

Clinton's statement was part of the other (unheralded) side of the Clinton globalization policy. The Clinton administration had in fact advocated for gradual labor rights inclusions in WTO and other international trade matters. What it was not willing to do was scuttle those agreements if labor rights were not honored in them. The Clinton administration was unprecedented in its advocacy of labor rights in international trade. It was quite normal in its willingness to make these less than highest priority.

President Clinton must have known that proposing the inclusion of an enforceable social clause in the WTO structure would antagonize developing country governments in the short run. It did. Developing country governments, claiming or fearing that a social clause would justify protectionist exclusion of their exports to rich country markets, successfully blocked further consideration (Jonquieres 1999). The end of the Seattle talks and the change of American administrations have now appeared to remove the inclusion of a social clause from the WTO agenda in the immediate or immediately foreseeable future. Although American media were not very interested, the international labor movement made, once again, an effort to force this issue on the WTO agenda at Doha in 2001, and it was, once again, unsuccessful.

The question is still very much alive in the global labor movement, however. As recently as January 2002, for example, a conference in Beijing, including Chinese labor officials, researchers, and labor rights and trade union researchers from the West and from Asia, debated the issue for three days.[8]

Strange Alliances

According to the conventional wisdom in the West and in much of the world's establishment press, there is a strange alignment of positions on world trade. Western bankers align with governments in the developing countries in favor of unrestricted trade. Western governments also favor freer trade, but third world governments criticize them for the remaining obstacles to imports that these governments tolerate. Opposing the blessings of free trade, in this view, are selfish rich country protectionist workers, misguided young radicals, and the occasional third world populist. In this model, the rich country bankers oppose their governments and ally with poor country nationalists; the rich country governments ally with their workers and oppose their bankers and commercial interests. Third world radicals, opposing the social clause in the name of development (trade), are allied, willy-nilly, with the rich country banks and their own governments, who they otherwise oppose.

No wonder editorial writers enjoy calling the critics of the WTO callous and foolish. In this confusion they can get away with almost anything. In a notorious column titled "Senseless in Seattle," Thomas Friedman, the *New York Times* laureate of contemporary globalization, said the anti-WTO demonstrators were "a Noah's ark of flat-earth advocates, protectionist trade unions and yuppies looking for their 1960's fix" (Friedman 1999, A23).

Mimicking the great metropolis, the *Boston Globe* also titled its editorial the next day "Senseless in Seattle":

> Ned Ludd was alive and rioting in Seattle this week. A new industrial revolution is upon us—one so vast and profound we cannot yet see where it will lead. A sign seen in Seattle—"Mobilization against Globalization"—expressed the fears of demonstrators who are trying to break the knitting machines of a new world economy. (*Boston Globe* 1999, A26)

Strange, indeed, would be a world alignment of forces that saw the financial sectors of the rich countries and their editorial apologists shoulder to shoulder with low-income and middle-income countries' governments and workers against high-income country workers and environmentalists.

Reality is not so strange as the polemical, editorial depiction of it. At a forum on labor standards in the apparel industry, I asked former Republican secretary of labor John Dunlop, an American labor relations expert, about the difference between some labor union confederation support for a social clause in trade agreements and their governments' opposition to it. Dunlop did a Jack Benny deadpan and said: "It is not surprising when unions and governments disagree."

Against the Stereotype: The Labor and
NGO Positions on the Social Clause

Those who oppose the inclusion of labor rights in international trade agreements sometimes argue that these rights depend on culturally relative, specifically Western, conceptions: freedom of association and the derived right to join a union and to collective bargaining. This claim was addressed in an ILO document written by Hoe Lim (2001):

> Numerous contemporary arguments against universal human rights, and by association international labor standards, hide behind the shield of cultural relativism but are often not supported by any discernible cultural basis. Arguments of cultural relativism tend to be made by economic and political elites. The very same elites who raise culture as a defense against external criticisms based on universal human rights often ruthlessly suppress inconvenient local customs, whether of the majority or the minority.
>
> All too often, leaders sing the praises of traditional communities—while they wield arbitrary power antithetical to traditional values, pursue development policies that systematically undermine traditional communities, and replace traditional leaders with corrupt cronies and party hacks. Such cynical manipulation of tradition occurs everywhere.
>
> For the most part, in undemocratic or closed political systems, it is only the views of the ruling elite which are given wide recognition. This should not be mistaken for an unchallenged consensus.

By contrast, the ICFTU takes pains to argue its case on behalf of a social clause in an inclusive language that takes in developing country supporters. The ICFTU participated in (organized) a Global Unions coalition that called for demonstrations on November 9, 2001—the opening of the Doha Ministerial meeting of the WTO—calling for global justice. The partners called for a "World trading system which includes fair rules and core labor rights as defined by the ILO, in order to achieve balanced and sustainable development" (ICFTU 2001).[9]

The ICFTU laid out its position in a working paper in 1999. At that time, the ICFTU addressed implicitly the question of whether its view was merely that of rich country unionists, the so-called Global North, by mentioning the developing country trade union federations that supported a social clause. The following table shows at least some social clause support in each of Latin America, Africa, and Asia.

Developing Country Supporters of a Social Clause

	National Trade Union Federation Country	Comment
Latin America	Argentina (1)	
	Barbados (1)	
	Chile (1)	
	Honduras (2)	
	El Salvador (2)	used U.S. GSP labor clause
	Guatemala (2)	same
	Nicaragua (2)	same
Africa (1)	Gabon	
	Madagascar	
	Malawi	
	Mauritius	
	Republic of South Africa	
	Senegal	
	Tunisia	
Asia	Korea (1)	
	Malaysia (2)	

Sources: 1 = ICFTU 1999; 2 = See text.

While many developing country governments use a rhetoric of nationalism or anti-imperialism to oppose the social clause idea, the impression that this is a unanimous developing country position is inaccurate. Here is an excerpt from the Korean Confederation of Trade Unions (KCTU):

> the KCTU believes "social clause" can be a significant and effective instrument to protect and achieve social rights and the basic trade union rights. . . .
>
> In subscribing to the social clause effort, the KCTU is aware of the . . . suspicion that it is motivated by protectionist intentions. . . . the social clause must be an instrument specifically oriented to the right of freedom of association, collective bargaining, the eradication of forced labor, child labor, and discrimination. The application of economic sanctions in conjunction with the social clause must be based on reasonable, objective, and transparent procedure, involving institutionally guaranteed participation of the concerned trade unions. (KCTU 1996)

Unions tend to support a labor rights approach to regulating trade in Central America. Perhaps the historic interaction between Central American and U.S. trade unions helps to account for this, but recent union rights campaigns reveal that struggling unions in Guatemala, Honduras, El Salvador, and Nicaragua have all made strategic use of threatened trade sanctions to attempt to secure their rights to organize.[10]

In Guatemala, workers formed a union at a factory working for the U.S. clothing giant Phillips Van Heusen in the early 1990s. In a long and bitter campaign their North American allies—including UNITE—filed at their behest a lawsuit under the U.S. Generalized System of Preferences (GSP) laws. The suit alleged that Guatemala was ineligible for trade concessions because, as illustrated by this case, it denied workers the right to organize, a right upon which GSP trade concessions were dependent. The threat of the lawsuit brought pressure on the company, through the Guatemalan government, and it recognized the union (Belanger 1996; Compa 1993).[11]

Similarly, in the successful stage of the campaign to organize a union at the Chentex factory in the Nicaragua free trade zone in 1998–2001, among the moments that were useful to the workers was the threat by the U.S. trade representative Charlene Barshevsky to withdraw Nicaraguan privileges under the Caribbean Basin Initiative Parity law for the same reason. As a member of a delegation investigating labor rights issues at Chentex, I asked the leadership of the trade union confederation leading the campaign in Managua about the use of the new labor rights conditionality in the Caribbean Basin Parity Act. Their response was as follows: they did not want Nicaragua to be the only nation reviewed for labor rights compliance, but they agreed that all nations should be subject to such a conditionality (for background on this issue, see Ross and Kernaghan 2000).

Israel Salinas, president of the Federacion Independiente de Trabajadores Hondurenos (FITH, or Independent Federation of Honduran Workers) and also of the Confederacion Unitaria de Trabajadores Hondurenos (CUTH, or Unitary Confederation of Honduran Workers), perhaps reflecting on these and similar incidents in his own country, told me that he supports social clauses in trade agreements. Similarly, unions struggling for recognition in El Salvador used workers' rights provisions of the GSP in U.S. trade law to induce their government to grant minimal rights and recognition (Davis 1995).

What these quick notes suggest is that the image that has been created—protectionist U.S. and European unions using labor rights issues to exclude low-income countries' products from their markets—is at best an oversimplified view of the international labor rights issue, and more probably it is simply an inaccurate reading of the complexity of the world trade union view of the social clause.

There is good reason for representatives of laborers in low-income countries to favor a social clause—one that goes beyond the use of access to rich country markets as a strategic lever. The more powerful reason is that competition among communities of workers in developing countries themselves threatens to erode or to hold back advancing labor standards and purchasing power for workers.

The standard argument against a social clause views the competition in world trade as one between the workers in the rich North against the workers in the poor South. If we examine a labor-intensive industrial sector, however—the apparel and textile sector—what becomes more apparent is that the ferocious competition of the last few years and the next decades is between developing countries. If this is so, then the reason for a social clause is the regulation of the terms of competition between developing countries—it is a South-South issue.

South-South: The Case of Competition for the North American Apparel Market

Contrary to the conventional view, the fiercest competition in many of the world export markets is not that between higher-income labor in the Global North and lower-income laborers in the Global South. Instead, it is competition among workers in the developing nations, a South-South competition. The North American (and European) apparel markets, and Mexican and Chinese suppliers to them, illustrate the matter.

The American apparel market is now dominated by imports from developing nations. Job loss is so extensive and has been so rapid that domestic production will not recoup those losses. The basic contenders for U.S. (and European) import market share are Mexico and China in the Western Hemisphere and China, Turkey, and some others in Europe. By inference, rules that define fair competition, including labor standards, are of interest to workers in all of these places, quite apart from whether they help U.S. apparel workers.

Apparel Imports to the United States

Apparel imports rose from about 2 percent of U.S. domestic consumption in the early 1960s to over 60 percent in the 1990s. In the largest categories of imports—men's and women's tops, for example—11 billion dollars of imports in each category furnish over 70 percent of the market by value and about 90 percent by quantity (U.S. Census Bureau 2001b). This steady rise in imports has, of course, had a drastic impact on apparel employment (see chap. 5, fig. 6). Since 1973, the high point of apparel employment in the United States, almost 800,000 jobs have disappeared (from 1.4 million to 660,000) and the rate of loss in the 1990s was 37,000 annually.

Since 1980, the period when import competition cut U.S. apparel employment industry in half, losing over 600,000 jobs, two great suppliers have become dominant in the U.S. market: Mexico and China. As of 2000, Mexico supplied just under 15 (14.7) percent of all imports to the United States; the Hong Kong Special Administrative Region and the People's Republic of China each supplied over 7 percent: the total is close to, but a bit more than, 15 percent (15.7).

The volume of apparel imports from both countries has grown even as they vie for market share. Figure 15 shows the dramatic competition in growth curves.

Competition for the European market is also fierce. The competition between Mexico and China for the U.S. market is similar to the competition between China and Turkey for the European market (with Rumania and Bangladesh trailing behind in third and fourth places). China's share of EU clothing imports grew from about 7 percent in 1988 to over 15 percent in 2000. Turkey went from over 8 percent to over 11 percent, with Rumania and Bangladesh at about 5 percent each. The competition we describe between China and Mexico for the North American market can serve as a model for the competition between China and Turkey as sup-

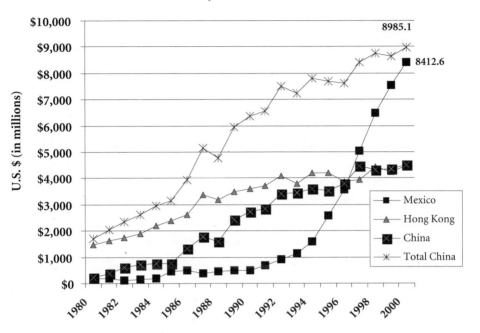

Solidarity North and South

Fig. 15. Growth of imports to the United States from China and Mexico, 1980–2000. Source: Office of Textiles and Apparel (OTEXA) 2001a, unpublished data (various years).

pliers to the EU market (International Textiles and Clothing Bureau 2001).

After 2005, when the MFA expires, exporting factories located in China will gain, or regain, some advantages they lost to entrepreneurs with facilities in Mexico after NAFTA. In the meantime, Mexican producers' advantages over other Caribbean exporters are ebbing since the law giving the Caribbean Basin countries parity with Mexico's advantages in the United States took effect in October 2000.

The apparel industry is perhaps more globalized than other ones, and the rapidity of the ebbs and flows of competition is arguably greater. Nonetheless, as the World Bank pointed out,

The share of manufactures in developing country exports rose from 20 percent to 60 percent between 1960 and 1990. Low and middle-income countries already account for almost 80 percent of the world's industrial work force. (World Bank 1995, 16)

Under the current regime of world trade, each national government that wants to boost export earnings may be tempted to sacrifice the interests of workers to the interests of investors. Mexico's central bankers may impress on Mexican regulators the importance of the fact that investors covet the low-wage attractions of Nicaragua. Korean investors in China may grow weary of their responsibility, however minimal, to build workers' dormitories—a cost they do not bear in Central America. Other governments may take note of the lack of motivation officials in Bangladesh evidence about enforcing the exclusion of children from Bangladesh's export sector. In China, child labor is rare in export factories.[12] With competition now from Vietnam and Bangladesh, will Chinese factory managers avoid close inspection of the work documents of young girls from the provinces? Without a common set of rules and expectations, the logic of the race to the bottom is powerful.

Evidence for a Race to the Bottom

The dramatic size of apparel exports from Mexico and China to North America led to employment growth in both countries. The export-oriented factories employ migrant workers from the poor rural areas. In China, beginning in the mid-1980s in Guangdong Province, the entire Pearl River Delta is now a manufacturing powerhouse churning out labor-intensive goods for the world market. Today some 12 million migrant workers from poor parts of China's countryside staff these factories' production lines.

A very similar phenomenon emerged in Mexico in the 1990s. Along the U.S.-Mexican border new investment created boomtowns where maquiladoras have mushroomed. These now employ about 1 million workers, an increase of 150 percent since 1990. The maquiladoras are spreading to other parts of the country as well.

There is evidence that South-South competition may be already a race to the bottom. Let us consider three items: wages and conditions of migrant export workers in China's export zones; wages and conditions for

Mexican manufacturing and apparel workers; and, a new concept, the trade-weighted wage of American apparel imports.

China

In China, as in the United States, minimum wages are weakly enforced. In the special economic zones and among foreign-owned enterprises, the zealously powerful state turns a tolerant eye toward labor scofflaws. The setting of a minimum wage is extremely decentralized. Each city or even a district in a city can set its own minimum wage based on a formula provided by the central government. This takes into account the cost of living in the locality, the prevailing wage, the rate of inflation, and so forth, and is adjusted each year. In 2001 Shenzhen City had two standards: inner Shenzhen, the commercialized sector of the city just north of Hong Kong, has the highest minimum wage level in China, at 574 yuan per month (U.S.$72), while the outer industrialized sector's minimum wage was set at 440 yuan per month (U.S.$55). Elsewhere in China, the legal minimum wages are lower, and local governments try to attract investments by granting numerous concessions to investors. On paper, these local governments comply with the central government's decrees about minimum wage levels; in many areas they leaped up in accord with inflation in 2001. In reality the wages of the migrant industrial workers are often considerably lower than that.

For one thing, the minimum wage is set by the month and does not take into account that many migrant workers labor for illegally long hours. According to a survey that Anita Chan conducted of China's footwear industry, the average number of work hours each day came to eleven, often with no days off. The official statistics do not take into consideration the staggering amount of wages owed but not paid to the migrant workers. Of the twenty thousand cases of workers' complaints lodged by letters and by personal visits to the Shenzhen authorities during the first nine months in 2001, 40 percent were related to unpaid wages. As a Shenzhen paper has editorialized, this has become a "normal practice" in southern China. When the illegally long work hours and unpaid wages are taken into account, a sizeable proportion of the workers is making considerably less than the legal minimum wage.

Minimum wage levels do not tell the whole story in other ways. Violence and physical abuse have become pervasive in Asian-invested factories owned and managed by Taiwanese, Koreans, and Hong Kong Chinese. Acute and chronic occupational health and safety ailments are an unhappy side to China's rapid integration into global capitalism. A startlingly high incidence of severed limbs and fingers has been recorded in Shenzhen City alone, where there were over ten thousand certified cases in 1999 among a migrant population of 4 million. As China has developed, the benefits have not trickled down to the assembly line workers from largely rural backgrounds who make the exported goods (see Chan 2001 for sources and more details).

Mexico

Wage levels in Mexico are nominally more regulated. There are only three minimum wage levels set for the entire country, and this also applies to the U.S.-Mexican border region: in 2000 these were equivalent to U.S.$93–108 per month. These minimum wages, though low, are almost double those in Shenzhen, the highest in China. But as in China, Mexico's minimum wages declined in the decade of the 1990s, with a sudden drop in 1996 after the peso collapse and after NAFTA's implementation. Indexed at 100 in 1990, they dropped to 55.8 by 1999.

Overall, the average Mexican wages in the manufacturing sector have also declined—dropping in real purchasing power by 20 percent since 1990 (Salas 2001). In the booming apparel sector, workers have had even larger losses. ILO figures show that their wages lost 28 percent of their purchasing power in the period 1994–99 (calculated from data extraction at ILO 2001).

Neither China's nor Mexico's workers who produce for export have benefited from the economic boom. There are more jobs, but in terms of work conditions and wages, workers' situations have degenerated. The reason is that they are caught in the internationally competitive global race to the bottom among assembly workers.

U.S. Trade

One way to summarize the process of the race to the bottom is by asking what the average wage is for imported clothing.[13] In Italy, for example, apparel workers earned about $12.55 per hour in total compensation (wages and benefits) in the late 1990s, while the official U.S. rate was $10.97. In the U.S. case, this was surely inflated because of the large number of violations of the minimum wage law (see Ross 2001). In any case, Italy was the origin of about 2.5 percent of U.S. imports (by dollar value) in the last year. If we weigh wages in China and Burma with Italy and Canada and all the other countries that send clothing, correcting for the size of the flow from each country, we can then estimate the hourly wage, on average, for the average imported garment. It's a soft estimate, given the varying ways countries report their data and the varying degrees of accuracy and honesty in them. For example, some of the reporting countries, such as China, combine footwear and apparel. The underlying database, from the ILO, includes some data by month and some by day or week. One must then estimate the number of hours in a working month in a given national setting and so forth.

A DOL report inspired by the antisweatshop movement was the initial basis for estimating the average apparel worker wage used in apparel imports for 1998 (Schoepfle 2000). It was between $1.75 and $1.87—depending on whether one used the DOL's official data or supplemented it with the National Labor Committee's reports from workers from the (few) countries the National Labor Committee reported.[14]

This number was recalculated for the year 2001 import profile (but continued using 1998 wage data, as these are the latest available for the whole list of countries). In the years since 1998, the mix of imported clothing to the United States changed. China's share declined, relative to Mexico's. However, Indonesia, Bangladesh, Guatemala, Nicaragua, and Peru all increased their share. Canada declined. The result of all these changes, calculated for thirty-three suppliers covering about 91 percent of American imports, is that the average import wage declined to a range from $1.77 to $1.63—a decline of about 6 percent. This shift in the import mix toward lower-wage countries is part of the competitive race to the bottom.

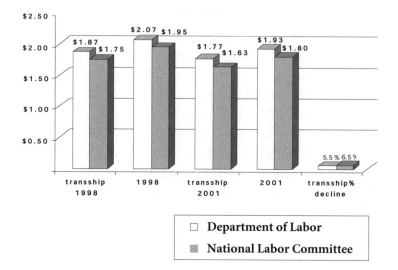

Fig. 16. Average hourly wage (U.S.$) of imported clothing. Source: Schoepfle 2000; OTEXA 2001a; National Labor Committee 1998; Textile Transshipment Team 2000.

Some may see a success story in this scramble to buy clothing made by lower-waged workers everywhere and anywhere. For example, workers in poorer countries are getting access to U.S. consumers. But there are at least two problems with this proposition: first, our own apparel workers, losing their jobs in the race to the bottom, are our own working poor. Our 245,000 full-time, year-round sewing machine operators, according to the overstated official statistics, earned on average $16,560 in 2000 (Bureau of Labor Statistics 2001d). Careful observers of our official poverty data believe the official definition should be 25 percent higher than it is. The sewing machine operators earn less than the expanded poverty definition for a family of three and are 15 percent above it for a family of two. The race to the bottom is a stampede that is crushing apparel workers.

The brothers and sisters of American apparel workers—often their literal relatives, as our own immigrants come from the countries from which we import clothing—do not always make the gains promised or hoped for in the canon of free trade. Inequality is growing in China; Mexican workers' compensation was lower in the late 1990s than it was in the early 1990s and late 1980s.

Solidarity North and South

The South-South Challenge

The debate regarding a social clause in the WTO appears to have reached a political impasse. There remains the problem of finding an enforceable mechanism to protect workers' rights on a global scale, because, as we have illustrated, the race to the bottom for workers, especially in labor-intensive industries, is a global reality, and it may get worse. The ILO, charged with this responsibility, does not presently have any means to enforce a lack of compliance with its conventions. There is no competent forum in which a verdict can be enforced when a nation, or even enterprises within a nation, contravenes fundamental principles of labor rights.

The challenge lies before the Southern governments and their labor movements. The complaint against Northern protectionism has not achieved much in the way of improving the lot of their workforces that make goods for export. Production in the Global South competes within itself. The retail giants—the eight-hundred-pound gorillas of the rag trade—may whipsaw concessions from Chinese officials or Asian factory owners in Guangdong by pleading that a Vietnamese location would be cheaper, so they need this concession or that price break. This only works because a Vietnamese official is willing to ignore his own labor law or to allow the firing of young union activists. A Mexican governor may consent to using police against strikers because the work has been fleeing his state and migrating back to China. When the unions and governments of the Global South allow such lawlessness, they themselves are coconspirators in the decline or stagnation in wages and labor standards.

The disturbing amount of wages owed to Chinese migrant workers is indicative of the fact that the bottom is, in real terms, continuing to fall. China is a key player in the South-South competition. Its size, labor surplus, and low wages, combined with high levels of social control, make Chinese industrial conditions a capitalist paradise. Unless other Southern countries and movements can convince China to form an international Southern consensus to put an international floor beneath labor standards, the scenario will only worsen. As William Greider (2001, 22) recently wrote, "China is defining the bottom."

Only through an enforceable floor to wages (locally relative) could these countries prevent Northern corporations and middleman suppliers from playing them off against each other. The WTO is a logical candidate to devise a regulatory regime in line with a labor social clause, with violators, both governments and corporations, sanctioned for violations. There may be alternatives to a WTO-embedded social clause; but if labor standards are to improve (or even be stabilized) there is little alternative to finding some means of an enforceable international regulatory structure.

Global capitalism is remaking the world: the question before the world community is whether workers can have a decent place in it.

13 Ascending a Ladder of Effective Antisweatshop Policy

when Maria Echaveste and Robert Reich considered how they might advance the cause of low-wage workers, they calculated that they were not going to be able to get enough budget authority to make a big difference through enforcement alone (Echaveste 2002).[1] They determined on a novel strategy that rode two horses: the FLSA and American voluntarism. The DOL used the threat of the "hot goods" provisions of the FLSA to encourage "manufacturers" (those who commission the production of clothing) to take responsibility to monitor the labor law compliance of their contractors. The result, well intentioned, was ambiguous. Having discussed earlier the decline in law enforcement over the last generation, in this chapter I will put the compliance monitoring strategy in the context of a universe of policies—discussing for each the virtues and limitations.

Figure 17 shows the hierarchical relationship of the various policies and practices that attempt to control labor abuse in the apparel industry, moving from less effective to more effective as one moves up the chart.

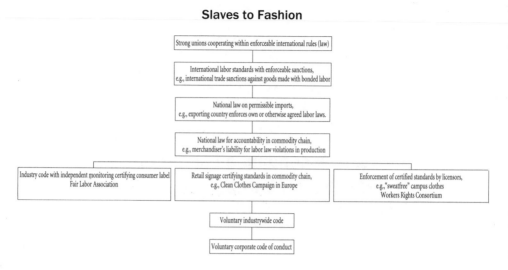

Fig. 17. Levels of effective antisweatshop policy

Corporate Codes of Conduct

Beginning at the bottom, corporations may institute their own codes of conduct—applying to their own plants but more to the point for the apparel industry—as expectations for their vendors. Since the embarrassing revelations of the El Monte slave case in 1995 and then the Gifford episode in 1996, corporate codes of conduct have become quite common. Varley and her colleagues reported on dozens of these codes in 1998 (Varley et al. 1998). The sweat-free campus movement also added momentum to corporate codes of conduct as firms sought a way of avoiding embarrassment and addressing the issue of labor abuses. Most studies and observations by reputable advocacy groups are skeptical of the overall efficacy of this way of approaching the problem (see, e.g., O'Rourke et al. 2000; HKCIC 2001; *Asian Labour Update* 2000–2001; Shepherd 2000–2001; Connor 2001). Briefly, when a vendor (contractor) fails to pay a legal minimum wage or adequately protect health or safety, the purchaser of the contractor's goods has no incentive except fear of external embarrassment to compel compliance. The vendor has every reason to evade compliance. If the code is voluntary and private, the relationship gives no one an incentive to enforce the code. That is probably why most studies of private and voluntary codes of conduct reveal that workers are usually ignorant of them and that violations are widespread (e.g., HKCIC 2001).

Add to these considerations the problem of complexity. Many contractors work for multiple corporations. Adidas and Nike shoes may be made in the same factory. A contractor may work for Champion one season and another firm the next year. The proliferation of codes is confusing for contractors and everyone else. Finally, corporate codes vary in their content, some being vague and hortatory while others specifically require compliance with local labor law—however inadequate it may be. Rarely, if ever, does a voluntary corporate conduct code commit the firm to enforce labor rights among its vendors or maintain some substantive standard (like a locally defined living wage for a family).

Industrywide Voluntary Codes of Conduct

The obvious next step up is an industrywide voluntary code of conduct. The American Apparel Manufacturers Association (AAMA) took one approach to such a code in 1998.[2] The Worldwide Responsible Apparel Production (WRAP) program involved the development of principles and then certification of factories that follow the principles. The principles essentially boil down to say that apparel production should be accomplished within local laws. For example, the WRAP hours of work code does not restrict the hours of work to a maximum of sixty with a normal workweek of forty-eight hours (unless lower by law), as do the other internationally oriented codes discussed as part of the emerging world consensus in chapter 1 (see chap. 1, table 6). Instead the WRAP code states:

> *Hours of Work*—Manufacturers of sewn products will assure that hours worked each day, and days worked each week, shall not exceed the legal limitations of the countries in which apparel is produced. Manufacturers of sewn product will provide at least one day off in every seven-day period, except as required to meet urgent business needs. (WRAP 1998)

WRAP certifies monitors; firms hire monitors to do compliance audits. To gain certification, firms submit the audits. So far, 615 factories worldwide have been accredited. There are similar schemes that are not specific to the apparel industry—for example SA 8000, discussed in chapter 1.

The virtue of the industrywide approach is succinctly stated by WRAP itself:

> Recognizing the potential for individual manufacturers to adopt inconsistent standards and unnecessarily duplicate monitoring efforts, several prominent apparel producers approached the American Apparel Manufacturers Association to coordinate the industry's role in addressing these issues. (WRAP 2002a)

> Factory certification places primary responsibility for improving workplace conditions on those who own and operate sewn product manufacturing facilities. In addition, *it eliminates costly and inefficient duplication of monitoring efforts, when different corporate customers spend money, time and energy monitoring the same factories in an uncoordinated manner.* (WRAP 2002b, emphasis added)

The problems with the WRAP approach are these: it gives consumers no way to distinguish which goods have been made in certified factories and which have not. It is governed by, and its code is determined by, industry owners and is not the result of consensus among the stakeholders—workers' representatives are excluded. The monitors report to the factory owners; even when recertification inspections are reported to the WRAP certification board, they are still confidential and private. Thus, there is little incentive for manufacturers to ride hard on their vendors and even less for vendors to strictly comply with codes.

The commission that governs the free trade zone of Nicaragua is an endorser of WRAP: it does not seem to prevent the Las Mercedes free trade zone from being a merciless sweatshop.

Voluntary Codes, Independent Monitoring, and Consumer-Oriented Labeling

After the Kathie Lee Gifford affair, Secretary of Labor Reich and WHD administrator Echaveste made use of the publicity surge to launch what would turn out to be a very long drawn-out effort to create a sweat-free label (Echaveste 2002). The result of the first round of negotiations for a code of conduct was announced on April 14, 1997. During that news conference President Clinton clearly and repeatedly alluded to the administration's hoped-for result. In order to "give American consumers greater confidence in the products they buy," he said, the signatories to the code of conduct would devise "an effective way to share this information with consumers, such as labels on clothing, seals of approval in advertising, or signs in stores to guarantee that no sweatshop labor was used on a given product line" (Clinton 1997). Although the FLA became more controversial than its political godparents had hoped, it remains oriented to signaling to consumers that they can buy "clean clothes." The FLA says that it will eventually

> [C]reate a "service mark" that a company certified to be in compliance may choose to use in its advertising, at the store where purchases are made, or on the consumer goods bought by customers. The service mark conveys that the company's products "have been produced in compliance with the Fair Labor Association standards." This means that the company has adopted the FLA Code, has met the FLA's monitoring requirements, and has successfully participated in the FLA's remediation procedure. (FLA 2002a)[3]

The steps toward this label are in process as this book nears completion. The first "service marks" could appear by sometime in 2004. The critics of this approach fear that the lack of transparency in the monitoring-reporting system, and inadequacies in the code of conduct underlying the effort, could lead to a worst-case scenario: sweat-free labels that deceptively cloak continuing bad conditions.

Another approach is that of the CCC, centered in Amsterdam but with look-alike groups in many European countries and capitals. The CCC has developed a code of conduct for global apparel production, and it works to get name brand labels (e.g., Nike) and big retail chains to agree to ensure that their commodity chains honor such codes. Ideally they would see retailers with emblems claiming that their sources are sweat free—and a system to ensure that it was.

Although pitted in fierce competition with one another, the university-based WRC also is based on voluntary codes—though it is free of producer/retailer influence and advocates stronger codes of conduct. The WRC, a smaller operation, is driven by complaints rather than by random monitoring. In two instances in 2001–2002 it was able to leverage change in two factories—one in Mexico and one in the Dominican Republic.

The contradictions of a voluntary code are evident from the structure and outcomes of the fight between the FLA and the WRC and the wide participation in WRAP. A code with broad enough support to garner industry leaders and widespread industry support is not apt to represent very high standards or embody rigorous enforcement (WRAP). A broad code—that is, one tolerable by some industry leaders, with independent monitoring but slow enforcement procedures, such as the FLA—is still repugnant to those who want to keep their affairs away from prying outsiders. This caused major producers to leave the FLA and is probably why few retail chains or large manufacturers have joined. Yet, without wide availability on shelves—that is, market share—a sweat-free label cannot have an impact on the lives of workers in the United States or elsewhere. In the meantime, all the incentives for the retailers and contractors move against enforceable high standards. So high standards make for narrow participation; wide participation leads to weak standards or toothless enforcement.

National Law for Accountability in the Commodity Chain

A law that held retailers or brand name labels accountable for the labor violations committed in the course of producing clothing at their initiation would, if properly enforced, give all the parties in the commodity chain reasonable incentive to clean up conditions. Strict law enforcement and the sanctions it ultimately employs—fines and even criminal penalties—have a way of getting the attention of practical people. Secretary Reich's use of the "hot goods" provision of the FLSA might have been a harbinger of a future law enforcement regime. This strategy would concentrate enforcement power at the top of the industrial commodity chain in apparel, using law enforcement as a weapon to leverage change all the way down. His threat was to freeze goods from entering commerce. The next step would be to threaten the Wal-Marts and Nieman Marcuses with civil and criminal penalties when their contractors are labor rights scofflaws. This is the goal of the long-waiting "Stop Sweatshops Bill" introduced in the 1990s by Representative Clay of Missouri and Senator Kennedy of Massachusetts.

A similar law was passed in the Netherlands, and, according to CCC staff (Van den Braber 1997) it had the effect feared for all strictly national regulatory attempts: it drastically reduced domestic production in the Dutch clothing industry. The size of the U.S. market and the lower level of (legal) wages argues for less drastic results; and many think that the U.S. industry is reaching its minimum level. Somewhere near the current level of employment, it is efficient to have a local "reserve" capacity for certain kinds of production, including the most standardized (more capital intense) and the most volatile (requiring fast turnaround and close consultation).

Nevertheless, there are strict limits to the effectiveness of strictly national regulation. We can clean up the worst of exploitative situations in the American apparel industry—and we should, even if this does reduce employment somewhat. But as long as there is a worldwide reservoir of intensely exploitative workplaces in the industry, stability may be fragile and gains weak. Cleaning up the supply chain within an *importing* country does not have leverage over conditions in exporting countries.

National Law on Permissible Imports

The United States consumes about 30 percent of the world's exported clothing; the EU imports another 26 percent of the clothing that is traded in the world economy.[4] If either or both of these governmental entities had taken steps to enforce standards in its own apparel industry, the next step would be to use access to its market to leverage change on a global scale. However ambitious a goal, as we have seen in our review so far, it is actually the only practical one. Only a world in which there is no place to hide for intense exploitation can protect workers in a thoroughly globalized industry. Between them, the EU and the United States consume 56 percent of the world's clothing exports. We have become uncomfortably aware that this market power is most usually employed to comfort the comfortable. Consider the possibility that it might be used to assist the exploited.

It may surprise some that the United States has had important features of labor standards leveraging in its trade law for a long while. But now these potential protections—never used vigorously—are threatened.

Under the Generalized System of Preferences (GSP), imports of a broad list of goods are admitted to the United States duty-free from developing countries as an aid to their economic development. There are a number of eligibility conditions that a low-income country must satisfy to be listed as a GSP beneficiary. These conditions include "to ensure internationally recognized worker rights," which the legislation specifically defines as:

> Right of association
> Right to organize and bargain collectively
> Prohibition of any form of forced or compulsory labor
> Minimum age for child employment
> Acceptable work conditions regarding, for example, minimum wages, work hours, and occupational safety and health standards. (Office of the U.S. Trade Representative 1999, 6, 49, 58)

This list is essentially the "core labor rights " concept of the ILO—even though the U.S. government has not ratified the underlying ILO conventions. The U.S. GSP legislation is actually somewhat more substantive than the ILO core concept, because it includes "acceptable work conditions," not just procedural rights.

Six of the top ten countries exporting apparel to the United States (as of 2001) are GSP nations (Honduras, Dominican Republic, Indonesia, Bangladesh, the Philippines, and Thailand) (cf. Office of the U.S. Trade Representative 1999 with OTEXA 2002). Other notable beneficiaries include most of the Central American countries. After the Reagan administration encouraged the implantation of an apparel industry in Central America through the Caribbean Basin Initiative, local unions, American labor, and NGO advocates used the GSP workers' rights provisions, inducing labor law and political practice changes in, for example, Guatemala (Belanger 1996). That they were used to help apparel workers is interesting because the GSP explicitly excludes apparel from the list of goods admitted duty-free. Instead, by threatening other exports from a country, it was used to leverage change in the apparel sector.

In October 2000 the Caribbean Basin Trade Partnership Act (CBTPA) went into effect. It includes very similar labor rights eligibility factors as the GSP for duty-free access to American markets.[5] Passed at the same time, the African Growth and Opportunity Act (AGOA) includes the same GSP language on labor rights. Both of the more recent laws include apparel and textile imports. Thus, in principle, eligibility for access to the U.S. market is conditioned on respect for labor rights for a large proportion of our clothing imports.

GSP actions—or actions under successive laws that embody similar features—have not generally been initiated by the U.S. government without extreme pressure from American labor unions. As those unions get weaker, their ability to exert such pressure also wanes. Indeed, the whole GSP approach may be in its twilight—especially in relation to the apparel industry. The eligibility process is one that includes high levels of political discretion. Whatever the rhetoric of successive presidents, none has put high stakes on labor rights. So the language in existing and recent laws gives only modest leverage to labor rights advocates absent a political establishment in Washington that made labor rights a priority. The problem will soon get worse.

The WTO agreement calls for an end to quotas of textile and apparel imports as of 2005. Then, all WTO members should have quota-free access to the markets of the rich countries insofar as textile and clothing are concerned. As distinct from the GSP system, the WTO does not link labor rights to trade access. As more tariffs are removed, under the long-run WTO system, more goods will move away from labor rights conditionality. Still, some tariffs and limits remain on a broader range of goods. So, in principle, duty-free access through the GSP, the CBTPA, and the AGOA may remain usable levers to ratchet up labor rights observances in our trading partners.

Considering the top ten apparel importers to the United States, among the four not part of GSP or Caribbean Basin preferences, Mexico is granted duty-free access under the NAFTA. The remaining three—China,

Korea, and Hong Kong—are members of the WTO. Each will enjoy market access under the ATC, which uses a quota system that began under the MFA—but it will expire in 2005.

If present Washington proposals are eventually ratified, however, even the GSP and Caribbean Basin labor rights language may become as extinct as labor rights within the WTO. Pending hemisphere-wide negotiations and eventually congressional approval, the U.S. government proposes the formation of the Free Trade Area of the Americas (FTAA)—critics call it "NAFTA on steroids." The present discussion of the FTAA does not include strong labor rights language.

The conclusion is this: the WTO system creates immense pressure to reduce or eliminate tariffs and quotas and to extend even greater privileges to trading blocs—for example, the Western Hemisphere and the EU. In the process, it appears that slightly useful labor rights protections in U.S. trade law are being lost and none is replacing them.

International Labor Standards with Enforceable Sanctions

National regulation attempting to leverage international labor standards can make a difference, but only at painstakingly slow rates and at relatively high political costs. When a nation seeks to unilaterally impose labor standards on another, employers and their allies are apt to mobilize all available political resources to resist—and this will predictably include demagogic nationalism. And so in today's environment, developing country labor unionists often find that their alliance with solidarity activists or unions from the Global North makes them vulnerable to nationalist attacks claiming that they are tools of protectionists from the rich countries and their unions. These appeals were used against the Chentex workers in Nicaragua, including a staged rally paid for by the employers.

It is also the rare political leadership that will endanger diplomatic relations or larger economic or geopolitical considerations for the concerns of a group of workers in a single industry or conflict. Finally, a country-by-country solution—with campaigns and actions each years long in both the importing country's political and legal arena and the exporting country's one as well—bodes a struggle of centuries, not decades.

The logical antidote to this concern is a truly international regime of enforceable labor standards. In such a structure the standards are the property of no one country—for example, Mexican workers could charge the United States with failure to enforce its own minimum wage laws—and enforcement would be through forums thoroughly international and impartial. Ah, and if paradise were here, now, we would all have wings. The international labor movement has, of course, proposed a regime of international labor standards with enforceable sanctions in relation to the WTO. This social clause idea is the subject of detailed discussion in chapter 12. It is not consensual in the world labor movement, and most developing country governments reject it.

Even if such international-level standards and enforcement mechanisms could be agreed upon, however, we would be back to the problem of ground-level enforcement and inspection. Maria Echaveste put it this way: the United States is a rich country. She reflected on her experience at the DOL by noting that it is hard, almost impossible, to convince the Congress to spend more money on labor inspection. What do we think will happen in Bangladesh, she asked (Echaveste 2002)?

If we were to construct an ideal system to protect workers' rights in a world of global exchanges, it would have the following features. The first and most important one is the principle that governs all the others: the aim is to create a global system where workers' rights are protected as well as investors' rights, a world in which no nation provides a safe haven for investors seeking to exploit labor in ways that transgress fundamental norms of decency. Thus no nation should have a comparative advantage in world trade by excessive abuse or exploitation of labor.

Labor standards would be clear, but concepts would be appropriate to different levels of development. For example, minimum wages should enable full-time workers to have a decent life, but that minimum level would be different in rich and poor countries. In another example, child labor minimum ages would have to respect both national law and school-leaving ages and levels of development.

319

Procedural rights should be universal—for example, the right to free association. On the other hand, a realistic process would take into account massive differences in political systems and cultures and would allow for protracted negotiation and transition—for example, the People's Republic of China.

On the other hand, enforcement should be impartial and fair. It should not be up to American jurists to judge whether the Chinese are enforcing appropriate minimum wages in their export factories (the Americans aren't doing it either). There should be impartial authorities to which parties can take disputes and claims.

Finally, standards must be enforceable. Ultimately, that means that sanctions—some punishments—are available to deter long-term, flagrant, and willful practices of labor abuse.

An example of a current failure in the enforcement of labor standards is the situation in Myanmar (Burma). After careful and slow investigation, the ILO found that Burma uses forced labor. The trilateral (business, labor, and government) structure of ILO discussions requires that such conclusions be consensual; they are consequently rare and slow. Despite this care, four years after such a finding and nine years after the charge was first made (1993), clothing imports from Burma to the United States had increased.

The problem with the ILO is that it simply has no enforcement powers—no sanctions. Short of war, the only effective forms of sanction on a world scale are economic and trade based: tariffs or embargos. The latter requires armed force in the final analysis. So it is to the former, trade sanctions, that most eyes fall when considering enforcement mechanisms for global labor standards. This is repugnant to many developing country activists and establishment members. It remains to be seen whether there are other, more effective ways to develop enforceable standards.

In our experiment, even if we had created a set of rules and impartial forums for adjudication and enforcement mechanisms appropriate in scale to transgressions, there would still be a problem of monitoring and action. For technical training and worldwide reach, the ILO is without peer. Yet, without the millions of eyes and ears and noses of workers alert to their own rights and workplaces, it is hard to imagine a worldwide—no less a U.S.—national enforcement regimen that would root out abuses. The industrialized countries learned early on (what we are now forgetting) that democratically organized workers are their own best defenders. There is simply no substitute for strong unions when it comes to defending workers' rights. Strong states and magnanimous employers are simply not the same as workers trained in their own self-defense.

So that is the final piece of the puzzle—strong unions cooperating with one another across international boundaries, including cooperation to use impartial enforcement mechanisms to raise labor standards that are the product of global agreement.

One example of how this would help in the United States is simple and straightforward. Our undocumented immigrant workers are terribly vulnerable to labor abuse. Yet it is easy for employers to resist labor union organization among them—call the INS! Consider the labor and immigration law reform that would make it impossible to deport a worker while his or her work unit was engaged in a collective bargaining or union organizing campaign. When this was proposed once at a conference that included a variety of stakeholders in the apparel industry, an industry representative opposed the idea, saying calmly, "It would make unionization a policy of the United States." He was correct.

14 Three Pillars of Decency

some policies are more powerful or strategic than others. The more permanent and far-reaching solutions to labor abuse are located at the global level—where the politics are so complicated that any conceivable time horizon of success ranges far into the future. So be it. That the task is long-range is not an argument against it: what is required is a strategic vision that is plausible. Our analysis and the history of working classes, unions, and parties of the older industrial regions suggest that there are three legs to the stool upon which working-class conditions rest—three pillars of decency: workers and their unions; middle-class reformers as a political force and as consumers; and government regulation. The context of globalized capital and global institutions of economic regulation that are far from the reach of domestic politics makes this era one in which change in the conditions of sweatshop workers will be more arduous than ever. One of the great Talmudic sages of Jewish tradition, Rabbi Tarfon, said, "It is not your obligation to complete the work [of perfecting the world], but neither are you free to desist [from it]."

Should one take up the obligation to start, one would have to know, however arduous the attainment, what needs to be done. Among the tasks most desperately needed is to change the so-called mainstream discourse about labor abuse and exploitation. This chapter first brings together themes of the arguments that have appeared throughout the book to confront directly both the liberal and conservative justifications for labor abuse. It then turns to the key legislative and domestic policies that would restrain unscrupulous employers and facilitate the revival of the labor movement. That revival, in turn, would be the basis for consumer cooperation and further government reform—a platform for global change.

Are Sweatshops Good for You?

Some mainstream figures in economics and intellectual life have mounted a defense of sweatshops. This defense has come in response to the social movements of the 1990s and to social criticism of global capitalism, but it builds upon what many economists believe are the fundamentals of their science. A vast gap has opened between mainstream economists, on the one hand, and social scientists and educated lay people who are concerned about labor abuse and global economic relations, on the other.[1]

The sweatshop defenders only rarely address the problem of sweated labor within the rich countries; so much of the concern in this book is not relevant to most of their contentions.[2] Instead, the apologists for harsh labor conditions tend to focus their attention on developing economies and the role of low-wage labor in the development process. These voices call out against attempts to tie labor standards to trade agreements, and some oppose consumer action to enforce voluntary codes of conduct on the merchandising brands or the retail chains (ACIT 2000; Lim 2000).[3]

In common among the defenders of sweatshop labor conditions is an argument that is also frequently used to justify labor abuse within the United States. It is the "better than" argument: workers choose these jobs because they are *better than* the alternatives open to them. The fact of choice appears ethically to justify the conditions of the jobs.

In the following discussion, the contentions that justify sweatshop conditions or that strongly reject the policies that might alleviate them are addressed in turn. Rather than an excursion in economic theory, the discussion addresses the broader social and historical context often neglected in the abstractions of contemporary economic theory.

In addition to the "better than" argument, here are some of the main points made by the defenders of sweatshops:

- Sweatshop jobs are a (necessary) part of the ladder of development; we (in the United States and other rich countries) had them; the poor countries must go through this stage, and soon they will be prosperous too (see Krugman 1997).
- Growth is what will alleviate suffering and bring progress (WTO 1996).
- Linking labor standards to trade—as, for example, a social clause for the WTO—is really a biased attack by rich country unions and other interests to protect their markets. The labor standards chosen are biased to the resources and legal structures of the West (Bhagwati 2000a, 2000b). However, the WTO believes that "economic growth and development fostered by increased trade and further trade liberalization contribute to the promotion of these standards" (WTO 1996).
- Sweatshop conditions in domestic industries cannot be solved by regulations or careful law enforcement: for example, the enforcement of minimum wages will cause the jobs to shift to lower-wage environments.

The "better than" argument doesn't deny that abuse is real: "Workers in those shirt and sneaker factories are, inevitably, paid very little and expected to endure terrible working conditions," admits Krugman (1997). "Some managers are brutal in the way they house workers in firetraps, expose children to dangerous chemicals, deny bathroom breaks, demand sexual favors, force people to work double shifts or dismiss anyone who tries to organize a union," say Kristof and WuDunn, who nevertheless note how much of an improvement these conditions are—since, rather than lose her daughter to malaria, the miserable wages a Cambodian woman earns at least allows her to get a mosquito net to protect her children (Kristof and WuDunn 2000, 70).

The structure of this argument should be carefully examined. It is simple but only apparently sophisticated. The simplicity is that the appearance of choice by the worker in taking a sweatshop job legitimates the bad conditions. In Krugman's somewhat notorious article the symbolic alternative to factory work is living on a waste dump and picking at it as a means of living; in Kristof and WuDunn's article "Two Cheers for Sweatshops" the alternative is dying of malaria.

Philosophers are acquainted with this problem—choice under constraint. Discussing Aristotle's *Nicomachean Ethics,* T. H. Irwin noted that coercion or constraint transforms the meaning of choice, "not because they compel someone against his rational desires, but because he is compelled to choose rationally actions that are against his rational plan" (Irwin 1981, 136).[4] It is rational for a worker to toil at a sewing machine if someone holds a gun to her head (or if her family's life is at stake) and she is ordered to do so. Is death by starvation, or pain inflicted by extreme want, less coercive than the bully's threat? Such economic behavior is not properly understood as "free choice" and not even importantly understood as simple "rational choice."

The problem with the "better than" argument is that its logic allows no limit; that is, quite literally, it is uncivilized, unrestrained by a moral boundary. "Better than" is a slippery slope: The sweatshop is *better than* picking garbage or breaking bricks; it is *better than* prostitution, which is *better than* bonded labor or sexual slavery.[5] Slavery is *better than* death. Two cheers for slavery?

The framers of our laws on indentured and bonded labor and human trafficking have thought more clearly than have our economists on this matter: that workers agree to the conditions that led to their indenture does not relieve abusive employers from the law against it. The operators of the El Monte "slave" factory were found guilty and went to jail, and three of the Saipan contractors who indentured young Chinese and Vietnamese women are awaiting sentencing (U.S. Department of Justice 2003).

The sweatshop defenders depend on a model of the garment economy that treats market forces as if they were physical laws—as if wages, like the weather, are a result that humans cannot affect. So Krugman says the workers are "inevitably" paid very little. By contrast, Robert Pollin and associates (Pollin, Burns, and Heintz 2001) found that U.S. or Mexican workers (both of whom are paid multiples of Asian workers) could double their wages and still have but a minor impact on U.S. clothing prices.

More than "necessity" is involved here—it is also power. In a market in which employment is growing and there is room for price increases, as Pollin's work shows there is, workers who are socially empowered could demand more wages. But in much of the garment-exporting world, workers are suppressed or repressed. They cannot share in or enjoy the fruits of growth. Contrary to the implications of Krugman and of Kristof and

WuDunn, their poverty and the exploitation of it are not inevitable in the way a rainstorm is: they are inevitable in the way the outcome of a fight between a gunslinger and a boxer is; only one has the firepower.

The argument of the sweatshop defenders goes beyond the individual level—they address an alleged social good. The overall view depends on two empirical claims: one at the global level, one at the national level.

At the global level the claim is that those nations that are most "open" to the global economy—that is, they put the least restrictions on foreign investments and on importing and exporting—have achieved the most growth in the recent period. At first glance this proposition is not germane to the sweatshop issue. However, policies tend to come in packages, and the package of neoliberal (unrestrained free market) policies is one that rejects rigorous labor standards in trade agreements and also in domestic arrangements. On the other hand, the package of antisweatshop policies tends to advocate regulation of labor conditions by using domestic law or trade or investment controls to enforce higher standards.

The usual claims about the virtue of globalization are dependent on a methodological oddity and a statistical artifact. The methodological oddity is the use of an anecdotal style that highlights East Asian "success stories" rather than a rigorously quantitative cross-national approach—the usual international economics method. In this mode Korea, Singapore, Hong Kong, and Taiwan—export-oriented economies that started their march to prosperity by making textiles and toys (low-wage industries)—are put forward as models.

There are numerous problems in this approach: all of the East Asian fast-growing economies were recipients of exceptional subsidies due to cold war spending; all but Hong Kong had notoriously strong, directive state policies and were not at all open or laissez-faire economies; all employed strong state policies to move from low-wage to high-wage industrial structures as rapidly as possible (see, e.g., Rodrik 2002).

The experience of these countries stands in contrast to the Western Hemisphere countries that shifted to low-wage export industries and foreign investment as a means of development: stagnation, especially for workers, has been more typical of the Latin American economies attempting to export their way out of poverty (see, e.g., Ross and Chan 2002; Chan and Ross 2003).

The positive claims about globalization (which amounts to openness to foreign investments and the use of low-wage export industries to earn foreign currencies) and poverty reduction also hinge on a statistical artifact. The laureates of globalization tout the poverty reduction of those countries most integrated into the world economy (World Bank 2001b).

China and India are included in the analysis; because of their immense populations and recent economic growth they have a statistically disproportionate impact on statistical results at an aggregated world scale. Absent them, the data are very different. On the other hand, for China, the period of increased openness and the development of markets has been one in which unemployment has soared, inequality has become among the highest in the world, and the rural health provision has crashed. In another analysis, one that contrasts the period of globalized capital of the last twenty years with the twenty years before that, growth in the developing world was much more rapid in the earlier period—not a good result from the point of view of the laureates of globalization (Weller, Scott, and Hersh 2001; Weisbrot and Baker 2002). The analytical problem continues: China is not neoliberal and only recently joined the WTO—it doesn't fit the model.

There are further problems with the globalization-neoliberal prescription: openness to foreign investment is associated, in quantitative studies, with repression, decline in provision for basic necessities, and increases in inequality (see London and Ross 1995; London and Williams 1990).

The results of statistical studies that analyze results for a panel of scores of countries—cross-national studies—are accompanied by observations equally valid to the anecdotal observations of the sweatshop defenders, of national stagnation, despite a desperate commitment to the low-wage export industry. Bangladesh and Mexico are examples.

The findings about inequality are particularly important. At its core the sweatshop defenders' argument is pristine "trickle-downism": success occurs if gross national or gross domestic product grows. They say "a rising tide lifts all boats."

Without a rising tide it is very hard indeed to lift any boats. But the cruel truth is that an economic pie might grow and workers might not prosper: instead inequality may grow. This, after all, is the course of the last twenty years in the United States: wage losses for the bottom 20 percent; immense gains for the top 20 percent (see, e.g., Smith 2001, 80). For workers to share the fruits of growth, a legislative, social, and political structure must exist in which they have voice and that ensures a broad participation in the fruits of growth. This is not true in many, if not most, of today's labor-intensive export platform societies.

Among the cautions that the sweatshop defenders give to those advocating more active regulation and a "leveling up" of labor standards is that higher wages will produce less employment. This is often and particularly aimed at those advocating strict enforcement of U.S. minimum wage laws. There are numerous defects in these arguments—here are a few:

- The advocates of higher standards for apparel labor know full well that sharp increases in wages or conditions in one place will tend to encourage investment to flow away from that place. They advocate, therefore, a universal application of standards.

  This is *not* the same thing as a world minimum wage of the same level—a living wage relative to each economy will, of course, have different levels, depending on the wealth and general circumstance of each society.

- Nations have different advantages in production. The U.S. production advantage in apparel is high productivity and proximity to fashion markets. Industry experts believe that these advantages will hold tens of thousands of apparel jobs inside the United States despite wage increases.
- Repeated surveys in the United States (Marymount University Center 1999; Program on International Policy Attitudes 2000) have found the population willing to spend a few percent more (which Pollin, Burns, and Heintz 2001 show is enough) to ensure a sweat-free clothing supply.

The sweatshop defenders are left with a mechanical reading of history: "We" (the older industrial regions, the West) started industrialization with miserable conditions for the working classes, but now we are prosperous; "they" (the developing world) must retrace our steps, and if policies of economic growth are followed, they will. At issue are which steps at what times.

The laureates of globalization and the defenders of sweatshops seem to converge around the idea that economic growth solves all. It is surely true that in cross-national studies higher levels of GNP per capita are associated with more equality and better working conditions. Or at least they were before the current era of globalization (Galbraith, Conceição, and Kum 2000).

Now there is a divide—some of the rich nations have become strikingly less equal than they were, with the United States and the United Kingdom in the lead. At the end of the nineteenth century, when the United States was catching up to England and Germany in industrial output, it had an immense internal market and high tariff barriers to protect its young industries. Despite economic growth its working classes were miserable (though better fed and largely better off than their European counterparts).

It was not until after the New Deal had erected a public policy safety net and World War II had created full employment—and in its aftermath political consensus sought to keep unemployment below 3 percent—that the idea of workers as "middle class" (middle income) took root. Tremendous postwar growth in the United States and among European countries underlay the decency achieved by workers in the older industrial regions. The history of sweatshops in the United States shows the rest of the story: great strife; prodigious political movements; generations-long struggles for decency; political coalitions and allies; and strong national legislation that enabled workers to share the abundance they had helped to create.

Absent the power they had developed and the laws they had caused to be passed, workers' conditions in the United States might have been like those in Mexico: a middle-income country by comparative indicators, but one in which the workers have been left out of the party (see, e.g., Rothstein 1994). Mexican per capita income in 2001—$5,560 (data extracted from World Bank 2003)—was approximately similar to that in the United States in the early 1940s (see U.S. Department of Commerce 2003). In the 1990s Mexico became more unequal, with the Gini coefficient increasing (from 0.43 to 0.48). In the 1940s the U.S. Gini measure of inequality among families was about 0.38, much less than Mexico's at the same level of overall wealth (Henwood 1993). In the 1990s U.S. inequality also grew. These data illustrate a simple proposition: Economic growth is no guarantee of shared abundance.

The sweatshop defenders counsel passive patience: the lesson of history is that justice and decency must be actively grasped. As Frederick Douglass said it: If there is no struggle, there is no progress.

The Three Pillars of Decency Agenda

The First Pillar: Rebuild Union Strength

Because undocumented workers are so vulnerable to exploitation and to unfair labor practices, unions who organize in low-wage industries will be given an important boost when we protect immigrant workers. Legalization is one path; the other is preventing the threat of deportation from being used for union busting and as a license to exploit workers. Create a legal zone of immunity for workers engaged in union campaigns—no deportation for union representation.

Workers themselves, we have said, are the best inspectors and defenders of their rights—but they must have the right to organize to exercise that ability. We should strengthen the human right to association and to collective bargaining to which so much of our law gives lip service but which current employer practice negates. Here are four points of labor law reform that would help redress the balance of equity in American labor relations:[6]

1. "Card check" recognition: If a majority of a company's employees freely sign "cards" designating a union to negotiate on their behalf, collective bargaining should begin. The current requirement of the NLRB is that, if 30 percent of the workers sign cards saying they want to be represented by a union, a supervised "election" is held. Originally a well-intentioned means of assuring freedom of choice, this becomes instead a way for antiunion employers and their consultants to delay and frustrate employee choice. A "card check" system has worked well in Canada, without abridging legitimate employer or employee rights, and it can work here as well.

2. First contract arbitration: If negotiations in a newly unionized firm stalemate, a neutral arbitrator should be called upon to set terms of an initial "get acquainted" contract, customized to the firm's special needs. Arbitration is

increasingly used as a tool in commercial conflicts, and labor and management typically now use it to resolve contract disputes. Too many newly
unionized employers, however, now take advantage of legal loopholes to pre-
tend to bargain in good faith, while throwing up obstacles to agreement.
Penalties for failing to engage in good faith bargaining are minor compared
to employers' perceived advantage for stonewalling. In a high percentage of
cases, this unfair labor practice causes newly elected unions to fail to get a first
contract, and eventually their support ebbs away. An arbitrator, jointly
selected by management and labor, can limit this practice.

3. Control of the *captive audience* advantage. Workplaces are for work. But if a
firm chooses to use its facilities and employee time for antiunion campaigning (captive audience meetings to propagandize against unions), unions
should have equal time and access to respond to such efforts. Today's NLRB
elections, where one side (management) can electioneer to a captive audience
for eight hours a day while the other side (labor) has little access to employees, would not pass muster as a fair election anywhere else in the world. Equal
access is a long overdue democratic reform.

Punish unfair labor practices—really. Employees' right to join a union
needs stronger protection. Unscrupulous employers fire far too many
workers for their attempt to organize or join a union. The NLRB's remedies for unlawful firings are minimal, and the process of adjudication
takes far too long. Speedier and more effective redress along with tougher
penalties for unlawful firings are needed.

Much of labor-intensive manufacturing has migrated and will continue
to migrate to developing countries. The goal of workers everywhere is that
they should be able to share in the fruits of the growth and the wealth that
they create themselves. They must be able to defend their just deserts, and
they must have protected rights to do this. Workers in our or any country
may have to compete with workers who live in countries with lower standards of living; they should not be made to compete with workers who
cannot call for a collective raise in their wages for fear of being jailed,
fired, or harassed.

The global justice movement should take up the call of the international labor movement to ensure labor rights in trade agreements. Those
international agreements that have been ratified should be amended;
none should be ratified that do not properly guarantee that the world
trade regime will put labor at the table when the treaties guaranteeing
rights are presented.

This is not a consensual matter among the world's critics of globalization. Perhaps among developing countries' critics of globalization there are more nationalists than working-class advocates; perhaps the critics of globalization are more concerned about national businesses than local workers. Perhaps hostility to the WTO is so great that reforms to the international system look less interesting than dismantling it. For whatever reasons, the linkage between trade and labor standards has not seen favor among developing country intellectuals—though the union picture is more diverse. Critical to changing those politics is the reframing that this book has suggested—understanding it not as a matter of rich country labor versus poor country exporters but rather as one of the rules of the game that includes competition among poor countries.

In the meantime, labor unions and justice advocates must reach out to workers and organizations in the developing world to reframe the entire issue of labor rights. Indeed, among the more important advances of the next ten years will be the cooperation of unions and advocacy groups ever more closely across national borders.

The Second Pillar: Government Policy

In addition to labor law changes, there are important policy and legal changes that can help, directly, to improve the conditions of sweatshop workers in the U.S. clothing industry. These are things that reformers—workers and their middle-class allies—should demand of their political representatives. Touched upon in the course of this volume, here is a summary.

To protect workers from unscrupulous (or desperate) employers, more investigators should be hired to enforce the FLSA. If there were twice as many investigators in the WHD of the DOL as there are now, it would still be less than the equivalent number during the Eisenhower administration.

Make retailers responsible in criminal and civil court for the labor law violations in the manufacture of store brands and other clothing items whose production they directly commission—the legislation is called "manufacturers' liability" and is the legal equivalent of the "joint liability contract" the garment workers union once could enforce.

Three Pillars of Decency

The U.S. legal code has numerous instances that reference internationally recognized labor rights as a basis for granting special trade consideration to nations, for example, the GSP. Even legislation that supporters of the labor movement oppose often makes reference to such concepts—for example, the so-called fast track legislation that empowers the president to negotiate trade agreements. Some administrations (e.g., Bill Clinton's) use this language somewhat more in their foreign negotiations than do others. Practically none administers agreements and our trade laws as if labor rights were actually central parts of the human rights concept that we, as a nation, often brandish as our special mission. Until more citizens inside and outside of the labor movement believe labor rights to be central human rights and rhetorical flair is supplemented by hard policy, workers will get short shrift in American trade policy.

The Third Pillar: Reformers and Consumers

Soon, sometime in the next two or three years, some clothes and athletic shoes in the American market may bear a label that refers to "sweat free" or "Fair Labor Association." Born in controversy and attacked by student activists, this Clinton-era initiative is, as this book goes to print, changing a bit in response to impassioned criticism. The campaigns to achieve workers' rights at Mexmode and to secure those rights at the BJ&B factory both included positive responses from the FLA. Its sponsors are, no doubt, hoping that its label will be trusted. Consumers should stay alert to the possibility that the label, which will be launched with some fanfare, is not meaningful, even while hoping that, by the time the group is ready to unveil it, they will have made important strides in guaranteeing decent labor conditions in production.

There are some who advocate the generation of a list of "clean clothes" suppliers—such as Los Angeles's *SweatX* or Massachusetts's *No sweat apparel*. These may be good guides for students or young people for whom T-shirts are the staple clothing; for those with more diverse clothing needs, such a list will have to wait on a larger union share of the clothing supply.

There is no easy path for the consumer with a conscience.[7] The place to start is to realize that right now there is no really large, dependable supply of "clean clothes." Conscientious consumers can try to learn about current controversies and, as may be called for from time to time, boycott a given brand or, better, make known to a store or a firm that their practices are abhorrent and should change. One's personal goal cannot be to become a saint free of the taint of sweat upon one's clothes but rather to become an ally with a strategic need to focus at any given moment.

As in the middle of the twentieth century in the older industrial nations, the apparel workers of the global rag trade require the three pillars of union strength, government policy, and allied reformers and consumers to support strongly the platform upon which decent conditions depend. Sooner or later: sooner would be better.

Personal Epilogue

Hearts Starve

In January 2002, having completed a conference on labor and globalization at the University of Beijing, I, along with my coworker, Anita Chan, and the historian-sociologist Peter Alexander, guided by a Beijing friend of Ms. Chan, went in search of a clothing factory. First we went to a market far on the southern side of the city. Beijing city authorities had built the market after they tore down a street bazaar. This part of the city holds many migrants from Zhejiang Province, where there is an active private clothing and textile industry.

The market sold soft goods of every description, at prices even lower than the bargains of the central city's famous "Silk Alley." The ritual of bargaining, though, is very similar.

We asked the owners of the small stalls selling jeans and blouses if they knew of a factory close by. In short order a young man selling jeans told us of a place in some kind of industrial park not very far away. We hopped a bus and after about two stops began to look about.

Typically in Beijing, empty parcels or pieces of ground that are not parkland or part of a mainstream economic enterprise are littered with plastic bags and other windblown trash. In one triangle of land near a highway interchange, an impromptu dump had developed, and as we walked by three or four people were picking through the day's leavings, looking, one supposes, for something of use. We came in sight of some fairly recent, though very dirty, buildings with an entrance gate. The wind was blowing grit from the nearby highway and from the ungrassed pieces of ground. On drying racks we saw dozens of chickens under preparation for some commercial process.

Beijing trimmer, January 2002. Photographer: Robert J. S. Ross.

We entered a small building and along a dark corridor opened a door to a small workroom. On this winter day a potbellied stove was on, and three people were working in the space. Within seconds of entering the space, the smallest person in our group of four began coughing and had to rush out, feeling faint; then the rest of us became allergic and faint, in order of smallest to largest (Peter, who was quite a bit over six feet tall). Clearly some dose-related toxin was in the air in that room, but the three workers carried on.

As we proceeded down the corridor, we did indeed find a coat factory. In a small office with a couch, a desk, and a bed, the owner was interested to show us the workroom next door. There, in a small room (one of us estimated it to be forty square meters) were twenty-two workers making overcoats—for the Russian market we learned. We chatted with the owner. She told us she and her husband had another factory in Zhejiang Province that was much larger, capable of producing tens of thousands of shirts a month.

In that impressively crowded workroom most of the people were women sitting at very tightly spaced sewing machines. A fellow was pressing by applying his iron to the coats draped on a dressmaker's dummy. When we asked if we could take a picture, the workers smiled and giggled with each other about what the foreigners were doing. The picture is one of amused operators, packed in but smiling.

At the front of the workroom was a very large pile of sewn coats. Two women were sitting on the floor, working on this pile. They were trimming—cutting off the loose ends of thread at buttons, buttonholes, and labels and otherwise tidying up the work. This is among the lowest paid work in a garment factory, and these workers didn't even get chairs.

The young women trimmers were not smiling. The coats were black, and their part of the room was not well lit (the sewing stations were bright with fluorescents), so my photograph of a young woman trimming coats is a bit dim. But as I close this work, it is to her that my thoughts flow. A migrant, no doubt without full residence papers, she will not have rights to the public schools or to the public health system. She will be boarding, many people to a room, where someone else is the nominal renter, because of her lack of a residency permit. We were at the shop late on a Saturday afternoon and were told that they would be working the next day. The woman's face seems to me vaguely pained—looking off at an angle from the camera.

Was she, like Mexican women in Los Angeles, thinking about when she might go out with her young man? Was she thinking about her parents back in the village? Did she dream that one day things might be easier? Did she hope that soon she could work at a sewing machine, where the pay is better and you get a chair? Our situation did not permit us to talk to her. But I wonder still, as she slaved for fashion, if her heart starves for roses.

Notes

Introduction

1. Fasanella's painting "Lawrence 1912, the Bread and Roses Strike" may be viewed online at <http://www.nyhistory.org/fasanella/lawrence.html>.

2. One scholar claims the children were sent away so their cries of hunger would not weaken their mothers' resolve (Harney 1999).

3. Kerri Harney (1999) first used Lincoln's phrase "mystic chords" in this context.

4. A combing of the newspapers of the period—recall that photojournalism was alive and well in that era—reveals nary an indication, and the slogan appears in no literature of the day (Sider 1996), nor is it used verbatim in the Italian language poems of the strike's orator–poet Arturo Giovannitti. I report here the trenchant scholarship of Harney (1999), whose work was an undergraduate honors thesis. She began her research by following up the search for evidence undertaken by Gerald Sider (1996).

5. The quote is from Kenneth MacGowan, "Giovannitti: Poet of the Wop," *Forum* (October 1914): 609, discussing the poet–orator Arturo Giovannitti, who played a leadership role in the Lawrence strike. It is taken from Harney 1999.

6. This quote is from a childhood memory of a Folkways record album liner. I am not able to document it.

Chapter 1

1. The great labor historian John R. Commons referred in 1901 to the "contractor" or "sweater" as the "organizer" of work often done in homes by immigrants (in Stein 1977, 44–45). Usage is not consistent, for others refer to the "sweater" as the "home worker" (Garnett 1988, 31).

2. Outerwear refers to clothing that is not underwear, excludes certain tailored garments. See chap. 6, note 5.

3. See "'Knee Pants' at 45 cents a dozen—a Ludlow Street Sweater's Shop" in Riis 1890. Available at <http://www.cis.yale.edu/amstud/inforev/riis/riis24.gif>.

4. But it would not have provided income above a more appropriate and higher poverty line. See later in this chapter for a discussion of different poverty criteria.

5. What is big? Christopher Jencks, reflecting on the partisan or interested use of the estimates of homelessness, thought 1 million was the magic number for an American social

problem. My estimate for the apparel industry fails this test; for all industries in the nation, I have no estimate, but, of course, labor abuse as I have defined *sweatshops* would have to be much more than 1 million: the issue would be where it is as concentrated as apparel. As discussed later in this chapter, sweatshop labor is nowhere as concentrated as it is in apparel work, with the possible exception of restaurants and agriculture. See Jencks 1994, 2–4.

6. Value-added is an economic concept that denotes the estimated value, in dollars, that is added to a product or material at each stage of its manufacture or distribution.

7. The GAO sample of violators was not representative because its sample was composed of the violators *known* to the DOL in the two states as a result of their investigations.

8. "There is no theoretical reason to exclude from the informal economy the unrecorded practices of large corporations, particularly since they have close linkages with the growth of other informal activities" (Castells and Portes 1989, 13, 15). When seventy-one workers, lured into slavery from Thailand, were discovered in a slave factory in El Monte, California, in 1995, the list of retailers for which the clothing was bound was a who's who of mainstream (and upscale) retailing in California, including Neiman Marcus and the Mays chain (Su 1997).

9. The method they used is called "input-output" analysis.

10. The EDD Tax Branch is one of the largest tax collection agencies in the nation and handles all the administrative and enforcement functions for audit and collection of unemployment insurance, disability insurance, employment training tax (ETT), and personal income tax (PIT) withholding.

11. The fact that there were so many violations for each violator firm makes it possible to use minimum wage violations as an indicator variable for multiple labor law violations. This is de facto the way the DOL treats the matter in its press releases.

12. Voluntary compliance monitoring is considered a failure by labor rights advocates. Despite, apparently, boosting compliance rates, almost half of those allegedly monitored are still labor law violators. Notoriously, among the first firms to claim that it monitored its contractors was the infamous Guess? jeans company, which was later found to have repeat violators in its contractor chain (Greenhouse 1997).

13. These estimates are derived from the method outlined in detail in appendix 1.

14. It should be noted that the restaurant industry, when examined by the GAO in 1989, had as high a level of FLSA violations as did the apparel industry. In general, they were of different types. Records-keeping violations were high, and child labor violations were much more frequent than in the apparel industry. Some fraction of these violations might be technical: for example, when a teenager works late during the school week. Restaurants are frequent violators of sanitary codes. Among the more serious sweatshop conditions occur when Chinese workers are smuggled into the country and held under conditions of indenture, often working in restaurants (Kwong 1998). There is no other known recent study of industrial concentrations of major FLSA violations; though the meat-packing industry has become notorious for health and safety issues.

15. The analysis that follows is based on violation reports of the 1990s and the turn of the decade. In March 2002, the DOL reported declining violation rates in New York City. Since the DOL had ceased publishing enforcement reports and the Bush administration had called for cuts in the Wage and Hour Division enforcement budget, a "wait and see" attitude seems more appropriate than that taken by the DOL's PR spinners: "Labor Secretary Elaine L. Chao Announces Increased Compliance in Garment Industry."

Chapter 2

1. The modern usage of this diasporic yearning continues. Bony M's "By the Rivers of Babylon" puts to reggae rhythm what Clara would have read in Hebrew.

2. In 1900 there were 94,000 clothing workers in New York, about half the national

total of 206,000. The growth had been 6,000 per year since 1870 nationally. By 1910 total employment would have been well over 100,000 (N. Green 1997, 48).

3. The number of workers in the factory at the time of the fire appears differently in different sources. Rosy Safran, a sewing machine operator whose recollection was published in the *Independent* a month after the fire, said "700 girls" were there (McClymer 1998, 89, 90). Stein, who wrote the definitive history, uses the five hundred worker figure (Stein 2001 [1962], 29). Gompers, in a fervent attack on the employers, said two thousand were on the payroll (1911). The *New York Times,* the next day (March 26), said six hundred workers were in the factory, five hundred of them women and girls.

4. A tale, perhaps apocryphal, perhaps an instructive fable about familiarity, is told by, among others, the left wing organizer Steve Max in regard to the flamboyant Reform Democrat congresswoman Bella Abzug, she of the large hats and Manhattan accent in the 1970s. At a talk she gave at a Manhattan Democratic club, the tale relates, Abzug's audience included two gents seated far back who exchanged knowing comments about how she had been a Red (i.e., a communist) at some time in the past. "Yeah," one is said to have replied, "she may have been a Red but she's one of ours." So too the lasses of the Triangle.

5. The industries in question were shoe production in Lynn and textile production in Fall River.

6. See Gereffi and Korzeniewicz 1994 and Bonacich et al. 1994 for discussions of commodity chains in general and apparel specifically.

7. As an act of disclosure I should note that my stepfather's father (whom I never met but about whom I have heard plenty) was among the leaders of the communist grouping in the ILGWU.

Chapter 3

1. Calculated from the Consumer Price Index data from the U.S. Bureau of Labor statistics at <http://data.bls.gov/cgi-bin/surveymost?cu>.

2. Among the positive surprises in Robert Caro's monumental and scathingly negative biography of New York's highway, parks, and housing tyrant, Robert Moses, is the story—detailed, warmly sympathetic, and nearly disappeared from contemporary memory—of the evolution of Al Smith as a progressive figure. See Caro 1974, from which much of this information is taken. Caro recalls that Smith was known as the best "bill drafter" in Albany, though he had never finished high school. He spent long hours in a spare Albany hotel, while the legislature was in session, studying bills and their precedents, that is, the special meaning of phrases used in them. It was his more malevolent protégé, Robert Moses, who was to take this title from him, with less happy results.

3. Girl Guides are the British Commonwealth equivalents to Girl Scouts.

4. For a discussion of research on European corporatism, testing a variety of theories of cause and effect, see Western 1991.

5. The bill was, as drafted by Perkins's people and later "Tommy" Corcoran and Benjamin Cohn, forty pages long; when Roosevelt later saw it he gave a "big sigh and said 'For heaven's sake, take it back and tell them to reduce it to 2 pages'" (Perkins 1957, 18). Perkins explained that it was meant for Supreme Court justices and not for "the man in the street."

6. No surprise, there is a vast literature on the history of the American labor movement. One that emphasizes the internal politics and contending philosophies of organization is Boyer and Morais's *Labor's Untold Story* (1955), a fairly politicized view from the left. A classic discussion of the evolution of business unionism is John R. Commons's *Trade Unionism and Labor Problems* (1922 [1905]). Commons's views are discussed in Barbash 1989.

7. "One Big Union" is the phrase the IWW—a syndicalist and colorful radical expression of working-class solidarity around the turn of the nineteenth century—used to describe its vision of all workers united in a single association.

8. Later, after industrial unions had remade the terrain of capitalism, the result would be called Fordism, first and most vividly by Aldous Huxley in his novel *Brave New World*. Mass production required mass consumption to sustain itself. Ford vaguely understood this when he made cheap cars and paid workers moderately decent wages. It took the rest of the mass production employers another generation to recognize this, an insight that their unions helped them to see. The result was mass production, mass consumption, and large governments to regulate the uneasy partnership that was later called Fordism, coined in social theory by French intellectuals. Strange echoes in the twenty-first century. Just as Huxley had noticed in his novel of 1932, President George W. Bush urged Americans to consume as a patriotic duty when the U.S. economy nose-dived after the attacks of September 11, 2001.

9. An older textbook that included some brilliant synthetic work made this argument: Szymanski 1978.

10. Over 3 million emigrated. The net was 5.7 million, the highest in history until 1980–90 and then 1990–2000 (U.S. INS 1996).

11. This argument is an extension of Goldfield 1989.

Chapter 4

1. Schlesinger was an attorney whose history of apparel industry organization was undertaken on behalf of the ILGWU, of which his father had been an early president.

2. For perspectives on the internal fight between socialists and communists in the ILGWU, see Tyler 1995 and N. Green 1997.

3. The quotation marks around *sweatshop* are in Hill's original.

4. The interviews are housed at the Centro de Estudios Puertorriquenos at Hunter College of the City University of New York. The center includes a collection of Puerto Rican oral history materials.

5. Repeated studies on the 1980s and 1990s showed that about 60 percent of New York contractor shops were labor law violators.

6. In another GAO study, over 89 percent of California sweatshops were registered or listed on tax rolls. If the 6 are 80 percent of the total, then the total is 7.5; to make sure the estimate is not too low, we round up to 10.

7. We omit Chinatown from these calculations. Its recent immigrant and total population was lower in the 1950s than in the 1970s and after. We also exclude Staten Island and Queens because neither borough had significant Puerto Rican populations in the 1950s.

8. Further calculations indicate that over this time span apparel workers averaged between 127 percent and 133 percent of the poverty threshold for a family of three. Many observers consider 125 percent of the U.S. official poverty rates an approximation of a more reasonable level of decent living standards.

Chapter 5

1. I discuss this procedure and its limits at some length in chapter 12.

2. Both interviewees and the NLC varied widely in reports of how many workers and/or union sympathizers had been fired. They are without access to lists of employees and are in a situation where the workers do not have telephones and the unions' own record keeping is minimal.

3. I have found that about 40 percent of news stories about domestic sweatshops in the *New York Times* and *Los Angeles Times* identify the immigrant status of ethnicity of the workers in either the headline or the lead paragraph and that over 50–60 percent mention these identifiers of the workers somewhere in the article.

Chapter 6

1. This proposition and the discussion that follows differ—by elaboration—from Gary Gereffi's original (1994) distinction between buyer- and producer-driven commodity

chains. I note too that competition may still occur among relatively powerful buyers or producers. Among the key hallmarks of the era of global capitalism, as distinct from monopoly capitalism, is the renewed price competition among relatively concentrated producers. See Ross and Trachte 1990.

2. This estimate, for 2000, is based on calculations in appendix 1. As rapid job loss has continued the numbers in any given industry category will also drop.

3. Cutters, working with mechanical blades about the size of a table saw, trace a pattern over dozens or scores of layers of cloth. The pieces are then sewn by sewing machine operators; the thread ends are trimmed; and the garments are then pressed.

4. Buck's accomplishment should be appreciated. As the new sweatshops appeared in the late 1970s the first guesses about the cause of their appearance confused effect and cause: the Mafia and unscrupulous contractors. This analysis did not last the decade.

5. Examples of outerwear are bathing suits, down coats, sweaters, jogging suits, outerwear pants and shorts, and windbreakers. The category excludes underwear, lingerie, nightwear, blouses, shirts, dresses, suits, tailored coats, tailored jackets, and skirts.

6. These figures have been calculated from U.S. DOL, Bureau of Labor Statistics, Office of Productivity and Technology data, available at <http://www.bls.gov/lpc/home.htm>.

7. *Save the Tiger*, a film for which Jack Lemmon won a best actor academy award in 1973, depicts him burning down his factory for insurance money and providing prostitutes to his customers.

8. Others were later added, and at least one was subtracted.

9. By comparison, in 1980, there were 5,900 employed persons and citizens held 62 percent of those jobs (Central Statistics Division 2001, 50, 51).

10. In its publication "Recent Trends in Population, Labor Force, Employment, and Unemployment Commonwealth of the Northern Mariana Islands, 1973 to 1999, Second Edition, September 2000," the CNMI Central Statistical Division says there were 7,700 garment jobs in 1995: this is more than 100 percent of the 1995 nondurable manufacturing sector they reported in the *Statistical Yearbook* for 2001..I thus assume that virtually all of the over 14,000 jobs in that sector in 1999 were also in the garment sector.

11. The description of working conditions in Saipan is drawn from *Doe I et al. vs. The Gap et al.* 2001.

Chapter 7

1. The 60 percent number is from repeated U.S. DOL random surveys in Los Angeles (California State Department of Industrial Relations 1994; U.S. DOL 1996, 1998, 2000) and New York (U.S. DOL 1997b, 1999). See chapter 1 for documentation.

2. Defense expenditures were 4.9 percent of GDP in 1981, rose to 6.3 percent in 1986, and were 5.7 percent in 1989. The Kennedy-Johnson (Vietnam) comparison is 9.4 percent in 1961, falling to 7.4 percent in 1965, and ending at 8.7 percent in 1969 (calculated from Council of Economic Advisers 1997, B-76, B-78).

3. Not counting the postal service, see Hatch and Clinton 2000, 8. Most of the decrease was after 1991—on the Clinton watch.

4. In 1995 all means-tested family support programs, of which AFDC was the largest, cost $18.1 billion. Total 1996 domestic discretionary spending was $533 billion—3.4 percent (Committee on Ways and Means 1997, tables I-5, I-1). When combined with the costs of Medicaid, health services for the poor, however, the budgetary impact is greater—especially on state budgets. Ironically, the only sane way to cut welfare involved extensions of Medicaid eligibility. I am grateful to S. M. Miller for this insight.

5. Another form of privatization stirs less controversy: turning over previously government-operated services to not-for-profit service agencies. Examples abound: mental health services, community-sponsored housing, and so forth.

6. These numbers are based on DOL budget documents, the Bureau of Labor Statistics'

Current Employment Statistics, and the Census Bureau's County Business Patterns, various years, and the Statistical Abstract of the United States, various years. The referent of 1957—and the uneven selection of years—is determined by the budget documents available at the DOL library, where many years' budget documents are missing.

7. Previous to 1974 one location per country was counted; after that each physically separate location was counted.

8. A similar dynamic caused Ronald Reagan to sign legislation calling for mandatory advance notice of plant closings in 1988—a campaign gift to his successor, Vice President George H. W. Bush.

9. Cal-Safety is a monitoring firm, and Kellwood is a large manufacturer.

10. "Thought experiments are devices of the imagination used to investigate nature" *(Stanford Encyclopedia of Philosophy)*. Available at <http://plato.stanford.edu/entries /thought-experiment>. Accessed on March 14, 2002. The data for this experiment are taken from Esbenshade's (2001) summary of the DOL's compliance surveys.

11. One symptom or indicator of this difference is that during Reich's time, and continuing through the administration of Alexis Herman, the DOL featured a prominent "No Sweat" Web page with informational links and quarterly reports of enforcement activity and educational material. Under the Chao/Bush administration, one must find one's way to "Garment" at the Wage and Hour division to find this material—and as of March 2002, none had been added since December 2000. Rae Glass, director of external affairs, told me on March 14, 2002, that they intended to post the garment enforcement reports. As of the summer of 2004 they were not.

12. The success in improving conditions became moot when Phillips Van Heusen removed its contract from the plant and it later closed.

13. These informants gave me their views on a "background" basis; that is, they wish to remain anonymous.

14. Compare "Commentary by UNITE on AIP 'Preliminary Agreement' of 11/2/98." Available at <www.sweatshopwatch.org/swatch/headlines/1998/unite_fla.html>. Accessed March 15, 2002.

15. The Reich-Clinton DOL did perform an elaborate study of official wage rates and poverty lines among apparel exporters to the United States (Schoepfle 2000).

16. The UFCW represents retail clerks at some department store chains.

17. In the longer run, after Harvey's retirement in 2001, the ILRF decided that his seat on the FLA board was personal and not institutional and demurred an invitation to send a representative (Collingsworth 2002).

18. For example, in Greenhouse's July 3 article (Greenhouse 1998a, A16), presaging the collapse of the consensus approach, Posner said: "I remain cautiously optimistic that we're going to find a path that leads to an agreement."

19. Made available to me by a staff member of the ILRF.

20. For the text, see "The Collegiate Code of Conduct for CLC Licensees." Available at <http://www.news.wisc.edu/packages/sweatshops/index.msql?get=clccode>.

21. See Ross 2001 for a discussion of this. The budget proposal number is from the Office of Management and Budget, Budget of the United States, Appendix, Department of Labor, p. 693. Available at <http://www.whitehouse.gov/omb/budget/fy2002/lab.pdf>. The CPI range is from the Congressional Budget Office, An Analysis of the President's Budgetary Proposals for Fiscal Year 2002, May 2001, table 13. Available at <http://www.cbo.gov/show-doc.cfm?index=2819&sequence=0&from=7>.

Chapter 8

The chapter is a revised version of a paper presented at the Marymount University conference entitled "An Academic Search for Sweatshop Solutions," on May 30, 1997. A still earlier version was jointly written with Ellen McCormack (Wellesley College) and Ellen Rosen

(Brandeis University) and presented at the annual meeting of the Society for the Study of Social Problems in 1996.

1. Though Americans associate the abuses of the garment industry with the victimization of people of color, it is the case that in many places, perhaps most, the people who are ground up in the apparel workshops of the world tend to be rural to urban migrants or, as in Saipan, immigrant or guest workers. They are not everywhere ethnically distinct or subordinate to the larger society, though they do tend to be predominantly women and migrants or immigrants.

2. *Gross* immigration is a larger number than *net* immigration. Net immigration includes emigration and estimates of undocumented entries and exists of illegal migrants. The INS has not yet released *net* immigration figures for 1990–2000. Ironically, although 1900–10 had higher gross immigration than 1980–90, the net figure was identical—5.7 million (U.S. INS and U.S. DOL 1999).

3. Calculated from U.S. INS 2002, table 2.

4. It is an error, though, to think that most shops are *completely* in the black, informal, or have an off-the-books economy. They blend aspects of regular and irregular features. See Ross 2002.

5. When they are slaves or held in illegal indenture, the heroic entrepreneur becomes the Dickensian exploiter. The academic acceptance moves to a note of moral outrage. In the shadows, though, are those who are forced to accept terrible conditions in order to work off debts of transportation. (e.g., the Saipan case in chapter 6 and Kwong 1999).

6. Stier (1991) and Loo and Ong (1987) found in a study of San Francisco's Chinatown that 85 percent of the employed women surveyed reported that they saw language as a major barrier to a better job.

7. Earlier in the twentieth century, union organizer lore put it this way: "The hardest thing to teach Jewish workers was that Jewish bosses were bosses."

8. Schumpeter, an Austrian economist, argued that entrepreneurs who do new things heroically "destroy" old ways—and firms—creatively making new things in new ways, thus creating the future of prosperity. Schumpeter (1975 [1942])

9. As noted in the discussion of Nicaragua and of Bonacich and Appelbaum's (2000) work on Los Angeles, when economic or political developments restrict men's access to factory employment, they filter into the traditionally female-dominated sewing jobs.

10. Examples of labor legislation and union strength include the FLSA in 1938, the prohibition of homework in 1942, and the relative strength of the ILGWU.

11. The U.S. Supreme Court has found that an employer must comply with the FLSA even if he has hired an undocumented, illegal worker. On the other hand, as this chapter was being finalized, the U.S. Supreme Court ruled that an employer who had fired an undocumented worker for union activity was not liable for $67,000 in back pay, because it couldn't be held liable for wages it would have been illegal to pay. The case, *Hoffman Plastic Compounds v. National Labor Relations Board*, 00–1595, was reported by the Associated Press on March 27, 2002.

Chapter 9

1. Leon Stein (n.d.) interview with Joe Glazer. *Padrone* refers to a system of labor gang recruitment by Italian labor recruiters. The boss ("lord") got a fee for the gang's work; the workers' share was up to the boss. The system exploited new immigrants, especially in construction. The usage connotes both arbitrary wage setting and exploitation based on coethnicity.

2. The Amalgamated Clothing Workers of America (ACWA) was founded in 1914 to represent workers in the men's wear industry, parallel to the International Ladies Garments Workers Union (ILGWU) in the women's wear industry (1910). The "Amalgamated," as it

was known, took the lead in the establishment (1939) of the Textile Workers Union of America (TWUA). In 1976 ACWA and TWUA became the Amalgamated Clothing and Textile Workers Union (ACTWU). In 1995 the ILGWU and ACTWU merged to form UNITE: the Union of Needle Trades Industrial and Textile Employees. UNITE is the official name.

3. Newspaper and popular sources often put the number of apparel workers in southern California and Los Angeles at about 120,000 and in New York at 80,000. The numbers cited here and in figure 11 include only the "apparel" category (SIC 23) of the Bureau of Labor Statistics Current Employment survey. Small numbers of employees from other industry branches are sometimes included in apparel data—but not enough to make the differences here. I think the larger numbers often cited are the result of (a) people rounding up from mid-1990s data of about 112,000 in Los Angeles and over 75,000 in New York; and (b) people not realizing how rapidly jobs are being lost in the industry.

4. On television, see Putnam 2000; on the concept of class consciousness and residential and other forms of community, see Szymanski 1978.

5. Workers with a conscientious objection to joining a union may pay the equivalent of dues to the union, known as an agency fee.

6. The unusual contractor structure of the apparel industry is actually the occasion of a Taft-Hartley exemption from this provision. There is a legal paradox: the main labor-repressive legislation of the post–World War II era exempts the apparel industry from one of its most antisolidarity features, recognizing the continuity of the web of production from "manufacturer" and contractor. Yet, other aspects of labor legislation, the FLSA, does not fully hold responsible the manufacturer who causes work to be done by contractors under sublegal conditions.

7. The "Contract with America" was the name given to their program by a group of ultraconservative Republicans who were led to power in 1994 by the aggressive new speaker of the house, Newt Gingrich of Georgia. It included strong antiunion features as well as a general animus against all of the strong government initiatives of the New Deal and after. Its most notable successes were welfare reform and budget cutting.

8. A slightly larger number—6.8 percent—was represented by unions. The difference is those workers who choose not to be union members but whose work units are represented by unions.

9. The Amalgamated had joined with the Textile Workers Union of America in 1976 (see note 2 in this chapter).

Chapter 10

Lisa Grandmaison, Clark University, collected and coded the student questionnaire data and helped summarize literature on media framing; Bruce London assisted in data analysis and interpretation of the student questionnaires.

1. This was a newspaper account of a study of nine of its contractor factories in Indonesia that Nike commissioned from its "front" group—the Global Alliance. The body of the report, though not the executive summary, indicated the workers were dissatisfied with their pay, despite acknowledging it was higher than other local factories. Unable to deal with this complexity, and perhaps not willing to read the whole report, the newspaper stories focused on the executive summary admission of harassment. See Global Alliance 2001.

2. Note that the difference in quantity is almost entirely due to different ways of counting: anywhere in story (*Los Angeles Times*) versus headline or lead (*New York Times*). If one counts the number of times *sweatshop* shows up anywhere in the *New York Times*, the number is more comparable: 121 (*Los Angeles Times*) versus 85 (*New York Times*). These counts are based on the Lexis-Nexis database for the *New York Times* and the *Los Angeles Times* archives.

3. Most studies have been on framing effects in television news rather than print news (Yows 1994).

4. After this search was accomplished in 1999, Lexis-Nexis database ceased carrying the *Los Angeles Times* archive (except for a rolling six-month window). It is therefore no longer possible to replicate the data with the same parameters.

5. When the various immigrant categories are searched in full text rather than in headline or lead, the story count for the major newspaper file goes from 145 to 198—indicating that only 53 additional stories are added beyond those that use the immigrant-ethnic frame in the lead.

6. See appendix to chapter 10 for the items in the index and statistical analyses.

7. Are student respondents a good indicator of how effects may flow through the mass public? On this issue they may be. They are responding to print materials—the sweatshop issue has been predominantly a print, rather than electronic, story. Students represent what analysts call "the educated public"—more likely to read, to pay attention, and to form opinions leading to actions.

8. "All possess alike liberty of conscience and immunities of citizenship. It is now no more that toleration is spoken of, as if it was by the indulgence of one class of people, that another enjoyed the exercise of their inherent natural rights. For happily the Government of the United States, which gives to bigotry no sanction, to persecution no assistance, requires only that they who live under its protection, should demean themselves as good citizens, in giving it on all occasions their effectual support" (Washington 1790).

9. As the minority party, the Democrats could not get the Republican committee chair to hold a formal hearing on the issue. Their "hearing" was therefore a forum with no technical status.

10. For the concept of a commodity chain applied to the apparel industry, see Appelbaum and Gereffi (1994) and Gereffi (1994).

11. The draft title of the conference paper for which this material was originally developed was "Kathie Lee Is an Atom Bomb." I think I meant she had really big impact. I am evading various friendly advisers who told me not to use the title by sneaking it into this note.

12. A selective incentive is a benefit available to movement participants but not to the general public who might otherwise benefit, as "free riders," from the achievement of the movement (Olson 1965; Fireman and Gamson 1979).

13. Though it did not use child labor, Modern Dress was eventually fined by both the DOL for overtime violations and by Boston authorities for safety violations. In both cases the focus on Modern Dress was a result of media exposure. The DOL learned (again) of Modern Dress from a radio report of an interview that followed the September field trip. A *Boston Herald* reporter brought the Modern Dress case to Boston health and safety inspectors after the reporter heard about the same interview.

14. While we did inspect the influence of race, we do not include it here because of the small numbers of minority group members in our sample and the fact that the variable had no impact on results.

15. We also found women significantly less likely to blame immigrants than men and conservatives considerable more likely to blame immigrants than liberals. The effects of occupation, immigrant background, and union background were not significant. This is probably because there were not enough cases with these characteristics, given the relatively low levels of immigrant blame.

Part 3

1. All of the active NGOs in the labor and labor rights field have vigorous and informative World Wide Web presence. Some of these Web sites will be given in notes as we proceed.

2. <http://www.nlcnet.org/nlc/History.shtml>.
3. <http://www.globalexchange.org/about/>.
4. <http://www.maquilasolidarity.org/aboutus.htm>.
5. <http://www.cleanclothes.org/index.htm>.
6. <http://www.jwj.org/AboutJWJ/History.htm>.

Chapter 11

1. The partial exception would be the general attitude of support given to Southern sitters-in at historically Black colleges; these events were, of course, off campus (McAdam 1982).

2. The top ten collegiate licensed apparel manufacturers for 2001–2002 were (1) Nike USA Inc., (2) Zephyr Graf-X, (3) Gear For Sports, (4) Top of the World, (5) Team Edition Apparel, (6) Champion Custom Products, (7) VF Imagewear (East) Inc., (8) Knights Apparel, (9) Colosseum Athletics, and (10) Red Oak Sportswear (Collegiate Licensing Company 2002).

3. The general idea was based on Notre Dame's pioneering 1996 code—a product of Jesuit social conscience rather than pressure from a campus movement.

4. The use of the WRC database has, of course, informed this passage.

5. The USAS Web site that claims 200 groups only lists 113—some number of which are inactive, e.g., the author's campus chapter. On other hand, tardiness in maintaining Web site lists is not so unusual.

6. The study from which that conclusion is based was not about movement participation.

7. Interestingly, the White (and Black) New Left of the 1960s and the current movement both began with demands on private parties (e.g., integrating lunch counters; imposing codes of conduct on clothing labelers) not, in the very first instance, governments.

8. In the 1960s SDS was critical of the labor movement and invested in (residential) community issues. This has been exaggerated in a legion of places. I do not want to distract from the main line of discussion to engage the matter in detail. Emblematic item: The Port Huron statement was written at a Michigan AFL-CIO summer camp, the use of which was obtained by one member whose mother was a UAW vice president; one of three UAW vice presidents whose children at one time or another were leaders of the Michigan SDS chapter. At Port Huron numerous leading figures (not including Tom Hayden) came from union homes.

9. More recently, however, the sphere of consumption has again become part of the discourse of the new movement: consuming less is a prescription against being part of the exploiting class—stop sweatshops by buying used clothes. In this regard, the current movement reproduces that aspect of 1960s cultural radicalism that came to be called "lifestyle politics."

10. Counterculture is that complex of opinion and symbol that rejected conventional jobs, careers, sex roles, and family patterns; approved experimentation with drugs; and celebrated the visible manifestation of cultural difference as a political badge of honor.

11. On September 7, 2001, Kukdong changed its name to Mexmode.

12. In English, the Confederación Revolucionario de Obreros y Campesinos (CROC) means Revolutionary Confederation of Workers and Peasants.

13. The Mexico Solidarity Center is a project of the AFL-CIO and one of fifty-five Solidarity Centers around the world. Alvarado had been one of the fifty-four students arrested during a sit-in at the University of Wisconsin, Madison, in February 2000, staged by students to convince the administration to join the WRC. In the summer of 2000, Alvarado returned to Mexico City, his birthplace, and joined the Solidarity Center.

14. Estimates range from six hundred to eight hundred workers who remained in the factory.

15. Three workers were hospitalized, fourteen were treated by the Red Cross, several others were tended to by neighbors of the factory, and a dozen wounded remained in the facility where riot police denied the Red Cross access to them. Two strike leaders were detained and questioned by police, released not until later that night (Centro de Apoyo al Trabajador 2001a, 14).

16. It should be noted that e-mail and Internet are the primary means of communication between the 150 USAS chapters spread across the United States. Between five hundred and a thousand students are members of the USAS general list serve and generate up to four hundred e-mail postings each month.

17. Bhumika Muchhala, a USAS activist conducting field research in Jakarta, Indonesia, reported: "After three strikes, workers in Kukdong-Indonesia were able to organize a plant-level union 3 months ago [October 2000]. Since then they've attained a wage increase of 30 percent and are struggling for collective bargaining agreement with the management right now" (Muchhala 2001).

18. Universities that had apparel produced by Kukdong during the years 2000–2001 are Boston College; Cornell University; Georgetown University; Northwestern; Purdue University; Tulane University; University of Arizona; University of Connecticut; University of Illinois, Urbana-Champaign; University of Iowa; University of Michigan; University of Minnesota; University of Missouri, Columbia; University of New Hampshire; University of North Carolina, Chapel Hill; and University of Washington.

19. For example, management classified some of the official petitioners as "confidential employees" and ineligible to be union members (Centro de Apoyo al Trabajador 2001a, 16).

20. Mexmode (at the time still Kukdong) produced more than 300,000 garments under contract with Nike from January to July 2001.

21. Despite local and international pressure to support workers rights and improve factory conditions, Matamoros Garment closed in March 2003 for "financial reasons" (Moreno 2003).

22. This was not the first time that an international coalition had come to the aid of Dominican free-trade workers. On June 22, 1994, workers at the Korean-owned Bibong Apparel plant became the first in the history of Dominican free trade zones to collectively bargain. Responsible in part for their success was an international coalition of the National Confederation of Dominican Workers (CNTD), the Federation of Free Zone workers (FENATRAZONAS), the ITGLWF, the AFL-CIO, and the U.S. apparel unions that have since merged to form UNITE (ICFTU 1996).

23. Interestingly, although Nike was the primary manufacturer represented at BJ&B, and Reebok was also a lead business partner, adidas-Salomon had no production at BJ&B and "only 5 of [their] products were developed there without [their] permission" (FLA 2002b).

Chapter 12

This chapter is partly based on work jointly done with Anita Chan from the Australian National University.

1. The following account is taken from Foner 1986, 17–70.

2. The actual proposal was somewhat more modest: to create a working group to study the eventual linkage. See Kamil (1999).

3. For one example, at the World Social Forum in Porto Alegre, Brazil, in February 2002, the "Call of Social Movements" included advocacy of union rights—with no mention of WTO or trade linkage. It did, however, condemn neoliberalism for neglecting rights of indigenous peoples (Convention 169 of the ILO) and excoriated the WTO for neocolonialism and called for rejecting the WTO position on patents (intellectual property). It did not adopt the ICFTU position on the WTO (World Social Forum 2002).

4. These rights correspond to the formal acts of the ILO: Freedom of Association and

Protection of Rights to Organise (ILO Convention No. 87, with 128 ratifications out of 175 member states); Right to Organize and Collective Bargaining (No. 98, with 146 ratifications); Forced Labor (No. 29, with 152 ratifications); Abolition of Forced Labor (No. 105, with 146 ratifications); Equal Remuneration (No. 100, with 144 ratifications) and Discrimination—Employment and Occupation (No. 111, with 142 ratifications); and Minimum Age Convention [Child Labor] (No. 138 with 85 ratifications).

5. The literature on this issue is vast. See, for example, Lipset, Seong, and Torres 1993.

6. The ILO has broken off official subsidies for training and other nonessential contacts with the regime. Some countries have cut aid as a matter of national policy. Myanmar imports of clothing to the United States have grown.

7. Without detailed financial information it is my distinct impression, gleaned from union activists and NGO staff, that two propositions are probably accurate: union support was critical to both media attention and funding the infrastructure of the Seattle demonstrations; and the United Steelworkers Union were particularly active and critical. Lest this be interpreted as *merely* a "protectionist" impulse, I note that Steelworkers representatives were extraordinarily active on behalf of garment workers in Nicaragua in the Chentex struggle—a matter in which I was involved as witness and investigator and in which they, as a union, had no simple material interest.

8. Anita Chan and I presented a version of this chapter to the international conference entitled "Industrial Relations and Labour Policies in a Globalising World" held at Beijing University in January 2002.

9. The ICFTU represents more than 156 million workers in 221 affiliated organizations in 148 countries and territories. The cold war counterpart to the ICFTU is the World Federation of Trade Unions (WFTU). Initially oriented to unions associated with Communist Parties, it is now more nearly based in developing country trade unions, including, e.g., the All China Federation of Trade Unions. WFTU opposes the use of WTO sanctions to enforce labor rights—the social clause. WFTU, rhetorically critical of the WTO, upholds the same position on labor standards—leave it to the ILO. See World Federation of Trade Unions 2001, 5–6.

10. I should swiftly acknowledge that the AFL-CIO history in Central America is checkered. For years, AFL-CIO international policy was dominated by cold war perspectives and infiltrated by state operatives. This legacy is extremely prejudicial in the period since John Sweeney's rise to the confederation presidency, when, to the disbelief and despite the ignorance of many third world activists, the AFL-CIO actually changed course in Central America. I was witness to this personally when union federation staff supported the Chentex workers in Managua—who, after all, were Sandinistas!

11. Unfortunately for the workers, the company eventually evaded the union by moving its contract away from the factory, which closed.

12. Labor rights advocates told me that there is such a labor surplus in China that "they don't need to use kids."

13. More technically, this is a "trade-weighted average wage of imported clothing" with the weight, in this case, by dollar value (not volume of garments).

14. My first attempt at this estimate was about 10 percent higher. My original calculations were based on (at least) one fiction in U.S. import data, a factor that would otherwise cause an overestimate of the average wage of imported clothing. That factor is the transshipment of garments from China to Hong Kong. By attributing 50 percent of Hong Kong's (higher waged) exports to China (much lower waged), the U.S. average wage embodied in imported clothing dropped substantially. The basis for this was Textile Transshipment Team 2000.

Chapter 13

1. In his stump speech for his campaign for governor of Massachusetts, Reich claimed that under his leadership the department was able to cut personnel and do more work (speech at a fund-raiser on April 10, 2002, in Worcester, Massachusetts).

2. In 2000, the AAMA joined the Footwear Industries of America and the Fashion Association to become the American Apparel and Footwear Association (AAFA).

3. As of January 26, 2004, the FLA no longer had an FAQ section on its Web site and nowhere claimed it intended to create a "fair labor" label or "service mark." Whether this marks a reversal of long-term strategy or merely gradualism was not possible to establish as this book went into production.

4. These figures are calculated from WTO 2000 (153, 154).

5. I am grateful to Jim Shea of the DOL for pointing out that the language on child labor enforcement in the CBTPA is a bit stronger than the older GSP language (Shea 2002).

Chapter 14

1. There are important dissenters among the economists, those who support the goals and the means of the antisweatshop movement and those who express reservation about neoliberal global policies (see Miller 2003; Elliott and Freeman 2000; Freeman 1998; and Rodrik 2002).

2. An exception is the prominent economist Jagdish Bhagwati, who acknowledges both the existence and undesirability of sweatshops in the United States. Bhagwati, however, raises labor abuse in the United States merely to scold those who would try to deal with the problem through world trade regulation. He is not known for addressing the regulatory matters domestically (Bhagwati 2000a).

3. Again, Bhagwati is an exception: he opposes trade sanctions to deter labor abuse but thinks consumer action is acceptable—in principle (Bhagwati 2002).

4. This pithy phrase was cited in an essay by Miranda Smith (1998).

5. It is startling how frequently child prostitution is used as the justification for factory exploitation (Bhagwati 2000a, 2002).

6. This passage is taken with permission and only minor editing from Rothstein 1997a. See also Rothstein 1996a.

7. Some young activists solve this problem by pledging not to buy new clothes. Clearly this helps no sweatshop worker anywhere. A better path for those with a need to clothe themselves righteously would be to buy *expensive* clothes—even if fewer of them. Apparel prices today take about a 50 percent smaller proportion of family budgets than they did a generation ago and are currently suffering price deflation. However unlikely, if Americans were willing to spend more for better clothes, it would make it easier for contractors and retailers to pay more for their production.

References

ABC. 1996. "Kathie Lee Gifford." *ABC Prime Time Live*. Transcript #455–2, May 22. Available at <http://www.lexisnexis.com>. Accessed January 24, 2004.

Abernathy, Frederick H., Janice Hammond, David Weil, and John Dunlop. 1999. *A Stitch in Time: Lean Retailing and the Transformation of Manufacturing*. New York. Oxford University Press.

Academic Consortium on International Trade (ACIT). 2000. Letter to University Presidents. September 25. Available at <http://www.fordschool.umich.edu/rsie/acit/Documents/Anti-SweatshopLetterPage.html>. Accessed July 9, 2003.

Andrews, Fred. 1999. "It's Not the Product That's Different, It's the Process." *New York Times*, December 15.

Apparel Industry. 1996. "Private Label Apparel Market." January, 54.

———. 2000. "Top Retailers." August, 10.

Appelbaum, Richard, and Gary Gereffi. 1994. "Power and Profits in the Apparel Commodity Chain." In *Global Production: The Apparel Industry in the Pacific Rim*, ed. Edna Bonacich, Lucie Cheng, Norma Chinchilla, Nora Hamilton, and Paul Ong, 42–62. Philadelphia: Temple University Press.

Asian Labour Update. 2000–2001. Codes of Conduct. Special issue, no. 37. Available at <http://www.amrc.org.hk/archive.htm>. Accessed January 26, 2004.

Ballinger, Jeffrey. 1999. Comments at "Forum on the Living Wage." Brown University Student Labor Action Coalition, March 23.

Barbash, Jack. 1989. "John R. Commons: Pioneer in Labor Economics." *Monthly Labor Review* 112 (5): 44–49.

Barbosa, Juan. 2000. Interview by author. July 13.

Barnet, Richard J., and John Cavanagh. 1994. *Global Dreams: Imperial Corporations and the New World Order*. New York: Simon & Schuster.

Bearak, Barry. 1996. "Kathie Lee and the Sweatshop Crusade; A Workers-Rights Activist Brought Gifford to Tears with Claims about Her Clothing Line. Now, They've Joined Forces and He Is Relying on Her TV Celebrity to Spotlight the Issue." *Los Angeles Times*, June 14, 1.

Beechey, Veronica. 1988. "Rethinking the Definition of Work: Gender and Work." In *Fem-*

References

inization of the Labor Force: Paradoxes and Promises, ed. J. Jenson, E. Hagen, and C. Reddy. New York: Oxford University Press.

Behar, Richard. 1996a. "Guess: What's behind This IPO." *Fortune,* October 14, 133–40.

———. 1996b. "Guess Gets Pressed: Blue Jeans and the Art of Politics." *Fortune,* November 11, 38.

Behindthelabel.org. 2001. "Dominican Collegiate Apparel Workers Still Waiting for Promised Changes." July 20. Available at <http://www.behindthelabel.org/sitemap .php#archives>. Accessed January 26, 2004.

Belanger, Amy. 1996. "Note and Comment: Internationally Recognized Worker Rights and the Efficacy of the Generalized System of Preferences: A Guatemalan Case Study." *American University Journal of International Law and Policy* 11 (1): 101–36.

Berg, Gordon. 1989. "Frances Perkins and the Flowering of Socioeconomic Policies." *Monthly Labor Review* 112 (6): 28–35.

Bernard, Elaine. 1998. Introduction. Speech at a conference at Harvard University on sweatshop issues and globalization, October 10.

Best, Harry. 1919. "Extent of Organization in the Women's Garment Making Industries of New York." *American Economic Review* 9 (4): 776–92.

Bezlova, Antoaneta. 2002. "China: Santa's Sweatshops." *Asia Times,* December 24. Available at <http://www.atimes.com/atimes/China/DL24Ad01.html>. Accessed June 19, 2003.

Bhagwati, Jagdish. 2000a. "Economic Sense and Nonsense." *Harvard International Review* 22 (3): 78 et seq.

———. 2000b. "Nike Wrongfoots the Student Critics: 'Anti-Sweatshop' Protesters Are Using Strong-Arm Tactics That Will Undermine Their Own Cause." *Financial Times* (London), May 2, U.S. ed., 11.

———. 2002. "Coping with Antiglobalization: A Trilogy of Discontents." *Foreign Affairs* 81 (1): 2 et seq.

Boje, David M., Grace Ann Rosile, and J. Dámaso Miguel Alcantara Carrillo. 2001. "The Kuk Dong Story: When the Foxes Guards the Hen House." March 25 (updated July 7, 2003). Available at <http://cbae.nmsu.edu/~dboje/AA/kuk_dong_story.htm>. Accessed July 7, 2003.

Bonacich, Edna. 2002. "Labor's Response to Global Production." In *Free Trade and Uneven Development: The North American Apparel Industry after NAFTA,* ed. Gary Gereffi, David Spener, and Jennifer Bair. Philadelphia: Temple University Press.

Bonacich, Edna, and Richard Appelbaum. 2000. *Behind the Label: Inequality in the Los Angeles Apparel Industry.* Berkeley: University of California Press.

Bonacich, Edna, and John Modell. 1980. *The Economic Basis of Ethnic Solidarity: Small Business in the Japanese American Community.* Berkeley: University of California Press.

Bonacich, Edna, Lucie Cheng, Norma Chinchilla, Nora Hamilton, and Paul Ong, eds. 1994. *Global Production: The Apparel Industry in the Pacific Rim.* Philadelphia: Temple University Press.

Booth, Charles. 1902–3. *Life and Labour of the People in London.* 17 vols. London: Macmillan.

Boris, Eileen. 1985. "Regulating Industrial Homework: The Triumph of 'Sacred Motherhood.'" *Journal of American History* 71 (4): 745–63.

———. 1994. *Home to Work: Motherhood and the Politics of Industrial Homework in the United States.* New York: Cambridge University Press.

Boston Globe. 1999. "Senseless in Seattle." December 2, A26.

Boyer, Richard Owen, and Herbert Morais. 1955. *Labor's Untold Story.* New York: Cameron.

Brakken, Eric. 1999. "For Folks (especially from the West) Interested in Civil Disobedience at the WTO." E-mail to USAS list serve. July 13.

References

Branigin, William. 1997a. "Reaping Abuse for What They Sew." *Washington Post,* February 16, A.01.

———. 1997b. "Clinton, Garment Makers Hail Accord on Sweatshops; Critics Say Pact Falls Short on Key Work Issues." *Washington Post,* April 15, A10.

Briggs, Barbara. 1998. Interview by author. October 19.

Brody, David. 1981. "Frances Perkins." *Dictionary of American Biography, Supplement 7: 1961–1965.* American Council of Learned Societies. Reproduced in Biography Resource Center, Farmington Hills, MI: Gale, 2001.

Bronfenbrenner, Kate. 1996. *Final Report: The Effects of Plant Closing or Threat of Plant Closing on the Right of Workers to Organize.* Ithaca: New York State School of Industrial and Labor Relations, Cornell University.

———. 2000. "Uneasy Terrain: The Impact of Capital Mobility on Workers, Wages, and Union Organizing." Paper submitted to the U.S. Trade Deficit Review Commission. Ithaca: New York State School of Industrial and Labor Relations, Cornell University.

Brown, Courtney. 1988. "Mass Dynamics of U.S. Presidential Competitions, 1928–1936." *American Political Science Review* 82 (4): 1153–81.

Brownstein, Ronald. 1998. "The Balanced Budget Is Liberating Democrats and Reshaping Politics." *U.S. News and World Report,* February 16, 30.

Brown University Student Labor Action Coalition (SLAC). 1999. Group interview by author, March 23.

Buck, Rinker. 1979. "The New Sweatshops: A Penny for Your Collar." *New York* 12 (9): 29.

Buhle, Paul. 1999. *Taking Care of Business: Samuel Gompers, George Meany, Lane Kirkland, and the Tragedy of American Labor.* New York: Monthly Review Press.

Bureau of Labor Statistics. U.S. Department of Labor. 1971. *Employment and Earnings.* Washington, DC: GPO.

———. 1991. *Employment and Earnings.* Washington, DC: GPO.

———. 2001a. Current Employment Survey. Public Data Query. Available at <http://146.142.4.24/labjava/outside.jsp?survey=ee>. Accessed September 18, 2001.

———. 2001b. Data from Industry Productivity Database. Office of Productivity and Technology. August 16. Available at <ftp://ftp.bls.gov/pub/special.requests/opt/dipts/ULC3Drt.TXT>. Accessed April 10, 2002.

———. 2001c. "Productivity and Costs: Manufacturing Industries, 1990–99." Press Release, May 15. Available at <ftp://ftp.bls.gov/pub/news.release/prin2.txt>. Accessed April 10, 2002.

———. 2001d. "SIC 23—Apparel and Other Finished Products Made from Fabrics and Similar Materials." In *2000 National Industry-Specific Occupational Employment and Wage Estimates.* Available at <http://stats.bls.gov/oes/2000/oesi2_23.htm#b51–0000>. Accessed May 8, 2002.

———. 2001e. "Consumer Price Index—Urban Wage Earners and Clerical Workers." *Consumer Prices Indexes.* Available at <http://www.bls.gov/cpi/home.htm#data>. Accessed January 28, 2004.

———. 2004a. *Current Economic Survey.* Available at <http://data.bls.gov/labjava/outside.jsp?survey=ce>. Accessed January 23, 2004.

———. 2004b. *Employment, Hours, and Earnings from the Current Employment Statistics Survey (State and Metro Area).* Available at <http://www.bls.gov/data/>. Accessed January 20, 2004.

———. 2004c. *Multifactor Productivity.* Available at <http://data.bls.gov/cgi-bin/dsrv>. Accessed January 24, 2004.

Burger and Comer. 2000. "October 2000 Economic Impact Study by Burger and Comer, CPAs." Available at <http://www.sgma-saipan.org/sgma_websmall/stats/er_00.htm>. Accessed March 1, 2002.

Burnett, John. 2001. "Effort by American College Students to Help Improve Working Con-

References

ditions at Mexican Plant That Makes Nike Sweatshirts." *NPR's All Things Considered,* August 14. Available at <www.lexisnexis.com>. Accessed May 12, 2003.

Bush, George W. 2001. "The President's Management Agenda." Executive Office of the President, Office of Management and Budget, Washington, DC. Available at <http://www.whitehouse.gov/omb/budget/fy2002/mgmt.pdf>. Accessed March 11, 2002.

Bythell, Duncan. 1978. *The Sweated Trades: Outwork in Nineteenth-Century Britain.* London: Batsford Academic Press.

California State Department of Industrial Relations. 1994. "Federal, State Labor Agencies Release Results of Compliance Survey on Garment Industry." April 14. Available at <http://www.dir.ca.gov/DIRNews/1994/94–17.html>. Accessed January 27, 2004.

California State Division of Labor Standards Enforcement (DLSE). 1996. Targeted Industries Partnership Program, *Fourth Annual Report.* Available at <http://www.dir.ca.gov/dlse/tipp4.htm>. Accessed January 13, 2004.

Campaign for Labor Rights. 2001. "Independent Union Leader Beaten by Croc Supporters, Then Punished by Kukdong." *Kukdong—Independent Union Leader Beaten by CROC Supporters,* May 17. Available at <http://campaignforlaborrights.org/alters/2001/kukdongindebycrocsupporters.html>. Accessed May 15, 2003.

Capella, Joseph N., and Kathleen Hall Jamieson. 1996. "News Frames, Political Cynicism, and Media Cynicism." *Annals of the American Academy of Political and Social Science* 546 (July): 71–85.

Caro, Robert. 1974. *The Power Broker: Robert Moses and the Fall of New York.* New York: Knopf.

Castells, Manuel, and Alejandro Portes. 1989. "World Underneath: The Origins, Dynamics, and Effects of the Informal Economy." In *The Informal Economy: Studies in Advanced and Less Developed Countries,* ed. Alejandro Portes, Manuel Castells, and Laura A. Benton, 11–37. Baltimore: Johns Hopkins University Press.

Central Statistics Division. 2000. *Recent Trends in Population, Labor Force, Employment, and Unemployment, Commonwealth of the Northern Mariana Islands, 1973 to 1999.* 2d ed. Saipan: Department of Commerce.

———. 2001. *Commonwealth of the Northern Mariana Islands Statistical Yearbook.* Saipan: Department of Commerce.

Centro de Apoyo al Trabajador (Collegiate Apparel Research Initiative—Mexico). 2001a. "La Lucha Sigue: Stories from the People of the Kukdong Factory." July. Available at <http://www.maquilasolidarity.org/campaigns/nike/pdf/La%20Lucha%20Sigue.pdf>. Accessed May 15, 2003.

———. 2001b. "La Lucha Sigue: Parte II." Available at <http://www.people.fas.harvard.edu/~fragola/usas/docs/LaLuchaSigue_Part_II.pdf>. Accessed May 20, 2003.

Chan, Anita. 2000. "Globalization, China's Free (Read Bonded) Labour Market, and the Chinese Trade Union." *Asia Pacific Business Review* 6 (3 & 4): 260–81.

———. 2001. *China's Workers under Assault: The Exploitation of Labor in a Globalizing Economy.* Armonk, NY: M. E. Sharpe.

Chan, Anita, and Robert Ross. 2003 "Racing to the Bottom: International Trade without a Social Clause." *Third World Quarterly* 24 (6): 1011–28.

Chandrasekaran, Rajiv. 2001. "Indonesian Workers in Nike Plants List Abuses." *Washington Post,* February 23, E1.

Chapin, Ralph. 1915. "Solidarity Forever." Lyrics available at <http://crixa.com/muse/unionsong/u025.html>. Accessed January 21, 2004.

Chow, Gon Ling. 1992. "Garment Sweatshops in the Ethnic Enclave: Alterations Needed." B.A. thesis, Harvard College.

Clinton, William Jefferson. 1996. "Remarks Announcing Measures to Improve Working Conditions in the Apparel Industry and an Exchange with Reporters." August 2. Public

References

Papers of the Presidents. *Weekly Compilation of Presidential Documents* 32 (31): 1347–96. Available at <http://www.gpo.gov/nara/pubpaps/srchpaps.html>.

———. 1997. "Remarks on the Apparel Industry Partnership." April 14. Public Papers of the Presidents. *Weekly Compilation of Presidential Documents* 33 (16): 515–550. Available at <http://www.gpo.gov/nara/pubpaps/srchpaps.html>.

———. 1999. "Telephone Interview with Michael Paulson of the Seattle Post-Intelligencer in San Francisco, California." November 30. Public Papers of the Presidents. *Weekly Compilation of Presidential Documents* 2:2180–84. Available at <http://www.gpo.gov/nara/pubpaps/srchpaps.html>. Accessed October 19, 2001.

———. 2000. "Remarks by the President at World Economic Forum." January 29. Available at <http://secretary.state.gov/www/travels/2000/000129clinton_wef.html>. Accessed October 18, 2001.

Collegiate Licensing Company. 2002. "CLC Names Top Selling Universities, Manufacturers for July 1, 2001–December 31, 2001." February 6. Available at <http://www.clc.com/Pages/home2.html>. Accessed January 27, 2004.

Collier, Robert, and Jenny Strasburg. 2002. "Clothiers Fold on Sweatshop Lawsuit: Saipan Workers to Get Millions; Levi Holds Out." *San Francisco Chronicle,* September 27, A1.

Collingsworth, Terry. 2002. Interview by author. January 10.

Commission of Inquiry. 1998. *Report of the Commission of Inquiry Appointed under Article 26 of the Constitution of the International Labour Organization to Examine the Observance by Myanmar of the Forced Labour Convention, 1930 (No. 29).* Geneva: International Labour Organization, July 2.

Committee on Economic Security. 1935. *Report to the President.* Washington, DC: GPO.

Committee on Ways and Means. U.S. House of Representatives. 1997. *The 1996 Green Book:* "Background Material and Data on Programs within the Jurisdiction of the Committee on Ways and Means." WMCP 104–14. Available at <http://www.access.gpo.gov/congress/wm001.html>. Accessed March 14, 2002.

Commons, John R. 1921 [1905]. *Trade Unionism and Labor Problems.* Boston: Ginn.

Compa, Lance. 1993. "International Labor Rights and the Sovereignty Question: NAFTA and Guatemala, Two Case Studies." *American University Journal of International Law and Policy* 9 (fall): 117–49.

———. 2000. *Unfair Advantage: Workers' Freedom of Association in the United States under International Human Rights Standards.* New York: Human Rights Watch. Available at <http://www.hrw.org/reports/2000/uslabor/index.htm#TopOfPage>. Accessed October 18, 2001.

Connor, Tim. 2001. *Still Waiting for Nike to Do It.* San Francisco: Global Exchange.

———. 2002. *We Are Not Machines.* San Francisco: Global Exchange. Available at <http://www.caa.org.au/campaigns/nike/reports/machines/index.html>. Accessed June 19, 2003.

Coughlin, Ginny. 1997, 2001. Interviews by author. May 14.

Council of Economic Advisers. 1997. *Economic Report of the President.* Statistical tables from Appendix B. Available at <http://w3.access.gpo.gov/usbudget/fy1998/erp_wk1.html>. Accessed March 9, 2002.

———. 2002. *Economic Report of the President Together with the Annual Report of the Council of Economic Advisers.* Washington, DC: GPO.

Crittendon, Jules. 1997. "Inspectors Close Alleged Sweatshop." *Boston Herald,* December 3, 7.

Cumbler, John T. 1979. *Working-Class Community in Industrial America: Work, Leisure, and Struggle in Two Industrial Cities, 1880–1930.* Westport, CT: Greenwood Press.

Daniels, Norman, Bruce Kennedy, and Ichiro Kawachi. 2000. "Justice Is Good for Our Health." *Boston Review,* February/March. Available at <http://bostonreview.mit.edu/BR25.1/daniels.html>. Accessed September 6, 2001.

References

Daugherty, John. 2000. *National Park Service: The First 75 Years. Biographical Vignettes. John D. Rockefeller, Jr. 1874–1960.* Available at <http://www.cr.nps.gov /history/online_books/sontag/rockefeller.htm>. Accessed January 23, 2004.

Davies, James C. 1962. "Toward a Theory of Revolution." *American Sociological Review* 27 (1): 5–19.

Davis, Benjamin N. 1995. "Note and Comment: The Effects of Worker Rights Protections in United States Trade Laws: A Case Study of El Salvador." *American University Journal of International Law and Policy* 10 (spring): 1167 et seq.

Deloitte Touche Tohmatsu. 2003. *The Challenge of Complexity in Global Manufacturing: Critical Trends in Supply Chain Management.* London: Deloitte Touche Tohmatsu.

Democratic Staff. 1997. *Economic Miracle or Economic Mirage? The Human Cost of Development in the Commonwealth of the Northern Mariana Islands.* Committee on Resources, U.S. House of Representatives, Washington, DC. <http://resourcescommittee .house.gov/105cong/democrat/cnmi_rpt.htm#five>.

Doe I et al. vs. The Gap et al. 2001. Case No. CV-01–0031, United States District Court Northern Mariana Islands. "Second Amended Complaint For Damages And Injunctive Relief."

Domke, David, Dhavan V. Shah, and Daniel B. Wackman. 1998. "Media Priming Effects: Accessibility, Association, and Activation." *International Journal of Public Opinion Research* 10 (1): 51–75.

Dopplet, Jack. 1994. "Marching to the Police and Court Beats." In *Public Opinion, the Press, and Public Policy,* ed. J. David Kennamer, 113–30. Westport, CT: Praeger.

Douglas, Susan. 1996. "Stupid Press Tricks." *Progressive* 60 (8): 19.

Douglas, Paul H., and Joseph Hackman. 1938. "The Fair Labor Standards Act of 1938 I." *Political Science Quarterly* 53 (4): 491–515.

Dubinsky, David. 1977 [1953]. "Out of These Slums." In *Out of the Sweatshop: The Struggle for Industrial Democracy,* ed. Leon Stein. New York: Quadrangle/The New York Times Book Co.

———. 1977 [1955]. "Remarks of David Dubinsky at the ILGWU Housing Dedication Ceremony." In *Out of the Sweatshop: The Struggle for Industrial Democracy,* ed. Leon Stein. New York: Quadrangle/The New York Times Book Co.

Echaveste, Maria. 2002. Interview by author. April 9.

Edelman, Rachel. 1999. "Living Wage Meeting Tomorrow Night." USAS list serve, October 5.

Edsall, Thomas B., and Mary D. Edsall. 1992. *Chain Reaction: The Impact of Race, Rights, and Taxes on American Politics.* New York: Norton.

Elliott, Kimberly Ann, and Richard B. Freeman. 2000. "White Hats or Don Quixotes? Human Rights Vigilantes in the Global Economy." Paper presented at the National Bureau of Economic Research Conference on Emerging Labor Market Institutions. August.

Ellis, Kristi. 1996. "LA Labor Probe Uncovers Homework Items for Guess." *Women's Wear Daily,* July 31, 4 et seq.

———. 1997a. "NLRB Sets Complaint on Guess." *Women's Wear Daily,* November 20, 12.

———. 1997b. "L.A.'s Anti-union Fervor." *Women's Wear Daily,* June 3, 8 et seq.

Encyclopedia Britannica. 2001. "sweatshop." *Encyclopedia Britannica Online* <http://search .eb.com/bol/topic?eu=72449&sctn=1>. Accessed September 18, 2001.

Entin, Lena. 2002. "A20 de-brief & Monday 5–20 WOGAN meeting." Worcester Global Action Network list serve, May 16. Available at <http://groups.yahoo.com /group/woganlist/messages/791>.

Entman, Robert. 1991. "Framing U.S. Coverage of International News: Contrasts of KAL and Iran Air Incidents." *Journal of Communication* 41:6–27.

References

———. 1993. "Framing: Toward Clarification of a Fractured Paradigm." *Journal of Communication* 43 (4): 51–58.

Esbenshade, Jill. 2001. "The Social Accountability Contract: Private Monitoring from Los Angeles to the Global Apparel Industry." *Labor Studies Journal* 26 (1): 98 et seq. Available from Infotrac One File database.

Ethical Trading Initiative (ETI). 2003. "What Is ETI?" Available at <http://www.ethical-trade.org/pub/about/eti/main/index.shtml>. Accessed January 20, 2004.

European Union. 2001. "Textiles and Clothing. Statistics." Available at <http://europa.eu.int/comm/enterprise/textile/statistics.htm#world_exports_of_clothing>. Accessed September 24, 2001.

Fair Labor Association (FLA). 2001. "Charter Document (Amended Agreement October 2001)." Available at <http://www.fairlabor.org/html/amendctr.html#top>. Accessed March 15, 2002.

———. 2002a. "Frequently Asked Questions." Available at <http://www.fairlabor.org/html/faqs.html>. Accessed April 18, 2002.

———. 2002b. "Interim Report Investigation into Third Party Complaint against BJ&B." Available at <http://www.publicinnovations.org/projects/Interim%20report%20on%20BJ&B%20investigation.doc>. Accessed June 13, 2003.

———. 2003a. "First Public Report: Towards Improving Workers Lives, August 1, 2001–July 31, 2002." Available at <http://www.fairlabor.org/all/transparency/Public%20Report%20Y1.pdf>. Accessed June 13, 2003.

———. 2003b. "Workplace Code of Conduct." Available at <http://www.fairlabor.org/all/code/index.html>. Accessed January 20, 2004.

Fantasia, Rick. 1988. *Cultures of Solidarity: Consciousness, Action, and Contemporary American Workers.* Berkeley: University of California Press.

Featherstone, Liza. 2002. "Strange Marchfellows." *Nation,* May 13, et seq.

Featherstone, Liza, and United Students Against Sweatshops. 2002. *Students against Sweatshops: The Making of a Movement.* New York: Verso.

Fireman, Bruce, and William A. Gamson. 1979. "Utilitarian Logic in the Resource Mobilization Perspective." In *The Dynamics of Social Movements,* ed. Mayer N. Zald and John D. McCarthy, 8–44. Boston: Little, Brown.

Fishbein, Jerry. 1996. Interview by author. September 23.

Fisk, Robert. 2001. "My Beating by Refugees Is a Symbol of the Hatred and Fury of This Filthy War." *Independent,* December 10. Available at <http://www.independent.co.uk/story.jsp?story=109257>. Accessed May 23, 2002.

Flacks, R. 1967. "The Liberated Generation: Social Psychological Roots of Student Protest." *Journal of Social Issues* 23:52–75.

———. 1971. *Youth and Social Change.* Chicago: Rand McNally.

Foner, Phillip S. 1986. *May Day: A Short History of the International Workers' Holiday, 1886–1986.* New York: International Publishers.

Food Research and Action Center (FRAC). 2001. "Health Consequences of Hunger." Available at <http://www.frac.org/html/hunger_in_the_us/health.html>. Accessed September 6, 2001.

Ford, Fred. 2001. "Dodging the G8 Protest Nonsense Is Great News for Ottawa." *Ottawa Citizen,* July 26, B4.

Fortune. 2001. "Fortune 500." April 16. Available at <http://www.fortune.com/fortune/fortune500> on March 2, 2002.

Foucault, Michel. 1980 [1975]. *Power/Knowledge: Selected Interviews and Other Writings, 1972–1977.* New York: Pantheon. Available at <http://www.thefoucauldian.co.uk/body-power.htm>. Accessed November 1, 2001.

References

Fraser, John. 1998. "Statement of John R. Fraser, Acting Administrator, Wage and Hour Division, Employment Standards Administration, U.S. Department of Labor Before House Education and the Workforce Committee, Oversight and Investigations Subcommittee." Hearing on Worker Exploitation in New York City Garment Industry, March 31, Washington, DC. Available at <http://edworkforce.house.gov/hearings/105th/oi/awp33198/fraser.htm>. Accessed January 20, 2004.

Frazier, Franklin. 1990. "Child Labor Violations and Sweatshops in the U.S.: Statement of Franklin Frazier, Director of Education and Employment Issues, Human Resources Division, before the Subcommittee on Employment and Housing, Committee on Government Operations." Washington, DC: GAO.

Freeman, Jo. 1972–73. "The Tyranny of Structurelessness." *Berkeley Journal of Sociology* 17:151–16. Another version available at <http://www.jofreeman.com/joreen/tyranny.htm>. Accessed May 23, 2002.

Freeman, Richard B. 1998. "What Role for Labor Standards in the Global Economy?" Harvard University and NBER. Available at <http://www.nber.org/~freeman/Papers%20on%20RBF%20owebsite/un-stan.pdf>. Accessed July 9, 2003.

Friedman, Thomas. 1999. "Senseless in Seattle." *New York Times,* December 1, A23.

Fruit of the Loom. 2000. "Annual Report for Fiscal Year Ended December 30th, 2000." U.S. Securities and Exchange Commission Form 10-K. Available at <www.lexisnexis.com>; also available through "EDGAR" at <http://www.sec.gov/edgar/searchedgar/webusers.htm>.

Galbraith, James K., Pedro Conceição, and Hyunsub Kum. 2000. "Inequality and Growth Reconsidered Once Again: Some New Evidence from Old Data." University of Texas Inequality Project, Working Paper No. 17. Available at <http://utip.gov.utexas.edu>. Accessed July 9, 2003.

Gallagher, John. 2002. "Technology Edge Helps Wal-Mart Beat Out Kmart." *Detroit Free Press,* January 18.

Gamson, W. A., and K. E. Lasch. 1983. "The Political Culture of Social Welfare Policy." In *Evaluating the Welfare State: Social and Political Perspectives,* ed. S. E. Spiro and E. Yuchtman-Yaar. New York: Academic Press.

Gamson, W. A., and A. Modigliani. 1987. "The Changing Culture of Affirmative Action." In *Research in Political Sociology,* ed. R. G. Braungart and M. M. Braungart, 3:137–77. Greenwich, CT: JAI.

Garnett, Henrietta. 1988. "The Rag Trade: A Study of the Jewish Inhabitants of the East End of London in the Clothing Industry." In *Components of Dress,* ed. Juliet Ash and Lee Wright, 29–36. London and New York: Routledge.

Gereffi, Gary. 1994. "The Organization of Buyer Driven Global Commodity Chains: How U.S. Retailers Shape Overseas Production." In *Commodity Chains and Global Capitalism,* ed. Gary Gereffi and Miguel Korzeniewicz, 95–122. Westport, CT: Greenwood.

Gereffi, Gary, and Miguel Korzeniewicz, eds. 1994. *Commodity Chains and Global Capitalism.* Westport, Conn.: Greenwood Press.

Getter, Lisa. 1999. "GAO Report Disputes Gore Claims On Red-Tape Cuts." *Los Angeles Times.* August 14, A6.

Gifford, Court D., ed. 1998. *Directory of U.S. Labor Organizations.* Washington, DC: Bureau of National Affairs.

———. 2001. *Directory of U.S. Labor Organizations.* Washington, DC: Bureau of National Affairs.

Gitlin, Todd. 1980. *The Whole World Is Watching.* Berkeley: University of California Press.

Global Alliance. 2001. *Indonesia.* Available at <http://www.theglobalalliance.org/section.cfm/6/30>. Accessed May 30, 2002.

References

Global Exchange. 2002a. "Frequently Asked Questions." Available at <http://www.glob-alexchange.org/economy/corporations/saipan/faq.html>. Accessed March 2, 2002.

———. 2002b. "Overview." Available at <http://www.globalexchange.org/economy/cor-porations/gap/overview.html>. Accessed January 28, 2004.

———. 2004. "Frequently Asked Questions [about Saipan Campaign]." Available at <http://www.globalexchange.org/campaigns/sweatshops/saipan/faq.html>. Accessed January 23, 2004.

Goldfield, Michael. 1989. "Worker Insurgency, Radical Organization, and New Deal Labor Legislation." *American Political Science Review* 83 (4): 1257–82.

Gompers, Samuel. 1911. "Hostile Employers See Yourselves as Others Know You." *American Federationist,* May, 356–61. Available at <http://www.ilr.cornell.edu/trianglefire/texts/newspaper/af_0511.html>. Accessed July 30, 2001.

Gonzalez, David. 1996. "In Quiet Bank, Dreams Grow for Immigrant." *New York Times,* August 28, B1.

———. 2003. "Latin Sweatshops Pressed by U.S. Campus Power." *New York Times,* April 4, A3.

Gourevitch, Alexander. 2001. "Awakening the Giant: How the Living Wage Movement Can Revive Progressive Politics." *American Prospect* Online, May 30. Available at <http://www.prospect.org/webfeatures/2001/05/gourevitch-a-05–30.html>. Accessed July 6, 2003.

Green, Nancy L. 1992. "Sweatshop Migrations: The Garment Industry between Home and Work." In *The Landscape of Modernity: New York City, 1900–1940,* ed. David Ward and Oliver Zunz, 213–34. New York: Russell Sage.

———. 1997. *Ready to Wear—Ready to Work: A Century of Industry and Immigrants in Paris and New York.* Durham, NC: Duke University Press.

Green, Susan. 1997. Interview by author. April 4.

Greene, Julie. 1998. *Pure and Simple Politics: The American Federation of Labor and Political Activism, 1881–1917.* New York: Cambridge University Press.

Greenhouse, Steven. 1996. "With $7,500 in Cash, Giffords Scramble to Save Face at Sweat-shop." *New York Times,* May 24, B3.

———. 1997. "Accord to Combat Sweatshop Labor Faces Obstacles." *New York Times,* April 13. A1.

———. 1998a. "Antisweatshop Coalition Finds Itself at Odds on Garment Factory Code." *New York Times,* July 3.

———. 1998b. "Union Organization Drive Exposes Flaws in Nation's Labor Laws." *New York Times,* July 10, A1, A11.

———. 1999. "Activism Surges at Campuses Nationwide, and Labor Is at Issue." *New York Times,* March 29, 14.

Greider, William. 2001. "A New Giant Sucking Sound: China Is Taking Away Mexico's Jobs, as Globalization Enters a Fateful New Stage." *Nation,* December 31, 22 et seq.

Grohl, Earl. 1997. Interview by author. April 10.

Guess? Inc. 1996. *Quarterly Report Pursuant to Section 13 or 15(D) of the Securities Exchange Act of 1934 for the Quarterly Period Ended March 31, 1996* (Form 10-Q). Filed May 14. Available at <http://www.sec.gov/Archives/edgar /data/912463 /0000912057–96–009425.txt>. Accessed May 11, 2002.

———. 2001. *Annual Report Pursuant to Section 13 or 15(D)of the Securities Exchange Act of 1934 for the Fiscal Year Ended December 31, 2000 Commission File Number 1–1189* (Form 10-K). Filed April 2. Available at <http://www.sec.gov/Archives/edgar/data/912463 /000091205701506544/0000912057–01-506544-index.htm>. Accessed January 28, 2004.

———. 2002. *Schedule 14a Proxy Statement Pursuant to Section 14(A) of the Securities Exchange Act of 1934.* Filed April 4. Securities and Exchange Commission. Available at

References

<http://moneycentral.msn.com/investor/sec/filing.asp?Symbol=GES>. Accessed May 11, 2002.

Haefele, Marc B., and Christine Pelisek. 2002. "Hot Fudge for Social Justice: The New Flavor for Ben of Ben & Jerry's Is Called: No Sweat Shop." *LA Weekly*, April 12–18. Available at <http://www.laweekly.com/ink/02/21/news-pelisek.shtml>. Accessed May 15, 2002.

Harney, Kerri. 1999. "Bread and Roses in United States History: The Power of Constructed Memory." Thesis, State University of New York at Binghamton.

Hatch, Julie, and Angela Clinton. 2000. "Job Growth in the 1990s: A Retrospect." *Monthly Labor Review* 123:12. Available at <http://stats.bls.gov/opub/mlr/2000/12/art1abs.htm>. Accessed March 9, 2002.

Hawley, Margaret. 2003. Correspondence (May 20) with Adam Tomczik on behalf of author. Original in Tomczik's possession.

Hegel, Georg Wilhelm Friedrich. 1942. *Hegel's Philosophy of Right*. Trans. and ed. T. M. Knox. Oxford: Clarendon.

Henwood, Doug. 1993. "Gini Says: Measuring Income Inequality." *Left Business Observer*, October 18. Available at <http://www.panix.com/~dhenwood/Gini_supplement.html>. Accessed June 18, 2003.

Herbert, Bob. 1994. "In America, the Sweatshop Lives." *New York Times*, December 28, 15.

———. 1997. "In America: A Good Start." *New York Times*, April 14, 17.

———. 1998. "In America, Sweatshop U." *New York Times*, April 12, sect. 4, p. 13.

Hermanson, Jeff. 2003a. "Report of Contract Signing." Memorandum (March 21) in author's possession.

———. 2003b. Letter (email) to author, June 6.

Herzog, Boaz. 2001. "Mexican Factory Making Nike Products Unionizes." *Oregonian*, September 27, D.01. Available at <www.lexisnexis.com>. Accessed May 12, 2003.

Hill, Herbert. 1974. "Guardians of the Sweatshops: The Trade Unions, Racism, and the Garment Industry." In *Puerto Rico and Puerto Ricans: Studies in History and Society*, ed. Adalberto López and James Petras. New York: Wiley.

Hinojosa Ojeda, Raul, with Dr. Robert McCleery, Enrico Marcelli, Fernando de Paolis, David Runsten, and Marysol Sanchez. 2001. "Comprehensive Migration Policy Reform in North America: The Key to Sustainable and Equitable Economic Integration." NAID Center Working Paper No. 12. North American Integration and Development Center, School of Public Policy and Social Research, University of California, Los Angeles.

Hirsch, Barry T., and David A. Macpherson. 1996–2001. *Union Membership and Earnings Data Book: Compilations from the Current Population Survey*. Annual editions. Washington, DC: Bureau of National Affairs.

Hoffman, Ann. 1997. Interview by author. April 10.

Hoffman, K., and H. Rush. 1988. *Microelectronics and Clothing: The Impact of Technological Change on a Global Industry*. New York: Praeger.

Holland, Josiah Gilbert. N.d. Available at <http://www.cyber-nation.com/victory/quotations/authors/quotes_holland_josiahgilbert.html>. Accessed January 23, 2004.

Hong Kong Christian Industrial Committee (HKCIC). 2001. *BOM!! Beware of Mickey— Disney Sweatshops in South China (2/2001)*. Hong Kong: HKCIC. Available at <http://www.cic.org.hk/download/whole%20report2.doc>. Accessed January 28, 2004.

———. 2003. "Integration with the Pearl River Delta—Unfair Trade for Unfair Toys." Press Release, January 10. Available at <http://www.cleanclothes.org/publications/HK-Press-Release-10-Jan-2003.pdf>. Accessed June 19, 2003.

Hooper, John, and Kate Connolly. 2001. "Focus: Germany in Turmoil: Is the Party Over? Germans Enjoy High Incomes and an Efficient Welfare State. But Now Europe's Economic Powerhouse Faces Radical Change That Its People Will Find Hard to Accept." *Observer*, August 26, 16.

References

Hornblower, Margot. 1997. "Guess Gets Out." *Time,* January 27, 48.

Houston Chronicle. 1994. "Stores Get Warning on 'Sweatshops'; Reich Says Don't Sell Illegally Made Clothes." September 10, Business 1.

Howard, Alan. 1997. "Labor, History, and Sweatshops in the New Global Economy." In *No Sweat Fashion, Free Trade and the Rights of Garment Workers,* ed. Andrew Ross. New York: Verso.

Howe, Rob, L. McNeil, R. Aria, J. S. Podesta, L. Wright, and A. Otey. 1996. "Labor Pains." *People,* June 10, 58–67.

Institute for Government Innovation. 1996. "No Sweat Eradicating Sweatshops 1996 Winner." John F. Kennedy School of Government, Harvard University. Available at <http://www.innovations.harvard.edu/winners/nsfed96.htm>. Accessed March 12, 2002.

Institute for Social Research. 2001. "How America Responds to Terrorist Attacks." Parts 1 and 2. October 9. Available at <http://www.umich.edu/~newsinfo /Releases /2001/Oct01/r100901a.html>. Accessed May 23, 2002.

International Confederation of Free Trade Unions (ICFTU). 1996. "Building Solidarity, Attacking Poverty, Creating Jobs." In *Global Market–Trade Unionism's Greatest Challenge.* Brussels: ICFTU. Available at <http://www.itcilo.it/english/actrav/telearn /global/ilo/seura/icftu2.htm>. Accessed June 13, 2003.

———. 1999. *Building Workers' Human Rights into the Global Trading System.* Brussels: ICFTU.

———. 2001. "ICFTU Online . . . WTO Must Tackle Workers' Rights at Doha." October 29. Available at <http://www.icftu.org/displaydocument.asp?Index=991214039&Language=EN>. Accessed April 15, 2002.

International Labor Organization (ILO). 1998. "Declaration On Fundamental Principles And Rights At Work." Available at <http://www.ilo.org/public/english/standards /decl/declaration/text/index.htm. Accessed October 18, 2001.

———. 2000. "Labour Practices in the Footwear, Leather, Textiles and Clothing Industries: Report for discussion at the Tripartite Meeting on Labour Practices in the Footwear, Leather, Textiles and Clothing Industries." October. Geneva: ILO. Available at <http://www.ilo.org/public/english/dialogue/sector/techmeet/tmlfi00/tmlfi-r.pdf>. Accessed February 11, 2002.

———. 2001. Laborsta Data base. Available from: <http://laborsta.ilo.org/>.

International Textiles and Clothing Bureau. 2001. "Developments in Textiles and Clothing Imports in the US—1990–2000 (Updated)." Table. Available at <http://www.itcb .org/Documents/ITCB-TD1.pdf>. Accessed March 24, 2002.

Irwin, T. H. 1981. "Reason and Responsibility in Aristotle." In *Essays on Aristotle's Ethics,* ed. Amelie Oksenberg Rorty, 117–56. Major Thinkers Series, Vol. 2. Berkeley: University of California Press.

Iyengar, Shanto. 1991. *Is Anyone Responsible?* Chicago: University of Chicago Press.

Jencks, Christopher. 1994. *The Homeless.* Cambridge and London. Harvard University Press.

Joffe-Block, Miriam. 2001. "Thai Workers Express Solidarity with Mexican Workers." USAS International Solidarity list serve, January 18.

Jones, Jackie. 1995. "Forces Behind Restructuring in U.S. Apparel Retailing and Its Effect on the U.S. Apparel Industry." *Industry Trade and Technology Review* March:23–27.

Jonquieres, Guy De. 1999. "Clinton Demands Threaten Turmoil at WTO Summit: President Outlines Long-Term Goal of Link between Trade and Labor Standards." *Financial Times,* December 2, P1.

Kamil, Mustapha. 1999. "Proposal to Include Labour Issue Attracts Flak." *New Straits Times* (Malaysia), December 4, Business 25.

Kearney, Neil. 2000 "Textiles, Globalisation and International Development." Curriculum

References

material for Transport and General Workers Union Training Program. Available at <http://www.tgwu.org.uk/TGWUInternatEd/Textiles/kearney.htm>. Accessed July 7, 2003.

———. 2002. "Trade Unions Also Need to Globalise." Speech delivered in January. Available at <http://www.itglwf.org/displaydocument.asp?DocType=Speech&Index=339&Language=EN>. Accessed July 7, 2003.

Keppler, Thomas M., and David Shaw. 1998. "Company Tries to Limit Sweatshops." *Daily Free Press* (Boston University) April 28. Available at <http://www.dailyfreepress.com/media/paper87/DFPArchive/frontpage/0428982.html>. Accessed January 28, 2004.

Kernaghan, Charles. 1996. Interview by author. October 4.

———. 1997. "Paying to Lose Our Jobs." In *No Sweat Fashion, Free Trade, and the Rights of Garment Workers*, ed. Andrew Ross, 79–94. New York: Verso.

Kessler-Harris, Alice. 1982. *Out to Work: A History of Wage-Earning Women in the U.S.* New York: Oxford University Press.

Kidd, Dusty, and Kit Morris. 2001a. "Statement from Nike." February 2. Available at <http://ur.rutgers.edu/news/ACLA/nikekukdongstatement3.htm>. Accessed May 14, 2003.

———. 2001b. "Nike Statement." March 28. Available at <http://ur.rutgers.edu/news/ACLA/nikekukdongmarch28.htm>. Accessed July 7, 2003.

———. 2001c. "Nike Report on Mexmode/Kukdong." November 30. Available at <http://ur.rutgers.edu/news/ACLA/nikenovember3001.htm>. Accessed May 14, 2003.

Kohl's Department Stores. 2000. *Annual Report.* Menomonee Falls, WI. Available at <www.kohls.com>.

Korean Confederation of Trade Unions (KCTU). 1996. "KCTU's International Policy." Available at <http://www.kctu.org/about/about.html>. Accessed November 9, 2001.

Kreider, Aaron. 2000. "Privilege and Our Movement." Messages (August 7) posted to <usas@listbot.com>.

———. 2001. "Differentiating High Cost and High Risk Activism: The Case of Anti-Sweatshop Student Sit-ins." M.A. thesis (draft), June 27. Available at <http://www.nd.edu/~akreider/essays/mastersdraft2.doc>. Accessed January 26, 2004.

Kristof, Nicholas D., and Sheryl WuDunn. 2000. "Two Cheers for Sweatshops." *New York Times,* September 24, sect. 6, 70.

Krugman, Paul. 1997. "In Praise of Cheap Labor: Bad Jobs at Bad Wages Are Better Than No Jobs at All." *Slate,* March 21. Available at <http://slate.msn.com/id/1918>. Accessed January 26, 2004.

Krupa, Gregg. 1999. "The Battle Cry against Sweatshops Resounds across College Campuses; Activists Score in Campaign Targeting Athletic Retailers." *Boston Globe,* April 18, F1.

Krupat, Kitty. 1997. "From War Zone to Free Trade Zone." In *No Sweat Fashion, Free Trade, and the Rights of Garment Workers*, ed. Andrew Ross, 51–78. New York: Verso.

Kuttner, Robert. 2001. "Harvard Now Sees the Error of Its Wages." *Boston Globe,* December 24, A15.

Kwong, Peter. 1987. *The New Chinatown.* New York: Hill and Wang Press.

———. 1998. *Forbidden Workers: Illegal Chinese Immigrants and American Labor.* New York: New Press.

Kurt Salomon Associates. 1992. *Perspective: Soft Goods Outlook for 1993.* New York: KSA.

Kwong, Peter, and Joann Lum. 1988. "How the Other Half Lives Now." *Nation,* June 18, 858–61.

Labaton, Stephan. 2002. "Mideast Turmoil: The Demonstrators; Thousands March in Washington in Support of Palestinians." *New York Times,* April 21, 1:13.

References

Labor Research Associates. 2001. "Union statistics." In *Union Trends and Data.* Available at <http://www.laborresearch.org/union_stats/Union_members.html>. Accessed April 6, 2002.

Lam, Leo L. 1992. "Designer Duty: Extending Liability to Manufacturers for Violation of Labor Standards in Garment Industry Sweatshops." *University of Pennsylvania Law Review* 141 (2): 623–67.

Laslett, John, and Mary Tyler. 1989. *The ILGWU in Los Angeles: 1907–1988.* Inglewood, CA: Ten Star Press.

Le, C. N. 2003. "Demographic Characteristics of Immigrants." Available at <http://www.asian-nation.org/immigrant_stats.shtml>. Accessed June 25, 2003.

Leichter, Senator Franz S. 1982. "Statement: The Reemergence of Sweatshops and the Enforcement of Wage and Hour Standards." Hearings before the Subcommittee on Labor Standards of the Committee on Education and Labor, U.S. House of Representatives, 97th Congress. Washington, DC: GPO.

Leichter, Senator Franz S., Glenn von Nostitz, and Maria Gonzalez. 1981. "The Return of the Sweatshop." February 26. Staff report (photocopy), Office of State Senator Franz Leichter, New York.

Leo, John. 1995. "The Oppression Sweepstakes." *U.S. News & World Report* 118 (July 24): 18.

Lewis, Diane. 1994. "Major Retailers Warned; Reich Says Stores Selling Sweatshop Goods Face Charges." *Boston Globe,* September 10, Economy 11.

Lim, Hoe. 2001. *The Social Clause: Issues and Challenges.* Turin: International Labor Organization, Bureau for Workers' Activities. Available at <http://www.itcilo.it/english /actrav/telearn/global/ilo/guide/hoelim.htm>. Accessed January 28, 2004.

Lim, Linda. 2000. Summary of sweatshop discussion. Global Summer Business Institute, University of Michigan Business School. May. Available at <http://www.ford-school.umich.edu/rsie/acit/Documents/LimStanfordSlides.pdf>. Accessed June 30, 2003.

Lipset, Seymour Martin, Kyoung-Ryung Seong, and John Charles Torres. 1993. "A Comparative Analysis of the Social Requisites of Democracy." *International Social Science Journal* 45 (2): 155–76.

Loew, Cori. 1999. "NE Regional USAS Conf. Middlebury, VT 10/29–31." E-mail to USAS list serve, October 12.

London, Bruce, and Robert J. S. Ross. 1995. "The Political Sociology of Foreign Direct Investment: Global Capitalism and Capital Mobility, 1965–1980." *International Journal of Comparative Sociology* 36 (3–4): 198–218.

London, Bruce, and Bruce A. Williams. 1990. "National Politics, International Dependency, and Basic Needs Provision: A Cross-National Analysis." *Social Forces* 69 (2): 565–84.

Loo, Chalsa, and Paul Ong. 1987. "Slaying Demons with a Sewing Needle: Feminist Issues for Chinatown's Women." In *From Different Shores: Perspectives on Race and Ethnicity in America,* ed. Ronald Takaki. New York: Oxford University Press.

Loucky, James, Maria Soldatenko, Gregory Scott, and Edna Bonacich. 1994. "Immigrant Enterprise and Labor in the Los Angeles Garment Industry." In *Global Production: The Apparel Industry in the Pacific Rim,* ed. Edna Bonacich, Lucie Cheng, Norma Chinchilla, Nora Hamilton, and Paul Ong, 345–61. Philadelphia: Temple University Press.

MacLean, Annie Marion. 1903. "The Sweat-Shop in Summer." *American Journal of Sociology* 9 (3): 289–309.

Mallia, Joseph. 1997. "The Return of the Sweatshop; Apparel Subcontractors Skirt Wage, Safety Laws." *Boston Herald,* May 18, 1, 24–26.

Manager, Vada. 2001. "Nike Statement. Nike Reiterates Its Support for an Independent, Accredited Monitor for Kukdong Mexico Factory." January 25. Available at

References

<http://ur.rutgers.edu/news/ACLA/NikeKukdongStatement2.htm>. Accessed May 14, 2003.

Mancini, Marikah. 2000. "Mexico Delegation." October 12. USAS Solidarity list serve.

Mankoff, Milton, and Richard Flacks. 1971. "The Changing Social Base of the American Student Movement." *Annals of the American Academy of Political and Social Science* 395:55–67.

Manners, Jane. 2001. "Joe Hill Goes to Harvard." *Nation,* July 2, 16 et seq.

Maquila Solidarity Network. 2001. "Nike: Kuk Dong, Mexico. 2001. Update #5." Available at <www.maquilasolidarity.org/campaigns/nike/kukdong.htm>. Accessed July 7, 2003.

———. 2002. "Nike: Kuk Dong, Mexico. Update #6." Available at <www.maquilasolidarity.org/campaigns/nike/kukdong.htm>. Accessed July 7, 2003.

Marshall, Adriana. 1987. "New Immigrants in New York's Economy." In *New Immigrants in New York,* ed. Nancy Foner, 79–101. New York: Columbia University Press.

Marx, Karl. 1998. "The Struggle between Capital and Labour and Its Results." In *Value, Price and Profit,* 144–49. In Karl Marx and Friedrich Engels, *Collected Works of Marx and Engels,* Vol. 20: *1864–1868.* New York: International Publishers.

Marymount University Center for Ethical Concerns. 1999. "The Consumers and Sweatshops." Available at <http://www.marymount.edu/news/garmentstudy/overview.html>. Accessed July 9, 2003.

May Department Stores Company. 2001. *Annual Report.* St. Louis, MO.

Mazur, Jay. 1997. "Announcement by President Bill Clinton. Topic: Apparel Industry." Federal News Service, White House Briefing, April 14. Available at <www.lexisnexis.com>.

McAdam, Doug. 1982. *Political Process and the Development of Black Insurgency, 1930–1970.* Chicago: University of Chicago Press.

McCall, William. 2001. "Workers at Mexican Factory Making Nike Products Plan to Unionize." *Associated Press,* September 27.

McClymer, John F. 1998. *The Triangle Strike and Fire.* New York: Harcourt, Brace.

McGrath, Molly. 2003. Interview with Kendra Fehrer on behalf of author. June 17.

Meislin, Richard J. 1980. "Caution in State Legislature: Record of 1980 Session in Albany Displays a Shift from Social Liberalism amid Financial Troubles." *New York Times,* June 16, B6.

Metz, Cara. 2001. Photograph of young girl. Available at <http://uniteunion.org/sweatshops/whatis/whatis.html>. Accessed August 30, 2001.

Meyer, David S., and Joshua Gamson. 1995. "The Challenge of Cultural Elites: Celebrities and Social Movements." *Sociological Inquiry* 65:181–206.

Meyer, Nancy. 2000. "Live! Kathie Lee Eyes Furniture." *Home Furnishings New,* April 17, 74 (16): 3.

Meza, Linda Rodriguez. 1997. "Testimony." In *No Sweat Fashion, Free Trade and the Rights of Garment Workers,* ed. Andrew Ross, 4–8. New York: Verso.

Miller, James. 1987. *Democracy Is in the Streets.* New York: Simon and Schuster.

Miller, John. 2003. "Why Economists Are Wrong about Sweatshops and the Antisweatshop Movement." *Challenge* 46 (1): 93–122.

Miller, Lenore. 1998. Letter to Pharis Harvey. November 18. Author's collection.

Moody, Nekesa Mumbi. 1996. "Gifford on Hand as Pataki Signs Anti-Sweatshop Legislation." *Associated Press,* July 2, A.M. cycle. Retrieved from <www.lexisnexis.com>.

Moreno, Jenalia. 2003. "New Grass-roots Movement Fosters Unions, in Past Discouraged." *Houston Chronicle,* June 14, Business: 01.

Morris, Charles J. 1998. "A Tale of Two Statutes: Discrimination for Union Activity under the NLRA and RLA." *Employment Rights and Policy Journal* 327: 317 ex seq.

References

Mort, Jo-Ann. 1997. "They Want to Kill Us for a Little Money." In *No Sweat Fashion, Free Trade and the Rights of Garment Workers*, ed. Andrew Ross, 193–98. New York: Verso.

Muchhala, Bhumika. 2001. "Kukdong-Indonesia—Support from Workers in Indonesia." USAS International Solidarity list serve, January 14.

Nadel, Stanley. 1985. "Reds versus Pinks: A Civil War in the International Ladies Garment Workers Union." *New York History* 66:49–101.

Nash, June, and Patricia Fernandez-Kelly. 1983. *Women, Men, and the New International Division of Labor*. New York: SUNY Press.

National Labor Committee (NLC). 1998. "Apparel; Wages around the World." Available at <http://www.nlcnet.org/resources/wages.htm.> Accessed February 5, 2002.

———. 2000. *Made in China: Behind the Label*. Available at <http://www.nlcnet.org/campaigns/archive/chinareport/introduction.shtml>. Accessed July 5, 2003.

National Labor Relations Board (NLRB). 2001. *The First Sixty Years: The Story of the National Labor Relations Board, 1935–1995*. Available at <http://www.nlrb.gov/publications/first60yrs/60yrs_entirepub.html>. Accessed December 3, 2001.

Nelson, Thomas E., Rosalee A. Clawson, and Zoe M. Oxley. 1997. "Media Framing of a Civil Liberties Conflict and Its Effect on Tolerance." *American Political Science Review* 91 (3): 567–84.

Newfield, Jack. 2002. Interview by author, May 15.

New York State Department of Labor. 1982. *Report to the Governor and Legislature on the Garment Manufacturing Industry and Industrial Homework*.

New York Times. 1911. "141 Men and Girls Die in Waist Factory Fire; Trapped High Up in Washington Place Building; Street Strewn with Bodies; Piles of Dead Inside." March 26. Available at <http://www.ilr.cornell.edu/trianglefire/texts/newspaper/nyt_032611_5.html>. Accessed May 28, 2002.

———. 1971. Untitled abstract of a report of a speech. Available at <www.lexisnexis.com>. July 14, p. 13.

Nicaragua Network. 2000. "Labor Crisis in Free Trade Zone Continues." Posted from *Nicaragua Monitor*, August, and available at <http://www.nicanet.org/news/freetradezone.html>. Accessed September 12, 2000.

Nicholson, Kathleen. 1997. "Private Label Finding a Welcome in Areas Where Designers Live." *Women's Wear Daily*, August 14, 174 (2): 1.

Nien Hsing. 2001. "Profile." Available at <http://www.nht.com.tw/english/eindex.htm>. Accessed January 23, 2004.

Nova, Scott. 2003a. Interview with Adam Tomczik and correspondence. June 3. On file with author.

———. 2003b. Group interview with Kendra Fehrer, Adam Tomczik, and author. June 10.

NPD Group. 2001. "Retail Apparel Sales Statistics and Trends." Available at <http://retailindustry.about.com/library/weekly/01/aa010319a.htm>. Accessed January 28, 2004.

O'Donnell, Guillermo A. 1973. *Modernization and Bureaucratic-Authoritarianism: Studies in South American Politics*. Berkeley: University of California Press.

Office of Public Affairs. 1995. "Labor Secretary Robert B. Reich, Apparel Manufacturers Announce Major Breakthrough in Effort to Eradicate U.S. Sweatshops." Press Release, U.S. Department of Labor, October 17. Available at <http://www.dol.gov/opa/media/press/opa/opa95421.htm>. Accessed March 12, 2002.

Office of Textiles and Apparel (OTEXA). 2001a. "Major Shippers Report." U.S. Department of Commerce, International Trade Administration. Available at <http://otexa.ita.doc.gov/msr/catv1.htm>. Accessed February 5, 2002.

———. 2001b. International Trade Administration on-line database. Available at <http://otexa.ita.doc.gov/scripts/tqsum2.exe/ctrypageracte>. Accessed January 22, 2004.

———. 2002. "Major Shippers Report." U.S. Department of Commerce, International

References

Trade Administration, April. Available at <http://otexa.ita.doc.gov/cats$.htm>. Accessed April 20, 2002.

Office of the U.S. Trade Representative. Executive Office of the President. 1999. *U.S. Generalized System of Preferences Guidebook.* Washington, DC: GPO.

Ordonez, Anastasia. 2003. Interview with Adam Tomczik on behalf of author. May 28.

Organization for Economic Cooperation and Development (OECD). 1994. *Foreign Trade by Commodities.* Paris: OECD.

Olson, Mancur. 1965. *The Logic of Collective Action.* Cambridge: Harvard University Press.

Orleck, Annelise. 1997. "Clara Lemlich Shavelson." In *Jewish Women in America: An Historical Encyclopedia,* ed. Paula E. Hyman and Deborah Dash Moore, 2:1238–41. New York and London: Routledge.

O'Rourke, Dara, and Business for Social Responsibility Education Fund, Investor Responsibility Research Center. 2000. *Independent University Initiative Final Report.* Washington, DC: Investor Responsibility Research Center. Available at <http://207.197.145.204/resources/IUI_Final_Report_2000.pdf>. Accessed April 18, 2002.

Ortiz, Altagracia. 1990. "Puerto Rican Workers in the Garment Industry of New York City, 1920–1960." In *Labor Divided: Race and Ethnicity in United States Labor Struggles, 1835–1960,* ed. Robert Asher and Charles Stephenson, 105–25. Albany: SUNY Press.

———. 1996. "Puerto Rican Women in the Garment Industry of New York City, 1920–1980." In *Puerto Rican Women and Work: Bridges in Transnational Labor,* ed. Altagracia Ortiz. Philadelphia: Temple University Press.

Palpacuer, Florence. 1997. *Development of Core-Periphery Forms of Organization: Some Lessons from the New York Garment Industry.* Geneva: International Labour Organization.

Pardun, Robert. 2002. *Prairie Radical.* Los Galos, CA: Shire Press.

Parsons, Maura, and Melinda St. Louis. 2001. "Chentex Union Officers Forced to Resign." *NicaNet.* Available at <http://www.nicanet.org/maura_chentex.htm>.

Penaloza, Nancy. 1996. Testimony to Fashion Industry Forum. Marymount University. Available at <http://www.dol.gov/opa/forum/penaloza.txt>. Accessed March 14, 2002.

Perkins, Frances. 1957. Lectures of Frances Perkins, Collection Box 2/3047, March 20. Kheel Center for Labor-Management Documentation and Archives, Cornell University.

———. 1964. Lectures of Frances Perkins, Collection /3047, September 30. Kheel Center for Labor-Management Documentation and Archives, Cornell University. Excerpt available at <http://www.ilr.cornell.edu/trianglefire/texts/lectures/perkins.html>. Accessed August 1, 2001.

———. 1965. Lectures of Frances Perkins, Collection Box 1/3047, Tape 14 (transcription), January 13. Kheel Center for Labor-Management Documentation and Archives, Cornell University.

Pessar, Patricia R. 1987. "The Dominicans: Women in the Household and the Garment Industry." In *New Immigrants in New York,* ed. Nancy Foner, 103–29. New York: Columbia University Press.

Pinsky, Robert. 1996. "The Shirt." In *The Figured Wheel,* 84. New York: Farrar, Straus, and Giroux.

Pollin, Robert, Justine Burns, and James Heintz. 2001. "Global Apparel Production and Sweatshop Labor: Can Raising Retail Prices Finance Living Wages?" Working Paper Series Number 19, Political Economy Research Institute, University of Massachusetts. Revised in 2002. Forthcoming in *Cambridge Journal of Economics.* Available at <http://www.umass.edu/peri>. Accessed July 9, 2003.

Pritchard, David. 1994. "The News Media and Public Policy Agendas." In *Public Opinion, the Press, and Public Policy,* ed. J. David Kennamer, 103–12. Westport, CT: Praeger.

Program on International Policy Attitudes. University of Maryland. 2000. "Americans on

References

Globalization: A Study of U.S. Public Attitudes." March 28. Available at <http://www.pipa.org/OnlineReports/Globalization/3.html>. Accessed July 9, 2003.

Proper, Carl. 1997a. Telephone interview by author with research staff of UNITE. November.

———. 1997b. In-house calculations from U.S. Bureau of Labor Statistics data. December.

Puerto Rican Forum. 1970 [1964]. A *Study of Poverty Conditions in the New York Puerto Rican Community.* New York: Puerto Rican Forum.

Putnam, Robert D. 2000. *Bowling Alone: The Collapse and Revival of American Community.* New York: Simon & Schuster.

Ramey, Joanna. 1992. "Guess-Labor Dept. Contractor Pact Only the First." *Women's Wear Daily,* August 6, 15.

———. 1997a. "Sweatshop Task Force, at Impasse, Called by White House for Meeting." *Women's Wear Daily,* March 28, 9.

———. 1997b. "Warnaco Quits Anti-Sweatshop group, Disagrees with Monitoring Proposal; Warnaco Group, Member of Pres. Clinton's Anti-Sweatshop Task Force." *Women's Wear Daily,* April 10, 18.

———. 1997c. "Karen Kane Is 2nd Company to Quit Anti-sweatshop Unit; White House Anti-Sweatshop Task Force." *Women's Wear Daily,* June 20, 14.

Rasky, Susan F. 1990. "The Nation; Deficit Reduction, Phase 1: The Staring." *New York Times,* May 27, sect. 4, 1.

Riis, Jacob. 1890. *How the Other Half Lives.* New York: Scribner's. Available at <http://www.cis.yale.edu/amstud/inforev/riis/title.html>. Accessed July 25, 2001.

Rockefeller, John D., Jr. 1941. Appeal on behalf of United Service Organizations and National War Fund. Radio broadcast, July 8. Available at <http://archive.rockefeller.edu/bio/jdrjr.php>.

Rodriguez, Clara. 1979. "The Economic Factors Affecting Puerto Ricans in New York." In *Labor Migration under Capitalism: The Puerto Rican Experience,* ed. Centro de Estudios Puertorigqueños, History Task Force. New York: Monthly Review Press.

Rodrik, Dani. 2002. "Globalization for Whom? Time to Change the Rules—and Focus on Poor Workers." *Harvard,* July–August, 29. Available at <http://www.harvard-magazine.com/on-line/070280.html>. Accessed July 9, 2003.

Rohter, Larry. 1996. "Hondurans in 'Sweatshops' See Opportunity." *New York Times,* July 18, A2

Roosevelt, Franklin Delano. 1937. Second Inaugural Address. Available at <http://www.feri.org/fdr/speech10.htm>. Accessed January 28, 2004.

Rosen, Ellen. 1987. *Bitter Choices: Blue Collar Women in and out of Work.* Chicago: University of Chicago Press.

———. 1994. "Women Workers in a Restructured Domestic Apparel Industry." *Economic Development Quarterly* 8 (2): 197–210.

———. 2002. *Making Sweatshops: The Globalization of the U.S. Apparel Industry.* Berkeley: University of California Press.

Ross, Andrew. 1997. "After the Year of the Sweatshop." In *No Sweat Fashion, Free Trade and the Rights of Garment Workers,* ed. Andrew Ross, 291–96. New York: Verso.

Ross, Robert. 1983. "Facing Leviathan: Public Policy and Global Capitalism." *Economic Geography* 59 (2): 144–60.

———. 1995. "Global Capital, Global Unions: Speculations on the Future of Global Unionism." In *Die Geburt der Weltwirtschaft,* ed. Karl. S. Althaler and Hardy Hanappi. Vienna: Sonderzahl Verlagsges.

———. 1995–96. "Global Capitalism and Labor at the End of History." *Socialism and Democracy* 9 (2): 1–23.

References

———. 1997a. "Restricting Immigration: A Sweatshop Nonsolution." In *An Academic Search for Sweatshop Solutions: Conference proceedings,* ed. Janice McCoart, 32–45. Arlington, VA: Marymount University.

———. 1997b. "Kathie Lee Makes a Difference: The Impact and Strategy of Celebrity in the Making of the Sweatshop Issue." Paper delivered at Eastern Sociological Society annual meeting. Baltimore, April 11.

———. 2001. "Sweatshop Police." *Nation,* September 3, 6–7.

———. 2002. "The New Sweatshops in the United States: How New, How Real, How Many, and Why?" In *Global Production, Regional Response, and Local Jobs: Challenges and Opportunities in the North American Apparel Industry,* ed. Gary Gereffi, David Spener, and Jennifer Bair, 100–122. Philadelphia: Temple University Press.

Ross, Robert, and Anita Chan. 2002. "From North-South to South-South: The True Face of Global Competition." *Foreign Affairs* 81 (5): 8–13.

Ross, Robert J. S., and Charles Kernaghan. 2000. "Countdown in Managua." *Nation,* September 4, 25–27.

Ross, Robert J. S., and Graham Staines. 1972. "The Politics of Analyzing Social Problems." *Social Problems* 20 (1): 18–40.

Ross, Robert J. S., and Kent Trachte. 1983. "Global Cities and Global Classes: The Peripheralization of Labor in New York City." *Review* 6 (3): 393–431.

———. 1990. *Global Capitalism: The New Leviathan.* Albany: SUNY Press.

Rothstein, Richard. 1989. *Keeping Jobs in Fashion: An Alternative to the Euthanasia of the U.S. Apparel Industry.* Washington, DC: Economic Policy Institute.

Rothstein, Richard. 1989. "Representative Democracy in SDS." In *Toward a History of the New Left: Essays from within the Movement,* ed. R. David Myers, 49–62. New York: Carlson.

———. 1993. "Without Higher Wages, Free Trade Doesn't Pay." *New Perspectives Quarterly* 10 (4): 42–47.

———. 1994. "The Global Hiring Hall." *American Prospect* March 21, 5:17. Available at <http://www.prospect.org/print/V5/17/rothstein-r.html>. Accessed July 9, 2003.

———. 1996a. "Toward a More Perfect Union." *American Prospect* 7 (26), May 1–June 1. Available at <http://www.prospect.org/print/V7/26/rothstein-r.html>. Accessed July 9, 2003.

———. 1996b. Lecture and Interview. Clark University, October 4.

———. 1997a. "Stagnation and Income Inequality: What We Can Do About It." Washington, DC: Economic Policy Institute.

———. 1997b. "Union Strength in the United States: Lessons from the UPS Strike." *International Labour Review* 136 (4): 469–91.

Ruggiero, Renato. 1998. "A Global System for the Next Fifty Years." Speech, October 30. Available at <http://www.wto.org/english/news_e/sprr_e/chat_e.htm>. Accessed October 18, 2001.

Ruiz, Miguel. 2000. Interview by author. July 13–16.

Safa, Helen I. 1999. "Women Coping with Crisis: Social Consequences of Export-Led Industrialization in the Dominican Republic." The North-South Agenda Papers Number 36, University of Miami. Available at <http://www.miami.edu/nsc/pages/pub-appdf/36AP.pdf>.

Salas, Carlos. 2001. *The Impact of NAFTA on Wages and Incomes in Mexico.* Washington, DC: Economic Policy Institute.

Sale, Kirkpatrick. 1973. *SDS.* New York: Random House.

Salem, D'Jamila. 1996. "Human Rights Group Targets Disney, Kathie Lee Apparel Lines; Labor: It Tells Congress That Imported Clothing Was Made by Abused, Underage Workers. TV Hostess and Companies Deny Charges." *Los Angeles Times,* April 30, 1.

References

Salmon, Charles T., and Chi-Yung Moh. 1994. "The Spiral of Silence." In *Public Opinion, the Press, and Public Policy*, ed. J. David Kennamer, 145–62. Westport, CT: Praeger.

Samuel, Howard D. 2000. "Troubled Passage: The Labor Movement and the Fair Labor Standards Act." *Monthly Labor Review* 123 (12): 32–37.

Sassen, Saskia. 1988. *The Mobility of Capital and Labor*. Cambridge: Cambridge University Press.

Savage, David G., and Nancy Cleeland. 2002. "High Court Ruling Hurts Union Goals of Immigrants; Labor: An Employer Can Fire an Illegal Worker Trying to Organize, the Justices Decide. Exploitation Is Feared." *Los Angeles Times*, March 28, 20.

Scardino, Emily. 2001. "Jeans Jumping, Shorts Slumping." *DSN Retailing Today*, August 20. Available at <http://www.findarticles.com/cf_0/m0FNP/16_40/77755755/p1/article.jhtml>. Accessed January 23, 2004.

Schattschneider, E. E. 1975 [1960]. *The Semisovereign People*. Fort Worth, TX: Harcourt.

Schlesinger, Emil. 1951. *The Outside System of Production in the Women's Garment Industry in the New York Market*. New York: Hecla.

Schmidley, A. Dianne. 2001. *Profile of the Foreign-Born Population in the United States: 2000*. U.S. Census Bureau, Current Population Reports, Series P23–206. Washington, DC: GPO.

Schmiechen, James A. 1984. *Sweated Industries and Sweated Labor: The London Clothing Trades, 1860–1914*. Champaign: University of Illinois Press.

Schoepfle, Gregory K . 2000. *Wage, Benefits, Poverty Line, and Meeting Workers' Needs in the Apparel and Footwear Industries of Selected Countries*. International Labor Affairs Bureau, Office of International Economic Affairs, U.S. Department of Labor. Washington, DC: GPO.

Scholars Against Sweatshop Labor. 2001. "Statement," October. Available at <http://www.umass.edu/peri/sasl/petition.htm>. Accessed January 25, 2004.

Schumpeter, Joseph Alois. 1983 [1942]. *Capitalism, Socialism, and Democracy*. Magnolia: Peter Smith.

Schwennesen, Tricia. 2000. "Labor Activists Rally in Front of Eugene, Ore., Nike Store." *Register Guard*, August 22, 2.

Seiden, Suzanne. 1997. Interview by author, April 10.

Shea, Jim. 2002. Interview by author. April 22.

Shepherd, Ed. 2000–2001 "Credibility Gap between Codes and Conduct—A Smokescreen for Poor Labour Standards." *Asian Labour Update*, no. 37 [Special Issue, Codes of Conduct]. Available at <http://www.amrc.org.hk/Arch/3700.html>. Accessed January 26, 2004.

Sider, Gerald. 1996. "Cleansing History: Lawrence, Massachusetts, the Strike for Four Loaves of Bread and No Roses, and the Anthropology of Working-Class Consciousness." *Radical History Review* 65:48–83.

Silverstein, Stuart. 1993. "Fashion Firms Told to Police Contractors; Labor: 'Hot Goods' Statute Is Being Used to Make Big Apparel Makers Stop Working with Companies That Violate Laws." *Los Angeles Times*, June 11, D1.

Simon, Rita J., and Susan H. Alexander. 1993. *The Ambivalent Welcome: Print Media, Public Opinion and Immigration*. Westport, CT: Praeger.

Smeeding, Timothy, and Lee Rainwater. 2001. "Comparing Living Standards across Nations: Real Incomes at the Top, the Bottom and the Middle." Luxembourg Income Study Working Paper No. 266, Maxwell School of Citizenship and Public Affairs, Syracuse University.

Smith, James P. 2001. "Race and Ethnicity in the Labor Market: Trends over the Short and Long Term." In *America Becoming: Racial Trends and Their Consequences*, ed. Neil J. Smelser et al., 2:52–97.

References

Smith, Mark. 1994. "Sweatshops to Pay Workers Millions Owed in Back Wages." *Houston Chronicle*, October 27, Business 2.

Smith, Miranda K. 1998. "Divergent Views of Choice, Voluntariness, and Coercion in the Nicomachean Ethics." *STOA* 1 (spring): 1. Available at <http://www.sbcc.cc.ca.us/academic/phil/cpe/Stoa/stoa1/Smith.html>. Accessed May 28, 2003.

Smithsonian Institution, National Museum of American History. 1998. "Between a Rock and Hard Place: A History of American Sweatshops, 1820–Present." Available at <http://americanhistory.si.edu/sweatshops/history/2t125.htm>. Accessed January 21, 2004.

Social Security Administration. N.d. "Social Security Pioneers: Frances Perkins." Available at <http://www.ssa.gov/history/fperkins.html>. Accessed November 2, 2001.

Solomon, Norman. 1996. "Kathie Lee, Disney, and the Sweatshop Uproar." *Albion Monitor* 2 (on-line). Available at <http://www.monitor.net/monitor>. Accessed September 29, 1998.

St. Antoine, Theodore J. 1998. "How the Wagner Act Came to Be: A Prospectus (Later Known as National Labor Relations Act; Sponsored by Sen. Robert F. Wagner in 1935)." *Michigan Law Review* 96 (8): 2201.

St. George, Donna. 2001. "Chandra Levy Spectacle Commandeers Media Stage." *Washington Post*, July 15, C1.

Stein, Leon. N.d. Interview by Joe Glazer. Audiotape released by Collector Records of Maryland. Copy in possession of author.

———. 2001 [1962]. *The Triangle Fire*. Ithaca: ILR Press.

———, ed. 1997. *Out of the Sweatshop: The Struggle for Industrial Democracy*. New York: Quadrangle/New Times Book Company.

Stetson, Damon. 1979. Untitled abstract of article on sweatshops. *New York Times*, September 18, 1. Available at <www.lexisnexis.com>.

Stier, Helen. 1991. "Immigrant Women Go to Work: Analysis of Immigrant Wives' Labor Supply for Six Asian Groups." *Social Science Quarterly* 72:67–82.

Stolberg, Benjamin. 1944. *Tailor's Progress: The Story of a Famous Union and the Men Who Made It*. Garden City, NY: Doubleday, Doran.

Strasburg, Jenny. 2002. "Gap Resists Settlement of Saipan Sweatshop Suit." *San Francisco Chronicle*, March 2, B1. Available at <http://www.sfgate.com/cgi-bin/article.cgi?file=/chronicle/archive/2002/03/02/BU67588.DTL>. Accessed March 6, 2002.

Strom, Stephanie. 1996. "A Sweetheart Becomes Suspect; Looking Behind Those Kathie Lee Labels." *New York Times*, June 27, D1.

Students for Social Change. 1999. "We Will be GROWing Soon!!!" E-mail to USAS list serve. St. Cloud State University, October 14.

Su, Julie. 1997. "El Monte Thai Garment Workers: Slave Sweatshops." In *No Sweat Fashion, Free Trade and the Rights of Garment Workers*, ed. Andrew Ross, 143–49. New York: Verso.

Sward, Susan. 1993. "U.S. Crackdown on Garment Makers: Big Companies Pressured Not to Deal with Firms That Violate Labor Laws." *San Francisco Chronicle*, January 11, A1.

Sweeney, John. 2002. Letter from AFL-CIO President John J. Sweeney to Members of the U.S. Senate and House Regarding the Debate on Iraq. October 7. Available at <http://www.aflcio.org/mediacenter/prsptm/tm10072002.cfm>. Accessed July 6, 2003.

Sweeney, John, and John Monks. 2003. "Heads of British and American Labor Movements Send Joint Letter on Iraq to President Bush and Prime Minister Blair." January 30. Available at <http://www.aflcio.org/mediacenter/prsptm/pr01302003.cfm>. Accessed July 6, 2003.

Szymanski, Albert. 1978. *The Capitalist State and the Politics of Class*. Cambridge, MA: Winthrop.

References

Taylor, Paul. 1991a. "25 Die as Fire Hits N.C. Poultry Plant; Locked Doors Are Said to Add to Toll." *Washington Post,* September 4, A1.

———. 1991b. "Ashes and Accusations; Charges Fly over Factory Fire Deaths." *Washington Post,* September 5, A1.

Textile Transshipment Team. 2000. *1999 Textile Transshipment Report.* U.S. Customs Service, Department of the Treasury. Available at <http://www.customs.ustreas.gov/quotas/ttr/index99.htm>. Accessed May 9, 2002.

Thomas, Karen. 1996. "Labels May Be Remedy for Sweatshops." *USA Today,* July 17, 1D.

Tomkins, Richard, and Neil Buckley. 1998. "Levi Strauss Shuts Six Plants." *Financial Times* (London), September 30, 29.

Traub-Werner, Marion. 1999. "Stop Sweatshops-Linking Workers' Struggles." *Against the Current* 81 (14): 3. Available at <http://www.igc.org/solidarity/indexATC.html>. Accessed May 14, 2002.

Tye, Larry. 1991. "Poultry Plant Blaze Lights Era of Neglect." *Boston Globe,* September 8, 1 et seq.

Tyler, Gus. 1995. *Look for the Union Label: A History of the International Ladies' Garment Workers' Union.* Armonk: M. E. Sharpe.

Um, Shin Ja. 1996. *Korean Immigrant Women in the Dallas-Area Apparel Industry: Looking for Feminist Threads in Patriarchal Cloth.* Lanham, MD: University Press of America.

Union of Needletrades, Industrial and Textile Employees (UNITE). 1998. "Was Your School's Cap Made in This Sweatshop?"Available at <http://www.uniteunion.org/sweatshops/schoolcap/schoolcap.html>. Accessed 13, 2003.

United Students Against Sweatshops (USAS). 2002. "Narrative Story/History." Available at <http://www.studentsagainstsweatshops.org/history.php>. Accessed May 14, 2002; at current address January 26, 2004.

———. 2003. "University Cap Manufacturer Refuses to Bargain in Good Faith." February 26. Available at <www.sweatshopwatch.org./swatch/headlines/2003/cap_feb03.html>. Accessed June 13, 2003.

U.S. Census Bureau. 1961. *United States Censuses of Population and Housing: 1960.* Census Tracts. Final Report PHC (1) 104, part 1, tables P-1, P-4, P-5. Washington, DC: GPO.

———. 1994. *Statistical Abstract of the United States: 1994.* Washington, DC: GPO.

———. 1998. *1997 Economic Census: Bridge between NAICS and SIC Manufacturing.* Available at <http://www.census.gov/epcd/ec97brdg/E97B1315.HTM>.

———. 2000. "Apparel—1999 Summary." *Current Industrial Reports.* MQ315A (99)-5 (MQ23A (99)-5). August. Available at <http://www.census.gov/cir/www.> Accessed May 20, 2002.

———. 2001a. "Annual Survey of Manufacturers: Statistics for Industry Groups and Industries," M99 (AS)-1. Available at <http://www.census.gov/mcd/asm-as1.html>. Accessed January 28, 2004.

———. 2001b. "Apparel—2000 Summary." *Current Industrial Reports.* MQ315A(00)-5. Available at <http://www.census.gov/cir/www>. Accessed May 21, 2002.

———. 2001c. "Poverty Thresholds." Available at <http://www.census.gov/hhes/poverty/threshld.html>. Accessed January 28, 2004.

———. 2001d. *Statistical Abstract of the United States: 2000.* Washington, DC: GPO.

———. 2002a. "Historical Income Tables Households (H6)." *Current Population Survey.* Available at <http://www.census.gov/hhes/income/histinc/h06.html>. Accessed January 28, 2004.

———. 2002b. *March 2000 Current Population Report.* Tables 14–1A and 14–1D. Available at <http://www.census.gov/population/www/socdemo/foreign/ppl-145.html>. Accessed March 22, 2002.

References

U.S. Congress. House of Representatives. 1963. "Testimony of Herbert Hill, January 31, 1963." 88th Cong., 2d sess. *Cong. Rec.* 109, Pt. 2, 159–1572. Washington, DC: GPO.

U.S. Department of Commerce. 2003. National Income and Product Accounts. Bureau of Economic Analysis. Available at <http://www.bea.gov/bea/dn/nipaweb/index.asp>. Accessed June 12, 2003.

U.S. Department of Justice. 2003. "Garment Factory Owner Convicted in Largest Ever Human Trafficking Case Prosecuted by the Department Of Justice." Press Release 03–108, February 21. Available at <http://www.usdoj.gov/opa/pr/2003/February /03_crt_108.htm>. Accessed July 9, 2003.

U.S. Department of Labor. 1996. "Industry Monitoring Credited for Improved Garment Industry Compliance with Minimum Wage and Overtime Laws." Press Release, Office of Public Affairs, May 9. Available at <http://www.dol.gov/dol/opa/public /media/press/opa/opa96181.htm>. Accessed October 29, 1996.

———. 1997a. "FY1997 First Quarter Garment Enforcement Report." Available at <http://www.dol.gov/dol/esa/public/nosweat/garment4.htm>. Accessed July 2, 1998.

———. 1997b. "U.S. Department of Labor Compliance Survey Finds More Than Half of New York City Garment Shops in Violation of Labor Laws." Press Release, Office of Public Affairs, October 16. Available at <http://www.dol.gov/dol/opa/public/media /press/opa/opa97369.htm>. Accessed July 2, 1998.

———. 1998. "U.S. Department of Labor Announces Latest Los Angeles Garment Survey Results." Press Release, Office of Public Affairs, May 27. Available at <http://www.dol.gov/dol/opa/public/media/press/opa/opa98225.htm>. Accessed July 2, 1998.

———. 1999. "Conditions in New York City's Garment Industry Unchanged, But Tougher Enforcement Leads to Arrests." Press Release, Office of Public Affairs, October 15. Available at <http://www.dol.gov/opa/media/press/opa/archive/opa99300.htm>. Accessed January 20, 2004.

———. 2000. "Only One-Third of Southern California Garment Shops in Compliance with Federal Labor Laws." Press Release, Wage and Hour Division, August 25. Available at <http://www.dol.gov/esa/media/press/whd/sfwh112.htm>. Accessed January 13, 2004.

———. 2001. "Hourly Compensation Costs for Production Workers in Manufacturing: 29 Countries or Areas, 40 Manufacturing Industries, 1975, 1980, 1985 and 1990–1999." Unpublished data, Bureau of Labor Statistics. Released June 25. Available at <ftp://ftp.bls.gov/pub/special.requests/ForeignLabor/ind2300.txt>. Accessed March 4, 2002.

———. 2002. "U.S. Department of Labor 2001 New York City Garment Compliance Survey." Available at <http://www.dol.gov/Opa/Media/Press/Opa/NewYork_Survey .htm#survey1>. Accessed June 5, 2003.

———. 2003. "Department of Labor Budget Overview FY 2003—Agency Information." Employment and Training Administration. Available at <http://www.dol.gov/_sec/budget2003/esa-staff>. Accessed June 30, 2003.

U.S. Department of State. 1999. *Country Reports on Human Rights Practices for 1998.* Bureau of Democracy, Human Rights, and Labor, February 26. Available at <http://www.state .gov/www/global/human_rights/1998_hrp_report/98hrp_report_toc.html>. Accessed January 23, 2004.

———. 2001. *Country Reports on Human Rights Practices.* Bureau of Democracy, Human Rights, and Labor. Available at <http://www.state.gov/g/drl/rls/hrrpt/2000 /wha/810.htm>. Accessed January 20, 2004.

U.S. General Accounting Office (GAO). 1988. "Sweatshops" in the U.S.: Opinions on Their Extent and Possible Enforcement Options: Briefing Report to the Honorable Charles E. Schumer, House of Representatives." Washington, DC: GAO/HRD-88–130BR.

References

———. 1989. "Sweatshops in New York City a Local Example of a Nationwide Problem: Briefing Report to the Honorable Charles E. Schumer, House of Representatives." Washington, DC: GAO/HRD-89-101BR.

———. 1994a. "Tax Administration: Data on the Tax Compliance of Sweatshops." Washington, DC: GAO/GGD-94-210FS.

———. 1994b. "Garment Industry: Efforts to Address the Prevalence and Conditions of Sweatshops." Washington, DC: GAO/HEHS-95-29.

U.S. Immigration and Naturalization Service (INS). 1996. "Emigration: Immigration and Emigration by Decade: 1901–90." Available at <http://www.ins.usdoj.gov/graphics/aboutins/statistics/300.htm>. Accessed December 6, 2001.

———. 2002. "Immigrants Fiscal Year 2000." In *Statistical Yearbook of the Immigration and Naturalization Service.* Washington, DC: GPO.

———. 2003. "Estimates of the Unauthorized Immigrant Population Residing in the United States: 1990 to 2000." Washington, DC: U.S. ISN. Available at <http://uscis.gov/graphics/shared/aboutus/statistics/Ill_Report_1211.pdf>. Accessed June 25, 2003.

U.S. Immigration and Naturalization Service [as of 2002 U.S. Department of Homeland Security, Bureau of Citizenship and Immigration Services] and U.S. Department of Labor, Bureau of International Labor Affairs. 1999. *The Triennial Comprehensive Report on Immigration.* Washington, DC.: GPO. Available at <http://uscis.gov/graphics/aboutus/repsstudies/tri3.pdf>. Accessed January 28, 2004.

Van den Braber, Ric. 1997. Interview by author. June.

Vanity Fair Corporation. 2001. *Annual Report 2000.* Greensboro, NC. Available at <www.vfc.com>. Accessed January 22, 2002.

Varley, Pamela, Meg Voorhes, Peter DeSimone, Brenda Bateman, and Kerry Breen. 1998. *The Sweatshop Quandary: Corporate Responsibility on the Global Frontier.* Washington, DC: Investor Responsibility Research Center. Available at <http://www.ustr.gov/pdf/gspintro.pdf>. Accessed April 20, 2002.

Veblen, Thorstein. 1902. *The Theory of the Leisure Class.* New York: McMillan.

Velazquez, Nydia. 1996. Remarks in support of Amendment to HR 3755, *Congressional Record,* 104th Cong., 2d sess., July 10, H7234. Available at <http://frwebgate2.access.gpo.gov/cgi-bin/waisgate.cgi?WAISdocID=89346421825+0+0+0&WAISaction=retrieve>. Accessed January 23, 2004.

Verité. 2001. "Comprehensive Factory Evaluation Report. Prepared by Verité on Kukdong International Mexico, S.A. de C.V. Atlixco, Puebla, Mexico." March. Available at <http://www.nike.com/nikebiz/gc/mp/pdf/nike_verite_report.pdf;bsessionid=00DWKW3LJJRAACQCGIUCF4YKAIZC2IZD>. Accessed July 7, 2003.

Vernon, Raymond. 1979. "The Product Cycle Hypothesis in a New International Environment." *Oxford Bulletin of Economics and Statistics* 41:255–67.

Vickery, Tim. 2001. "Case Study: Monitoring a Source of Nike's Sweatshirts." *Christian Science Monitor,* April 30, 15.

Wakefield, Dan. 1959. *Island in the City.* Boston: Houghton Mifflin.

Waldinger, Roger. 1984. "Immigrant Enterprise in the New York Garment Industry." *Social Problems* 32 (1): 60–71.

———. 1986. *Through the Eye of the Needle: Immigrants and Enterprise in New York's Garment Trades.* New York: New York University Press.

Waldinger, Roger, and Michael Lapp. 1993. "Back to the Sweatshop or Ahead to the Informal Sector?" *International Journal of Urban and Regional Research* 17 (1): 6–29.

Wallace, Bill. 1995. "70 Immigrants Found in Raid on Sweatshop; Thai Workers Tell Horror Stories of Captivity." *San Francisco Chronicle,* August 4, A12.

Wall Street Journal. 2000. "Universities Asked to Ease Sweatshop Stance." September 18, 17C.

References

Washington, George. 1790. Letter to the Hebrew Congregation in Newport Rhode Island. Available at <http://gwpapers.virginia.edu/presidency/hebrew/hebrew2.html>. Accessed July 14, 2003.

Washington Post. 1992. "Poultry Producer Gets 20 Years in Deaths of 25 Workers in Fire." September 15, A12.

Weaver, Dale. 2001. "Charges Dropped against S.F. Niketown 7." USAS list serve, April 7.

Weingarten, Randi. 1981. "The Reemergence of the Sweatshop in the Downstate New York Area." *Industrial and Labor Relations Forum* 15 (2): 61–120.

Weisbrot, Mark, and Dean Baker. 2002. "The Relative Impact of Trade Liberalization on Developing Countries." Center for Economic and Policy Research, June 11. Washington, DC. Available at <http://www.cepr.net/relative_impact_of_trade_liberal.htm>. Accessed July 9, 2003.

Weller, Christian E., Robert E. Scott, and Adam S. Hersh. 2001. "The Unremarkable Record of Liberalized Trade. After 20 Years of Global Economic Deregulation, Poverty and Inequality Are as Pervasive as Ever." Economic Policy Institute Briefing Paper, Washington, DC. Available at <http://epinet.org/content.cfm/briefingpapers_sept01inequality>. Accessed July 9, 2003.

Welling, Deanna. 2000. "The Top 50 Apparel Retailers." *Apparel Industry Magazine* 66 (8): 32–34.

Western, Bruce. 1991. "A Comparative Study of Corporatist Development." *American Sociological Review* 56 (3): 283–94.

White, George. 1995. "Workers Held in Near-Slavery, Officials Say." *Los Angeles Times,* August 3, A1.

———. 1996. "El Monte Case Sparked Efforts to Monitor, Root Out Sweatshops." *Los Angeles Times,* August 2, A1.

Williams, Jessica R. 2001. "Mexico Delegation, October 16, 2000." USAS International Solidarity list serve.

Wilson, William J. 1996. *When Work Disappears.* New York: Knopf.

Witness. 2001. *Behind the Label: Garment Workers on U.S. Saipan.* Video documentation. Available at <http://www.oddcast.com/witness/saipan/saipan_story3a.html>. Accessed January 26, 2004.

Wolfson, Bernard J. 1998. "Ted K. Joins Anti-sweatshop Campaign." *Boston Herald,* June 10, Finance, 34.

Women's Wear Daily. 1995. "Dresses, Suits & Eveningwear." Fairchild 100 Supplement, November, 40.

Wong, Morrison G. 1983. "Chinese Sweatshops in the United States: A Look at the Garment Industry." *Research in the Sociology of Work* 2:357–79.

Worcester Global Action Network (WoGAN). 2002. "Mission Statement—Comments/Alterations Requested." WoGAN list serve #438, February 11. Available at <http://groups.yahoo.com/group/woganlist/message/438>.

Workers Rights Consortium (WRC). 2001a. "WRC Investigation re Complaint against Kukdong (Mexico): Preliminary Findings and Recommendations, January 24, 2001." Available at <http://www.workersrights.org/Report_Kukdong_1.pdf>. Accessed July 7, 2003.

———. 2001b. Historical Factory Disclosure Database. Available at <http://www.workersrights.org/fdd_historical.asp>. Accessed April 4, 2001.

———. 2002. "Model Code of Conduct." Available at <http://www.workersrights.org/coc.asp>. Accessed January 28, 2004.

———. 2003. "Affliated [sic] Colleges and Universities." Available at <http://workersrights.org/as.asp>. Accessed July 6, 2003.

References

World Bank. 1995. *World Development Report 1995: Workers in an Integrating World.* New York: Oxford University Press.

——. 2001a. "Nicaragua at a Glance." Country Data. Available at <http://www.worldbank.org/data/countrydata/countrydata.html#AAG.> Accessed January 26, 2004.

——. 2001b. "Draft Policy Research Report: Globalization, Growth and Poverty: Facts, Fears and an Agenda for Action." Washington, DC: World Bank.

——. 2003. Data by Country. Data Profile Tables. Available <http://worldbank.org/data/countrydata/countrydata.html>. Accessed January 26, 2004.

World Federation of Trade Unions. 2001. Memorandum from World Federation of Trade Unions (WFTU) to 4th Ministerial Conference of World Trade Organisation. Doha, Qatar, November 9–13. Available at <http://www.wftu.cz/>. Accessed May 9, 2002.

World Social Forum. 2002. "Porto Alegre II Call of Social Movements." Available at <http://www.forumsocialmundial.org.br/eng/portoalegrefinal_english.asp>. Accessed May 9, 2002.

World Trade Organization (WTO). 1996. "Ministerial Declaration." Available at <http://www.wto.org/english/thewto_e/minist_e/min96_e/wtodec_e.htm>. Accessed January 26, 2004.

——. 1999. "Trade and Labour Standards: Subject of Intense Debate." Available at <http://www.wto.org/english/thewto_e/minist_e/min99_e/english/about_e/18lab_e.htm>. Accessed November 26, 2001.

——. 2000. "Trade by Sector." *International Trade Statistics.* Available at <http://www.wto.org/english/res_e/statis_e/chp_4_e.pdf>. Accessed January 27, 2004.

——. 2001. "Trade by Sector." In *International Trade Statistics 2000.* Geneva: WTO. Available at <http://www.wto.org/english/res_e/statis_e/tradebysector_e.htm>. Accessed April 22, 2002.

——. 2002. "Agreement on Textiles and Clothing." Available at <http://www.wto.org/english/docs_e/legal_e/16-tex.pdf>. Accessed July 14, 2003.

Worldwide Responsible Apparel Production (WRAP). 1998. "Principles." Available at <http://www.wrapapparel.org/infosite2/index.htm>. Accessed April 18, 2002.

——. 2002a. "Worldwide Responsible Apparel Production." Available at <http://www.wrapapparel.org/index.cfm?page=home>. Accessed January 26, 2004.

——. 2002b. "Certification." Available at <http://www.wrapapparel .org/index .cfm?page=certification>. Accessed January 26, 2004.

Yows, Suzanne R. 1994. "Towards Developing a Coherent Theory of Framing: Understanding the Relationship between News Framing and Audience Framing." Ph.D. diss., University of Madison—Wisconsin.

Yupoong Incorporated. 2002. "Company History" and "Company Locations." Available at <http://www.yupoong.co.kr/company/history.jsp> and <http://www.yupoong.co.kr/company /location.jsp>. Accessed June 13, 2003.

Zepeda, Evelyn. 2003. Interview with Adam Tomczik on behalf of author. June 8.

Zernike, Kate. 1999. "College Activism, '90s Style, Unites Two Sides; Students, Administrators Agree on Protests." *Boston Globe,* February 15, A1.

Zhou, Min. 1992. *Chinatown: The Socioeconomic Potential of an Urban Enclave.* Philadelphia: Temple University Press.

Zwick, Jim. (2002) "Bread and Roses: The Lost Histories of a Slogan and a Poem." Available at <http://www.boondocksnet.com/labor/history/bread_and_roses_history.html.> In Jim Zwick, ed., *Bread and Roses: Poetry and History of the American Labor Movement.* <http://www.boondocksnet.com/labor/history/>. Accessed June 3, 2004.

Index

Index

Index

Index

Index

Employers, 321; abusive, 325; control by, 21, 23; deception by, 200; Korean, 180; and labor standards, 318; unscrupulous, 332; weak, 188. *See also* Contractors; Factories; Manufacturers and manufacturing; Retailers; Subcontractors; *names of specific companies*

Employment: barriers to decent, 177–78; decline in, 105, 204, 328; full, 85, 86, 199, 329; high, 82; jobs, 175, 178, 240, 304; jobs, loss of, 138, 191, 198, 299, 300, 306; increase in, 302, 325; statistics on, 107, 152, 192. *See also* Layoffs; Workers

Enforcement, 309; of codes of conduct, 144, 314; compliance monitoring as, 156–59; of the FLSA, 150, 151, 153, 170, 332; of homework ban, 247; of industrial codes, 78; of labor standards, 12, 18, 38, 244, 315, 320; in the media, 208–9; of minimum wage, 84, 163, 307; privatized, 100, 170; of union contracts, 58; by U.S. DOL, 32, 155, 321, 340n. 15

Enforcement, lack of, 103, 171, 205; in China, 39, 102, 303; of codes of conduct, 311; in Mexico, 112, 282; in the U.S., 151, 238, 303, 319; and wage laws, 39; and the WTO, 292. *See also* Deregulation; Privatization

Entman, Robert, 211

Environment, 112, 287

Environmentalists, 250, 293, 295

Environmental law, violators of, 32

Esbenshade, Jill, 157, 159

Ethics, 169, 237, 261; and employers, 156, 180; and labels, 161, 168; lack of, 216, 239

Ethnicity: co-, 179–80; in the media, 212–13, 217–18; of workers, 15, 17, 80, 82, 177

ETI (Ethical Trading Initiative), 39, 40, 41, 49–51

EU (European Union), 289, 318; imports to, 108, 110, 133, 288, 300–301, 315

Europe, 2, 76, 104, 329; antisweatshop groups in, 38, 245, 247, 313; capital in, 103, 128; Eastern, 5, 15, 81–82, 174; exports from, 299; labor movement in, 101, 188; Northern, 81–82; Southern, 5, 81–82, 174; unions in, 290, 293; Western, 37, 82. *See also names of specific countries*

Executives, 129, 133, 135, 146, 202

Exploitation, 12, 21, 24, 122, 262, 315; in the Caribbean, 226; comparative, 102; discourse about, 322; in the Dominican Republic, 276; of homeworkers, 178, 247; of immigrants, 124, 179, 216, 330; of male workers, 58; in the media, 206; and Nike, 12; "super," 28; in the U.S., 10, 202

Exports and exporters, 104, 122, 166, 247, 328; and competition, 288, 302; low-wage, 326–27; U.S., 121, 143. *See also* Free trade zones; Imports

Factories, 16, 40; in Asia, 177; BJ&B, 169, 238, 256, 266–67, 333; certified, 312; Chentex, 114–16, 118–20, 298, 318; in China, 110–11, 282, 335–37; closing of, 126, 196, 280, 349n. 21, 350n. 11; in CNMI, 141, 143; conditions in, 160–61; Dominican, 169, 238, 256, 266–67, 314; exits to, 71, 141; in free trade zones, 114–16, 118–20; Global Fashions, 224, 225, 227; growth of, 68, 86, 189; in Indonesia, 270, 349n. 17; inspections of, 71, 166, 225, 271, 275; Kukdong/Mexmode, 169, 238, 266, 267–74, 333; Leisorson's, 18, 52, 54, 56; locations of, 127–28, 134–35, 145, 169, 188, 196; Mandarin, 143, 164; Matamoros Garment, 268, 272; Mexican, 112, 113, 314; Moca, 275; Modern Dress, 234–35, 347n. 13; New Era, 169; owners of, 212, 336; Seo Fashions, 223, 226. *See also* Contractors; Doors; Production; Subcontractors; Sweatshops; Triangle Shirtwaist Company; Union shops

Factory Investigating Commission, 67–68, 73, 74, 75

Fairfield University, 249, 252, 259

Families, 49, 233, 240–42, 260; poor, 27; and poverty level, 36–37, 99; roles in, 178; size of, 39, 41, 47–48; and wages, 163; working, 19, 51, 63, 213, 264

Fashion, 69–70

Fashion design and designers, 37, 125, 127, 133, 135

Fashion Industry Forum, 227

Federated Department Stores, 131, 132

Feigenbaum, Benjamin, 56

Feminism, 92, 261, 263

FENATRAZONAS (Federacion Nacional de Trabajadores de Zonas), 275, 277, 280

Fielden, Samuel, 285

Finland, 70, 109

Fire, 24, 141, 176, 324; in poultry plant, 211–12; in Thai factory, 208; at Triangle

Index

Index

Guatemala, 297, 298; imports from, 105, 305, 316
Guess? Inc., 156, 200–203

Haiti, 217, 226
Harassment, 253, 272, 279, 281, 346n. 1; by police, 57, 286; prohibition of, 40, 50–51, 163; by supervisors, 115–16, 119
Harris, Isaac, 61, 63, 189, 213
Harvard University, 156, 164, 168, 258, 276, 281; living wage campaign at, 248, 265–66
Haymarket Square, 285–86
Health, 52, 104, 112; mandates for, 52, 64, 163. *See also* Sanitation
Health hazards, 275–76, 278, 304, 324, 336
Health insurance, 86, 95
Health laws, violators of, 26–27, 29, 177, 310
Health standards, 77, 316; poor, 181, 304, 327
Hegel, Georg Wilhelm Friedrich, 190–91
Herbert, Bob, 164, 208
Hermanson, Jeff, 280–81, 282–83
Hernandez, Ignacio, 280
Hernandez, Juana, 268
Hill, Herbert, 91–92, 183
Hillman, Sidney, 83, 84, 198
Hinojosa Ojeda, Raul, 185
Hiring, 58. *See also* Rehirings
Holland, Josiah Gilbert, 145
Homework, 90; decline of, 87, 94–95; legal, 247; prohibition of, 26, 58, 77, 84, 95; proposals against, 99; regulation of, 84, 94–95; restrictions on, 84
Homeworkers, 12, 14, 29, 189; in Britain, 14–15; competition with and among, 13, 18, 178; desperation of, 16–17; illegal, 99, 202; sewing machine operators, 34, 44, 46, 69
Honduras, 227, 297, 316; child labor in, 153, 222; sweatshops in, 143, 223; unions in, 297, 298
Hong Kong, 119, 123, 143, 304; imports from, 110, 111, 300, 318, 350n. 14; textile industry in, 97, 326
Hours, 13; of homeworkers, 84; limits on, 58, 64, 75, 76, 311; long, 114, 176, 178, 187; long, in China, 110, 303; long, in sweatshop definitions, 14, 18, 20, 36; and political platforms, 79, 83; standards for, 86, 316; violators of laws of, 30, 36, 303. *See*

also Days off; Overtime; Workdays; Workweeks
Housing, substandard, 94, 95, 116, 117
Houston Chronicle, 209
Howard, Alan, 190
How the Other Half Lives (Riis), 9, 19
Human rights, 165, 291, 296, 333; violations of, 12, 139, 169, 195
Human rights groups, 141, 163, 164, 166, 227, 291; lawyers', 162, 167
Hungary, 109

ICCR (Interfaith Center on Corporate Responsibility), 162, 167
ICFTU (International Confederation of Free Trades Unions), 39, 296–97, 350n. 9
Identity, 261, 264
ILGWU (International Ladies Garment Workers Union), 4, 83, 87, 93, 243; and benefits, 95; contracts with, 59, 87, 89–90; critics of, 89; discrimination in, 94; factions of, 68, 190; and imports, 97; Local 25 of, 52–53, 54, 55, 65, 70; in Los Angeles, 191; membership of, 58, 59–60, 71, 190; and merger, 198, 200, 202, 254; officials of, 90–91; and strikes, 52–53, 57, 58, 60, 64; women of color in, 92
Illegal enterprises, 29, 30, 34
Illinois, 175, 286; University of, 276. *See also* Chicago
ILO (International Labor Organization): data from, 304, 305; and enforcement, 292, 307, 320; and labor rights, 38–39, 291, 293, 296, 316; standards of, 40, 50, 118, 270, 349–50n. 4
ILRF (International Labor Rights Fund), 162, 167, 344n. 17
Immigrants, 19, 67, 76, 135, 172–86; Asian, 5, 172, 174, 175, 217; Black, 172; blame of, 214, 216, 219, 239, 242, 347n. 15; Caribbean, 180, 217; Central American, 172, 180, 185; Chinese, 172, 175, 177, 178–80, 185, 217; communities of, 175–76, 188; as contractors, 128; entrepreneurs, 175, 176, 177, 179–80, 181, 184; European, 5, 82, 172, 174, 200; exploitation of, 100, 124, 154, 179, 216, 330; Hispanic, 5, 174; and homework, 94; illegal, 192, 218; Jewish, 81, 172, 200; Korean, 174, 175, 180, 217; in the media, 206; and media frames, 208, 214, 216–21; Mexican, 34, 172, 174, 180, 217; organization of, 204;

Index

Korea, 109, 123, 217, 268, 278, 297, 318; corporations in, 140, 274; investors from, 114, 266, 267, 302, 304; textile industry in, 97, 326

Kreider, Aaron, 258

Kristof, Nicholas, 237, 324, 325

Krugman, Paul, 324, 325

Kukdong/Mexmode, 169, 238, 266, 267–74, 281, 333

Kurt Salomon (firm), 130

Labels, sweat-free, 204; and AIP/FLA, 161, 165–66, 167, 312–14, 333, 351n. 3

Labor: bonded, 40, 50, 139, 142, 325; cash only, 29, 30; cheap, 103, 120, 122, 292; control of, 122–23; fair, 260; indentured, 40, 50, 139, 142, 340n. 14; low-wage, 323; migrant, 12; restrictions on, 50; slave, 160, 209, 213–15, 221–22, 225, 310, 325; supply of, 219, 350n. 12. See also Child labor; Immigrants; U.S. DOL; Workers; Workers, women

Labor, forced, 324; in Asia, 104, 292, 320; in Central America, 114, 224; and codes of conduct, 40, 50, 163; prohibition of, 291, 297, 316; in the U.S., 139, 214

Labor abuse, 153, 164; in Central America, 164; deterrents to, 244, 320; and policy, 211, 322; regulations against, 284, 309–10; support for, 244, 323; in the U.S., 75, 205, 220, 321. See also Scandals

Labor Day, 286

Labor laws, 78, 115; reform of, 12, 183, 197, 330. See also Enforcement; FLSA; Health laws, violators of; Monitoring, compliance; NIRA; NLRA; Protocols of Peace; Regulation; Violations; Wage laws; Wagner Act

Labor market, 175, 185, 186, 244

Labor movement, 66, 76, 124, 163; alliances with, 262, 273; European, 101; history of, 3, 292; and human rights, 333; international, 286, 294, 319, 331; and labor law, 77, 78, 80; in Mexico, 113; in New York, 68, 75–76; Northern, 288; organizing by, 254; Southern, 288, 307; split in, 167; structure of, 80–81; weakening of, 194, 197; and the WTO, 293. See also names of specific labor organizations

Labor practices, unfair, 203, 331. See also Labor abuse; Violations; Wage, minimum, failure to pay

Labor rights, 102, 291; of the ILO, 38, 39, 296, 316; in trade policy, 317, 331, 333; violators of, 12, 114, 139, 275, 291; and the WTO, 294, 318

Labor standards, 41, 85, 283, 292, 316; absence of, 100, 243, 244; of the AIP, 162–63; in China, 288; enforcement of, 315, 320; of the FLA, 165; high, 314; international, 296, 318–19, 328; monitoring of, 38–39; raising of, 161, 168, 321; and trade agreements, 324, 326, 331–32; violations of, 118; weak, 314; and the WTO, 287, 290. See also Health standards; Reform; Reformers

Labor standards, lowering of, 183, 208; caused by competition, 73, 77, 102, 120, 299; caused by relocation, 104, 105; and immigrants, 185, 221. See also Race to the bottom

Language, 53, 54; abusive, 20, 23; and immigrants, 17, 177, 182, 188, 213

Laos, 175

Lapp, Michael, 28–30, 33, 34

Latin America, 281, 296–97, 326. See also Central America; South America; names of specific countries

Lawsuits, 298; class-action, 144; federal, 139, 142; state, 139, 142. See also Court cases

Lawyers, 144, 157, 278

Lawyers Committee for Human Rights, 162, 167

Layoffs, 126, 137, 138, 149, 272

Lee, Sammy, 129–30, 144, 145

Leftists, 81, 245, 251; New, 258, 260, 261, 262, 264. See also Feminism; Radicals; Revolution

Leichter, Franz, 208

Lemlich, Clara, 54–56, 101

Lesotho, 126

Levasseur, Emile, 19–20

Levi Strauss & Co., 39, 126, 127, 142, 144

Lexington Herald, 253

Lexis-Nexis, 217–18, 220, 230

Liability, 129, 197, 231, 332; joint, 89, 190

Liberalization, 290, 324

Liberals and liberalism, 122, 155, 241, 255, 323

Licensing, product, 254–55, 257, 271, 273

Life (magazine), 87, 88

Lighting, 17, 56, 267, 337

Lim, Hoe, 296

Index

Index

Index

Index

Triangle Shirtwaist Company, 18, 189; fire at, 52–58, 60–64, 65, 67, 73–74, 212, 341n. 3; strikes against, 52–58; workers at, 19, 221

Trimmers, 19, 126, 336–37

TRIMS (Trade Related Investment Measures), 289–90

Tulane University, 253, 259, 275

Tunisia, 47, 297

Turkey, 47, 109, 299, 300

Tyler, Gus, 96–97

UE (United Electrical Workers), 269

UFCW (United Food and Commercial Workers), 167

UMW (United Mine Workers), 83

UN (United Nations), 22, 139, 291

Unemployment, 77, 102, 189, 198, 211; high, 72, 182, 183–84, 327; and insurance, 76, 177; low, 329; threat of, 178

Union busting, 115, 184, 236, 330. *See also* Strikebreakers

Union contracts, 89, 95, 257, 267; enforcement of, 58; evasion of, 69, 73, 190; first, 330–31

Unionism: business, 80; dual, 70; industrial, 80–81, 83

Unionists, 4, 21, 40, 68, 296; developing country, 318

Unionization, 69, 71, 85, 97, 213, 321. *See also* Right of association

Union organizing, 283, 324, 331; right to, 78, 298, 316, 330; top-down, 89–90, 190, 202

Unions, 39, 67, 220, 260, 322, 332; company, 119, 268; and demonstrations, 250; in developing countries, 350n. 9; European, 290, 293, 298; evasion of, 189, 192; federations of, 281, 296–97, 298; fights in, 190; firing of activists from, 115, 118, 269, 280; firing of leaders of, 269, 279, 280; firing of members of, 115, 116, 269; formation of, 252; growth of, 193, 246; hostility to, 112, 143, 188, 196; independent, 170, 266, 268–69, 270, 271, 272; and labor standards, 299; leaders of, 114, 265; legal status of, 116, 118; legitimation of, 76; locals of, 248; lumber workers', 285; membership of, 191, 193–95, 197–99, 208, 241; mergers of, 203, 346n. 2; in Mexico, 113, 266, 272; and Mexmode, 267; negotiations with, 118; in Nicaragua, 114, 116; Northern, 290, 318; officers of, 116, 118;

organizers for, 63, 234–35, 273; recognition of, 266, 267, 277–78, 298; repression of, 41, 51; right to form, 40, 165, 194, 267, 268, 277; right to join, 40, 78, 110, 111, 296, 331; Southern, 307; strength of, 145, 183, 189, 239, 244, 321; and students, 198, 237, 254, 262; support for, 239, 241; U.S., 281, 297, 298, 317; and wages, 161. *See also* Workers, unionized; *names of specific unions*

Unions, weak, 103, 186, 197, 205; as cause of labor abuse, 219, 244; in the U.S., 82, 100, 317

Union shops, 60, 86, 93, 194, 257

UNITE (Union of Needletrades Industrial and Textile Employees), 26; and agreements, 162, 164, 166, 167, 168; and BJ&B, 275–76; creation of, 200; and the FLA, 38; and Guess? Inc., 156, 202–3; and international struggles, 115, 298; and Kathie Lee Gifford, 222, 226, 227, 232; and labels, 204; and labor abuse, 139, 153; membership of, 198, 245; and student movement, 254, 256

United Kingdom, 39, 47, 109, 131; England, 15, 101, 329; Parliament, 13, 18; sweatshops in, 13–15

United States: activists in, 41; capitalism in, 25; Census Bureau of, 46, 120, 130, 151, 198; clothing industry in, 15–16, 136, 138; contractors in, 128–29; exports to, 110, 111, 166, 288, 315–18, 320; income in, 107; inequality in, 185, 329; labor costs in, 109; new sweatshops in, 124; retailers in, 131; rights in, 195; State Department of, 163; Supreme Court of, 77–78, 345n. 11; sweatshops in, 9–12, 14, 41, 351n. 2; sweatshop workers in, 35–36, 42–47; unions in, 281, 297, 298, 317; violations in, 30, 34, 291; wage laws in, 38, 39, 303; wages in, 305, 325, 328; work conditions in, 37; and the WTO, 287. *See also* CNMI; GSP; INS; NRA; U.S. Congress; U.S. DOL; *names of specific cities, states, and presidents*

United Steelworkers Union, 115, 350n. 7

Universities and colleges, 168, 219, 257, 278, 281. *See also* CLC; Licensing, product; Logos, university/college; *names of specific institutions*

USAS (United Students Against Sweatshops), 248; and BJ&B, 256, 267, 276–77,

Index